ARMS AND WARFARE

Studies in International Relations

Charles W. Kegley, Jr., and Donald J. Puchala, General Editors

ARMS AND WARFARE
Escalation, De-escalation, and Negotiation

Michael Brzoska and Frederic S. Pearson

UNIVERSITY OF SOUTH CAROLINA PRESS

Copyright © 1994 University of South Carolina

Published in Columbia, South Carolina, by the
University of South Carolina Press

Manufactured in the United States of America

Library of Congress Cataloging–in–Publication Data

Brzoska, Michael.
    Arms and warfare : escalation, de-escalation, and negotiation /
Michael Brzoska and Frederic S. Pearson.
        p.   cm. — (Studies in international relations)
    Includes bibliography references and index.
    ISBN 0–87249–982–0 (hardcover : acid free)
    1. Arms transfers. 2. War. 3. Diplomatic negotiations in
international disputes. 4. Developing countries—History, Military—
Case studies.   I. Pearson, Frederic S. II. Title. III. Series:
Studies in international relations (Columbia, S.C.)
UF500.B79   1994
327.1' 74—dc20   93–46038

Contents

Tables	vi
Abbreviations	vii
Preface	x
Acknowledgments	xiii
1. Defining the Questions	1
2. Research Tools: Controversies about Arms-Transfer Data and Methodology	17
3. India-Pakistan Kashmir War, 1965	25
4. India-Pakistan Bangladesh War, 1971	43
5. The Central American Football War, 1969	61
6. The South Atlantic War, 1982	71
7. The Yom Kippur-Ramadan War, 1973	90
8. Israeli-Arab War in Lebanon, 1982	112
9. The Iraq-Iran War, 1980–88	134
10. The War in the Western Sahara, 1976–91	160
11. The Ogaden War, 1977–78	180
12. The Tanzania-Uganda War, 1978–79	200
13. Recent Trends, Analysis, and Projection	213
Appendix: Short Chronologies of the Wars	241
Notes	264
Bibliography	280
Index	307

Tables

1.	Arms Supplies or Embargo Effects on Ongoing War	15
2.	Arms Shipments to India, 1962–65	28
3.	Arms Shipments to Pakistan, 1962–65	29
4.	Arms Shipments to India, 1966–71	52
5.	Arms Shipments to Pakistan, 1966–71	53
6.	Arms Shipments to El Salvador, 1966–69	64
7.	Arms Shipments to Honduras, 1966–69	64
8.	Arms Shipments to Argentina, 1979–82	75
9.	Arms Shipments to Israel, 1970–73	95
10.	Arms Shipments to Egypt, 1970–73	96
11.	Arms Shipments to Syria, 1970–73	97
12.	Israeli and Arab Force Balances in 1973	98
13.	Arms Shipments to Israel, 1979–82	114
14.	Arms Shipments to Syria, 1979–82	115
15.	Israeli and Arab Forces Engaged in the 1982 War	117
16.	Arms Shipments to Iraq, 1977–79	136
17.	Arms Shipments to Iran, 1977–79	136
18.	Values of Major Weapons Deliveries to Iraq, 1980–88	146
19.	Values of Major Weapons Deliveries to Iran, 1980–88	147
20.	Arms Shipments to Morocco, 1972–74	163
21.	Arms Shipments to Morocco, 1975–91	165
22.	Arms Shipments to Ethiopa, 1974–78	183
23.	Arms Shipments to Somalia, 1974–78	184
24.	Arms Shipments to Uganda, 1975–78	201
25.	Arms Shipments to Tanzania, 1975–78	205
26.	Impact of Arms Resupply	215
27.	Impact of Arms Resupply on Wars Ongoing in 1991	222

Abbreviations

AAM	Air-to-Air Missile
ACDA	US Arms Control and Disarmament Agency
AEW	Airborne Early Warning
APC	Armored Personnel Carrier
AShM	Air-to-Ship Missile
ASM	Air-to-Surface Missile
ASW	Antisubmarine Warfare
ATM	Antitank Missile
CACM	Central American Common Market
CENTO	Central Treaty Organization
CIA	Central Intelligence Agency
CNR	Croatian National Resistance
CRS	Congressional Research Service
CSCE	Conference on Security and Cooperation in Europe
DMZ	Demilitarized Zone
EC	European Communities
ECM	Electronic Countermeasures
EEZ	Economic Exclusion Zone
EW	Electronic Warfare
FAC	Fast Attack Craft
FMS	Foreign Military Sales
FNLA	National Front for the Liberation of Angola

HMS	Her Majesty's Ship
IAF	Israeli Air Force
ICP	Iraqi Communist Party
IDF	Israeli Defense Force
IMF	International Monetary Fund
JKLF	Jammu and Kashmir Liberation Front
JNA	Yugoslav National Army
LDC	Less Developed Country
MAP	Military Assistance Programme
MBT	Main Battle Tank
MINURSO	United Nations Mission for the Referendum in Western Sahara
MPLA	Popular Movement for the Liberation of Angola
MRS	Multiple Rocket System
NATO	North Atlantic Treaty Organization
NIC	Newly Industrializing Country
NSC	National Security Council
OAS	Organization of American States
OAU	Organization of African Unity
PC	Patrol Craft
PFLP	Popular Front for the Liberation of Palestine
PLO	Palestinian Liberation Organization
Polisario	Frente Popular para La Liberación de la Saghia el Hambra y del Rio de Oro
SADR	Democratic Republic of Sahara
SALT	Strategic Arms Limitation Treaty
SAM	Surface-to-Air Missile

SShM	Surface-to-Ship Missile
SEATO	South East Asia Treaty Organization
ShAM	Ship-to-Air Missile
ShSHM	Ship-to-Ship Missile
SIPRI	Stockholm International Peace Research Institute
SLA	South Lebanese Army
SSM	Surface-to-Surface Missile
STDF	Slovene Territorial Defense Force
TPDF	Tanzanian People's Defense Forces
UN	United Nations
UNIIMOG	United Nations Iraq-Iran Military Observer Group
UNITA	National Union for the Total Liberation of Angola
UNLA	Uganda National Liberation Army
WSLF	Western Somali Liberation Front
ZANU	Zimbabwe African National Union

Preface

In *Major Barbara,* published in 1905, George Bernard Shaw ridiculed the hypocrisy of moralists who grew excited about arms salesmen supposedly fueling wars. Was it not the free will of buyers to obtain weapons? Similar reasoning allowed Sam Cummings, of Interarms Inc., to become the world's leading private arms dealer in the post–World War II period (see Brogan and Zarca, 1983, for an account of Cummings's remarkable career). Why should arms sellers be blamed and not politicians? Why should some people or governments have the right to deny others the means to defend themselves? Can it be assumed that some national leaders will use weapons more responsibly than others?

Much can be learned from the fact that these questions are as relevant today as they were almost a century ago. For one thinking in the "Realist" tradition, this relevance provides yet another indication that little has changed in the sphere of international relations, and that since realpolitik still reigns supreme, there is little point in trying to alter that situation. For one more attuned to the "Idealist" legacy, it offers another confirmation that the last decades—the "short century" between the beginning of the World War I and the end of the cold war—have been a disappointment in terms of conflict resolution mechanisms, but also a boost for hopes of arms-trade restraint in the post–cold war era. A third conclusion, for one less attached to specific knowledge systems than to the advancement of knowledge in general, would stress the importance of mere perseverance in the search for answers to the above questions.

As authors we place ourselves in the third category. As a result of our concerns about the scourges of war, our goal is to determine, through analysis, either positive or negative pre-war and mid-war effects of arms shipments. We want to know whether arms shipments generally lead toward peace or further warfare, and under what circumstances. As the reader will discover, much of our analysis, both in the formulation of hypotheses and in the subsequent case studies, is within the Realist tradition, with emphasis on military events, power relations, and narrow calculations of interests. For Idealists there may be too much of this, though consideration of the effects of weapon use—the destruction, sorrow, and ethical dilemmas entailed—as well as possible ameliorative solutions are offered. Indeed, our conclusions turn out not to fit entirely well with either the Realist or the Idealist paradigm.

This tension becomes obvious when our conclusions are compared with the gist of the numerous supposed efforts to control arms transfers and military technology in the early 1990s. Much of the activity was inspired by the Iraqi annexation of Kuwait in 1990 and the subsequent war for the "liberation" of Kuwait. There was much chest thumping about prior uncontrolled arms transfers that had allowed Iraq to rank among the best-armed and most-militant Third World states. Arms suppliers guiltily and belatedly proposed reform. Continued arms sales to "reliable" clients in the Middle East and elsewhere, however, indicate that negotiations and public declarations among the G-7 (a group formed among the seven largest economies) and the five permanent UN Security Council powers were mostly rhetorical and of little substance.

Although there has been little success in attempts to coordinate and jointly control the sale of conventional weapons to volatile regions, there has been more substance in efforts to control the transfer of weaponry that directly threatens industrialized countries. Thus, earlier restrictions on chemical, biological, and nuclear weapons and missile technology have been considerably strengthened. The end of the cold war seemed to improve prospects for future agreements on the control of conventional weapons, but due to renewed conflicts and continued, even increased economic pressures and incentives associated with arms production and sales, it now appears that the emphasis remains on easing threats to major powers rather than on arms control in general.

Approaches designed to protect primarily the direct interests of the industrialized world are, in our view, inadequate. They often entail attempts by the industrial North to manipulate the South while profiting in the process. During the cold war, such manipulations often involved East-West competition and occasional cooperation, in which arms transfers, as seen in our case studies, played a critical role. Now it is argued that cooperative denial of certain military technologies will play a stabilizing role. The earlier attempts generally failed, and we are doubtful of the latter as well. They ignore the power interests and internal dynamics of conflicts. The availability of technologies and the magnitude of supplier interests make it unlikely that such control will work unless those to be controlled agree with the limitations or are offered alternate security assurances.

Our analysis does not aim to answer all the provocative questions raised by the venerable Shaw. Indeed, as we proceeded with the study, our humility grew. The complexities of individual cases make generalizations difficult and sometimes contradictory. We deliberately selected diverse cases representing wars of various types, duration, and regional context. This produces differences of circumstance and nuance, but amidst the details we learn much about the various patterns of arms influence. We followed the "focussed" case-study approach popularized by Alexander George, asking similar questions of each case, so that it is possible to derive generalizations with a sense of data comparability and reliability.

Conclusions, nonetheless, must remain tentative. Over the course of our two-year study, the East-West conflict unravelled. Our results, therefore, are of historic interest in the cold war period; the validity of our findings for the coming decades can only be determined in the testing. Still, it would appear that the political dynamics between recipient and seller, both within and outside the shadow of superpower competition, remain relevant.

Our inquiry is limited to one particular, though central, aspect of the many problematiques of arms transfers in international relations. The focus is on the effects of such transfers on the course of wars—their origins, progress, and outcomes. Such inquiry has been largely neglected in the past. We hope that this focus will add some useful perspectives for policymaking as well, beyond the many studies of the dangers of arms proliferation for industrial countries.

The book's structure is shaped by these purposes. Initial hypotheses are proposed from the literature on arms and war, and subsequent case studies of Third World conflicts since 1960 (the time of origin for many new states) test these expectations. Through a combination of primary and secondary sources, an effort was made to collect refined arms-trade data in order to pinpoint as closely as possible the exact arrival of new weapons or agreements to supply them. We present an analysis based on three concurrent chronologies, summarized for each case in the appendix: arms shipments, hostilities, and diplomatic activity. Thus, we hope to learn whether and under what circumstances arms drive wars toward escalation or toward negotiated settlements.

Acknowledgments

This study has been made possible by the generous support of the John D. and Catherine T. MacArthur Foundation and the United States Institute of Peace. The approach and conclusions, of course, are the responsibility of the authors and do not necessarily reflect the views of either the MacArthur Foundation or the U.S. Institute of Peace.

An earlier version of parts of chapter 13 was published in the SIPRI *Yearbook,* 1982. We are grateful for the support provided from SIPRI in the preparation and publication of relevant material.

The authors would like to thank the following individuals: Elizabeth Agius, Robert Baumann, David Bunch, Carla Cox, Christer Crantz, Maike Petersen, Jeffrey Pickering, Suchitra Rath, Thomas Richardson, Mark Sandmann, Mark Schuler, Astrid Seyferth, Carol Sholy, and Mark Suprun for their able assistance in data collection and the preparation of chronologies; Ulrike Borchardt, Peter Körner, Rolf Hofmeier, and Volker Matthies for commenting on individual chapters; Ian Anthony, Gerd Hagmeyer-Gaverus, and Herbert Wulf, of the Stockholm International Peace Research Institute, for their help in tapping SIPRI's information base on arms transfers; and, certainly not least, Elizabeth Sherman and David Nelson for manuscript preparation.

In addition we thank our families, and our respective institutions: the Forschungsstelle Kriege, Rüstung, und Entwicklung at the University of Hamburg; the Center for Peace and Conflict Studies at Wayne State University, Detroit; and the Center for International Studies at the University of Missouri-St. Louis, as well as the editorial staff at the University of South Carolina Press.

Finally, we appreciate the operators of Bitnet and Internet. Without this electronic link our transatlantic project would have taken much longer to complete.

This book is dedicated to the countless millions who have lost their lives through the failure to stop wars once begun.

Arms and Warfare

CHAPTER 1

DEFINING THE QUESTIONS

INTRODUCTION

The Iraqi takeover of Kuwait in 1990, sometimes termed the first "post–cold war" world crisis, was a stark reminder of the importance of accounting for and controlling arms transfers. The arms of more than forty countries (SIPRI, 1990; Grimmett, 1989) had poured into the Gulf region during the ten-year Iran-Iraq war of the 1980s. Many of those systems, plus the "dual use" technologies related to chemical and nuclear weaponry and missile-delivery capabilities provided by Western sources to Iraq, threatened to come into play as President Saddam Hussein was confronted by a multinational, but largely US, array of force under UN auspices. The realization that the prior war's arms supplies enabled Iraqi leadership to undertake subsequent expansive operations, potentially at a high cost to those very arms donors, reminded leaders and the general public of how little is known, not only about the details of arms traffic, but also about the ultimate consequences of arms-supply policies.

Arms are supplied internationally for a host of reasons; arm-supplying nations are guided by combinations strategic and commercial motives (Pearson and Kolodziej, 1989). Strategic motives include the desire to bolster friendly states and to obtain base and overflight rights. Often, arms transfers are used as an instrument in the struggle against competitors and perceived enemies, both other states and political groups. A related, more domestically oriented, strategic motivation for arms transfers is the supplier's desire to strengthen domestic industry and maintain production teams necessary for defense through the income generated by arms exports.

Commercial motives are less kaleidoscopic. Actors involved include arms-producing companies and arms traders as well as politicians interested in bettering the economic situation in a particular industry or region.

Partly because of these dual motives, most states' arms-export policies contain elements of restraint.[1] The strategic motive implies a fairly clear restraint pattern: no weapon technology should fall into the hands of a potential enemy or be useful later against the supplier's regional interests. The commercial motive fairly quickly leads to the consideration not to annoy a better customer by delivering to its rival. In addition, a strengthening of the otherwise mostly defunct law of neutrality can be found in established arms-exporting countries where commercial motives are dominant; for countries such as Germany, Italy, and Switzerland, the transfer of arms to countries at war is forbidden by law.[2]

Now that the cold war has ended, major powers conceivably could revert to more open commercial arms trading in order to make up for the lost guaranteed markets of their respective alliances. However, Saddam Hussein's challenge to the established Middle Eastern "order," conceivably the precursor of other regional challenges by relatively disadvantaged but ambitious states, could be the occasion to rationalize the continued strategic distribution of US, Russian, British, or French arms to prop up favored-client states or factions under duress. In this sense, as well, NIC (Newly Industrializing Country) arms producers, including China, Israel, North and South Korea, and Brazil, could become more important sources of weapons for or against the regional challengers. Thus an arms transfer system resembling both the pre–World-War I situation, with freely roving and hardly restrained arms merchants, and one similar to the interwar period, when unilateral restraint put limits on arms transfers, is conceivable in the 1990s and beyond. (Harkavy, 1975; on historical and emerging systems see also Laurance, 1992, and Krause, 1992)

Do either or both of these courses signal the exacerbation of regional conflict and more destructive warfare? Or will one or the other contribute to a lessening of militant conflicts? To construct a methodological approach that allows one to formulate an answer to that question is a major aim of this study. Since prediction has to be based on the analysis of the past, we will first study wars of recent decades and then extrapolate trends to the 1990s. Our focus is the relationship between arms transfers, or restrictions thereon, and hostilities vs. peacemaking. But in order to judge these specific relations we have to study a range of issues in each war, including the existing order of battle, the political and diplomatic factors leading to and accompanying military activity, the military conduct of war and resultant attrition rates and, finally, the choices available to the decision makers involved, including available arms sources and outside diplomatic pressures.

AN ENDURING QUESTION: THE RELATIONSHIP OF ARMS AND WARFARE

In a way, the relationship between arms transfers and war is similar to that between armaments and war. After all, weapons are the implements of war, regardless of whether they are produced in the country at war or elsewhere, and regardless of whether they are already in place or delivered after the beginning of hostilities. What do we know, then, about the overall relationship between armaments and the conduct of war? There is no easy and quick answer to this question. At least two distinct strands of literature are relevant to this discussion because they contain conceptual clarifications and factual insights.

The first is the literature on deterrence. Often theoretically complicated, it in effect is built upon and extends into age-old controversies over the validity of the statement so effectively summarized by Vergetius, "Si vis pacem para bellum" (If you want peace, prepare for war). Can the promised use of military force cool aggressive behavior? J. David Singer, for one, argues to the contrary: "The greater a nation's military capabilities at any given time, the greater its likelihood of being involved in war within five years." (Singer, 1990b)

The assumptions underlying deterrence theory are fairly well understood (Morgan, 1983), though the practical consequences are debatable, at least when nuclear weapons are not part of the analysis (Weede, 1985 and 1988; Huth and Russett, 1988). The historical evidence, both on certain cases and in aggregate form, is less helpful than one might hope. There is, for example, no historical consensus on the question of deterrence in studies of either of the two most devastating wars in our century. Was it rational of German and Austrian decision makers in August 1914 to ignore the prospect of a two-front war against superior enemies? How could Hitler have been so adventurous in 1938–1939 given the balance of military forces in Europe? Similarly Saddam Hussein defied standard military logic in refusing to back away from a confrontation with forces of twenty-seven countries led by the foremost military power on earth.

Asking these and related questions, it becomes obvious that deterrence is a complicated concept. It is simplistic to assume that it arises merely from the numerical balance of military forces alone. In addition, there are questions of preparation, surprise, communication, resolve, risk-acceptance (Bueno de Mesquita, 1981), and strategic and tactical competence. Rather than looking only at the numerical balance of forces, we should distinguish a concept of deterrence that includes all relevant factors of decision making. Yet we also cannot ignore the tautological pitfall that such a concept also could suffer from an epistemological birth defect in that it is non-falsifiable: that is, when there is no military aggression, then deterrence is viable; when aggression has occurred, then deterrence has failed.

Rather than thinking of deterrence as failing once war has begun, it is useful to consider deterrence possibilities over the whole period of peace, war, and peace again. In this view, war is not necessarily a failure of deterrence, and peace no proof of its efficacy. A decision maker's calculus includes considerations about the balance of forces, during peace, war, and in terminating wars. Here the relevance of the availability of armaments during war becomes apparent. Deterrence of further fighting leads to peace.

The second strand of literature linking armaments and wars looks at the darker side of the relationship, which can be captured in a twisting of Vergetius' dictum a la Singer: "If you prepare for war you will get war." Is the preparation for war, as expressed in the accumulation of weapons or arms races, a major factor in the occurrence and exacerbation of wars? At least since the days of Quincy Wright and Lewis Richardson this question has been intensely studied and debated. Despite the intellectual energy spent there is rather little conclusive outcome.

Again, epistemological questions abound. What is an "arms race"? How does one measure it? Are all kinds of increases in military capabilities the same, or do intentions or number of opponents count? How does one determine "causes" of wars, or escalation of violence? Empirical studies of historical trends have shown that increased armaments and arms races do not generally "cause" wars. Nor do arms races invariably lead to fighting. (George, 1993) However, most wars have been preceded by some degree of arms buildup, and rising arms levels can aggravate existing tensions and lead to violence, especially when interpreted as an ominous sign of hostile intent, as in the Arab-Israeli or India-Pakistan fighting (Ziegler, 1987; Beer, 1981; Kemp, 1990b; Safran, 1969; Thayer, 1969, pp. 226–29). While too little is known about the complex psychological and strategic mechanisms by which such signs are interpreted or misinterpreted (i.e., about the accuracy of threat perception and the outbreak of war), even less is known about the effects of arms supplies once war is underway or, as in Saddam Hussein's case, the effects on subsequent wars. Judging by the frequency of historically misjudged threat, however (Brecher and James, 1988; and Lebow, 1981), it appears that accumulating arms levels further complicate an already blurred picture in which political interests (domestic, international neutrality, etc.) often condition a government's threat interpretation (reduction or exaggeration).

The transfer of arms adds extra dimensions to the complex perceptual relationship between wars and weapons, in that, through the transfer of weapons one or more outside actors becomes involved. Decision making by the parties in conflict becomes influenced and potentially even dependent upon decision making by parties originally not involved. The war-making capabilities or potential of actual combatants are curtailed or expanded by the whims and wishes of weapons and technology suppliers and—if arms transfers lead to subsequent involvements—by outside interveners.

War exacerbates the distinctions between types of suppliers. When arms are predominantly supplied to help or make friends, a war (or, often, the crisis preceding it) triggers a reassessment of the relationship in arms since it now is to become a de facto alliance. If transformation takes place, it provides extra incentives to deliver. This incentive may be offset by a desire not to destabilize a regional military balance, or not to aggravate tensions with other friends or foes. Conversely, a war also may lead to the reconsideration of strategic or tactical friendships. The supplier government has to assess its stake in the conflict and the recipient. Does it want its client to survive or to win the war or to pressure it into accepting a negotiated settlement? Suppliers also will consider their relationships with other states, such as potential intermediaries for weapons supplies or "regional policemen," as in the US "Nixon Doctrine" of the 1970s.[3]

Commercially oriented suppliers will respond to increased demand in the case of war. If the customer can pay, the obvious response is one of increased supply. But as noted above, there is generally considerable restraint even connected with commercial interests, operating especially in circumstances of war; one issue is consideration of payment prospects, another is potential pressure from strategic suppliers. Suppliers operating a strict policy of neutrality will stop all deliveries once fighting seems inevitable.

Therefore, supply of weaponry from the outside complicates the analysis of the relationship between armaments and wars in distinct ways, but does not alter its basic importance. It adds the necessity to look at dependence on deliveries, supply patterns, and decision making in supplying states, as well as in warring states.

Deterrence and peace theorists have argued about the overall pacification effects of arms supply. Indeed one rationale for supplying arms in general, as well as resupply during specific wars, is that it affords the donor some important restraining or policy influence over the recipient (Neuman, 1988). Dependencies on parts and ammunition as well as on the training of cadres supposedly allow the donor to encourage or discourage war-making decisions or stifle an ongoing war by closing the spigot on the arms-supply pipeline. On the other hand, skeptics have noted that arms recipients often pursue strategies to neutralize such restraints, seeking diverse and sometimes private or clandestine arms sources, and utilize reverse influence over the donor by stressing donor interests in the survival of the recipient states (Pierre, 1982; Quandt, 1978). This is especially effective in arms "buyers markets" and when donors lack political consensus to block supplies (see Wheelock, 1978; Ra'anan, 1978; Roeder, 1985).

Thus the question of the ultimate overall effects of arms transfers, especially during ongoing warfare, remains unanswered. Arms and spare parts clearly afford the wherewithal to continue a war or even escalate it, and thus constitute both a moral and political problem. Yet conceivably they also can hasten the conclusion of war either through battlefield victory or through the conviction they bring to the less well-armed side that it cannot keep up (i.e., mid-war deterrence). Indeed it has been argued that one of the problems of the Iran-Iraq war was that arms supply, arranged for both commercial and strategic purposes, was managed so as to promote stalemate and heavy attrition, thus prolonging and magnifying the war. Alternatives to such patterns would include asymmetrical supplies to one side to win decisively or symmetrical embargo to choke off the fighting.

In a sense, then, arms supplies or embargoes have both deterrent and precipitant effects. By changing power balances they can raise the costs of war and discourage the use of force. Yet by complex psycho-political processes, they also can hearten the recipient and lower the estimated costs of using force. Furthermore, difficulties in obtaining arms can be largely ignored as states seek to compensate not by making peace but by employing more diverse forms of violence.

Finally, arms suppliers, especially those concentrating on strategic goals, frequently fall into the trap of using arms as a surrogate for diplomacy, either to prevent or to end a war—i.e., assuming that by manipulating supplies and thus presumably the power balance, clear-cut decisive political outcomes ("sue for peace," "deterrence," "keep the aggressor from winning," etc.) can be achieved. Supplying Saddam Hussein's government might have enabled it ultimately to prevent Iran's victory and Gulf dominance. In the long run, however, it fueled the next war and Iraq's own hegemonic designs, and did not shut Iran permanently out of influence. In fact, arms balances are seldom the source of political agreement, but rather arms control or arms races generally reflect the state of such agreement or disagreement (Kemp, 1990b). In other words, arms supply is no substitute for effective political coalition-building.

This is not to say that arms transfers or their denial have never been useful in managing conflict. The military balance between Iran and Iraq in the 1970s may have led to the rough stability and grudging accords of the 1975 Shatt al Arab agreements (Neuman, 1990). The problem is that we have no systematic evidence of the effects of arms transfers in various types of warlike or crisis situations, particularly as they might lead either to negotiations or escalation of fighting. Harkavy, for example, has noted "the almost complete absence of any focused, comparative analysis of arms transfer diplomacy *after* the onset of and during conflict" (original emphasis; Harkavy, 1985, p. 6). George (1993) has echoed these sentiments regarding specific effects of arms races on deterrence in various contexts. Arms may be supplied to combatants for economic gain, but governments frequently also claim a desire to preserve or hasten peace, to influence the outcome of diplomacy or war, or, as in the Nixon Doctrine for example, to offset the need for more direct forms of military intervention in the foreign dispute.[4] Embargoes usually are justified by similar reasoning. The US-UK arms embargo of India and Pakistan in 1965 often is credited with bringing their South Asian war to a grinding halt, but unexpected consequences included stimulation of indigenous Indian and Pakistani arms industries and the search by both for alternative arms suppliers and strategic patrons—i.e., the USSR and China; the Indians and Pakistanis were able to fight another war just six years later.

DEVELOPING HYPOTHESES ON ARMS SUPPLY AND WAR ESCALATION

We know a bit more about the effects of arms supply on the initiation of war than we do about the effects on the conduct of war. Harkavy and Neuman, for example, (1985, vol. 1, pp. 20–21) note that foreign armed attacks on relatively strong regional powers have been undertaken even by smaller neighbors, emboldened by an expected uninterrupted flow of weapons that appeared to offer the attacker a "window of opportunity" (e.g., Somalia vs. Ethiopia, 1977, and Iraq vs. Iran, 1980). Obversely, Israel's "preventive" attack on Egypt in 1956 appeared driven in part by the fallout of Egypt's Czech and Soviet arms deals of 1955. At least when speaking of war outbreak, therefore, we generally have clear indicators of arms-supply effects, since there is usually a discrete moment of war initiation, if not a clear decision to fight. We can then associate that discrete moment to prior arms-supply patterns (see, for example, Safran, 1969).

The exact effects in on-going wars are more vague, however. On the one hand, active combatants that have already risked war participation are potentially more dependent on outside suppliers (especially if they lack indigenous production capabilities) than are states only contemplating war. The stakes of arms-acquisition diplomacy are higher when the die of war has been cast. On the other hand, because battles are ongoing and the heat of war potentially high, warring parties can extend their search for new and unconventional arms sources— battlefield pickup or clandestine sources—thus obscuring the effects of arms offers or denials by other governments.

Commentators such as Harkavy and Neuman have concluded that in lengthy wars of attrition, arms resupply has been "a major determinant of outcomes" (1985, vol. 1, p. 20), citing examples such as prolonged fighting and multiple arms suppliers in the Horn of Africa and Iran-Iraq wars. As in peacetime, however, it is difficult to trace the exact arrival of new arms in wartime, and their effect on specific fighting or peace decisions.

Since we suspect that arms supply crucially affects crisis escalation, de-escalation, and deterrence, a clearer understanding is needed concerning the likely consequences of such supply or denial during fighting. For practical purposes and policymaking this would afford a better understanding of the problems and payoffs of arms control, the peaceful settlement of conflicts, and the prospects of repeated warfare among the same parties. In this volume we propose to focus on the effects of arms flows just before and during selected international wars in the Third World. We will look for effects on escalation of fighting, on diplomatic negotiation and settlements, and on third-party intervention in the conflict. By registering as closely as possible the exact arrival of arms shipments and tracing government refusals to ship arms, we hope to show chronologically the outcomes under various conditions of conflict in various regions from the 1960s to the 1980s. This means that we will examine international wars of different duration and magnitude, sometimes in long-standing repetitive disputes (Arab-Israeli, India-Pakistan) and sometimes in ad hoc confrontations (Central America).

The basic rival hypotheses to be tested are: (1) the arrival of new arms supplies tends to fortify recipients so that violence is most often averted or abated, the need for third-party intervention precluded, and the prospect for negotiated settlements improved; (2) the arrival of new arms supplies tends to increase the likelihood of crises breaking into warfare, of escalation in on-going warfare, of third-party military intervention, or of the failure of negotiation; and (3) arms embargoes or limitations of resupply have pacification effects, similar to those in hypothesis one.

The reasoning behind these expectations follows from premises of realpolitik and action-reaction theories of crisis decision making. On the one hand, war preparations are sometimes seen as the most effective means of war avoidance or termination through the rise in potential political, military, and economic costs. On the other hand, defensive arms buildups increase security dilemmas for states that thereby pose threats to neighbors and rivals, causing these others to arm in response, thus raising tensions associated with war-making decisions. Arms receipt also presumably then lowers perceived costs of war and puts a premium on employment of forces before opponents undertake counterbalancing force increases, i.e., increasing the temptation to exploit force advantages. Finally, denial of arms supplies either freezes or erases force advantages, leading one or both sides to face higher costs and greater losses, thus presumably hastening the search for negotiated settlements.

The prospects of third-party military intervention can be affected by arms supplies in a number of ways: in fortifying recipients so that they do not require help; in raising the supplier's stake in the recipient's survival so that interventionary forces are sent if the fighting appears to be going badly; in deterring intervenors unwilling to confront heavily armed opponents; or in relieving concerns of potential intervenors who perceive the relative strengthening of their clients. In general, negotiations and diplomacy to end or limit fighting can be expected in situations of higher than expected war costs.

Those who have studied the impact of wartime arms resupply have made generalizations about the outcome of a particular war—who wins and who loses—and about differences in resupply patterns by various major or minor powers and according to war context. These findings are not as specific as those we seek concerning the effects on the course of wars, i.e., escalation, de-escalation, intervention, negotiation, but they do serve to inform our expectations regarding such effects. For example, the Soviet Union, at least during the cold war period, was found to respond "consistently with massive arms resupply to its beleaguered clients, while the United States, often 'Hamlet-like' in its ambivalence regarding client support versus arms control and 'conflict termination,' has exhibited a long and tortuous history of half-hearted and temporary embargoes, quarantines, non-lethal weapons support" (Harkavy and Neuman, 1985, vol. 1, p. 21). Thus, we would expect Soviet clients to show quick resilience in recovering from initial war setbacks, and for US clients to be at somewhat more prolonged distress but, because of US technological advantages, ultimately a qualitative advantage in prosecuting a war.

Once fighting begins, changes from prewar arms-supply patterns generally occur. In a survey of eight Third World international and insurgency wars, Neuman found high prewar dependence on one primary arms supplier (sixty-four percent of warring states), with half of warring states largely dependent on one of the superpowers. During the fighting, however, the pattern shifted markedly, with long wars generally disrupting the prewar supply relationship. Most warring states continued to rely heavily on the superpowers during international wars, but the volume (monetary value) of superpower military supply generally declined during the course of the fighting as supply slowdowns or restrictions were imposed. Usually the slack was picked up by other suppliers, as arms recipients increasingly diversified their arms sources. In other cases, depending upon the success of the war effort and the ease in acquiring weapons, states such as Ethiopia narrowed the scope of their arms acquisition, foregoing previously diverse suppliers and becoming more reliant on one (Neuman and Harkavy, 1987, p. 120). Similarly, during insurgencies states became more dependent on superpower and single suppliers. On the whole, overall military assistance and supplies increased during long wars, whether from one or a combination of suppliers. Short international wars, by contrast, did not disrupt prewar supply relationships.

As noted earlier, countries with larger prewar weapons inventories, or on-the-spot weapons advantages (e.g., Argentina in the

Falklands), appear to have been more likely to initiate war, at least in the Third World, than countries with smaller stocks; however, the quality of weapons available and troop morale and training also have served defenders well in repelling such attacks and bringing wars to a close (Neuman, 1986a&b; Neuman and Harkavy, 1987, p. 132). While military superiority is a major factor in winning wars, industrial superiority over the long run has been found to be a greater factor (see Wayman, Singer & Goertz, 1987).

Despite differences in their supply patterns, during the cold war the superpowers were circumspect about escalating fighting in wars among less developed countries (LDC). Both exercised supply restraint, particularly during the early stages of wars or until a favored client appeared badly hit. Neuman speculates (Neuman and Harkavy, 1987, p. 132–33) that this was due to fears of driving the opposite combatant further into the arms of the other superpower, or drawing the superpowers into more direct intervention. The US-Soviet relationship was characterized by a mixture of regional conflict escalation and conflict control, of competition and at least tacit cooperation (see George, 1986, and Kolodziej and Kanet, 1991). With scattered exceptions, generally in the Middle East, neither superpower released many new weapon technologies to LDCs during warfare.

Stephanie Neuman (1986a&b) also found that the importance of strategic motivation for arms supplies declined during wars. She interpreted this as a shift among suppliers nominally independent but factually within the camps and under the influence of the superpowers. Her argument is not fully convincing. The claim that, for instance, British and French arms deliveries are dependent on US decision-making seems overstated. Certainly, possible US reactions are taken into account in British and French decision-making over arms transfers, as during the Iraq-Iran War. But Neuman does not present evidence that this consideration dominates decision-making. Nor is the US position on deliveries of weapons to specific combatants always clear. We know even less about traditional arms-transfer decision-making in what was the East. But we think that it cannot simply be presumed that the politburo or some military council controlled all transfers from all former Soviet Bloc countries.[5] Neuman's analysis suffers, to an extent, from an overestimation of the superpowers' control over the behavior of other supplier states.

Generally, then, the major suppliers' policies were meant to defend the status quo, to afford control and leverage over the course of fighting, and to keep equipment from ending up in the wrong hands. Soviet direct presence in Vietnam, for example, increased markedly through aid in the 1979 fighting against China (Neuman and Harkavy, 1987, p. 134), which could be construed either as increasing Moscow's leverage or dragging out ever deeper Soviet commitments to Hanoi. Dangers of confronting other major powers in such supply commitments, along with sphere-of-influence politics, also could be the reason why the US and Soviets appeared readier to aid traditional clients (Central America or South Asia) rather than more geographically or politically remote states. Thus, it took many years and a changed political calculus regarding North Africa for the US to respond to Moroccan arms pleas in the Saharan war (Neuman and Harkavy, 1987, p. 135)

Although in some cases refusals or threatened refusals to resupply needed arms evidently hastened the termination of conflicts, this influence is complicated in that extensive initial supplies are necessary for subsequent withholding or resupply to have much effect on the recipients' policies. Even so, for example, "in no [Arab-Israeli] cases were any superpower goals achieved [through arms transfer or restriction policies] against the perceived interests of its clients. . . ." (Krause, 1987, p. 14). Major powers, particularly in cold war competition, ultimately underwent pressures to prove their support for clients and allies by resupplying them, so that even relatively weak or dependent clients could achieve considerable reverse leverage on the supplier. Arms recipients can be especially resistant to outside diplomatic pressure when it is perceived that crucial issues of national survival are at stake (see Nachmias, 1988, pp. 75–76).

A further study of eight recent conventional Third World cross-border wars has shown that in all but one case, arms resupply played an important role in providing clear advantages to one side in the fighting. In such cases, which included the Bangladesh independence war of 1971, Arabs vs. Israel (1973 and 1982), China vs. Vietnam, Ethiopia vs. Somalia, Zaire's Shaba crises, Morocco vs. Polisario, and Iran vs. Iraq, combatants with such advantages generally were able to repel initial attacks, recoup losses, or at least hold their own in the fighting. Such defensive success did not necessarily translate into favorable long-term settlement of issues, however (Harkavy, 1985, table 3).

REFINING HYPOTHESES

Commercial interests aside then, arms-resupply patterns are driven on the one hand by demand generated through wartime attrition rates, by the degree of the combatants' dependence on one or more arms supplier counteracted by each recipient's alternate sources of supply—either from battlefield acquisition, domestic production, or private trade. On the other hand, arms are supplied by states interested in affecting the war's progress and outcome and for reasons of traditional foreign policy alignments. Suppliers may wish to see certain parties win, or at least not lose the dispute, or to bolster their own image of power, credibility, or reliability, to bolster existing relationships with combatants or third parties, to test and prove weapons or doctrines under fire, to forestall reversion to more dangerous weapons (e.g., nuclear) or outside intervention (Harkavy, 1985, p. 15).

By the same token, suppliers might refuse resupply for fear of being drawn into open-ended commitments, depleting their own weapons stocks, exacerbating conflicts with political or arms-supply rivals or with disgruntled or worried allies, violating principles of legal or ethical restraint, releasing sophisticated, confidential, or dangerous technologies, or of embarrassment at the need for overflights or the prospect of client defeat even with assistance. Calculations about supply restrictions also could entail desire to pressure clients for concessions before resupply, to bring down an undesirable client government, or (e.g., France-Israel, 1967) to reorient foreign policy (Harkavy, 1985, pp. 15–16). A given supplier can, of course, be cross-pressured by a variety of such concerns in any single case.

Taking economic advantage of a situation further complicates these concerns. Commercial interests play a greater role in spurring arms transfers the more excess equipment a supplier has, the more concern about insufficient return on arms production investments, the more a supplier has been shut out of markets or seeks to enter new ones, and the smaller the supplier's own consumptive capabilities (Harkavy, 1985, pp. 17–18). Governments starved for foreign exchange also will be tempted to export arms without much heed of political consequences—as in the cases of China and ex-Czechoslovakia in recent years (though the revenue benefits of Chinese transfers appear thin; Anthony et al., 1993, p. 453) and despite the latter's original post–cold war pledge to leave the arms business.[6]

Since the heat of war generates the demand for weapons resupply, it is likely that intensity of motives will be asymmetrical—recipients presumably are under greater pressure to find arms than suppliers are to provide them. Suppliers in essence risk close identification with the cause of the recipient (though in recent wars many suppliers have backed both sides). If this basic pattern is true, then wartime supply patterns could be expected to deviate from peacetime patterns, reversing such phenomena as "buyer's markets" for example (see Catrina, 1988, pp. 14, 68).

A highly dependent recipient, under severe battlefield pressure, can be expected to accede more readily to supplier efforts to influence the conduct of war than would more resilient arms recipients. Recipients suffering high wartime attrition also would accede more readily. One normally assumes that the chances of negotiated settlements to wars increase the more clearly one side is beaten and the less its prospect for weapons resupply or other bail-outs. Fighting can be expected to escalate when the beleaguered side gains outside support, at least until a stalemate is reestablished.

The basic pattern above may indeed be too simple for real warlike situations. For example, stalemates can be either painful or relatively tolerable. After all, weapons attrition goes down in the lulls of a stalemate where the warring parties refrain from attack. Some weapons supplies or changes in fighting doctrine—as when the US assisted in building Morocco's Saharan wall against the Polisario—can bring on stalemates at relatively tolerable attrition levels, and hence low pressure for talks. Withdrawal of assistance (as when Algeria reduced support levels of Polisario) can generate more serious talks.

Therefore, an unrestricted flow of arms to a combatant generally is expected to increase levels of violence, but a flow regulated or moderated by restrictive suppliers can lead to stalemates that again conceivably engender a search for negotiations (see Table 1). Carte blanche resupplies would seem to be destabilizing for war outcomes and solutions, while embargoes or carefully managed resupply would presumably diminish overall violence levels. Yet embargo effects can vary depending on whether one side or both are disadvantaged.

We must extend our basic hypotheses, therefore, to allow for all these effects. Harkavy (1985) predicts that the complex interplay among previous arms dependencies, intensity and duration of fighting, supplier resupply and political policies aimed at political control

Table 1

Arms Supplies or Embargo Effects on Ongoing War

Factors Leading to Escalation	Factors Leading to Deescalation
Symmetric arms supply	Arms supply strongly favoring one side (particularly defenders)
Multiple arms suppliers or sources	Dependence on single suppliers
Combatants' revenge motives	High war attrition; painful stalemate
Low war attrition rates; tolerable stalemate	Embargoes and international pressure

or economic gain, and recipient war goals, motivation, and resupply options, will determine whether arms supplies during war escalate the carnage, as many arms-control advocates would assume, or generate pressures for peaceful settlement, as most supplying governments would argue. From the foregoing analysis, additional factors also must be considered in detailed analysis: the recipient's capability to purchase weapons and adopt various war-fighting tactics, the suppliers' stakes in the war or recipient regimes, and the previous level of armaments, both in terms of the balance of forces among combatants and in terms of the need for resupply.

It can be expected that "symmetrical" arms resupply, which tends to equalize the military capabilities in a two-party war, thus promoting stalemate, will diminish searches for negotiated settlements if the level of fighting remains low. If fighting and attrition levels are high, a more determined search either for arms or for negotiations, or both, can be expected. Here the restraining influence of arms suppliers can be greatest. If arms resupply or embargo affords great unilateral advantage to one party, and if the other party has little immediate prospect for matching the armaments, the weaker party can be expected to sue for peace.

Aside from military balances, if the arms suppliers include with their shipments significant political conditions or efforts to limit fighting and stimulate talks, then greater movement toward negotiated settlements can be expected. If recipients are more dependent upon single suppliers, the pacification effects of embargoes also can be more pronounced. Thus, the effects of arms embargoes could be expected to diminish in wars of the 1980s as compared to the 1960s, since states generally have diversified their arms sources. Successful embargoes now would appear to require a wide international participation of suppliers as well as inspection and enforcement.

Peace negotiations also are unlikely in the first flush of attack and successful occupation of foreign territory. If an attacker suffers a setback, however, it will be more likely to offer talks. Whether the defender agrees will be conditioned partly by its immediate prospects for reversing disadvantages and by revenge motives. These will be indirectly influenced by available arms. Therefore, arms resupply to defenders is more likely to be crucial in ending wars than supplies to attackers, since the attacker must be chastened but the defender not so encouraged that it is tempted to carry the war back to the attacker's homeland. Of course, manipulation of arms to this extent is difficult, since motives for war concern unachieved political goals rather than solely optimism or pessimism about armament or the course of the war.

CONCLUSION

Conceivably these hypotheses and expectations could prove mistaken as we review the details of specific wars. Leaders' motivations and calculations can be quite complex, and it is necessary to trace carefully the role of arms arrival or expectations in their decision-making. The methodology of doing so also bears careful discussion, as seen in the next chapter.

CHAPTER 2

RESEARCH TOOLS:
CONTROVERSIES ABOUT ARMS-TRANSFER DATA AND METHODOLOGY

INTRODUCTION

The research questions and hypotheses formulated in chapter one concern the relationship between the preparation, conduct, and termination of wars and the supply of weaponry. Because of many relevant structural and situational factors, as well as intervening variables, we need both time-specific data and methods to sort out the various relationships, yet, because of the limitations of available arms-transfer data, the range of useful methods is also restricted.

What arms-transfers data do we want? It would be good if we had both very detailed and highly aggregate accounts of arms shipments. Data should be detailed in the sense of accounting for major military goods transferred and the political and financial conditions of their transfer. We are interested in the perceived or actual military use-value of weapons transferred to the respective battlefields—so we need to know when they arrived and what they were capable of doing. Additionally, we want to know about support equipment and logistical backup, since they can be even more important than the weapon systems. Timing—and the perception of time—is of utmost importance, not only because weapons arriving at the wrong time might be useless, but also because the timing of weapon deals affects political and military decision-making calculus even before the arms are delivered. For the analysis of decision-making in recipient countries, it may be more important to know the dates of agreement on weapon deals than actual delivery dates; decisions regarding the fulfillment of prior contracts can be politically charged and highly influential in the course of wars. Thus for understanding the impact on fighting and political calculation, both agreement and receipt dates are crucial.

Unfortunately, however, timing is among the most difficult aspects of weapon deals to specify. Ideally, we would like to be able to determine at least the month of agreement or delivery in order to associate transfer agreement or delivery with effects on the fighting or negotiations. Due to reporting difficulties, specific dating is problematic and depends on ad hoc reports in various primary and secondary sources.

At the macro level we also want to know about the economic burden of arms importations, how much an individual supplier delivered and at what terms, and we want to know about the strings attached to arms transfers. We are interested in the open and hidden agendas of arms suppliers and recipients. We need to know about the debates surrounding arms exports decisions as well as about the debates in arms-importing states. Unfortunately, though, such agendas can be as obscure as the dates of arms deliveries.

DATA AVAILABILITY AND QUALITY

What arms transfer data do we have?[1] A variety of sources is available. Some, such as newspapers and special arms-trade publications, provide very detailed, though often not comprehensive material. Other, secondary sources, including historical studies of particular wars, yearbooks, current-affairs data collection, etc., present data in aggregated formats of various types. None of the various sources fully satisfies our data demands—especially those on timing; but they are all of some value for our purposes. Among the associated practical problems are governments' tendencies to conceal shipments and their value, and the difficulty of evaluating the combat effects of arms totals based on dollar value versus amount of equipment.

One theoretically useful source for arms-transfer data are normal trade statistics. Special categories generally are included for some weapons, such as guns, tanks, and war ships, while other relevant goods, such as most types of aircraft and electronics, are lumped together with civilian goods. Of course it is possible—and standard practice in some countries—to separate civilian and military goods into various subcategories. The US, for instance, publishes an enormous amount of information on sales of weaponry in its foreign-trade statistics; the USSR, on the other hand, used to report no figures for arms sales and only left a gap between civilian exports and total exports that one could infer was representative of arms sales. Even with Russia in the 1990s there has been uncertainty about conflicting official arms transfer totals. (Anthony et. al., 1993, pp. 446–451).

In practice, trade statistics are of only limited use for empirical research. Surveys show that the large majority of countries in the world do not publish complete and detailed data on arms imports, or exports for that matter (SIPRI, 1971; Arbeitsgruppe, 1980). In some cases, certain types of arms transfers are specifically excluded, and in other cases, transactions connected to armaments are not reported in the appropriate categories but rather are reported sketchily at the end of the trade statistics. In many cases, it is not clear from the available data whether and where arms transactions are included.

There is a large difference between what is recorded in trade statistics and what is known about arms transfers. Political, military, and economic interests combine to put considerable information into the public media, though it is scattered among numerous outlets. Such information is primarily from two types of sources: special periodicals and the general press, or a combination of the two. Several dozens of arms sellers' journals are currently published, mostly in Western Europe, but also in the US, in Asia, Australia, and Latin America. These include *Military Technology, Asian Defense, Defensa, Countermeasures,* and the like. There also are regular sales catalogs of weapon systems, mostly issued by governments, such as Britain, Israel, and Brazil, but also by specialized publishers, e.g., the British Jane's and the German Moench groups. In most cases, journals and catalogs only provide a forum for communication between weapon producers and possible buyers. The properties of certain weapon systems are described, sometimes in the form of competitive "consumer reports," advertisements, and sales-success stories. This last category is built upon press reports from companies ("nothing sells like success"), or recipient countries ("deterrence can only function if the enemy knows about it"). The specialists producing these publications often add information of their own—gossip and hard information—so that in the end an amazing amount of information becomes publicly available.

This information generally is good on technical aspects of weapon systems. It is less good on timing aspects (exact shipment dates are seldom reported). Sometimes dates can at least partially be reconstructed, for instance by examining the spread of information through the network of various specialized publications. Such publications are better on larger and more costly items than on cheaper ones; advertising in all its forms is expensive and only makes sense for costly items. Additionally, some of the deals announced in these publications are never consummated. Also, this type of source also has not been very good on arms transfers from the Soviet Union and other closed societies, unless their governments or agencies decide to engage in advertising.

Reports on deliveries from such states usually are based on accounts or information from government intelligence reporting.

Newspapers of all kinds are another important primary source on arms transfers. Reports about newly detected weapon systems can make a good story, so reporters are willing to go to some lengths to get them. Even more important is documentation of discussions about arms transfers, within and outside government circles. Not all reports make it into the major international papers—in the league of the *New York Times,* the *Washington Post,* the *Wall Street Journal,* the *Financial Times,* the *London Times,* or *Le Monde.* So the researcher must look both at major international papers and at regional papers. The search process then becomes dependent upon financial and time constraints. For this project, we were luckily able to draw upon the clippings and resources of a number of research institutes, including the Stockholm International Peace Research Institute (SIPRI).

Our admittedly sketchy impression is that in times of war, reporting in the major international newspapers is quite comprehensive. Reporters pick up stories from the regional papers and do investigative work on their own. The more "newsworthy" the war and the larger the weapons involved, the better is the reporting. Thus, reporting on the Middle East wars was very informative, while in cases such as the Uganda-Tanzania war, great gaps remained in the information provided by the major newspapers.

Because of the diversity of these sources, considerable effort is necessary to collect one comprehensive database. SIPRI provides the most painstakingly researched database, but only for "major weapons".[2] SIPRI publishes aggregated and tabulated data, and even more details on individual arms deals are available upon request. We have made extensive use of these data in this study.

In the area of aggregate arms-transfer data, there is only one alternative to SIPRI data: US government data. Official US tabulations are issued in various formats by a number of agencies, quoted during Congressional hearings, and squeezed out of the government by researchers and the press. Two regular publication outlets stand out: the US Arms Control and Disarmament Agency (ACDA) and the Congressional Research Service (CRS) of the Library of Congress, in recent years personified by its senior researcher, Richard Grimmett. These data, to which various US government agencies contribute and which are maintained by the US Defence Intelligence Agency, remain largely secret; ACDA and CRS are only allowed to publish certain versions in highly aggregated form: export and import series for individual countries; two-dimensional annual statistics for regions; and two-dimensional country statistics for major exporters over longer time periods. Only in selected cases—e.g., to document Soviet transfers to Nicaragua in the 1980s (United States Department of Defense, 1986)—have more detailed data been published.

In both the SIPRI and ACDA aggregated series, information on weapons hardware is translated into monetary values. Quite often, actual prices for weapons are not known or do not reflect the military use value of the weapons transferred. In such cases, prices have to be estimated on the bases of the information available (Brzoska and Ohlson, 1987, appendix). The most difficult pricing problems concerned Soviet arms transfers. Thus, in 1986, the US government decided to increase substantially its estimate of Soviet supplies, because it had changed its assumptions about the amount of support material that was supplied alongside weapons. These revisions, it was said, "generally do not affect underlying estimates of the number, type of value of major military equipment deliveries, but rather the estimated dollar value of supporting material deliveries, particularly those to countries engaged in ongoing hostilities" (United States Arms Control and Disarmament Agency, 1987, p. 145). Thus, the estimate of total Soviet exports of arms increased substantially, for example for the period of 1981 to 1985, from US $56.775 million to $86.153 million, or almost fifty-two percent (ACDA, 1986, 1987; in constant prices of 1983).

The gaps in the original reports and the difficulties in pricing put severe limits on both US government and SIPRI data. These collections are better suited for trend analysis than intercountry comparisons. They are even less suited for comparisons with economic data such as trade and financial figures. However, until better data are available (e.g., through the arms-trade register at the UN, as established through resolution 46/36L by the General Assembly in November 1991) these collections are the best sources available. Both aggregate sources are used sparingly in this study with due consideration of their limitations. SIPRI's unpublished "raw data" are surveyed to augment published series.

Aggregate and primary sources also are supplemented here with extensive use of secondary materials contained in scholarly studies. Often, this research provides rough dates for arms deliveries, and analysis has to put them in both decision-making and war scenario contexts. To improve reliability, we have used multiple sources wherever possible, and specify when the authors have a governmental role on one side or another. For battle analysis, we stress the type and amount of equipment received rather that the monetary value. For diplomatic analysis, we use both.

ANALYTICAL METHODS

A number of statistical methods are used to study relationships between variables. None seems appropriate here. There are two analytical reasons for this. First, the above discussion about our most straightforward variable, arms transfers, indicated that there could be little confidence in rigorous statistical exercises (Brzoska, 1982; Fei, 1979). Secondly, we are concerned with decision-making processes—about going to war, the conduct of wars, outside support for wars through arms deliveries, acquiescence in cease-fires, and the termination of wars. Statistical measurement based upon the assumption of random samples, such as regression analysis, is not well suited to the type of problems we are trying to tackle here.

The hypotheses formulated at the end of chapter one are fairly complex. To test them empirically demands the consideration of a large spectrum of circumstances and intervening factors. One can easily argue that only the comprehensive study of the origins, conduct, and terminations of wars could do justice to such a complex task, yet such comprehensiveness might require a book-length study of each war. Since we are interested here in generalizations, not in the individual case studies as such, we want to survey briefly several cases that combine to reveal the range of possibilities: long wars and short ones; wars directly related to major power interests and some of only local importance; some with wealthy combatants and some with very poor ones; cases involving various regions and types of regimes. Our hope is that there is something to generalize about, that each case is not only a unique script; we can only determine that by asking roughly the same questions of each case, i.e., employing focused case-study analysis (George and Smoke, 1974; George, 1993).

Another reason not to use a comprehensive single case study is that the specific problem of arms transfers during wars—while related to a number of other factors—might get lost in a study stretching into all aspects of a war. Comparison, while not insuring against neglect of important intervening factors in single cases, is more robust than comprehensive studies against the consideration of some factors and the exclusion of others.

Furthermore, one often implicit methodological consequence of the comparative approach is that relevant factors already are put into a hierarchy when the research questions are defined. Comparative analysis only makes sense when it is about a certain topic under certain circumstances—but not if it is about the totality of topics under all circumstances. Some of the variables are designated as more important than others for answering the questions posed. This does not imply that it is not possible to restructure hierarchies of variables if it becomes necessary during the research process. Indeed, theory-building is facilitated as the comparative process itself leads to the rearrangement of what are considered to be key variables.

This leads us back to the earlier question of the variable selection in relation to arms transfers. Following our line of argumentation so far, we should pre-select possibly important variables into a hierarchy and start looking for relations with arms transfers from the top of the list down. What are our perceptions about the most important variables linking arms transfers to wars? Thinking and discussing this, we came up not with a hierarchy of single variables but rather with two bundles of variables we thought to be proper reference points for the comparison of our individual case studies.

One bundle involves the military situation, including perceptions by relevant actors. We argue in chapter one that the importance of weapon deliveries, spare parts, and ammunition is dependent on the battlefield situation, actual or prospective. This in turn also impacts on decisions to end wars. The delivery even of seemingly unimportant spare parts can make a great difference in the conduct of war, or the perception of the possibilities to make war. On the other hand, given disintegration of forces or home-front support, even massive weapon infusions could occur without noticeable effect on the battlefield.

The other variable cluster involves warring states' diplomatic contacts. Here we try to capture the whole spectrum of political efforts to increase support for wars as well as political initiatives toward war termination. While the first factors capture what one might call the "material base" of warfare, this bundle of factors reflects the "political superstructure" of state behavior in war situation.

SYNOPSIS OF TOPICAL CHRONOLOGIES

In addition to the two variable bundles just described we have a third one of arms transfers, including the attendant political decision-making. The specific analytical method used here is the comparison of topical chronologies for each case. As the basis of our analysis, we generated three types of case chronologies: a chronology of the war fighting, including escalations and de-escalations; a chronology of diplomatic contacts and third-party political interventions, including initiatives to settle the war; and a chronology of arms transfers and the diplomacy surrounding them. In order to answer our research questions and test our hypotheses, we compared events in these chronologies, with the aim of establishing temporal links between arms transfers and events in one or the other chronology. The raw information derived from the chronologies was then augmented and compared with insights gained from the relevant literature, i.e., case studies of individual wars. Relying on the chronologies alone would be dangerous, since events may correlate in time by coincidence. The larger picture is necessary in order to assess the relationships between arms transfers and war events.

The method chosen for this study is best described as synoptical. It is not texts that are compared, but rather our variable bundles, in practice represented by chronologically ordered occurrences. The synopses are the starting points for generalizations, not more. Where case studies demonstrate the importance of other variables, we go beyond the mentioned variable bundles and accept better explanations of the chains of events.

CONCLUSION

The synoptical method falls short of providing definitive results. As an interpretive method, it is better suited for highlighting differences and suggesting generalizations and, hopefully, subtle insights not found either in statistical analysis or case studies. We do not find this disconcerting, but rather appropriate in light of the complexity of the subject matter and the dearth of knowledge about armament effects on the politics of war. We turn now to the series of representative cases.

CHAPTER 3

INDIA-PAKISTAN KASHMIR WAR, 1965

INTRODUCTION: THE BACKGROUND OF WAR

The India-Pakistan Kashmir War of 1965 has been cited as the foremost example of effective arms restrictions in ending hostilities. The US and UK imposed an arms embargo that, with the combatants highly dependent on them as suppliers, seemed to choke off the fighting. This example, then, could be the yardstick against which to measure other arms-control efforts in other wars. Yet we must first confirm that indeed the embargo, as opposed to other factors, was responsible for the settlement, and we must specify factors unique to this case that might differ from other wars.

The 1965 war had its origin in lingering and sporadic territorial and ethnic conflict dating to Indian independence, and in the particularly troublesome and persistent issue of Kashmir. The former princedom, largely Muslim in population, was ceded to India via a disputed decision of the maharajah in 1947. After more than a decade's worth of fruitless attempts to agree on a UN mandated plebiscite to determine the popular will, India gradually moved to absorb the territory. However, Pakistani-inspired armed infiltration periodically renewed the crisis atmosphere.

After the failure of an Anglo-American peace initiative in 1962–63, this atmosphere was reheated with Indian extension of constitutional provisions to Kashmir in 1964–65. Included were constitutional changes in 1964 and early 1965 to make Kashmiri administration essentially the same as the other Indian states. Unsuccessful Muslim raids and renewed attempts to foment rebellion followed.

The 1965 Kashmir crisis came during an especially tense period in a dispute and display of power over remote coastal marshlands on the Arabian Sea known as the Rann of Kutch. Indian and Pakistani troops clashed there in April and May, with Pakistan getting slightly the better of the fighting. Neither side appeared ready for the implications of full-scale fighting at that time, however. With a June cease-fire and promised arbitration, Pakistani military confidence appeared bolstered in pushing the Kashmir issue yet again (Ziring, 1984). Responding to Kashmiri uprisings attributed to Pakistani instigation, Indian troops occupied key points on the Pakistani side of the Kashmiri cease-fire lines in August 1965; the Pakistani army invaded Jammu on September 1, and the Indian army carried the war to three sectors of Pakistan a week later. A cease-fire was proclaimed under UN auspices on September 23 (Day, 1982).

The war's diplomatic background related to mutual competition and distrust not only about territory but also about the power balance on the subcontinent. Both India and Pakistan reacted to China's growing assertiveness, and tried to make use of superpower cold-war interests for their own regional purposes (Brines, 1968, ch. 11). Indian rearmament in the wake of the Indo-Chinese fighting of 1962 alarmed Pakistan, which took the initiative in trying to pressure, weaken, and isolate India.[1] Pakistan cultivated China to put added, if vague, diplomatic pressure on India to relinquish Kashmir (Brines, 1968, pp. 252–53). US interest in the Pakistani-American alliance also was spurred with the added stimulus of growing Pakistani-Chinese relations, even as Washington and London aided India. While taking pride in their American weaponry, Pakistani leaders felt relatively restricted to one major source of arms, with accompanying supply uncertainties in war (Brines, 1968, pp. 274–75).

ARMAMENT AND THE APPROACH OF WAR

Armament acted as a precipitant of war in this case (Brines, 1968, p. 263). India's unilateral buildup after 1962, driven partly by the Sino-Indian war and partly by the rationalization of US-Pakistani partnership, had a rebounding effect on Pakistan. New Delhi made little effort to reassure its suspicious neighbor. The US and the UK sought to shore up Indian defenses against China, but not to tip the armament scales against Pakistan, trying to confine the supplies to mountain forces, associated transport and trainer aircraft, air defense radar and control, and road building and communications, all provided at a relatively slow pace. Even this limited assistance, however, freed other forces for the Pakistani front and, when combined with India's growing domestic arms production, greatly alarmed Rawalpindi (Brines, 1968, pp. 264–65).[2]

At the same time, the Western powers' refusal to supply India with sophisticated supersonic aircraft and tanks to match those of Pakistan caused New Delhi to turn increasingly to Moscow. Washington and London wanted to limit the regional arms race, and did not think defense against China required advanced equipment (Brines, 1968, pp. 266–67). The Soviets nevertheless stepped in with renewed commitments even to build Indian factories for MiG production. Financial terms for Soviet military assistance were far more favorable, and Soviet supply agreements were more massive than those of the West, tending further to exacerbate the region's mutually perceived threats.

By 1964, Soviet military commitments to India totalled $131 million, compared to $110 million by the US (*New York Times,* May 13, 1964, p. 6). Table 2 shows the key equipment supplied to India by its arms patrons from 1962 to 1965. The pace of shipments picked up considerably throughout 1965 until the outbreak of war, with the UK and USSR leading the way. Corresponding figures for Pakistan in Table 3 show predominant US and then Chinese prewar roles. However, Washington clearly slowed the pace of deliveries to Pakistan in 1965, even before the embargo was announced when the war started, and China and West Germany only inadequately picked up the slack. The bulk of UK and US arms supplied to India after 1962 were rationalized as opposing Chinese power, while aid to Pakistan was seen largely as an antidote to the USSR, altogether a strange mix of conflicting priorities (see Burke, 1973, p. 277; see also Anthony, 1992; Thayer, 1969; Gupta, 1967, vol. 1; *Newsweek,* September 20, 1965, p. 33)

As China's influence on the subcontinent grew with the 1962 war, then, the Soviet Union joined the UK, France, Australia, Belgium, Canada, Japan, and the US in bolstering India's traditionally eclectic range of weaponry (Thayer, 1969, p. 226). Pakistan protested to Washington, to little avail (*New York Times,* May 13, 1964; and Chaudhri, 1966, p. 496). Pakistanis feared that a strengthened India would close its grip firmly on Kashmir; the constitutional reforms of 1964 seemed to confirm it. By the same token, India became alarmed over Pakistan's growing strategic partnership with China, which included a Sino-Pakistani boundary agreement covering northern Jammu and Kashmir and Sinkiang Province, and Chinese backing of Pakistani demands for a Kashmiri plebiscite (Butterworth, 1976, p. 393).

Table 2

Arms Shipments to India, 1962–65[*]

Major Arms Shipped to India, 1962–64

Canada	16 Caribou transport aircraft; 36 T-6 Harvard trainer aircraft; 5 DHC-3 Otter transports; 6 C-47 transports
France	40 AMX-13 tanks; 4 Chetak helicopters (produced under license); 20 Alouette-3 helicopters
Indonesia	8 Vampire T-55 fighter
UK	150 Hunter jet fighter; 100 Gnat jet fighters (Indian assembly); 80 Canberra bombers; 5 Viscount transports; 213 Centurion tanks; 80 Stuart tanks; 1 HS-748 transports (Indian assembly); 5 AOP-9 WWII vintage aircraft; 12 Sea Hawk fighter-bomber
US	25 C-119 Packet transports; 2 DHC-4 Caribou transports; 2 Model 47G helicopters; 30 Sherman Tanks; 3 L-1049 transports
USSR	10 MiG-21 jet fighters; 2 Ilyushin transports; 24 Antonov transports; 30 AA-2 Atoll AAM; 89 PT-76 amphibious tanks; 8 AN-12 Cub-A transports; 22 Mi-4 Hound helicopters
Yugoslavia	200 M-48 76mm towed guns

Major Arms Shipped to India, 1965

France	7 Chetak helicopters (Indian licensed production)
UK	5 Vijayanta tanks (Indian assembly); 6 Canberra B-I-8 bombers; 2 HS-748 transports (Indian assembly); 15 Gnat jet fighters (Indian assembly)
USSR	120 SA-2 Guideline SAM; 11 MiG 21 jet fighters; 89 PT-76 trainers; 33 AA-2 Atoll AAM; 20 SA-2 SAM launchers; 36 Mi-4 Hound helicopters

Sources: Estimates collected from Anthony, 1992; Singh, 1982; *Newsweek*, September 20, 1965; SIPRI files; authors' files.
[*]Including licensed production.

Table 3

Arms Shipments to Pakistan, 1962–65

Major Arms Shipped to Pakistan, 1962–64

US	180 M-113 Armored Personnel Carriers; 40 M-109 155mm artillery; 100 M-114 155mm artillery; 32 Model-47 helicopters; 12 F-104A jet fighters; 3 F-104B jet fighters; 300 AIM-9B AAM; 2 Bluebird Class coastal patrol and minesweepers; 4 C-130B Hercules transports; 25 T-37B trainers; 2 Queen Air A65 light aircraft; 4 HH-43B Huskie helicopters; 1 Tench Class submarine (WWII vintage)

Major Arms Shipped to Pakistan, 1965

China	4 MiG-15 UTI jet fighters; 40 Type-69 tanks
FRG	250 Cobra-2000 ATM
NET	1 F-27 MK-100 transport aircraft
UK	4 Ton Class coastal patrol ships
US	1 T-37B trainer; 1 Baron light aircraft; 20 M-109 155mm artillery

Source: Estimates collected from Anthony, 1992: SIPRI files; Dupuy, 1972, p. 326; *Newsweek,* September 20, 1965; authors' files.

Despite each side's scare headlines, neither appeared to have genuinely overwhelming military superiority at the outbreak of the 1965 fighting (Brines, 1968, pp. 268–69). India enjoyed advantages of numbers, Pakistan a slight edge in weapon sophistication and mobility (*Asian Recorder,* October 8–14, 1965, p. 6708; *New York Times,* August 29, 1965, pp. 1, 7; Burke, 1973). While some considered India's costly 1962 experiences with China as a sign of weakness, Indian troops were more "battle tested" than those of Pakistan. Indian planning for a cross-border counteroffensive also was quite extensive and despite the long difficult border, the Rann of Kutch episode had provided ample warning of tactics to be encountered later (Singh, 1982, p. 33).

India had begun employing Soviet equipment, such as nine MiG aircraft, along with British Hunters and French Mysteres. Yet India's arsenal also featured vintage US and UK equipment, such as Sherman tanks dating to the 1940s. Pakistan relied on US-supplied Sabre jets equipped with air-to-air missiles, and also featured an arsenal of US Patton tanks (both delivered in the late 1950s), much feared by the Indians. A great many of these ultimately were lost in the fighting. Reportedly NATO countries also had supplied Pakistan with early model antitank missiles and complex mines (Burke, 1973; SIPRI, 1971, pp. 500, 836–37).

The complex perception of military threat on each side, therefore, combined with mutual hostility over Kashmir to prevent much needed reassuring diplomatic agreements and to set the stage for preemptive or redressive attack (Brines, 1968, ch. 11). In dealing with the question of whether arms supplies "caused" this war, we have some rather definitive claims. Former US ambassador to India, John Kenneth Galbraith, for example, argued that, "The arms we supplied to Pakistan under this policy caused, and I underline the word, the war . . . between India and Pakistan. . . . if we had not supplied arms, Pakistan would not have sought the one thing we wanted above all to avoid; namely a military solution" (quoted by Thayer, 1969, p. 229).

Yet others maintain that the combined supplies to India to confront China after 1962 set off the chain reaction of counter-armament and military provocations and clashes throughout 1964 which led to the major war. It is difficult to know that any single set of arms supplies, rather than the interaction of preparations, helped trigger this war. Certainly neither side could have been confident in its weaponry if there had been none, or no likely resupply, but the political rivalries that drive wars might have spawned a successful search for alternate arms suppliers so that some level of fighting could have occurred had the major powers embargoed the region in 1964 or early 1965. Nevertheless, the openness of prewar supply to both sides tended to encourage those considering the military solution, about which Galbraith spoke, at a time when both "national liberation struggles" and territorial defense generally were oriented to the barrel of a gun. We had the spectacle then, as Thayer described it, "of Pakistanis in American *Patton* tanks fighting Indians in American *Sherman* tanks. . . ." (Thayer, 1969, p. 227).

THE COURSE OF WAR

By spreading the Kashmir fighting over one-thousand miles with air attacks into both west and east Pakistan, India fared better in the war than it had in the Rann of Kutch episode, but Pakistan also gained the backing of China, which delivered an ultimatum to New Delhi threatening to join Pakistan. (India's costly 1962 border clashes with Beijing were still fresh in the minds of those in New Delhi.) India received quiet Soviet support, but with a US-UK arms embargo to both sides, a quick resolution of the war appeared preferable to prolonged bloodletting. A UN formula for withdrawal and cease-fire and Soviet sponsored negotiations followed, with no real territorial change from the fighting.

However, the fight had both diplomatic and domestic repercussions, including deepened bitterness on the two sides, with Indian determination to retain Kashmir; new and important roles for both the USSR and China in the region with corresponding erosion of trust for the US and UK; changes in both the Indian (death, during peace talks, of harried Prime Minister Bahadur Shastri) and Pakistani (President Muhammad Ayub Khan's ultimate fall from power) governments; and accelerated efforts on both sides to become more self-reliant and generate more alternatives in arms procurement (Ziring, 1984). Comparison of chronologies of fighting, diplomacy, and arms supply reveal more specific effects of arms acquisition prior to and during the warfare.

The Rann of Kutch fighting—the prelude to the Kashmir war—was a time of testing for Pakistan's equipment (largely new American armor) and strategy, and a gauge of Indian armament and motivation (Gupta, 1969, p. 174; and Ganguly, 1986, p. 84). It is generally contended that Pakistan seized the opportunity presented by Indian police expulsions of Pakistani border guards from the disputed swampland of the Rann. Reinforced Pakistani guard units in turn wiped out the Indian outposts, and in the midst of the skirmishing, regular Pakistani forces were introduced in relatively large numbers to intimidate the Indian forces in this remote and difficult location, where Indian troops had little motivation to fight. The action also was seen by many, particularly in India, as a first venting of frustration building over Kashmir, a first round of fighting aimed ultimately at Kashmir itself (Brines, 1968, pp. 287-89). Pakistan was encouraged both by the general results of the Rann fighting (India fought only a holding action), and by the international response, including Washington's rather ineffectual protests about unauthorized use of US-supplied arms in violation of the US-Pakistani alliance treaty. The relative success of the Rann offensive is believed to have led senior Pakistani military officers and Foreign Minister Zulfiqar Ali Bhutto to press President Muhammad Ayub Khan ever more insistently for a Kashmir offensive (Ganguly, 1986, pp. 84–85).

In mid-May, even prior to the guerrilla offensive of August 5, incidents of firing along the Kashmir cease-fire lines reached a peak, and several hundred Indian forces occupied three Pakistani mountain observation posts. Designed to dissuade Pakistan from risking aggression, the mission served only to confirm Pakistani expectations of Indian aggression, and provide a *causus belli* (Brines, 1968, pp. 298–99). Though India's popular pride swelled with the assault, the Indian government soon agreed to a UN-sponsored withdrawal from the outposts.

India maintained the conviction that counterinsurgency warfare demanded attacks on the insurgents' sanctuaries (Brines, 1968, p. 317). They had demonstrated this on August 15, with a trek back to the same mountain outposts from which they had recently withdrawn—again evidently to dissuade Pakistan from supporting further uprisings (Pakistani artillery reportedly had rained down on Indian forces on the fourteenth; Brines, 1968, p. 318-319). Skirmishing between regular armed forces along the Kashmir cease-fire lines continued through August, with India penetrating into Pakistani-held Kashmir (Azad Kashmir) and Pakistani mountain territory (Ganguly, 1986, p. 57). Although India and some foreign observers maintained that the guerrilla offensive in Kashmir, organized as early as May, also included Pakistani army commanders and units, the first admitted involvement of regular Pakistani forces in support of the guerrillas was September 1. Indian forces then launched their own offensive beginning the formal cross-border war on September 5. Pakistan's tactic of instigating guerrilla insurrections resembled the 1947 Pakistan-India fighting, as well as the "national liberation" struggles of the 1960s (Brines, 1968, pp. 302–10).

Pakistan relied on its tank forces all through the escalating hostilities of August, attempting to reverse Indian momentum and compensate for the failure to inspire a general Kashmiri uprising. On September 1, they mounted their major offensive on the Southwest Kashmiri front, driving into Indian Kashmiri territory in the terrain best suited to mobile armor. A breakthrough in this sector could have cut off Indian access to Kashmir. This series of reprisals and ripostes blew up into the broad Indian offensive of the sixth, designed to shift to terrain favorable to India, i.e., the Pakistani Punjab near Lahore (Brines, 1968, pp. 322–29). The diversionary Indian attack succeeded in easing the pressure on Kashmir, as Pakistani armor was redeployed to defend key western cities.

Once Indian forces reached the outskirts of Lahore, they either were driven or merely pulled back (depending on the account) after encountering a canal turned into a moat by destroyed bridges. The Punjab fighting then settled into battles for strategic bridges, waterways, and villages. Pakistani counter-thrusts on September 8 included nighttime tank offensives toward Amritsar, utilizing relatively sophisticated US infrared-vision equipment. Indian defenses, though badly outnumbered, set an effective ambush (once the Pakistani tanks were detected by reconnaissance aircraft), and the attack was blunted (Brines, 1968, p. 339). Indeed, the superior firepower of the Patton tanks was useless and the gasoline-fueled tanks tended to catch fire, effectively ending use of such fuel in US tanks thereafter (Ganguly, 1986, p. 89). In breaking this offensive, then, a key to the war, India relied on skillful use of territorial barriers (such as canals and breached dikes) and equipment, often in ambush. Newly acquired high-velocity tank guns and jeep-mounted, Indian-manufactured (US design) recoilless rifles were very effective in neutralizing Pakistan's tank force advantages (Brines, 1968, p. 340).

Near Sialkot, fifty miles northeast of Lahore, the largest tank engagements at that time since World War II were fought, by most international interpretation essentially to a draw. India lost roughly twenty-seven percent of its tanks and Pakistan thirty-two percent.[3] Thus any Pakistani advantages in more sophisticated US equipment was washed out in difficulties of deployment and logistical support. Nevertheless, Pakistan's defenses blunted Indian advances, and at the time of the cease-fire on September 23, each side still possessed chunks of the other's territory seized in the initial fighting and could probably have continued fighting for several more weeks (Ganguly, 1986, p. 89). However, UN and major-power pressures mounted for the cease-fire, and the general sense of stalemate was growing on both sides (Brines, 1968, p. 347).

Relatively little air power was used in the war, and then mainly in tactical support roles, although each side tried strategic bombing of the other's airfields. India called upon air strikes in the face of the

Pakistani tank assaults of September 1 and the Pakistani air force retaliated on the second. Air support was a constant in the war thereafter (See Khan, 1979, pp. 22–23), but neither Pakistan's advanced F-104s nor India's latest MiGs played much of a role (the latter evidently suffering maintenance problems). Modern US-supplied Sidewinder air-to-air missiles also were not prominent.

The limited nature of the air war and overall offensives might have been due to mutual fears of touching off communal and public-opinion reactions to failure, to outside diplomatic pressures, and to technical difficulties. Clearly, no breakthroughs were scored because of the import or acquisition of new advanced weapons, despite persistent fears on both sides (Brines, 1968, pp. 348–49). (See Appendix, Chronology 1, "India-Pakistan War, 1965.")

DIPLOMATIC PRESSURE AND ARMS FLOW

Despite preoccupations in Vietnam and elsewhere, a worldwide diplomatic reaction to the emerging Indo-Pakistani crisis in August was followed by a concerted UN push for a truce. Some individual countries took sides. China lent mainly moral support to Pakistan, and was joined in this by Indonesia and a few other Muslim states. Turkey pledged some arms and Iran offered oil, but no "Islamic bloc" emerged. This significantly reduced Pakistan's prospects of obtaining large-scale arms or spares to continue the fighting. India had few willing patrons, as well, and became increasingly dependent upon Moscow (Brines, 1968, p. 353). Both sides evidently resented world opposition and pressure for a cease-fire. India insisted on the status-quo ante, particularly regarding Kashmir, which Pakistan was compelled finally to accept in return for face-saving UN commitments to seek an overall Kashmiri political solution (Brines, 1968, p. 355).

The cease-fire was achieved basically through joint major-power pressure inside and outside the UN. The Security Council was able to function with Soviet-US cooperation, and the US and UK applied the brunt of the pressure. Indeed, this was the first time in the cold-war period that the US and USSR voted together in the Security Council on a major war-peace matter.

The war's escalation from the confines of Kashmir to a general Indian attack on west Pakistan caused a heightened sense of international urgency, and an unusually swift (one day) reaction in the form of the arms embargo. The September 6 attack was viewed as a new war, and one far more dangerous to the international balance of power than the initial hostilities. While India might have won sympathy as the victim of guerrilla attacks in Kashmir, it was roundly criticized for crossing a recognized international border in widening the war (Brines, 1968, p. 361). China chimed in with border threats against India on September 8, in coincidence with the US-UK arms embargo and just as Pakistani forces tried to rebound in the Punjab fighting.

A particular focus of Indian concern was the Sino-Sikkim border (Brines, 1968, p. 362). Indian sensitivity to Chinese threats was magnified by the Soviet position of neutrality in the war (first stated on August 24 and reiterated on September 7). In this, the Soviets appeared to value approaches to Pakistan designed to keep the latter out of China's arms (Brines, 1968, p. 364). However, Moscow's gambit was made palatable to India by a notable Soviet reluctance to join the arms embargo. Some Soviet military and economic assistance continued to flow to India. An Indian military mission to Moscow early in the conflict negotiated a series of naval-weapon shipments, with agreement on provision of four submarines and reference to further supplies, including armor. However, relatively little Soviet equipment ultimately was used in the fighting.

The US-UK suspension of military assistance to the belligerents on September 7 and 8 had impact on both sides, but predominantly on Pakistan, which was more heavily reliant on US arms and had fewer prospects for alternative supply.[4] The embargo's effect was heightened by prior US policy, which had allowed Pakistan a relatively minimal stockpile of ammunition and spares, enough only to hold off an attack, rather than launch one against India. Pakistan had collected a thirty-day stockpile during the summer of 1965, partly by cutting back on training (Anthony, 1992, p. 77). Indeed, before India's escalation of September 6, jittery Pakistani air-force personnel already were exploring alternate sources of equipment supply in anticipation of insufficient US support and in light of almost complete dependence. India also lost spares for her British equipment, especially Centurion tanks. Perhaps more tellingly, Western economic assistance was also suspended, causing an even greater potential strain on the Indian economy.

The alternative arms suppliers explored by Pakistan, with indifferent results, were Turkey, Iran, and later, during the war, China and Indonesia (see Khan, 1979, pp. 10–11 and ch. 4). The army required ammunition, antiaircraft guns, and explosives; the air force required replacement fighter aircraft.

The Turks, bound by NATO ties to the US and wholly dependent on US equipment with attendant "re-export" restrictions, could promise Pakistan only some munitions and small arms, rather than the requested aircraft, spare air parts, and tanks. Similarly, Iran was slow to move promised supplies to Pakistan, but vowed to be forthcoming with explosives and ammunition. Both Turkey and Iran, in addition to the US limitations, had misgivings about China's role (Khan, 1979, pp. 56–57).

The Indonesians dispatched a number of MiG fighter aircraft,[5] together with two submarines and four missile boats (this in partial violation of Soviet provisions in their original supply to Indonesia and in spite of the pressing Malaccan Straits and Malaysian problems). However, these supplies did not arrive until after the cease-fire and were not sufficient to assure top Pakistani leaders of adequate resources to continue the fight (air-force advisors were confident of at least minimally sufficient supplies though) (Khan, 1979, pp. 46–47).

The Pakistanis also sought Chinese equipment to be sent via Indonesia, which perplexed the Chinese, who maintained that direct supplies were easier. Chinese leaders also seemed uncertain of whether Pakistan would fight to the finish for its political objectives, and weighed heavily the international costs of becoming involved militarily against India (Khan, 1979, pp. 40–42, 48–49). Chinese skepticism about Pakistani motives evidently was justified given the generally confused nature of war aims cited by most commentators, and the serious talk of peacemaking beginning after ten days of combat.

Thus, the "bite" of the embargo coincided with other factors, such as political uncertainties and battlefield stalemate. Though some of these factors eventually would have worked to India's advantage as the larger state, the UN provided a welcome locus for talks once the cost-benefit disadvantage of continued fighting became clear to both sides. Indeed, it is reported that Pakistani president Ayub Khan was so dismayed by the poor showing of his armored brigades that his will to fight on past the final UN deadline was nil. His military advisors reinforced his own pessimistic assessments of outnumbered forces low on ammunition and resources. Ayub Khan came to believe the air force too would be worn away (Khan, 1979, pp. 97–98).

In the negotiations for a cease-fire, India remained adamant on settlement terms, and evidently part of the cabinet sought to delay the cease-fire past the proposed September 13 date (UN Security Council resolution) until a relatively telling blow could be dealt to

Pakistan's armor, thus reducing future vulnerability. The Indian cabinet was split on this tactic, however, in view of mounting economic difficulties; the prime minister, favoring the acceptance of an early truce, won out. As many Indians anticipated, however, Pakistan resisted an early cease-fire at that time, so the fighting continued with the onus on Pakistan (Brines, 1968, pp. 367-69).

Battle attrition was quite heavy during these final days, September 13-17. Pakistan, stung by US "neutrality," pointedly invited American peace overtures on September 15, conceivably as a face-saving way out after the dust of tank battles settled and as supplies ran out. China weighed in with further border demands against India on September 17. Neither Washington's nor New Delhi's intelligence sources predicted a large-scale Chinese intervention, but troop concentrations facing Sikkim and Ladakh led to some concern over diversionary intrusions. Washington evidently had secretly warned Beijing about large-scale involvement in a direct meeting on September 14 and also expressed disapproval to Pakistan (Brines, 1968, pp. 372-73; Mankekar, 1966, pp. 128-29). India reportedly consulted US officials about possible air support if China did attack (conceivably this would have amounted to transport and supply as in 1962).

From about September 18, in the midst of the battlefield stalemate, the British high commissioner addressed cease-fire appeals to the two combatants. A discouraged President Ayub Khan, despite last minute efforts by some civilian and defense ministry advisors to paint more rosy battlefield and supply assessments, seized upon these appeals in private meetings with the high commissioner. Afghani mobilization added to the pressure on Pakistan, as it was interpreted as a symbolic pro-Indian gesture to balance Chinese moves (Khan, 1979, pp. 99-100).

The Security Council passed its third resolution on September 20, setting a September 22 deadline for cease-fire and withdrawal to positions held on August 5. On September 19, the USSR had invited the parties to meet at Tashkent; India had readily accepted—though rejecting passages about an eventual Kashmiri political settlement—while Pakistan, in the midst of domestic rioting, held out until the precise UN deadline. The Ayub government threatened to withdraw from the UN if progress toward a Kashmir settlement were not forthcoming. A Chinese three-day ultimatum on the Indian border issue was extended and then expired, with some exchange of shooting but, as predicted, no large-scale intervention. China had diverted a battalion of Indian troops, but had provided only psychological assistance to Pakistan (Brines, 1968, p. 376).

It appears, then, that the US-UK arms embargo conditioned the pattern of final settlement, but that the war ended mostly out of stalemate and overall domestic and diplomatic pressure. The embargo's differential impact on Pakistan coincided with some greater Indian boldness and a larger Pakistani "climbdown" in the final settlement. Pakistan's high commissioner in London had lamented on September 10 that India's war production was eighty percent indigenous while Pakistan had to import eighty percent of her supplies (Gupta, 1967, vol. 2, p. 5). Yet India, enjoying tactical advantage, appeared more anxious for a cease-fire than Pakistan.

Other key factors were notable as well in bringing about the settlement. India's economy was threatened by the economic sanctions. Moscow's diplomatic neutrality, despite the fact that it continued arms supplies to India, also raised New Delhi's concerns, especially about confronting China. Indeed, in response to India's call for renewed UK-US arms shipments in view of China's September 16 ultimatum, the British foreign secretary indicated that the ultimatum might speed the end of the fighting (Gupta, 1967, vol. 2, p. 165) Thus, while Chinese-Western strategy may not have been coordinated, it constituted quite effective concerted and comprehensive pressure on the warring parties not relying solely on an arms embargo; China's role was not fully lamented in Western capitals.[6]

Following sporadic cease-fire violations, and the ultimate success of the January Tashkent agreement on mutual withdrawal, Pakistan would basically revert to "national liberation" tactics in encouraging separatism and uprisings across the border (Brines, 1968, p. 381). The Egyptian press also reported that, despite an embargo that in the US case would extend officially through the 1960s, Pakistan's requests for fresh US arms supplies in the latter stages of the war may have resulted in an earmarked portion of a joint US-UK $300 million sale to Saudi Arabia; subsequent arms shipments occurred as well. (*Arab Observer*, 1966; see also ch. 4 below).

The Tashkent negotiations as well as the US-UK arms embargo brought the USSR to diplomatic prominence in the region. Moscow wanted a settlement that would limit the prospects and necessity of further Chinese inroads on the side of Pakistan, while also maintaining its own growing ties to India. Indeed, China too probably focussed mainly on the Soviet threat at this time; during his visit to consult Chinese leaders prior to the Tashkent talks, President Ayub was assured, jokingly, by Chou En-lai that China valued Pakistan's role as a Chinese "friend in SEATO," and that since China was not in a position to provide much hardware, it might be best for Pakistan to obtain it from Washington (Khan, 1979, p. 113).

Overall, the war ended with little lost by India and little gained by Pakistan. Indians agreed to give up positions captured in Azad Kashmir, and Pakistan mutually agreed to withdraw to August 5 positions, while bringing its frustrations about Indian absorption of Kashmir to public light. Pakistan had seen both a challenge (threat) and opportunity as it initiated the moves toward war in early 1965—a challenge in India's arms buildup and ties to the West after the 1962 Chinese war, and an opportunity as measured by the success of the Rann of Kutch fighting. Yet the war's results jarred its favored relationship with the US while bolstering those of India with the USSR. Indeed part of the reason the arms embargo had its effect may have been the rather limited and ill-defined Pakistani aims in initiating the conflict. Rawalpindi was, in part, swept along by the Rann of Kutch successes, and there never was much stomach for a prolonged war and the sacrifices necessary to replace destroyed equipment in time to continue fighting.

Hence, embargoes may be most effective in situations of relatively low motivation or limited war objectives, and in conjunction with broader multilateral sanctions. In this war, Ayub Khan did not even see fit to meet personally with Chinese leaders (as they had requested) to enlist greater assistance, or at least to push for it (Khan, 1979, ch. 4). The war itself, on both sides, was largely a "tit for tat" exercise in finding militarily suitable and favorable locations (especially for tanks) to retaliate for the opponent's prior foray. It had little of the flavor of all-out warfare for total victory. As is so often the case with inconclusive wars in persistent conflict systems, the 1965 fighting set the stage for the next round, which would focus on different issues and threats. The warriors on both sides had rather carefully avoided east Pakistan, and those in the east were not nearly as devoted to the Kashmiri issue as those in the west—a fact to be politically exploited by India (See Ganguly, 1986, pp. 92–93).

CONCLUSIONS

In a sense this case is a study of arms withheld rather than infused during war. The supplemental supplies sought by India and Pakistan during the fighting were symbolic, since the war ended before supplies from the USSR, China, France, or Indonesia were received and before the warring parties' supplies were exhausted. At least one observer maintained that considerable quantities of war materiel from Iran and Turkey were entering Pakistan by the time of the cease-fire, but both governments withheld the major weapons Pakistan sought (Singh, 1982, p. 4). We also know that India employed only about a third of her air force and relatively little advanced Soviet equipment, and that Pakistan was appraised that its own supplies were sufficient for at least a few more weeks of fighting. Therefore, the timing of the cease-fire decision was not wholly dependent on the arms embargo, though leaders could clearly see the prospect of equipment running out.

Indeed, the hypothesis that an arms embargo will have dampening effects on violence (see chapter one) is technically borne out in this case. But we should also note that this was a short war, not premised on complete victory over the opponent. Pakistan tried to confine action to the favorable terrain of Kashmir, and India, even in spreading the war, did not exploit potential east-west Pakistani frictions or involve its air force in large-scale attacks on the east. Rates of attrition in armor were high, but the air war could have continued longer, and navies were hardly even deployed. Therefore, the context and goals of the war, as well as conditions of arms dependency and overall multilateral diplomacy, affected embargo prospects.

This was a stalemate at relatively high attrition levels, at least in armor, although the casualty rates were not as high as in more recent Third World combat. Once the decision was made that a breakthrough would be too costly and risky, and that international pressures were compelling, the lost pride of having the opponent control land and prisoners led to the final talks and disengagement. The stalemate was more politically than militarily uncomfortable, and combined with the impact of the embargo, it moved Pakistan to swallow its pride, even as Indian pride, damaged by China and at the Rann of Kutch, was restored.

In this case, the arms embargo was felt by both sides but the effect was differentially greater on Pakistan—the government that ended up backing down further in negotiations. It has been noted that Pakistan's president became pessimistic both about immediate battlefield performance and long-term combat prospects while his forces were locked in stalemate with a larger foe possessing arms in reserve, with his own supplies running low. Pakistan began the war with the more modern equipment, with an example of relative US tolerance over its use in the Rann of Kutch, but with levels of arms relatively limited by US administrations interested in the regional power balance and India's viability vis-à-vis China.[7] Negotiations followed both sides' realization of higher than expected costs, and in India's case, of satisfactory gains as well.

Prewar supply patterns were partially suspended in this case, with hasty Pakistani efforts to diversify sources. India was able to overcome the technological sophistication of US weapons through battlefield tactics, but no particular surge in Soviet supplies was received. Except for some MiG attacks, most Soviet systems were kept in reserve or presented operational problems.

The war occurred at a time of dependence on major-power arms supplies, and was another in a series of such cases that saw relatively little US or Soviet resupply during the fighting. The superpowers were interested in containing and controlling the conflict. Pakistanis argued that the US, increasingly committed in Vietnam and decidedly anti-Chinese, took too little interest in the war and allowed the USSR too much latitude in promoting the settlement. In fact, US and UK interests called for the survival of both India and Pakistan as counterweights to socialist powers in Asia; this would explain the quick and resolute resort to an arms embargo, UN resolutions, and private diplomacy to end the war.

Pakistan's contacts with China and China's responses also appeared somewhat restrained by Western pressure on both parties. However, neither the US nor UK could have relished the idea of carrying through with threats to intervene (possibly by air) if China became involved in the war. USSR military aid was correlated to the Chinese threat, and evidently neither Pakistan nor India would have been left defenseless by their patrons. In this sense, both the supply and embargo of arms seemed carefully managed.

Interestingly, while the UK and Soviets resumed arms shipments to the combatants (mainly India) immediately upon the cease-fire, the US persisted in the embargo even after the Tashkent agreement; in February 1966 shipments of "nonlethal spare parts and end items" were resumed, obviously facilitating Pakistan's military recovery. Nevertheless, Pakistan was alarmed by this delay in full resupply from its main patron and sought more diverse arms sources, initially China, and by 1968, the Soviet Union as well (Thayer, 1969, pp. 233–34).

Washington was reluctant to refuel the region's arms race, but US leaders, based on Townsend Hoopes's Senate testimony in 1967, evidently concluded that "with the passage of time, a policy of total arms suspension was dissipating our influence and producing side effects of serious concern. All these developments are destabilizing and their cumulative effect could produce an uncontrolled arms race which no one wanted or intended. . . ." (quoted in Thayer, 1969, pp. 228–29). Arms embargoes, especially when unilateral, are difficult for major powers to maintain over time in part because they seem to deprive those powers of desired levers of influence in a given region, even as the embargoes themselves are forms of influence.

The India-Pakistan Kashmir War ended close to stalemate on the Punjabi plains, as mutual mistakes and resolute armored defenses blunted momentary breakthroughs. Evidently, it was less the supply of arms, or lack thereof, than political restraints and battlefield tactics that led to this stalemate and cease-fire agreement. The embargo constituted a background reality of poor prospects for breaking the stalemate, especially in Pakistani thinking. While India insisted that Pakistan pull back to August cease-fire lines, Pakistan dropped effective insistence on a Kashmir plebiscite.

If this is the "model" case of the efficacy of arms embargoes, the evidence for their effect is only partially compelling. The political goals of the war were quite limited. Clearly, though, emotions could have been carried away in further retaliation and intransigence if the support, including arms resupply, by major power patrons had been more reliable, encouraging, or extensive. In this sense, dampening the arms supply, including pre-embargo ceilings on ammunition and spares, markedly dampened perceptions of benefit in or enthusiasm for prolonged combat.

In a sense, as Brines notes (p. 348), the battlefield stalemate also relieved some of the psychological threats of weapons supplied to both sides. Pakistan's US supplied Sidewinder air-to-air missiles found few effective targets in the low and relatively slow-flying indigenously produced Indian Gnat fighters; Pakistan's Patton tanks were far from invincible, indeed proving quite vulnerable, especially when maneuvered with questionable tactics; India's MiGs appeared largely inoperable; Pakistani Sabre jets and F-104s were not decisive. However, neither side chose to draw much subsequent security reassurance from these calculations, especially in view of their mutual vulnerability to internal turmoil. We encounter these lingering insecurities in the next chapter.

CHAPTER 4

INDIA-PAKISTAN BANGLADESH WAR, 1971

INTRODUCTION: THE BACKGROUND OF WAR

The issues in dispute between India and Pakistan shifted gradually in 1970–71 to focus on the Bengali autonomy struggle inside Pakistan and ultimately on the resultant civil and international armed conflict. Kashmir was by no means a forgotten issue, and the Kashmir front was reopened in the course of what, in December 1971, became the third major India-Pakistan war. No less than the monumental dissolution of the Pakistani state itself was the main result, especially in view of India's support for the Awami League, the main political party of East Pakistan, for a guerrilla struggle when the League was repressed, and finally for the creation of an independent Bangladesh. The violent Pakistani internal crackdown on the Bengalis also caused a massive influx of millions of desperate refugees to an overburdened India. This case, then, is characteristic of the internationalized civil disputes so rampant in the Third World since the 1960s.

Much had changed in and around South Asia since the conclusion of the 1965 Indo-Pakistani fighting and the Tashkent agreements. The Soviet position in the region had been strengthened both by the Tashkent negotiations and the relative decline of US interest during the Vietnam years. Moscow in effect sought improved relations with both India and Pakistan, especially in hopes of containing Chinese influence. Coincidentally, similar US anti-Chinese interests finally had begun to wane, with the long wind-down of the Vietnam conflict and the Nixon-Mao initiatives. Indeed, Pakistan, enjoying (however briefly) open relations with all three powers, made itself helpful in fostering US National Security Adviser Henry Kissinger's secret trip to Beijing in 1971, thereby throwing the regional political calculus into some disarray. Washington had less pressing need for India as a counter to China, and more perceived need for Beijing to counter the Soviet Union; basically the Nixon Administration accommodated itself to larger regional roles for both Communist powers (Kissinger, 1979, pp. 684–787; Siddiqui, 1972, pp. 170–73; Wilcox, 1973, ch. 3). Therefore, as the three major powers viewed the growing India-Pakistan friction after 1970, they looked more than ever beyond immediate regional issues to their wider geostrategic competition and to ways of using regional partners to strengthen their overall position.

Changes also had occurred in the armaments field, changes largely wrought by the 1965 war. Washington remained reluctant to rearm the region in a major way, extending the nominal embargo but allowing the transfer of selected equipment and ammunition to maintain Pakistan's basic viability. Thus, the fast paced Pakistani arms buildup characteristic of the early 1960s was not repeated, and Pakistan lost its qualitative edge in weaponry over India. The latter had been busy building its indigenous weapons manufacturing capabilities in armor and aircraft, as well as smaller arms, and cultivated important arms-client relationships with the USSR, France, and Britain as well. The lesson learned from 1965 was diversification of arms sources, greater self-reliance, and less overall dependence to insure against future embargo effects (Anthony, 1992, chs. 6 and 7; Jackson, 1975, ch. 5).

As in 1965, the intensification of hostilities in this case occurred over a number of months in 1971, but instead of cross-border skirmishes, the diplomatic storm blew up mainly over domestic Pakistani repression. Eventually, guerrilla warfare was supported across the border, as in 1965, but this time by India against Pakistan; this escalation of involvement led to formal bilateral warfare in December. Unlike the 1965 escalation, however, though third parties attempted to intercede, no direct India-Pakistan talks occurred concerning the crisis—a remarkable example of diplomatic failure.

The main Bengali nationalist party, the Awami League, and its leader Sheikh Mujibur ("Mujib") Rahman, had won a major victory in renewed Pakistani elections in 1970, and was in a position to dominate the newly restored parliament. The League generated a six-point set of demands for virtual autonomy of Bengali territory in the east (the central government would be confined basically to defense and foreign policy without even taxing authority), which was resisted by the west Pakistani political elite (particularly dominated by Zulfiqar Ali Bhutto), the army (again largely dominated by the west), and eventually by martial-law president Yahya Khan, who was influenced strongly by these elites. The army particularly was concerned about Pakistani "territorial integrity" (a unitary state), defense spending, and resistance to India. Basically, however, Mujib and the League refused to play the traditional western back-room game of power allocation prior to the parliament's reconvening, which would have reassured the power brokers. These elites in turn conspired successfully to delay and finally preclude the parliamentary opening until the League had been displaced (Sisson and Rose, 1990, ch. 4).

The die was cast for massive eastern protests and brutal counter-repression in March. The army in that sector was expected to enforce the martial-law regime, but immediately began experiencing logistical problems and supply shortages that would dog them, despite initial successes, throughout the coming months. The president offered a new parliament, and aimed to preserve the unitary state, but never regained the confidence of the League, which in turn had tried to assure west Pakistan about its respect for the constitution. Essentially Yahya Khan came to treat the League as rebels, and jailed their leadership while disarming eastern forces and police (Wilcox, 1973, pp. 27–29).

After initial vacillations—partly because of elections in March 1971—the Indian government by May had come to the decision to support Bengali secession. As refugees from Pakistan's unrest arrived in large numbers, a League headquarters in exile was established near Calcutta. From here, liberation forces gradually were trained and supplied during the course of the conflict-ridden summer (Ganguly, 1986, p. 121). Regular Indian troops reportedly served as rebel advisors inside east Pakistan, and Indian border security forces intervened across the border to help League and rebel forces rein in Indian Naxalite and Marxist rebels based there (Siddiq, 1979, pp. 97–98; Sisson and Rose, 1990, p. 144). Indian army units were strengthened to compete with the bolstered Pakistani forces in the east; unlike 1965, therefore, deployments were seen by both sides in mid-crisis to constitute a credible threat of attack in both the east and west.

India was confronted with a choice of either quick intervention in Pakistan, before the monsoon made massive action impossible, or a gradual military buildup for such a confrontation late in the year. It chose the latter after consultations among service chiefs; among other factors, a lack of heavy equipment in the area, spare-parts and naval shortages, understaffed units, insufficient MiG production, internal security needs, and the necessity of neutralizing China and world opinion were noted.[1]

The Pakistani army was capable in six weeks of destroying most of the rebel positions near the Bengali-Indian border, but the longer the confrontation dragged on without effective political negotiations or settlement, the more aimless the army's mission became and the greater the effect of Indian supported guerrillas (Khan, 1973, pp. 115–17). During this first phase of guerrilla war, the rebels reportedly lacked arms and ammunition as well as organization and training. Later, however, supplies and training improved as weapons were captured in ambushes, brought by Bengali defectors from the Pakistani army, or supplied by "friendly sources" (purchased by Bengali groups in Europe or supplied by India). While small arms abounded, the guerrillas lacked armor and heavy equipment (Chowdhury, 1972, pp. 158–68).

Pakistani prewar diplomacy initially was successful, building a general international consensus to keep hands off an internal Pakistani problem despite Indian pleas for refugee relief (Sisson and Rose, 1990, ch. 8). However, as India pressed its public case, and as the refugee burden and human-rights abuses mounted, the World Bank aid consortium decided on June 21 not to renew Pakistani assistance, which in turn led to the Congressionally induced termination of US bilateral assistance. President Yahya Khan suffered a growing realization that his nearly bankrupt government could no longer afford, either economically or politically, massive military operations in the east (Ganguly, 1986, pp. 123–24). With the League leadership jailed, the Pakistani government tried unsuccessfully to win Bengali support with offers of partial amnesty and a new constitution.

Henry Kissinger visited both India and Pakistan in July on his way to China, warning Pakistan of India's war mood. But the Pakistani leadership was not impressed. They did not believe that India considered war an option; if so they were sure they would win. When Henry Kissinger mentioned—"as tactfully as I could"—the Indian military advantage, Yahya Khan and his colleagues retorted with heroic stories about Muslim fighters (Kissinger, 1979, p. 861).

In turn, Yahya Khan warned India on July 19 that any move to take Pakistani territory would result in general war. Evidently he expected both US and Chinese support in this, due to his instrumental role in setting up the unprecedented Washington-Beijing meeting, an expectation that proved highly unrealistic. Nevertheless, the belligerent Pakistani position and the excuse it gave India's leaders to cite an implied US-Chinese-Pakistani axis led to a closer Indian alignment with the USSR.[2] Having obtained intelligence information that China was not committed to backing Pakistan with force (the 1965 scenario was a further indication), and knowing the Washington-Beijing links were only at the formative stage, Indian leadership nevertheless attempted to win Moscow firmly away from its openings to Pakistan, and to insure a diplomatic ally in the UN Security Council if war were to erupt.

India previously had been only lukewarm about Mr. Brezhnev's call for a South Asian security system (presumably aimed at China), concluding a vague agreement with Moscow emphasizing economic cooperation in 1970. In July and August 1971, however, a full-fledged "friendship treaty" was finalized, based on a text Moscow proposed in mid-1970; it contained mutual promises not to assist each other's enemies. Offering similar treaty terms to others, India went to great pains to reassure Washington that the agreement did not compromise nonalignment. In negotiating the final document in August, New Delhi informed the Soviets of the planned military move against Pakistan. After hedging on approval (Moscow had held back from endorsing Pakistani dismemberment), the Soviets finally chose to support India fully in preparations for such an eventuality over the next three months. Simultaneously, Mrs. Gandhi embarked on a diplomatic offensive both to garner world support for the impending hostilities and to give diplomacy one last chance (Sisson and Rose, 1990, pp. 201–4, 210–11; Ganguly, 1986, p. 125).

Fearing a post-monsoon Indian offensive, Pakistan alerted forces in the west (rather than indulging in a further major build-up in the east), implying, for deterrent effect, renewal of the 1965 fighting scenario and a Kashmir crisis. Political reforms (new elections and a new constitution, but not the release and recognition of the Awami League leadership) were offered, along with a mutual Indo-Pakistani border pullback. However, on October 22 the Pakistani air force also was put on alert. These preparations merely allowed India to justify a counter-buildup in the west, and after increasing military assistance to the Bengali rebels in late October and early November, to mount a full-scale troop movement into East Pakistan on November 21, the date some choose as the start of the formal war (see Sisson and Rose, 1990).

During the long months of prelude to war, India had sought to neutralize third-party pressure on behalf of Pakistan, and refused repeated Pakistani and US proposals for mutual, UN observed pullbacks from the border, pullbacks that would have weakened India's support for the guerrillas. In July, India reportedly precluded a Bangladeshi government-in-exile initiative for Washington to mediate talks between the Awami League and the central Pakistani government (Sisson and Rose, 1990, pp. 193–94). Pakistan, on the other hand, remaining adamant about suppressing the League, tried to deter India from attacking in the east in force by adopting its conspicuous "defend the east through the west" strategy, hoping that captured Punjabi Indian territory could be traded back ultimately for lost Bengali territory if deterrence failed (Jackson, 1975, ch. 5).

The Pakistani government, as distinct from the military high command, was slow to realize the extent of Indian designs, evidently concluding in November that New Delhi's military incursions were meant only to establish border enclaves for the guerrillas. However, on December 3, finally despairing of a US or Chinese supported rescue, President Yahya Khan stubbornly and rather irrationally made good on his threat of general war by launching relatively ineffectual air and then ground attacks in the west (Khan, 1973, ch. 11; Sisson and Rose, 1990, ch. 11; Ganguly, 1986, p. 129; Siddiqui, 1972, pp. 174–75). If nothing else, Islamabad hoped for a territorial breakthrough, and to engage enough major-power concern for either a diplomatic or military intervention to end the war quickly, as with the diplomatic efforts of 1965 (Sisson and Rose, 1990, ch. 11). The Pakistani high command, after all, retained a relatively low assessment of India's fighting potential.

ARMAMENT AND THE APPROACH OF WAR

Once the major powers had entered the prewar crisis, efforts to employ arms-transfer diplomacy ensued. In April, the US, seeing the rise of tensions without constructive Pakistani reforms or settlement prospects and reacting to growing human-rights criticisms, began a contradictory arms-supply crackdown on Islamabad, hoping to induce needed reforms while not threatening Pakistani national viability (Sisson and Rose, 1990, ch. 9). China also pressed Islamabad quietly for an East Pakistani political settlement prior to Indian intervention, a fact known as well to Indian intelligence.

With the friendship treaty negotiations in August, India used her new Soviet opening to press, quite successfully, for major arms support; Soviet Air Marshal P. S. Koutakhov finally arrived in late October to oversee the shipment of urgently requested equipment (commencing by air- and sea-lift in early November). Evidently, Moscow had decided that India would attack Pakistan even without further Soviet assistance, and that influence with the region's dominant power and in the new Bengali state was worth the risks inherent in destabilizing Pakistan (Sisson and Rose, 1990, pp. 201–4, 243–45; Siddiqui, 1972, pp. 170–73).

Pakistan by no means had been totally deprived of arms transfers in the interwar period, with supplies coming mostly from China and France, but also from the US and USSR (Anthony, 1992, ch. 7; International Institute for Strategic Studies, *Strategic Survey,* 1972, p. 50; *New York Times,* November 9, 1971, p. 1). Step by step, Washington lifted the embargo, allowing the transfer of spare parts for nonlethal items from March 1966. The US also successfully negotiated with first West Germany, then Belgium and Italy, to sell one hundred older tanks to Pakistan. These countries received, in turn, newer NATO models (Anthony, 1992, pp. 102–3; Bowles, 1971 and 1969). The embargo was eased further in April of 1967 to allow both India and Pakistan to buy American spare parts, ammunition, communication equipment, medical supplies, vehicles, etc.[3] Washington authorized the sale of one hundred Turkish M-47 Patton tanks to Pakistan; but the Turks in the end decided to keep them (Anthony, 1992, p. 102). In March 1970, the US government began a further review of arms-transfer policy toward Pakistan and India.

Washington agreed to provide Pakistan further military aid in October 1970, but the arrangement was announced as a one-time exception to the arms ban in order to respond to renewed Soviet assistance to India (*New York Times,* October 11, 1970, p. 30). The agreement included three hundred armored personnel carriers (APCs), seven replacement (attrition) B-57 bombers, six F-104 fighters, four sea reconnaissance planes, and some "nonlethal" supplies, worth about $90 million. Actually, the deal was a condition imposed by the Pakistanis for help in bringing together Chinese leaders and Henry Kissinger (Kissinger, 1979, p. 849; Anthony, 1992, p. 102).[4] None of this equipment had been delivered by early 1971, but the State Department, which held up new export licenses on March 27, allowed shipments already contracted and licensed to go through, causing a storm of congressional protest. With holds on various categories of weapons, however, by mid-August only a total of about $3.8 million had reached Pakistan, mostly spare parts for pre-1965 equipment, along with drone aircraft and parachutes, and a priority airlift of $500,000 worth of spare parts.⁵ When a more complete US embargo was imposed in December (sales ended on November 8, with unused licenses revoked thereafter), the total delivered still reportedly was less than $5 million, which was justified to India on the basis of the need to keep at least minimal influence with Islamabad.⁶

US economic and military assistance to India, running only at about $5 million per year, continued largely uninterrupted during 1971, until in a last futile attempt at pressure in response to Indian border incursions in the east, Washington banned new (mainly ammunition) arms-export licenses and suspended license renewals on December 1. This still left approximately $11.5 million in valid licenses, mostly for anti-Chinese air-defense systems; as in Pakistan's case, these licensed exports were not shipped before the war (*New York Times,* December 2, 1971, p. 1; December 4, 1971, p. 10; Sisson and Rose, 1990, p. 260).

In line with its regional policy initiatives after 1968, the Soviet Union also had instituted a sizeable Pakistani military-assistance program, including spare parts for Chinese equipment such as MiG 19s, as well as sixty T-54 and T-55 tanks, rocket launchers, artillery, and helicopters at discounted rates.⁷ Gravitating back toward India when Pakistan maintained its Chinese ties, however, Moscow suspended such assistance in April 1970 (having tried to make the price of such suspension an Indian friendship agreement in 1969). As with US military aid, some shipments in the pipeline to Pakistan continued well into 1971 (mainly replacement parts and small quantities of arms), even after the failure of Soviet calls for a peaceful east Pakistani settlement in April. Conceivably, Soviet relations with Muslim Middle Eastern states, however tenuous, also conditioned these lingering Pakistani ties (see Sisson and Rose, 1990, ch. 12; Choudhury, 1975, p. 205; and Ganguly, 1986, p. 124).

China had soured on Pakistan's military chances against India in 1965, and strictly limited the extent of its Islamabad commitments short of military intervention. India cited substantial Chinese arms shipments to Pakistan in mid-1970, including 6 squadrons of jet fighters (evidently MiG 19s), 2 bomber squadrons, and more than 150 T-59 tanks, to go along with antiaircraft guns, radar installations, and other equipment. Since 1965, an estimated five new Pakistani divisions had been outfitted with Chinese equipment, but the overall supply was limited by China's own needs at a time of confrontation with the USSR (*New York Times,* September 9, 1970, p. 12; November 12, 1970, p. 9). Chinese military aid continued after Pakistan's March

25, 1971, Bengali crackdown, with a large load arriving (dispatched before March 25) in April. Prior commitments were honored, but Beijing, on an increasingly parallel course with Washington, refused new orders through the spring and summer. Evidently President Yahya Khan was ill-advised of these Chinese reservations, and thus made errors of overcommitment in east Pakistan. For political reasons those returning from the April 1971 consultations in Beijing sought to portray a deceivingly rosy picture of support against India (see Choudhury, 1975, pp. 212-13).

China delayed several months on a Pakistani request for aircraft, and confined shipments to small arms and ammunition in the latter half of 1971. An emergency Pakistani delegation arrived in November seeking thirty fighter aircraft and other supplies, but again despite contrived optimistic reports to Yahya Khan, most of the larger equipment arrived only after the December war was over (Sisson and Rose, 1990, pp. 250-53). Nevertheless, when India sought reassurances (during and after Kissinger's visit in July) from both China and the US on support for Pakistan, Mrs. Gandhi evidently got little detailed response—though as noted, Indian intelligence on Pakistani options was quite good, and in October, President Nixon sought personally to reassure her and plead for time (see Siddiqui, 1972, p. 173; Kissinger, 1979, pp. 873-85; and Choudhury, 1975, pp. 209-12). While the bulk of its 1971 prewar arms came from China, in the final months of war, Pakistan also bought needed parts and ammunition from North Korea and Romania (*New York Times,* October 15, 1971, p. 3; November 9, 1971, p. 1).

Both sides sharply increased military preparations in 1971, but with few crucial last-minute arms acquisitions. On the whole, pre-hostility arms supply patterns (see Tables 4 and 5) favored India much more conspicuously than they had in the 1965 war. Pakistan struggled to obtain spare parts and ammunition through the Nixon Administration's leaky embargo; from China she sought whatever aircraft and tanks might be available. Although French deliveries of Mirage fighter aircraft were sizeable, requirements to pay cash limited Pakistani purchases from Europe in light of foreign exchange shortage compounded by a cut in American grants and loans. India enjoyed massive Soviet, and to a lesser extent, East European, British, French, Swiss, and reportedly, even Israeli commitments to provide direct arms shipments or facilitate licensed Indian production of fighter aircraft, tanks, and other equipment (Wilcox, 1973, pp. 46-56; see also, Khan, 1973, p. 149).

Table 4

Arms Shipments to India, 1966–71

Major Arms Shipped to India, 1966–70

Canada	4 DHC-4 Caribou transport aircraft
Czechoslovakia	170 T-54 tanks; 150 OT-62 APC; 75 OT-64 APC
France	34 SA-316B Chetak helicopters (Indian licensed production); 50 AS-30 ASM; 3600 SS-11 wire-guided ATM (Indian licensed production); 3 Breguet Alize antisubmarine aircraft; 50 ENTAC ATM
Poland	2 Polnocny Class ships
Switzerland	4 Superfledermaus antiaircraft fire control systems
UK	24 HS-748 transports (Indian assembly); 170 licensed Vijayanta tanks; 100 Gnat fighters (Indian assembly); 12 Hunter T-66 fighters; 36 Hunter F-56 fighters; 2 Ham Class minesweepers; 50 Abbot 105mm guns; 6 Canberra B-15 bombers; 5 Canberra B-I-8 bombers
USSR	40 MI-4 Hound helicopters; 30 SA-2 SAM launchers and 360 SA-2 Guideline SAM; 10 AN-12 Cub-A transports; 225 M-46 130mm artillery; 350 M-1944 100mm artillery; 100 D-20 152mm howitzers; 100 D-30 122mm howitzers; 14 MiG-21 fighters; 70 MiG-21-FL fighters (Indian assembly); 140 SU-7B Fitter-A fighters; 165 AA-2 Atoll AAM (Indian assembly); 170 T-55 tanks; 4 Foxtrot Class submarines; 5 Petya-2 Class frigates

Major Arms Shipped to India, 1971

Czechoslovakia	55 T-54 tanks; 75 OT-62 APC; 75 OT-64 APC
France	8 SA-316B Chetak helicopters (Indian licensed production); 200 SS-11 wire-guided ATM (Indian assembly)
Italy	50 Model-56 105mm howitzers
Switzerland	4 Superfledermaus antiaircraft fire control systems
UK	6 Sea King SH-3D naval helicopters; 6 Canberra B-15 bombers; 5 Canberra B-I-12 bombers; 25 Abbot 105mm guns; 6 HS-748 transports (Indian assembly); 20 Gnat fighters (Indian assembly); 50 licensed Vijayanta tanks
USA	4 Model 300 helicopters
USSR	48 SSN-2 Styx and Styx L SSM; 5 SA-2 SAM and 120 SA-2

Guideline SAM; 55 T-55 tanks; 8 OSA-1 Class missile boats; 1 T-58 Class minesweeper; 100 D-30 122mm howitzers; 20 MiG-21-FL fighters (Indian assembly); 60 AA-2 Atoll AAM (Indian assembly); 100 M-1946 130mm artillery; 20 MI-8 HIP transport helicopters

Source: Estimates collected from Anthony, 1992; SIPRI files; authors' files

Table 5

Arms Shipments to Pakistan, 1966–71

Major Arms Shipped to Pakistan, 1966–70

China*	4 IL-28 bombers; 60 F-6 fighters; 95 Type-69 tanks
USSR†	9 Mi-8 HIP transport helicopters; 100 T-54 tanks; 50 T-55 tanks; 50 M-1937 152mm howitzers; 100 M-46 130mm artillery; 20 PT-76 amphibious tanks
France	3 Mirage-3R fighters; 18 Mirage-3E fighters; 3 Mirage 3-D fighters; 4 Alouette-3 helicopters; 96 R-530 AAM; 3 Daphne Class submarines
US	2 C-130 Hercules transports
FRG	750 Cobra 2000 ATM
Iran	90 CL-13 Sabre jets (from Germany); 4 C-130B Hercules transports
UK	1 Trident bomber
Belgium	3 ex-US TF-104G fighters; 100 older tanks

Major Arms Shipped to Pakistan, 1971

China	55 Type-69 tanks; 40 F-6 fighters
France	2 Mirage-5DP fighters; 14 Mirage-5P fighters; 64 R-530 AAM
Jordan	10 ex-US F-104A fighters
US	4 T-37C trainers
USSR	3 MI-8 HIP transport helicopters

Source: Estimates collected from Anthony, 1992; SIPRI files; authors' files
*There were no reported Chinese arms shipments to Pakistan for 1968–69.
†The USSR was Pakistan's only major arms supplier in 1969.

By 1971, Indian militarily related production was extensive and included almost the full range of weapons (SIPRI, 1971, pp. 741–58). Pakistani domestic production was far more limited because of lack of industrial infrastructure and funds. Products included small arms, a light aircraft of Swedish design, and ammunition (Khan, 1973, p. 275; Katz, 1984, pp. 265–76).

Despite Pakistani hopes, there was little international or UN response to the growing Bengali crisis in September or October. Over the summer and early fall Washington and Moscow, as well as Paris and London, discussed ways to head off war, and the Soviets initially urged India to accept agreements on the refugee and East Pakistan reform issues. On September 21, however, a General Assembly debate on East Bengal was ruled out on the grounds that it was an internal Pakistani matter, despite Soviet pleas to the contrary. Britain and France tried to hold the middle ground and press for a Bengali political settlement—with India refusing (Chowdhury, 1972, p. 250). On October 10, India proposed a settlement but Pakistan still resisted moderate US pressure and inducements and would not deal with the Awami League leadership (a plan for talks with a Mujib delegate in Calcutta eventually was accepted, but evidently came too late) or formulate a plan acceptable to India (Jackson, 1975, pp. 79–92; Wilcox, 1973, pp. 39–46). Thereafter, despite lingering American efforts with Pakistan, and in view first of Pakistani and then Indian border reinforcements, Moscow probably would have vetoed Security Council proposals disadvantageous to India, even as the Secretary General came to support mutual border pullbacks. The General Assembly responded to Pakistani complaints by passing such a border-inspection proposal in November, but New Delhi refused (Siddiq, 1979, p. 113). India's end-of-the-year deadline for action was fast approaching.

Washington tried unsuccessfully to translate its managed arms supplies into political influence for a settlement, formally reminding Pakistan as early as April of restrictions on domestic uses of American weapons under their 1959 agreement. However, failure to enforce restrictions in 1965 left little prospect of restraint in 1971, although Pakistan made some effort to use primarily domestically produced and Chinese, French, and USSR supplied weapons in the east. As late as November 19, the Nixon Administration evidently thought significant progress toward political settlement was being made, first in interceding for the life of Sheikh Mujib, and then in conjunction with Iran in pushing for an acceptable autonomy arrangement with the

Awami League by year's end. India was not persuaded (Choudhury, 1975, pp. 208–10; and International Institute for Strategic Studies, 1972, p. 48).

As prospects of political settlement waned, Washington's main concern was to assure the survival of at least the western portion of its Central Treaty Organization (CENTO) ally. With the conclusion of the Indian-Soviet treaty, the Nixon Administration became increasingly suspicious of Indian motives, and tried to devise a publicly acceptable level of support for Pakistan. At their meeting in October, aware of Pakistan's untenable position and the unavoidable loss of the east, President Nixon tried to impress the Indian leader with news of his decision to stop Pakistani arms shipments still in the pipeline. He further offered Mrs. Gandhi both humanitarian relief and vigorous efforts for an eventual East Pakistani settlement.[8] However, while affirming her military restraint, the Indian leader viewed US offers as unproductively slow, and continued with military preparations for a December 6 offensive. In turn, Nixon and Kissinger tried to fortify Pakistan, within the framework of the technical embargo, enough to keep the west from falling. They never were able or willing to back Pakistan sufficiently to deter India, however. At the same time, the Pakistani government apparently deceived itself, or at least its gullible president, into believing it would be saved by major-power patrons, and proceeded doggedly to attack the Indian Punjab and Kashmir on December 3, despite patently bleak overall military prospects.

THE COURSE OF WAR

The full-scale, two-front war launched on December 3 itself lasted only two weeks, with India dominating in the east and settling for another basic stalemate in the west. False hopes, including the expected availability of arms, conditioned this outcome to a considerable extent, evidently affecting certain strategic calculations, especially by Pakistan.

The initial air attack in the west, for example, was insufficient (only sixteen planes participated) to do major damage to Indian defenses, partly because of Pakistan's evident fear of overcommitting frontline aircraft and risking their loss in view of uncertain resupply and advanced Indian air-defense systems. There was little prospect of replacing F-104s and F-86 Sabre fighters, and after heavy initial losses, Pakistani involvement in air combat remained sporadic throughout the war. Similarly, Pakistani armor commitments were reserved because of successful Indian attacks on oil and rail facilities, leaving only twelve days of assured fuel (Sisson and Rose, 1990, p. 231; Jackson, 1975, pp. 116–22).

In contrast, and unlike 1965, the Indian air force could bring nearly all its weapons into play with assurance both of domestic and Soviet resupply (Sisson and Rose, 1990, p. 245; Jackson, 1975, p. 122). Every major Pakistani city and air base was attacked; Indian ground forces were heavily supported and dropped into key locations by air; and both eastern and western Pakistani ports were shelled and effectively blockaded by the Indian navy (which unlike 1965 was fully engaged in the war, especially utilizing Soviet-supplied missile boats). Both sides ultimately suffered heavy casualties and lost considerable equipment during the fighting (Jagdev Singh, 1988, pp. 198–203; Butterworth, 1976, p. 457; Jackson, 1975, p. 122).[9]

The political goal of denying an independent Bengali enclave in eastern territory led Pakistan to an ill-devised forward-border defense strategy centered on key towns over widely scattered territory. Once air superiority had been won, this static point defense allowed Indian forces to use mobility (light vehicles, mobile artillery, helicopters, and bridging equipment) and air drops to proceed, despite difficult river terrain, rapidly toward Dacca before Pakistani forces could coalesce around the regional capital. Because of Pakistan's "strong in the west" strategy and denial of reinforcements, eastern forces, depleted by defections, were both outmanned and outgunned. Yet basic supplies and ammunition had been heavily stockpiled, and if Pakistani forces had been able to reach Dacca with some hope of relief, they might have held out much longer (International Institute for Strategic Studies, *Strategic Survey, 1971,* 1972, p. 50; Jackson, 1975, ch. 5). The war's truly decisive and costly battles mainly were over by December 10.

The hope for a western sector breakthrough against Indian defenses never emerged, largely because of Indian air dominance. Pakistan's initial evening air strikes of December 3 were not immediately followed by further sorties, and Indian SAM defenses and aircraft dispersal mitigated the effectiveness of the raid (Sethi, 1972, pp. 132–37). India enjoyed a 2:1 advantage in combat aircraft, quickly repaired damage to its airfields, and ruled the skies by December 6. The immediate Pakistani Kashmir ground offensive, over much of the same terrain as 1965, was no more effective than those six years earlier, and might have been restrained as well by Pakistani concerns about being branded aggressors. In fact, Pakistan lost some territory to Indian advances in other western sectors, but India's overall strategy remained limited so as not to provoke too much major-power opposition (Jackson, 1975, ch. 5; International Institute for Strategic Studies, *Strategic Survey, 1971, 1972,* p. 53; Sisson and Rose, 1990, pp. 231–32). (See Appendix, Chronology 2, "India-Pakistan Bangladesh War, 1971.")

DIPLOMATIC PRESSURE AND ARMS FLOW

As Pakistan's cause sank, US concern grew for its ally's ultimate survival. Partly on the basis of a controversial CIA report of impending Indian plans for a major western offensive, and in view of insufficient perceived Indian reassurances, on December 10th Washington dispatched a Seventh Fleet armada from the Pacific and ultimately (by the fourteenth) into the Bay of Bengal. Much was made of this supposed American military threat, shadowed as it was by a Soviet fleet (formally reinforced on the sixth and thirteenth, but with reinforcements only arriving on the eighteenth), but it appears mainly to have been a diplomatic signal of support for west Pakistan and an involvement to reassure China, i.e., a counter to the Soviet presence and an effort to keep Islamabad hanging on (Sisson and Rose, 1990, p. 262).[10]

Washington also explored potential Pakistani arms resupply routes during the war, but abandoned plans to have Jordan or Saudi Arabia quietly transfer US equipment; the State Department concluded that this would violate arms-aid provisions. However, Jordan reportedly nevertheless delivered ten US planes to Pakistan (Libya illegally shipped three US F-5 aircraft after the cease-fire as well; *New York Times,* December 31, 1971, p. 1; June 3, 1972, p. 1). An internal government debate on the extent of treaty commitments to Pakistan also ended on the State Department's contention, with Henry Kissinger dissenting, that no binding defense obligation existed (Kissinger, 1979, pp. 894–96; Jackson, 1975, pp. 136–38).

Indian forces raced to Dacca to stay ahead of US efforts to rouse the UN toward a cease-fire resolution. Indeed, in the face of collapsing defenses on December 7 and 8, east Pakistani commanders and the regional governor began pushing their president for a settlement. Amidst confused communication, Yahya Khan first authorized such an initiative through the UN, suggesting destruction of the maximum amount of equipment in the process, and then angrily rescinded the offer (which had included an elected eastern civilian government) as inadequate to preserve Pakistan's unity. Reportedly, Washington had counselled strongly against any settlement without an accompanying western sector cease-fire (Jagdev Singh, 1988, p. 202). This reconsideration left India free to pursue territorial gains without UN counter-pressure (Sisson and Rose, 1990, pp. 231–33). After Dacca's fall, there was further brief suspense about whether India would halt in the West, whether the US might somehow intervene by air to assure a halt, and whether President Yahya finally would accept a settlement and a unilateral Indian cease-fire (Jackson, 1975, pp. 114–16; Jagdev Singh, 1988, pp. 203–5).

Thus, it was apparent by December 10 that UN and other multilateral diplomatic initiatives would not stop the war, as they had been poised to do in 1965. Beginning with Security Council deliberations on the fourth, the USSR vetoed two main US-initiated and Chinese-backed cease-fire proposals calling for mutual pullbacks and UN observation. In turn Moscow's substitute proposals calling for an east Pakistani settlement were blocked by China and withdrawn. This left the matter in the General Assembly's hands, one of the infrequent uses of the Uniting for Peace Resolution. The US proposal was passed resoundingly on the seventh (even here, Britain and France abstained; see Sethi, 1972, p. 148), but with little effect. Washington tried to combine UN diplomacy with military and economic-aid pressure on India, revoking arms-sales licenses on the third, suspending economic assistance on the sixth, and striking India from the 1972 aid budget on the eighth—all to no avail (Jackson, 1975, pp. 122–27).

On December 9, Pakistan announced its acceptance of the General Assembly resolution. Zulfikar Ali Bhutto, then deputy prime minister, met with Henry Kissinger on the eleventh to discuss further pressure to save west Pakistan (Kissinger, 1979, pp. 907–8). India refused the cease-fire on the twelfth, as the war's military turning point had been reached. Assurance of Indian restraint mentioned only Kashmir at that point, and Washington and Beijing prepared to reopen the matter in the Security Council. There, the Soviet Union vetoed a further US attempt to halt the fighting and save west Pakistan on the thirteenth, and Bhutto walked out of the council during debate of Japanese and Italian cease-fire proposals on the fourteenth, further complicating pacification efforts (Jagdev Singh, 1988, pp. 204–5).

In a move reminiscent of the 1965 "end-game" diplomacy, on December 15 Beijing protested alleged Indian troop incursions on the Sikkim-Tibet border, and flew in more than 200,000 rounds of tank and anti-aircraft ammunition for Pakistan (*New York Times,* December 25, 1971, p. 2). However, as it became clear that decisive third-party intervention was precluded, Pakistan's alternating statements of belligerence and submission gave way to the cease-fire agreements (west and east) of the seventeenth and eighteenth. These were ratified formally by the Security Council on December 22. Once again street demonstrations protested a Pakistani military capitulation and the president soon resigned (Jackson, 1975, pp. 124-30; Sisson and Rose, 1990, pp. 232-35, 250-55).

Subtle US-Soviet signalling also accompanied the cease-fire accords. With Washington's vague references to Pakistani military assistance, punctuated with the Seventh Fleet's presence, and China's last-minute arms shipments, the Soviet deputy foreign minister arrived in New Delhi on December 12 and stayed until the sixteenth. Indian representatives also visited Moscow from the eleventh to the fifteenth, and evidently at these meetings restraint on the western front was counselled, if indeed such counsel were necessary (Jackson, 1975, pp. 139-41).

CONCLUSIONS

In this case, therefore, arms transfers appear to have conditioned fighting strategies and limitations more than they determined the war's instigation and ultimate settlement. There seems to have been little or no effect on willingness to negotiate either in the crisis months or the weeks of combat. Pakistan clearly was constrained in military strategy by its relatively inferior qualitative position, but not constrained notably in either domestic political repression or foreign military assertiveness at the war's outset. Indeed, increasing American efforts to employ arms-transfer diplomacy afforded insufficient clout with either Pakistan or India. Pakistan erred badly in its evident expectation of active US and Chinese backing because of its diplomatic "go-between" role, and may have interpreted the very limited military assistance and vague statements of support received in 1971 as a sign of further commitment. India evidently was heartened in its interventionist approach by relative arms-supply security through a steady multiyear buildup and source diversification, culminating in the boost of British and Soviet arms shipments in 1971 (the latter just prior to the war) on the basis of forewarning in October and November.

Unlike 1965, a degree of major-power consensus existed only on keeping west Pakistan intact. Even Britain and France diverged from America's pro-Pakistani UN policy during the war, remaining neutral or tilting a bit toward the Indian position (*New York Times,* December 14, 1971, pp. 1, 10). Washington and Beijing developed a roughly parallel approach both to the crisis (attempting, unsuccessfully, to restrain Pakistan) and the war (posturing to push Soviet restraint on India). The overall effect was to the advantage of India, with its greater connections for arms supplies.

Once again, basic strategic aims and the major-power diplomatic balance, as opposed to arms supply per se, seemed to have the primary impact on peace prospects. The major powers' impact on peace negotiations was delayed mainly because of their conflicting signals and priorities. The superpowers were on opposite sides, and the US and China tried both to restrain and preserve Pakistan—thus leading to confusing messages about armament and commitments. Pakistan abandoned large weapons stores in the east to advancing Indian troops, and could probably have held out longer with a more realistic defense strategy, a well-defined mission, and reinforcements. However, having lost the air war, the long-term prospect was dim in any case.

A disadvantageous weapons balance and poor strategies therefore conditioned fighting both on land and in the air. Pakistan's reluctant patrons, the US and China, recognized and accepted the loss of the east, but tried to cover over any humiliation and disintegration in the west. Although her eastern military commanders wanted to concede, Pakistan did not immediately conform to our expectations—as expressed in chapter one—of concessions from a weaker and losing power, perhaps because of a general perception that foreign powers would prevent the ultimate fall, and because of advice from those patrons not to give in unconditionally.

The impact of arms supply and supply restrictions, then, clearly depends on the degree of consensus among major powers. In 1965, that consensus was there, and although the embargo did not immediately end the fighting, it combined with effective diplomatic pressures to offer face-saving ways out for the stalemated military opponents. In 1971, with less of a stalemate and less major-power consensus, the weaker party (Pakistan) became essentially a pawn to major-power diplomacy while the stronger party (India) set the basic terms of settlement.

CHAPTER 5

THE CENTRAL AMERICAN "FOOTBALL WAR," 1969

INTRODUCTION: THE BACKGROUND OF WAR

In certain respects the 1969 dispute and war between El Salvador and Honduras resembled the 1971 India-Pakistan affair. The so-called "football war" of Central America actually had roots not so much in two hotly contested soccer matches as in the frustrations and resentments caused by a cross-border refugee problem, similar to that involving the Bengalis in 1971. Along with economic privation, land tenure and crowding led to the Central American refugee dilemma. A highly restrictive landholding pattern in one of the region's most crowded states, El Salvador, over a period of years had caused the exodus of over 300,000 peasants to relatively sparsely populated Honduras. By the late 1960s this amounted to roughly twenty percent of Honduras's rural population. Going back to the beginning of the century, such illegal immigrants had been welcomed by labor-hungry Honduran and US agribusinesses, and had found vacant tracts of land. However, when economic conditions worsened, even in the 1950s, Hondurans cracked down on this emigre group (Armstrong and Shenk, 1982, p. 56).

The Honduran government resented both the exportation of Salvadoran poverty and also El Salvador's export-trade success within the Central American Common Market (CACM). In essence it seemed that Honduras was being asked to pay twice for El Salvador's economic policies. Honduran leaders saw increased political advantage in antiforeign campaigns (Anderson, 1981, pp. 74–75). In the late 1960s, landowners, confronted with a growing peasant political movement and unions, tried with various degrees of success to turn public opinion and the Honduran government against the Salvadoran peasants. Government leaders and a progressive agrarian institute spoke of land reform in 1968 and 1969, but proposed to take the acreage from Salvadoran immigrants rather than from Honduran hacendaderos (La

Feber, 1984, p. 183; Lapper and Painter, 1985, pp. 60–61; Morris, 1984, pp. 110–11; *New York Times,* July 5, 1969, p. 2; Durham, 1979, p. 164; Langley, 1985, p. 182).

Relations between the two states became increasingly strained. Soon after the arrest of a Honduran citizen along the border in 1967, approximately forty heavily armed Salvadoran soldiers, who had purportedly strayed across the border, were interned in Honduras on suspicion of interference in Honduran politics (*New York Times,* June 28, 1969, p. 1; Anderson, 1981, pp. 81–89; Langley, 1985, p. 181). In 1968, El Salvador, controlling most of the undemarcated territory along the border, failed to ratify a border treaty proposed by the Honduran government (Anderson, 1981, p. 77; Durham, 1979, pp. 1–2).

In 1968 Honduras determined to enforce agrarian ownership restrictions against foreigners, and notes were sent to Salvadoran settlers in April 1969 ordering them to vacate. Bitter feelings contributed to rioting during the World Cup qualifying football matches in mid-June. The Honduran government seized the occasion to expel several thousand Salvadoran peasants amid widely reported and rumored atrocities (Dunkerly, 1985, pp. 81–82). El Salvador responded with an escalation of border tensions, and a full-fledged invasion of its neighbor on July 14. Thus, as the influx of foreign Bengali refugees added to pressures and temptations leading to India's 1971 invasion of east Pakistan, El Salvador's reaction to the influx of its own expelled nationals in the Football War resulted from a type of economic and social dislocation and victimization all too common in world politics.

ARMAMENT AND THE APPROACH OF WAR

The Football War was fought by two small ill-equipped armies, and ultimately ground to a halt with El Salvador enjoying the better of the quite bloody fighting. The war ended at least partly because of insufficient equipment, fuel, ammunition, and spare parts. The US was the principal military supplier to both sides, having viewed these two states as part of its anti-Cuban Latin American military assistance program, which at that time still involved largely grant-in-aid shipments of obsolete equipment and massive training missions. In 1968, Washington had supplied Honduras with about $800,000 in military assistance, and El Salvador with $500,000, while cumulative US military aid from 1945–68 amounted to $6.4 million to El Salvador and $8.2 million to Honduras (*New York Times,* July 16, 1969, pp. 1, 12; *Congressional Record,* 91st Congress, 1st Session, Senate, July 30, 1969, p. 21356). Indeed, critics of US policy blamed Washington for making the war possible not only through arms supply and failure to use it as a lever for restraint, but through bloated military training programs; in 1963 and 1964 more US officers staffed the San Salvador embassy's air-force mission than there were pilots in the entire Salvadoran air force (La Feber, 1984, p. 176).

Both armies had, up to 1969, been developed mainly for counterinsurgency and domestic control (Rosenberg and Shepherd, 1986, pp. 184–85). Each side participated in the joint Central American Defense Council, an organization supported by the US and designed to coordinate strategy for regional defense, and to standardize command, training, and equipment. The efforts of the council were aimed vaguely and primarily at Cuba, but despite occasional joint exercises, there never was much effective preparation or coordination, as each army tended to look mainly for a domestic political role (Morris, 1984, pp. 109–10).

At the time of the war, El Salvador could muster more than 8000 combat troops as compared to Honduras's 2500; each side was armed mainly with US and West European rifles and machine guns. El Salvador also had a few light tanks, mostly inoperable at the time of the war, along with mortars and bazookas that were used in the fighting. Honduras was at a severe disadvantage in land equipment, possessing only one battery of 75mm howitzers in contrast to El Salvador's more modern 105mm cannons, delivered in 1969 (see Table 6). El Salvador also was able to engineer some converted armored personnel carriers during the war (*Keesings Contemporary Archives,* vol. 15, August 23–30, 1969, pp. 23526–27; Anderson, 1981, pp. 116–22).

Honduras enjoyed a countervailing slight advantage in air forces, with a grand total of twenty-three combat aircraft to only eleven for its opponent. However, reportedly only eight World War II vintage fighter planes on each side were functional at the start of the fighting: US P-51 Mustang's for El Salvador and Corsair subsonic jet fighters for Honduras (*New York Times,* June 28, 1969, p. 1; July 18, 1969, p. 9). Transport capabilities amounted to old DC-3's and C-47's, which also doubled as bombers, with crews releasing explosives by hand without bombsights (*Newsweek,* July 28, 1969, p. 54; Anderson, 1981, pp. 114–15).

Table 6

Arms Shipments to El Salvador, 1966–69

Major Arms Supplied to El Salvador, 1966–68

US   8 Model-180 light aircraft; 4 C-47 transports; 5 Bird Dog light observation planes; 1 used DC 4 (Canadian built) transport; 4 B-26 Invader planes; 6 used F-51 Mustang jets

Major Arms Supplied to El Salvador, 1969

FRG   20 UR-416 APC
US   30 M-101-A1 105mm howitzers; 6 used F-51 Mustang jets (war replacement); 1 Fairchild FH-1100 light aircraft

Source: Estimates collected from SIPRI files; authors' files.

Table 7

Arms Shipments to Honduras, 1966–69

Major Arms Supplied to Honduras, 1966–68

US   3 C-47 transports; 3 Model-185 light aircraft; 4 SS-55 utility helicopters

Major Arms Supplied to Honduras, 1969

Venezuela 4 F-86K Sabre jets (ex-German-Italian)
US   2 C-47 transports

Source: Estimates from SIPRI files; authors' files.

Only El Salvador had even minimal domestic arms production capability, producing small arms, ammunition, and mortars. Both sides were directly sensitive to arms supply and highly vulnerable to an arms cut-off (SIPRI, 1971; Keegan, 1983, pp. 252, 499; Kidron and Smith, 1983, p. 23).

THE COURSE OF WAR

Rioting at the football matches in mid-June touched off the diplomatic crisis later in the month, as the flight of more than ten thousand Salvadorans from Honduras into El Salvador and Nicaragua began. Diplomatic relations were broken first by El Salvador on the twenty-sixth, and a day later by Honduras; El Salvador also closed its border, attempting to stem the returning refugee tide (Durham, 1979, p. 164). Charges of human-rights abuses were exchanged as each side called for support from the Organization of American States (OAS). By July 3, skirmishing along the border was alleged. On the fourth El Salvador mobilized its armed forces.

In launching the war, Salvadoran military leaders were confident of their superiority against Honduras and openly imitated Israel's 1967 six-day war against the Arab states. Evidently their somewhat newer arsenal added to that tactical confidence (Dunkerly, 1985, p. 82). Admiring Israeli daring and despite considerable policy and armament differences from the Middle East, they styled themselves as beleaguered by larger neighbors, and designed a two-pronged pincer movement, complete with surprise air attacks against Honduran bases. Reportedly, intelligence gathering for such an offensive had been going on since late June (Anderson, 1981, pp. 110–11). The aim evidently was to cut off Honduran defenses and penetrate as far as Tegucigalpa to topple the regime if possible, but at least far enough to acquire a foothold to trade for concessions on the refugee issue.

Initial Salvadoran advances were successful. Their edge in the ground fighting was partly due to more modern automatic rifles (not a "major weapon" by SIPRI reporting standards), a recent acquisition from West Germany (*New York Times,* July 18, 1969, p. 1; *Facts on File,* vol. 29, July 17–23, 1969, p. 445; Anderson, 1981, p. 116).[1] However, Honduran troops reportedly fought back doggedly, even using machetes effectively. El Salvador's initially successful thrust bogged down—as much because of lack of ammunition and overextended supply logistics as because of effective Honduran resistance (Dunkerley, 1985, p. 83).

The Salvadoran attack failed utterly to wipe out Honduras's air force, as pilots collided on the ground, got lost, and failed to hit their targets. Officials admitted that El Salvador's fliers were "green kids;" the hoped-for night raids to take advantage of Honduras's lack of navigational aids fizzled. Honduras, stung and eager for revenge, responded with fairly effective bombing against an oil depot and port, thus depleting El Salvador's fuel supplies; the Honduras air force reportedly received some spares and fuel from Nicaragua. Honduran crews proved better trained (although both sides were American schooled) and bases were more dispersed (El Salvador had only one functional air base) (Anderson, 1981, pp. 116–17; Rosenberg and Shepherd, 1986, p. 10). Still, it did not take long before most of the planes on both sides were grounded by lack of parts and war damage (Anderson, 1981, pp. 114–15).

Like its supposed Middle Eastern counterpart, the war, which was termed "the most serious armed conflict between Latin American States in more than thirty years," also lasted only approximately 100 hours. Even so, and despite basically primitive weaponry, at least 250 military and probably more than 2000 total deaths were reported (Sivard, 1987–88, p. 29, estimates a total of 5000 deaths but other estimates were lower. See Durham, 1979, p. 165; Anderson, 1981, p. 126; Dunkerley, 1985, p. 82).

Both sides suffered from supply shortages, as outside diplomatic pressure began to have an effect. Armed forces' morale quickly drained, as evidenced by desertions and looting on both sides three days into the war. After the OAS arranged a cease-fire on July 18, it was not until July 30 that Salvadoran forces, which had penetrated up to twenty-five miles into Honduras (sometimes using oil company road maps) were withdrawn under a threat of OAS economic sanctions. (See Appendix, Chronology 3, "The Central American Football War.")

DIPLOMATIC PRESSURE AND ARMS FLOW

Despite more than two weeks of mounting military hostilities prior to the outbreak of war, no specific threats or sanctions appear to have been employed by the US or other states to halt the slide toward combat. Indeed, US policy toward the crisis as it developed appeared intentionally low-keyed in order to avoid charges of dictating policy in Central America. Washington, preoccupied in Vietnam and elsewhere, preferred to let OAS officials initiate mediation in response to the parties' requests for assistance (*New York Times,* June 28, 1969, p. 1). The US government, along with other states in the region, tended to dismiss the three-year record of growing bitterness between El Salvador and Honduras as a minor diversion in an otherwise seemingly harmonious relationship. Moreover, in a remarkable show of insensitivity, Washington dispatched Nelson Rockefeller, symbol of resented American business interests, to Honduras during the prewar crisis; his visit sparked fresh rioting as Hondurans evidently came to believe that the US was behind the influx of Salvadorans (Langley, 1985, p. 183).

The disputing parties had appeared to welcome a joint Guatemalan-Nicaraguan-Costa Rican OAS mediation team on June 29 (*New York Times,* June 29, 1969, p. 15). The diplomatic mission was backed on July 4 by an OAS Council resolution calling on the parties to show restraint (*United Nations Year Book,* 1969, p. 183). Troop clashes, begun on July 3, continued, however. The mediators demanded restraint and withdrawal of forces from the border, but El Salvador refused on the twelfth. Political leaders on each side reportedly felt insecure in the face of powerful domestic economic and political interest groups (Anderson, 1981, pp. 108–9). Honduras sought arms aid and support from the OAS, but withdrew the arms request before seeking a cease-fire (*London Times,* July 15, 1969, pp. 1–4). On July 14, the same day Salvadoran troops crossed the border in force, the OAS Council constituted itself the Organ of Consultation under the OAS charter.

With war underway, diplomatic pressure intensified, and, along with military exhaustion and the impact of heavy rains on the battlefields, finally brought first a cease-fire and ultimately a Salvadoran withdrawal (*Facts on File,* vol. 29, July 17-23, 1969, p. 445). These pressures included an arms embargo by the US, the leading arms supplier (seen by Hondurans as favoring the better-armed Salvadorans) from the first day of the war (*New York Times,* December 3, 1969, p. 8). Washington was highly alarmed and reportedly surprised at the outbreak of fighting. Some replacement arms evidently were shipped to El Salvador and Honduras during the course of fighting, but not enough to sustain the war effort of two sparsely armed and nearly destitute states. Fearing the consequences for regional stability, Guatemala quickly joined Washington's pressure for a cease-fire (Dunkerley, 1985, p. 83).

The OAS called for an immediate cease-fire on July 14, and contributed to the end of the hostilities and the negotiation process by dispatching a peace mission with representatives of Nicaragua, the US, Argentina, and Ecuador. Both the UN Secretary General and the Pope also tried to intercede. The OAS reinforced its peace demands with a unanimous vote on July 18, calling for mutual withdrawal, the dispatch of an observer team to separate the belligerents, and protection of foreign nationals. The seven-nation team was drawn from a broad sampling of OAS membership, including Central and North Americans; it arrived on the nineteenth to observe the cease-fire, which only slowly went into effect on the twentieth (Anderson, 1981, p. 124). Despite the formal embargo, diplomacy was only effective when both sides came to share negative assessments of the continued prospects of fighting.

With the cease-fire, however, Salvadoran troops maintained their Honduran footholds. Pointed economic threats by the US, CACM members, and the OAS at large, communicated by the foreign ministers of Peru, Colombia, and Paraguay, and by other senior OAS officials on July 23 and 28, brought El Salvador finally to withdraw its forces despite only sketchy assurances of the rights of the Salvadoran emigres (Durham, 1979, p. 1). Thus, the threat of trade sanctions appeared more telling than the arms embargo itself, though the two in tandem seemed to preclude further war-making, much as the combination of sanctions had done in the 1965 Indo-Pakistani war.

An additional ploy had been the OAS Council's decision early in the war, at Washington's urging, to defer decision rather than refuse Honduras's urgent request for defensive-arms shipments, i.e., antiaircraft guns, fighter planes, machine guns, mortars, and ammunition (*New York Times,* July 18, 1969, p. 8). Thus, an implied threat was left for El Salvador that if a cease-fire were not effected, Honduras might be rearmed by multinational agreement. It is doubtful that arms replenishment would have mattered much to either side's fighting capabilities, however, since low prewar military capabilities could not sustain the war effort long enough for the new weapons either to be delivered or to take effect.

CONCLUSIONS

The Central American case shows the effect of military exhaustion, partly induced by an arms embargo, on two small, poorly armed states. For all practical purposes there was no military resupply during this ultimately stalemated war. Yet these states still inflicted relatively massive damage on each other, involving thousands of casualties, great economic dislocation, and the uprooting of hundreds of thousands of people, in less than one week of fighting. Due to the combination of outside pressures and high attrition rates, the parties were quite ready for a cease-fire by that time, however.

A slight prewar arms buildup in El Salvador contributed to that state's initially aggressive response to perceived grievances and fear of economic burdens, but at the end, neither state seemed in the position to absorb and make immediate use of more arms. Both sides lacked effective military organization and leadership, despite intrusive training programs, and both became caught in a fatal combination of mass xenophobia and manipulation by their respective political elites.

The war's initiator did not withdraw from enemy territory, despite the embargo, until further heavy multilateral diplomatic and economic pressure was applied. Fearing the return of exiles, Salvadoran leaders held out against international pressure for such a settlement; indeed, a peace treaty between the parties was not signed until 1980. Economic sanctions were more effective than the arms embargo alone; the arms embargo led to the cease-fire, while the economic threats produced the withdrawal of Salvadoran forces.

Thus the status of both states' armed forces before the war and the efforts of the OAS were more important in determining the war's duration and outcome than were arms-supply policies. Nevertheless, the arms-supply pattern and restrictions greatly enhanced US and OAS leverage once the fighting began, and helped shorten the combat. These states were highly dependent on a single arms source, one which denied them wartime resupply, but which opened the gates shortly afterward to a massive arms buildup. Washington moved to provide significant immediate military assistance (agreeing to replace six downed Salvadoran Mustang fighters in July) despite the spectacle of inept Central American leadership, regional carnage, and resistance to a negotiated settlement.

Thus the two sides fought a war that in itself devastated their economies for years to come—costing El Salvador an estimated $54 million in war damage and dislocation, lost trade involving the collapse of CACM, and postwar arms replacements in what became a new regional arms race. Honduras for its part had to issue ten-year defense bonds to pay for the war (Dunkerley, 1985, p. 83; *Keesings Contemporary Archives,* August 23–30, 1969, p. 23527). Politically the war served as a short-lived boost to both governments despite its almost farcical nature and cost. Salvadoran President Sanchez Hernandez and Honduran President Oswaldo Lopez Arellano, both military men, mythically proved their mettle. Lopez Arellano especially redeemed his reputation from the beating it had sustained in Honduras during the controversy over Salvadoran immigration. He had, in fact, been presumed on the verge of overthrow when El Salvador attacked (Langley, 1985, p. 187; Morris, 1984, p. 112). Conversely, El Salvador's leadership had been making hesitant but marked progress in economic and political reform, but the return of as many as 150,000 expellees from Honduras worked to reverse these promising trends (Schmidt, 1983, pp. 55–56).

The Football War was a case of relatively successful arms embargo and crippling wartime attrition in a situation of high arms-supply dependency. Such situations were especially characteristic of the 1960s. As in the 1965 India-Pakistan war, though, the embargo itself did not substitute for concerted international diplomacy in bringing the war to conclusion. The India-Pakistan cases differed from the Football War, however, both in the much more sophisticated armament available in South Asia and in the demonstrably more limited war aims there. Indeed it was partially fear of losing more of the sophisticated armament that evidently conditioned Indian and Pakistani decisions to terminate fighting. Yet South Asian international rivalries also remained more intense than those of Central America, where domestic class, as opposed to ethnic conflict, seemed to condition most arms acquisition and most of the cross-border warfare. By way of further comparison, we turn now to a later Latin American war.

CHAPTER 6

THE SOUTH ATLANTIC WAR, 1982

INTRODUCTION: THE BACKGROUND OF WAR

The struggle over a number of islands in the South Atlantic adjacent to Argentina, the two largest of which the Argentineans call Malvinas and the British the Falklands, brought back memories of the kind of warfare many believed obsolete in the late-twentieth century. Fought between an old established sea power and a "newly industrializing country," the encounter had trappings of former colonial days, of contests over prestige, naval set-piece fighting, and the expression of domestic political troubles through foreign policy adventures.

In one sense, it was war over territory. Not that the islands themselves were very valuable territory: only a small part of the land was arable or populated (with 1800 "Kelters"); the climate was rough, and the islands had little intrinsic strategic importance. Deposits of minerals and oil were present in the vicinity, but it was unclear whether profitable exploitation was possible. One of the disputed islands, South Georgia, provided a convenient link to the Antarctic, but generally the territories were more important in a symbolic than an economic sense.

The newly sovereign Argentinean republic had taken possession of the main islands in 1823, but lost control to Britain just a decade later. Periodically thereafter, Argentine resentment of this colonial remnant ran high. British governments were intransigent, even in the second half of the twentieth century, when most other imperial conquests were surrendered. The latest round of diplomatic negotiations over the islands, which had begun in 1965 and continued under UN auspices, stalled on the question of the status of inhabitants. Buenos Aires wanted them to become Argentineans; the islanders forcefully asserted their desire to remain British subjects, and London yielded to their pressure.

In early 1982, both governments had internal difficulties, though on different scales and of differing intensities. After seizing power in

1976, the Argentine military leadership had run the country into deep economic crisis. The economic upswing of the military government's early years, largely financed by foreign borrowing, had given way to recession in 1980. Public discontent grew, even among those who had supported or acquiesced in the military coup of 1976; political opposition, murderously silenced in the preceding years, sprang up again partly because of a loosening of repression and partly due to the economic morass.

In December 1981, a small "autogolpe," a coup within the coup, occurred. The junta leadership was reshuffled, with Army General Leopoldo Galtieri becoming head of government, and Admiral Jorge Isaac Anaya, head of the navy—the dominant military service since 1976—becoming strongman behind the scenes. The new junta soon began a foreign-policy review, focussing primarily on the recovery of the Malvinas as a chance to rebuild political support. The year 1982, heralding the sesquicentennial of British occupation, was seen as a symbolically propitious date for liberation. Therefore, in January a "double decision" was taken: Britain was to be pressed to negotiate more seriously than before; and at the same time preparations for a military capture of the islands sometime after October would be planned in case the negotiations proved fruitless (Freedman and Gamba-Stonehouse, 1990, pp. 114–17; Moneta, 1984, p. 318; Makin, 1983, p. 398).

Negotiations were still going on and no particular move for a military intervention had yet been made when Argentine scrap dealers set up a station on South Georgia Island in mid-March. After British authorities attempted to expel them, the junta decided on the twenty-sixth to dispatch marines in a full-scale invasion on April 2; leaders in Buenos Aires perceived that any other course would further erode their shaky popular standing (Freedman and Gamba-Stonehouse, 1990, pp. 62–71). Indeed, militant nationalism initially carried Argentina away as masses celebrated under blue-and-white flags; an uncontrolled escalatory process was set in motion. When the war ultimately was lost, many of these celebrants would blame the military, and the armed forces, which had wanted to transform Argentinean society and economy from top to bottom, would surrender power ignominiously.

Britain's conservative government, which came to power in 1979, also was in trouble in early 1982. Though Prime Minister Thatcher remained confident, opinion polls indicated dwindling support for the Tories, with elections due in 1984 at the latest. The successful Falkland campaign generally is judged as an important factor in the government's eventual electoral victory.[1]

Although reminiscent of an earlier era, the war was to take on new political symbolism as well. By stressing the anticolonial theme, the Argentineans tried to project a North-South image of injustice, somewhat as Saddam Hussein tried to do nearly a decade later in the Gulf War. At least among their Latin American colleagues and in the Middle East, Argentine leaders were quite successful politically in this attempt. The war also did not fit into the then prevalent East-West conflict pattern. The clash between two countries considered staunchly "Western" and capitalistic, close to the United States and decidedly anticommunist, generated considerable cross-pressure, particularly among Western allies.

In subsequent analyses of the war, the Falkland-Malvinas episode became a prime example of multiple misjudgments, false assumptions, misinterpretations, and faulty intelligence. The British did not think it probable that the Argentineans, with whom they were negotiating about the islands' future, would stage a military attack. Thus, Britain remained a supplier of Argentine armaments right up to the beginning of hostilities. The destroyer *Santissima* left Portsmouth after an extensive modernization only in early March 1982. On the other hand, the Argentine government did not believe that a British counterattack was likely. They reasoned that rational British leadership would not spend large sums of money to pursue a risky campaign to recapture the distant, barren, and scarcely populated islands. Some in Buenos Aires even thought that London had given indirect signals to that effect. In addition, the Argentine government was confident that the US would support it or at least remain neutral (Freedman and Gamba-Stonehouse, 1990, pp. 33, 80–81; Gamba, 1987, pp. 79–82; Falcoff, 1990).

ARMAMENT AND THE APPROACH OF WAR

The geostrategic location and industrial capacity of the two states was reflected in their prewar armament supply. The British side could rely on a large and diversified arms industry and full access to NATO procurement channels. Most material was produced in Britain, with some critical high-technology goods coming from the outside, mainly from the US. The Argentineans, on the other hand, largely depended on imported arms. Argentina's sizeable domestic arms industry was only capable of delivering certain types of weapons and munitions. Most advanced systems and components came from Western countries, particularly from Western Europe during the 1970s and early 1980s. The weapons fielded by both sides, therefore, were often similar; indeed British weapons themselves loomed large in the Argentine arsenal, and particularly in the navy. Looked at from the armament side, the Falklands-Malvinas struggle was to be a West-West war.

Already before the junta took power in 1976, a massive rearmament program had begun in Buenos Aires. Its origin was the "Plan Europea," a project designed by an earlier military government in 1967. In response to US restrictions on various types of weapons, the armed forces planned to switch procurement to West European suppliers. Not only would this provide access to modern weaponry, but technical assistance could launch a modern domestic arms industry. Since the 1950s, Argentina had enjoyed sizable domestic aerospace capacity, whose main product in the 1970s was the Pucará, a small turbo-prop aircraft optimized for combat against lightly armed forces, i.e., counterinsurgency. The army also was authorized to buy a tank design from West Germany in 1974; indigenous production of the TAM medium tank and derivatives began in 1978. The air force and army both benefitted from other such purchases as well (see Table 8).

Argentina's main emphasis, though, was on procurement for the politically influential navy. In 1969, two West German coastal submarines of the U-209 class were bought, and in 1971, an order for two Type-42 British destroyers followed, one of which was built in Argentina. In 1977–78, six large conventional submarines of the TR-1700 class and 10 Meko type frigates and corvettes were bought from West Germany, with four of the former and six of the latter to be built in Argentina. The navy also took the opportunity to purchase French corvettes originally intended for South Africa, which were offered on the international market after the South African arms embargo in the Fall of 1977. To round out this major expansion, beginning in 1979 new armament was installed on the only Argentine aircraft carrier, which had been built in Britain in 1945. More significantly, fourteen modern French Super Etendard naval fighter-bombers were ordered for use on the carrier. The emphasis on the navy naturally followed the junta's rhetoric about an expanded role in the South Atlantic, and was to intensify the ongoing Beagle Channel territorial dispute with Chile.

Table 8

Arms Shipments to Argentina, 1979–82

Major arms shipped to Argentina, 1979–81

Austria	57 Cuirassier MBT
Belgium	5 BDX APC
France	7 Mirage-3E fighter; 2 VBC APC; 1000 HOT ATM; 9 SA-316B; 24 SA-330J helicopters; 5 Super Etendard naval fighters; 3 D'Orves Class Corvette with MM-38 Exocet ShShM
Israel	16 Dagger (Mirage-3C)
Italy	10 MB-339A, 8 MB-326GB trainers; 18 A-109 Hirundo helicopters
Netherlands	3 F-27 MK-500 transports
Switzerland	35mm antiaircraft guns
UK	Sea Dart ShAM; 35mm ammunition
US	3 CH-47 Chinook helicopters; 2 AN/TPS-43 3-D mobile precision radars; 3 Learjet-35A transports

Major arms shipped to Argentina, 1982

Brazil	3 EMB-111 transport
France	24 Roland-1 SAM
France	9 Super Etendard naval fighters with AM-39 Exocet AShM
Israel	Artillery ammunition
Peru	10 Mirage-5 fighters; Ammunition and spare parts, rockets
Switzerland	Radar-directed antiaircraft gun (35mm?)
UK	1 Type 42 destroyer with Exocet ShShMs, Sea Dart ShAM
Venezuela	Ammunition and spare parts

Source: Estimates from SIPRI files; authors' files.

In sum, then, arms procurement contracts signed between 1976 and the beginning of the war totalled about $10 billion US dollars (Millan,

1986, p. 36). But by early 1982, only a fraction of the items ordered had been issued to the armed forces. Very little naval equipment had been delivered; none of the submarines ordered in 1977 and none of the frigates and corvettes ordered in 1978 were ready. Completions were planned for dates between 1983 and 1985 (Moore, 1983, pp. 8–12). The weapons systems which were in service included the two British Type-42 destroyers, three of the French D'Orves Class corvettes, and some of the aircraft for the carrier *Ventecinco de Mayo,* including fourteen US A-4P Skyhawks acquired secondhand from the US. The project to install Super Etendard aircraft on the carrier was in progress, with six planes delivered by March 1982. The other eight ordered were still in France, and of the AM-39 Exocet Air-to-Ship-Missiles (AShM) to arm the Super Etendards, only six or seven had been delivered at the outbreak of hostilities.

The situation was only marginally better for the other Argentine services. The army had taken delivery of about 160 TAMs and several hundred smaller armored vehicles from Germany, France, Austria, and Switzerland, about a dozen helicopters from France and the US, and four French-German Roland air-defense systems. More TAMs, helicopters, and Rolands were on order but not yet delivered. The air force had received about 30 domestically produced Pucarás, 2 mobile TPS-43 radars, some additional patrol aircraft and helicopters from the US, and an additional group of Mirage-III bombers and 2 squadrons of Mirage-derived Neshers from Israel. Still unfulfilled were orders for more Pucarás and 24 A-4P Skyhawks from Israel (with US engines), a sale blocked by the US government.

When the war began in 1982, therefore, none of the services had completed the planned force-modernization program. Major projects were still in the pipeline; the navy especially awaited more potent weapons, perhaps a factor in their sporadic wartime performance.[2] All of the services had additional deficits in training and operational planning because of their preoccupation with domestic repression in the 1970s. Again it was the navy, heavily involved in that repression campaign, that was least prepared to fight a conventional war. Nevertheless, the rearmament program had added to Argentina's fighting confidence and stature. In the decision-making to initiate the war, the opportunity to boost morale and carry on with rearmament were major considerations, though one can hardly say that the new arms themselves led directly to the invasion. Had the war started even half a year later, as suggested in Junta planning, Argentina's armed forces would have been stronger, and British capability to recapture the islands weaker.

For Britain, the prewar armament program had aims opposite those of Argentina, and incompatible with the unanticipated need to launch a long-distance naval armada. The main trend of British military procurement since the 1960s had been to de-emphasize the imperial mission. Instead of being able to project power at great distance, the main naval objective was to support the NATO roles of North Atlantic convoy protection and antisubmarine warfare. Thus, larger ships, such as the Leander-class destroyers, were replaced by smaller, faster ships such as the Type-22 frigates. The last of the large aircraft carriers in the Royal Navy, the *HMS Hermes,* was due to be decommissioned in 1983. Of a new class of light aircraft carriers, only the first of three ships, the *HMS Invincible,* was completed by early 1982, and in February its sale to Australia for £175 million was announced (another sign of how unexpected the Falklands invasion was; Moore, 1983, p. 550). The two carriers, with their flights of Sea Harrier fighters, proved to be Britain's most valuable asset during the Falkland-Malvinas war, and without them, a reoccupation of the islands would have been virtually impossible, at least without foreign assistance.

Thus, while the Argentineans were still in the middle of their rearmament program, the British fortuitously had not yet reduced their long-range force projection capability as fully as planned. Considering comparative armament between the two sides reinforces the impression that in deciding to go to war, Argentina's top military brass did not expect major and prolonged British resistance. There was no interservice planning of what to do in case Britain sent a naval task force, nor much coordination once it got there. Argentina massed ammunition on the main airstrip on the West Falklands, but there was no clear planning in case of a British land attack (Cordesman and Wagner, 1990b, pp. 238–361; Middlebrook, 1985 and 1989; Burden, 1986; Dartford, 1985; Ethell and Price, 1983; Huertas and Briasco, 1987; Moro, 1989).

A combination of political pressure and opportunism—with a large dose of misjudgment—was the war's main igniting factor. Indeed, the actual date of the invasion was militarily inconvenient for Buenos Aires because the annual army draft cycle ended in May; army personnel stationed on the islands after the initial occupation would be inexperienced recruits.

THE COURSE OF WAR

Hostilities on the Falkland-Malvinas began early on April 2, 1982. Spearheaded by a marine landing party, Argentine forces overwhelmed the islands' eighty-four-man contingent of Royal Marines. On April 3, South Georgia Island, recently reenforced by twenty-two Royal Marines, was occupied. With great public enthusiasm at home, the Argentine junta declared that sovereignty had been reestablished over the Malvinas.

Improbable as it might have seemed, on April 1, with reports of the imminent invasion coming out of Buenos Aires, the British government already had decided to send a naval task force to retake the islands by force if necessary. The task force was assembled from regular naval units, naval auxiliary forces, and civilian ships requisitioned for this purpose. On April 5, sixteen warships and nineteen support vessels, led by the aircraft carriers *Hermes* and *Invincible,* sailed from Portsmouth to the South Atlantic. The nuclear-propelled submarine *HMS Conqueror* already was on its way.

Argentine transport aircraft had begun to bring troops, weapons systems, ammunition, and support material to the islands from within minutes of their capture. They traveled nine-hundred km from the main base, Commodore Rivadavia, on the Argentine mainland. The five transport squadrons of the Argentine air force with their US supplied C-130 E/H Hercules and Dutch F-27 Fokkers were soon supported by requisitioned civilian aircraft and naval transport ships in bringing material to both the West and East Falklands. Mirages, helicopters, and Pucarás were ferried to Port Stanley. Two radars, including the new Westinghouse-supplied TPS-43, were moved to the West Falklands; Roland and Tigercat surface-to-air missiles (SAMs) were brought in for air defense. Thus, by the end of the month, twenty-thousand Argentine soldiers camped on the Falklands, amply supplied with artillery, ammunition, and a few armored vehicles.

Meanwhile, the British task force had grown to include fifteen surface warships, three submarines, thirty-eight civilian ships, and seventeen Royal Fleet Auxiliary ships, carrying a total of forty Harrier fighter aircraft and hundreds of helicopters. It reached its predetermined position near the Falklands-Malvinas on April 30. From April 16 to 22, ships of the task force had stopped at Ascension Island for refuelling and to take on added stocks, including certain new US high-technology weapons.

As early as April 25, British marines from the *HMS Endurance* reoccupied South Georgia, sinking the Argentinean US-Guppy-class submarine *Santa Fe* in the process. From May 1, Argentine positions on the Falklands were bombed by Sea Harriers, operating from the *HMS Hermes,* and Vulcan bombers operating from the nearest British base, Ascension Island. The Vulcans were greatly hampered by a lack of range as well as tankers for mid-flight refuelling. For each trip from the Ascensions, a Vulcan had to be refuelled three times by Victor tankers; thus, only one bomber at a time could make the trip. The main target of British air attacks was the landing field at Stanley. However, it was only marginally damaged during the campaign and remained operational for aircraft such as C-130s and Pucarás until the Argentine surrender.

Answering these British moves, Argentine forces immediately began to attack the task force. Surface ships and Argentina's two remaining submarines took to sea. On the evening of May 1, Israeli-supplied Daggers and an aged ex-British Canberra bomber swooped in on British ships. At least one Dagger and the Canberra were shot down by Sea Harriers; after this encounter, the Argentine air force stopped using Canberras on such missions. On May 2, the Argentine battle-cruiser Belgrano was sunk by a torpedo from the destroyer *HMS Conqueror,* with a loss of 368 lives. As a result, those Argentine naval units that had not yet been sent to the Falklands remained close to the coast, outside Britain's self-declared "Total Exclusion Zone." One of the two Argentine submarines continued to harass the task force, while the other was disabled by engine trouble.[3] Argentine aircraft fared somewhat better than ships: attacks with French-supplied Exocet and antiship missiles received worldwide attention that continued after the end of the conflict.

However, use of the feared Exocets was limited from the start by the low number in the Argentine arsenal, reportedly no more than five air-launched AM-39s and about two dozen ground-launched MM-38s (Colombo, 1984, p. 17; Tilford, 1984, p. 44). The only aircraft in the Argentine forces capable of launching the AM-39s were Super Etendard fighters. Although pilots had received training in France in the preceding year, the naval air arm, aided by French experts, was still in the early stages of adapting to the aircraft when the war started. The Super Etendards were intended to replace A-4 Skyhawks on the aircraft carrier *Ventecinco de Mayo* but the transformation had not been made. They operated instead from the naval base of Rio Gallegos, which was just as well, since the *Ventecinco de Mayo* did not leave harbor, officially because of difficulties with the propulsion system, but possibly because of fears about British submarines.

All tolled, British losses from Exocet attacks were less severe than those due to conventional "iron" bombs and guns. Conventional bombs were dropped from a variety of aircraft, including Pucarás, Skyhawks, and Mirages. Altogether the Argentines conducted at least nineteen successful air strikes and damaged or sank sixteen British ships (Cordesman and Wagner, 1990b, p. 319). However, only about twenty percent of the bombs exploded, mainly due to problems with setting the fuzes (Wood and Hewish, 1982, p. 977), so in ten cases the damage was limited. Military analysts have concluded: "It seems at least possible that if these bomb hits had resulted in explosions, they might have forced the British task force ships to withdraw or had a political effect on the course of the war" (Cordesman and Wagner, 1990b, p. 319).

The aircraft attacking the naval task force were guided by various maritime patrol aircraft and the radars stationed near Stanley. Although the Argentineans were quite successful in guiding aircraft, the lack of a more modern electronic warfare capability, such as US-supplied AWACS radar planes or satellite-based intelligence, limited their effective range. The British task force similarly lacked airborne radar surveillance (their own version of AWACS had been plagued by delays), but ultimately received valuable US satellite information. Still, airborne command and control electronics were later analyzed as one of the task force's major shortcomings (United Kingdom, "Report of a Committee of Privy Councellors, Chairman: Lord Franks," 1983). Argentine aircraft often flew at such low levels that they were not detected by shipborne radar. Nevertheless, Argentina's aircraft loss rate was high; more than one-hundred aircraft were destroyed during the war, with about thirty-two downed by British Harriers, eighteen with Sidewinder AIM-9L Air-to-Air Missiles (AAMs) (Cordesman and Wagner, 1990b, pp. 303–5; Middlebrook, 1985, pp. 284–5; Ethell and Price, 1983). The AIM-9L proved early in the war to be one of the most deadly weapons in the British arsenal.[4]

On May 21, British forces finally landed on the West Falklands-Malvinas near San Carlos. Under heavy fire from Argentine aircraft coming both from the mainland and from nearby airstrips, they secured a beachhead. Although the Argentine troops were more than double the size of the British contingent, they were soon overrun. This was mostly due to lack of training and poor command coordination. In addition, the inexperienced recruits were neither used to nor equipped for the cold weather. There was no lack of weapons and ammunition, however. By June 2, British forces were in sight of Port Stanley, where about five thousand Argentine defenders were dug in. Although the British government authorized the attack against this last Argentine foothold on June 3, British task force commanders delayed the assault in order to strengthen their position and to try to persuade the opposing commanders to give in. As the British closed in, the Argentine garrison surrendered on June 14 under heavy fire.

The British victory was no foregone conclusion when the task force set sail to the South Atlantic. In fact, given Argentinean equipment and geographic advantages, it was a risky endeavor. Given the effective Argentine air operations and penetration of UK defenses, British forces were fortunate not to suffer higher losses. Had Argentine forces on the islands been able to use their numerical advantage to stop or prolong the British advance, the task force could have run into serious problems. Given their high sortie rates, for example, operation of the Harriers and other vital systems probably would have become difficult beyond the end of June.

On the whole though, British weak points proved less decisive than Argentine deficiencies in planning, training, and command. Argentine forces also suffered from short supply of certain weapons systems, as in the frustrating lack of an effective antisubmarine warfare (ASW) capability. In addition, deadly as the air force and the naval air arm were in sinking British ships, they lacked sophisticated maritime air-control capability. Argentine airborne forces also had too few refueling aircraft to operate at a distance of more than four-hundred miles from base (a problem to some extent shared by the British), and aircraft that were most successful against the task force, i.e., A-4P and A-4Q Skyhawk bombers and Super Etendards, were in short supply or poor repair (Colombo, 1984, p. 13). Finally, supplies of missiles generally were insufficient, including AM-39 Exocets and effective air-to-air and air-defense systems. Up-to-date conventional bombs would probably have wreaked more damage as well.

Most of these shortcomings were known to the Argentine high command before the war. In fact, better ASW capabilities, as well as more Skyhawks and Super Etendards were on order when the war began. Such gaps could not have been closed during a three-month war, although Buenos Aires did approach several arms sources during the conflict.

Ironically, Britain had to contend with many similar supply, maintenance, command, and control problems over a tremendously long distance. For example, when the task force sailed it lacked latest-generation missiles both for air-to-air combat and for shipborne air defense. The former capabilities were, however, greatly enhanced by US supplies of AIM-9L Sidewinders as the task force passed Ascension Island. Thus, the active support of America as an ally, won by Britain and lost by Argentina in the war's diplomatic struggle, proved especially decisive.

The war remained relatively confined to the issue in contention. Britain refrained from attacking the mainland, an option much feared by the Argentine military. Also, there was the thorny issue of British nuclear weapons. Evidently, British ships sailing toward the Falklands carried such weapons, but they were removed before the South Atlantic was reached. Had the fighting turned for the worse, it is interesting to speculate whether London would have tried or threatened to widen the war in order to add to the diplomatic pressure, particularly in Washington or Moscow (Freedman and Gamba-Stonehouse, 1990, p. 130). (See Appendix, Chronology 4, "The South Atlantic War, 1982.")

DIPLOMATIC PRESSURE AND ARMS FLOW

When London announced its intention to fight, it also began a major diplomatic offensive to isolate Argentina and cut off strategic military supplies. This soon paid off in the European Community; on April 9, the European Council discussed several economic-warfare measures against Buenos Aires, including an arms embargo, which went into effect on the sixteenth. The most immediate effect was in France, which agreed to cancel shipment of additional Super Etendards and AM-39 Exocets scheduled for delivery in the spring of 1982. French technicians also were recalled and prohibited from advising Argentine pilots and maintenance crews. In addition, spare parts for the many weapon systems previously bought by the Argentine military were withheld. Instead, a stream of technical information flowed from France to Britain to help counter French-supplied weapons (Freedman and Gamba-Stonehouse, 1990, p. 154). The West German government likewise announced that it would not allow arms or ammunition to go to Argentina as long as hostilities lasted. At the same time, though, work continued on ships ordered by the Argentine navy.

The Italians, while voting in favor of the embargo, reportedly allowed the transfer of some nonlethal items ordered earlier (Goldblat and Milan, 1983a, p. 42).

Other governments also embargoed arms sales. Spain officially barred deliveries to either side, though reports persisted of some spare parts getting through to Argentina. The Austrians likewise stopped delivery of Argentina's Kürassier tanks, and Ottawa and Tokyo both placed an embargo on the export of military goods to Buenos Aires. Another important Argentine supplier, upon which British diplomacy focused, was Israel. Although the Israeli government decided on an arms embargo on April 7, it is not clear whether it was fully enforced and covered both new and continuing contracts. Among the items reported to have slipped through were spare parts for the A-4 Skyhawks and ship-to-ship missiles similar to the MM-38 Exocet (called "Gabriel" in Israel).[5]

Despite the diminished US role as arms supplier, Argentina's arsenal still featured many American systems, including its fleet of C-130 Hercules transport aircraft, the A-4 Skyhawks, and P-2 Neptune maritime surveillance aircraft. Washington confirmed its continued official embargo, in force rather ineffectively since 1978 due to the disturbing political situation in Buenos Aires. On April 30, this was extended to cover dual-use items destined for the Argentine military.

Thus by the end of April, all main Argentine suppliers had joined in embargoing the transfer of weapons, ammunition, and spare parts. Still, some military material reached Argentina. Israel was mentioned as one probable source, though other governments, particularly in Latin America, sent symbolic quantities of military goods to express solidarity with the Malvinas cause. Reportedly, these also included Libya (some air-to-air and surface-to-air missiles), Ecuador (small arms and ammunition of Israeli origin), Venezuela (spare part for Mirages and Canberra bombers), Peru (Mirage or Sukhoi-22 aircraft), and South Africa (ammunition, Exocet type missiles).[6] The black market involving spare parts for US supplied weapons also was probably active from various sources. None of these deliveries involved large quantities or was of much military significance, however.

That might have been different had the Argentines taken weapon deliveries from the Soviet Union or one of its allies. There are indications that Moscow offered support, though Argentine decision-makers later claimed to have refused it; details are far from clear.[7] One of the items mentioned at the time and also later were SAM-7 air-defense missiles, but none were found by the British forces conquering the Falklands. Another support measure often mentioned was satellite information. The Soviets collected massive amounts of satellite information (Jasani, 1983, pp. 429–31), but it is unlikely that they passed this on to Buenos Aires.

The British side was, as explained above, much less dependent on foreign supplies. Some Latin governments (including Spain, with arms restrictions) introduced trade sanctions against Britain, but none was a significant supplier of goods let alone weapons or ammunition. Others were less anti-British in their statements, raising the possibility that they might have been willing quietly to help London's logistical effort. First choice, from the British viewpoint, was Brazil, Argentina's main regional competitor. However, the Brazilian government rejected London's request for access to ports on April 16. Despite the Beagle Channel dispute, Chile also officially announced that it did not support the British military effort. But when a helicopter carrying UK scouts crashed in the mountains near the Chilean border, Argentine mistrust was stirred.

The only foreign government crucially important for military support and logistics was the US. As was revealed bit by bit in the years following the war (*Economist,* 1983b; Costa Mendez, 1985; Falcoff, 1990; Freedman and Gamba-Stonehouse, 1990), US support of the British military effort was prompt and massive. Among other things, the US military opened its strategic stockpile, helped with an extension of the runway on Ascension Island, sent large amounts of fuel, provided satellite intelligence, and delivered AIM-9L AAMs (Cordesman and Wagner, 1990b, p. 263).

However, until April 30, when President Reagan announced full support of Britain, both London and Washington tried to conceal this assistance. Neither wanted to validate the Argentine argument that this was a North-South war. In view of its cross-pressuring OAS alliance ties, Washington tried to act as mediator and therefore wanted to preserve the image of impartiality. There was serious internal disagreement in Washington about policy toward the combatants. Put simply, in view of NATO ties the Defense Department under Caspar Weinberger wholeheartedly supported the British military effort, while the UN mission under Ambassador Jeane Kirkpatrick did not want to aggravate the Argentineans; the State Department was divided and Secretary Alexander Haig tried steering a middle course (Kaufman, 1988; Freedman and Gamba-Stonehouse, 1990, pp. 165–245; Kinney, 1989).[8]

Even before the Argentine invasion, diplomatic efforts to limit the fighting had set in. On April 3, UN Security Council Resolution 502 was adopted, demanding a withdrawal of Argentine forces and requesting both sides to seek a peaceful negotiated solution. Britain considered the resolution a vindication of its position. Buenos Aires rejected it but viewed it as a partial success in projecting the Falkland-Malvinas issue to the forefront of international concern while avoiding condemnation as an aggressor.[9]

The two hostile states readily agreed to American mediation, and others, such as UN General Secretary Perez de Cuellar, also offered their services. Indeed, when they decided to attack, Argentine leaders had counted on Washington's involvement as neutral mediator, i.e., on "triangularizing" the Falkland-Malvinas issue (Gamba, 1987, p. 150).[10] The British, of course, saw the US as a natural ally. In view of London's strategic dependence on Washington, the Suez crisis of 1956 weighed on the minds of those meeting at 10 Downing Street (Gamba 1987, p. 156). The British side was aware of its need to cooperate closely with its leading ally to avoid a repeat of American efforts to scuttle Britain's use of force outside the NATO area.

Unfortunately, the Haig mediation effort failed to achieve any results, and was abandoned on April 20. According to published accounts, this was due to the intransigent position of both governments. Both insisted on sovereignty over the islands. Haig had proposed an interim multilateral administration by the US, Britain, Argentina, and possibly other countries, with negotiations continuing about ultimate sovereignty. While both governments agreed to negotiate, the British wanted the negotiations to be unconditional, while the Argentineans insisted on guarantees that negotiations would end with a transfer of sovereignty to Buenos Aires before 1983. Facing an increasingly suspicious and hostile junta (suspecting US bias toward Britain), the final Haig position on this issue was to give no such guarantees, but to offer US undertakings to reach a final settlement within six months if negotiations were not successful by December 31, 1982 (Haig, 1984, chapter 13; Gamba, 1987, pp. 154–57).[11]

Additional asymmetrical leverage was available to Haig, but went unused. Since the US had operated an arms embargo since 1978, Washington could have offered the Argentineans the resumption of normal relations, including an end to the arms ban. Haig also could have threatened an extension of the embargo to dual-purpose items. The British on the other hand were clearly dependent on US help. Naval analysts, for instance, had informed the administration of the fragility of the British logistical position (Cordesman and Wagner, 1990b, p. 262). But Haig did not seize such potential for diplomatic leverage. One reason for this was his personal view that, as a NATO partner, Britain should be supported. Another problem was his relative isolation in the administration, a situation that would lead to his resignation. While he had President Reagan's support as a mediator, he had little else. In National Security Council discussions about his mandate it had become clear that the administration was not capable of strong action.[12] A threat by Haig to limit supplies to the British side would not have been credible.

In late April, Peru's President Belaunde Terry privately offered to serve as intermediary. On May 2, he presented a seven-point peace plan, which resembled the last Haig proposal. Instead of the US, a group of smaller countries would act as island trustees, and the date for final decision was set for April 30, 1983. The Peruvian plan was accepted by the Argentine Foreign Minister Costa Mendez and General Galtieri early on May 2, but rejected by the full junta later the same day, after the *Conqueror* had torpedoed the *Belgrano*. A slightly amended Peruvian initiative was accepted by the British government on May 5, and finally rejected by Argentina on May 6, since it did not meet their demand for guaranteed transfer of sovereignty.

Simultaneously, Argentina took up an offer of mediation by UN Secretary General Perez de Cuellar. Intense discussions at a more junior level than the Haig meetings were conducted at UN headquarters in New York. On May 19, after the British landing party had been assembled, Perez de Cuellar tried to reconcile remaining differences, which again focussed on the question of the timetable for transfer of sovereignty. On May 20, however, he reported to the Security Council that his mission had failed.

Arms transfers played no role in either the Peruvian or the UN mediation effort. Neither of these mediators shared Haig's leverage over the two governments, although the Peruvians had offered substantial support and supplied some material at the beginning of the crisis. They were in no position to either help or hinder either side's military effort substantially, or to protect the Argentineans from their adversaries.

CONCLUSIONS

Despite being incomplete, the large-scale Argentine armament program probably influenced decision-making on the effort to "liberate" the Malvinas. Similarly, Britain's access early on to American military assistance clearly bolstered London's resolve and ability to resist and pursue its distant quest. Argentina's buildup both contributed to its difficult economic situation and resultant domestic political unrest in 1981–82, though it instilled self-confidence in the armed-forces leadership. It also ironically presented British military strategists with the unwelcome task of counteracting Argentina's British and European weapons in the South Atlantic.

Shortly after the beginning of hostilities, a number of countries, including all of Argentina's major prewar suppliers, decided to embargo the transfer of arms and related material to Buenos Aires. Argentine forces thus were, perhaps unexpectedly, confronted with relative shortages of certain weapons systems and spare parts. British armed forces, on the other hand, could draw on an almost unlimited supply of critical items because of their domestic stocks and allied support. Their problem was that the battle zone was eight-thousand miles from home. To overcome such logistical problems the British needed and obtained help, particularly from the US, a factor probably more crucial to their victory than the arms embargo.

In this case, arms supplies during the war bolstered the defending side, Britain, while the denial of arms to the attacker, Argentina (though in strictly military terms the circumstances were reversed after April), did not clearly lead to its backing down on the battlefield or in negotiations. The war was too short for the arms embargoes to have decisive effects, and involved only segments of the respective armed forces. In the Argentinean case, the whole air force, a small part of the navy, and about twenty-thousand army personnel were engaged; the British task force of a sizable portion of the Royal Navy, but only numerically small units from the air force and the army, numbering about twenty-eight-thousand men in all. Resupply problems were limited to certain items, which in the case of Argentina were embargoed, and in the case of Britain were not brought in fast enough. In general, though, both sides could have benefitted from more and better weapon systems, such additions also could have created more organizational and operational problems for either party. Certainly the Argentineans would have benefitted from additional Super Etendards and AM-39 Exocet missiles due for delivery during the war. But conceivably Britain, especially with US help, could have devised further antidotes to such threats. Therefore, none of these supply problems can be construed to have determined the course or the end of the fighting.

Clearly Argentine leaders were aware of their technological disadvantages in confronting the British, but fell back on logistical advantages, the belief that London would not fight, and the hope of some major-power diplomatic assistance. Indications of Soviet and Chinese support for Argentina's position at the UN seemed to bolster such hopes, vain as they ultimately proved to be. Encouraged, nevertheless, by worldwide diplomatic attention and Latin American support, the junta continually balked at concessions on the key issue of sovereignty, while remaining flexible on terms of British withdrawal and shared interim administration. Despite an increasingly comprehensive embargo, and looking for "back door" sources of arms resupply, e.g., from Venezuela, South Africa, Brazil, Libya, Peru, Uruguay, and Israel, the junta resolved to fight to the finish, mainly relying on its air force.

On the other side, US supplies to the British forces were quite crucial, especially in extending the time-frame within which the Royal Navy could operate in the South Atlantic. Without satellite intelligence, US logistical help, and the supply of AIM-9L Sidewinders, the already precarious British situation would have been even more difficult. As Sir Nicolas Henderson has concluded: "From my discussion with service leaders since the events I conclude that it is difficult to exaggerate the difference that America's support made to the military outcome" (Henderson, 1983, p. 31).

Furthermore, even had the British armada been forced to withdraw from hostilities, this would not necessarily have meant an ultimate Argentine victory. With the arms embargo in place in the longer run, British superiority and American pressure might have been overwhelming, though the reality of Argentine control of the Malvinas could have proved diplomatically nettlesome as well. Indeed, the swift British military response in April could have been due at least partly to a perception of dwindling military superiority vis-à-vis the Argentineans in the South Atlantic.

Nevertheless, Washington did not use the full leverage stemming from its supplier position. Internal divisions in the administration over whom to support, lack of leadership, as well as a reluctance to pressure Britain, seem to have been factors influencing US decision-making on this issue.

In a sense, then, this case resembles the second India-Pakistan war, in that a regional power, with poor overall military prospects against a better armed foe, nevertheless embarked on a sustained military struggle in hopes that the international community would secure its rights to sovereignty over a remote territory. In neither case were such expectations accurate, but military rulers nevertheless felt compelled to uphold their "destiny" in combat. The side with the more diversified access to arms supplies prevailed in both cases, and indeed the loser in each case was subject to an arms embargo. However, the outcomes appeared to hinge more on the overall power advantages, including third-party support, of the ultimate winners, Britain and India. Pakistan delayed its capitulation while the US scurried to preserve Pakistan's remaining territories; India enjoyed massive Soviet support. Argentina refused to capitulate until the last, as the US aided its opponent and tried to foster a neutral image. In neither case was outside diplomatic pressure on the respective parties as concerted and extensive as in the 1965 South Asian and Central American football wars.

Argentina's overall intransigence does not closely comport with the expectations developed in chapter one about belligerents having trouble gaining access to arms. As in the Football War, it seems to indicate the additional importance of overall political pressure and will in determining what to fight for and how long to hold out. We will further explore the complex behavior of those at war and under pressure as we turn next to the Middle East at roughly the same periods.

CHAPTER 7

THE YOM KIPPUR-RAMADAN WAR, 1973

INTRODUCTION: THE BACKGROUND OF WAR

As with Indian-Pakistani hostilities, the various rounds of Arab-Israeli fighting form an action/reaction chain extending back decades. Each individual war has had its own context as related to a particular set of irritants, but unresolved issues from the previous rounds set the stage for the next. Theoretically, such repetitive hostilities constitute an ongoing hostility "system," in which the effect of arms supplies can be highly destabilizing, and which can contrast quite sharply to one-shot nonrepetitive wars such as those between El Salvador and Honduras or Britain and Argentina.

For one thing, arms supplies build cumulatively from one war to another, with replenishment often constituting step-level increases both quantitatively and qualitatively. This does not necessarily mean that war is more likely to break out at any particular point in time than it is between new enemies; indeed, old enemies can gauge their competition within limits and may not be subject to as much miscalculation as relative strangers. Yet the fact of relatively focussed hostilities, of revenge motives, and of mounting arms stockpiles, would seem to raise the overall probability of warfare. Remedies for past disadvantages are sought; ghosts of prior wars condition arms acquisition efforts; defense establishments are strengthened with growing stakes in outmaneuvering the enemy.

Therefore, key arms suppliers are likely to be cultivated by states in such ongoing conflict systems. This in turn increases the suppliers' potential arms leverage. It is in such long-term conflict systems that we might expect the greatest restraining effects of arms-transfer diplomacy, if the suppliers can coordinate their positions. Thus, we examine two wars in perhaps the most notorious such conflict system, the Arab-Israeli dispute: the 1973 Yom Kippur-Ramadan war, covered in this chapter, and the 1982 Israeli invasion of Lebanon, covered in the next. Theoretically, the US and Soviet capability to influence the outbreak and continuation of fighting should have been very great in these instances, particularly since the wars lasted longer than Israel's relatively easy Six-Day War victory in 1967.

ARMAMENT AND THE APPROACH OF WAR

During the 1960s, a spiralling regional arms race took place. Israel read the arms preparation of each individual Arab state as a threat, and in turn armed for multifront fighting, thus compelling its Arab opponents to respond as much as possible in kind, and strain their economies to do so. In the 1967 war, arms-transfer diplomacy had not played a great role. The superpowers had been rather restrained in their Middle Eastern arms transfers. Relatively massive Soviet supplies to both Syria and Egypt and Washington's aid to Israel after 1962 had been designed to preserve influence and maintain power balances and defenses, but not to foster uncontrolled combat. Indeed, Moscow denied Syria SAM-2 antiaircraft missiles in January 1967 and withheld spare parts and ammunition from Egypt in the months before the war precisely for this reason. France, shifting its Middle Eastern policies, also joined in these efforts during the prewar Israeli-Syrian clashes, applying an arms embargo against Israel, a state then still heavily dependent on French weapons (Krause, 1987; Krause, 1990, pp. 398–99).

Nevertheless, these restraining efforts failed to prevent the 1967 fighting, especially in view of Soviet efforts to generate a strong Egyptian-Syrian alliance and relative US inattention to the developing crisis during its Vietnam preoccupation (Kerr, 1971; Laqueur, 1968). Cairo's stunning military setback was soon redressed with massive Soviet military resupply. Moscow began to promise this aid even during the war, when the Arab side was losing badly and needed an effective cease-fire. Concomitantly, the US replaced France as Israel's primary, indeed virtually sole, arms supplier; thus, overall arms transfer volumes to the region increased markedly (Krause, 1990, p. 399).

Dangerous fighting broke out again in 1970, the "War of Attrition," along the Suez Canal. Still refusing Egyptian requests for advanced offensive capabilities, Moscow nevertheless sent MiG-21s (instead of 25s) and decided to commit Soviet air forces on behalf of Egypt, the first such engagement outside Europe. The resulting close encounters between Israeli and Soviet pilots, together with US diplomatic pressure, seemed to chasten both sides, and hesitant negotiations began. Yet new surface-to-air (SAM) missile emplacements, manned by Soviet personnel, also heartened the Egyptians in defending against Israeli raids along the Canal and in the Egyptian interior. Thus, despite its growing interest in detente with the Nixon administration, Moscow continued to compete heavily with the US for Middle Eastern regional influence.

Generally, both superpowers seemed relatively content with the status quo between the Egypt-Syria alliance and Israel, which allowed Washington and Moscow significant regional influence without much evident risk of full-scale war. Indeed, the Nixon administration tried a bit of arms diplomacy against Israel in 1970, slowing response to Tel Aviv's requests for fighter aircraft in reaction to Israel's employment of newly delivered Phantom jets to bomb civilian targets in Egypt (Kissinger, 1979, pp. 564–65, 570–72). Israel's acceptance of a cease-fire along the canal has been attributed by some to its continuing need for US equipment, while the Soviets reputedly were able to exercise arms influence in bringing Egypt to this agreement as well. Yet apart from superpower pressure, Cairo and Tel Aviv both needed to lessen the tension and attrition. Furthermore, even if arms pressures facilitated the cease-fire, they could not alone produce a further diplomatic settlement (Krause, 1987). The precedent had been set, however, in Washington to attempt to time the flow of arms, within the overall continuing supply relationship, in order to affect the prospect and pace of negotiations and movement toward settlement (Bar-Siman-Tov, 1987, pp. 180–85).

As the US-Israeli relationship solidified again in 1971, due largely to common interests, such as the 1970 Jordanian expulsion of the Palestine Liberation Organization (PLO) and clashes with Syria, Egypt's President Anwar as-Sadat became ever more restive at the lack of progress toward the return of Israeli-occupied territory. He maintained pressure for additional sophisticated and offensive Soviet armament and technical assistance (Mets, 1986, pp. 91–93). In November 1972, after first failing in diplomatic overtures to the Israelis and Americans about "land for peace" (Bailey, 1990, pp. 294–97; Kissinger, 1979, pp. 1292–1300), President Sadat embarked on a plan for limited war to convince Tel Aviv and Washington that the status quo was no longer tenable. Diplomatic contacts and discussions proceeded amidst arms build-ups. Egypt's general command prepared for a joint military operation with Syria to seize strategic territory in both Sinai and the Syrian plateau. Syria would be expected to break Israel's hold on the Golan Heights, and reach the Jordan River and the shores of Lake Tiberius.

While planning, Egyptian military leaders recognized certain Israeli advantages, including air superiority and the close US supply relationship, but they also posed Israeli disadvantages vis-à-vis Egypt's greater manpower, bi-frontal attack strategy, and improved Soviet-supplied air defense surface-to-air missile (SAM) system, as well as Israel's overextended communication lines. Forces of second-line Arab states were expected to join the fighting through integrated units as well, as joint planning and command coordination continued right up to the October 6, 1973 attack date (El Badri, et al., 1977, pp. 15–25).

Both sides had substantially improved their military capabilities since the 1967 war. By 1970 the Soviets had installed an Egyptian air-defense system based on the SA-2, and the US had countered it for Israel with electronic countermeasures (ECM) developed in Vietnam. In the spring of that year, Moscow "upped the ante" with SA-3 air defenses and MiG 21s, as well as Soviet pilots; the new SAMs were effective against lower-altitude attacks. However, at that time the Soviets drew the line at largely defensive equipment, dodging most Egyptian requests for offensive infantry armament, and insisting that the new supplies be used in combat only with Soviet permission. Moscow kept relatively close control, wanting to maximize restraints and influence over a war if it were to come in this volatile region (Mets, 1986).

Angry at such limits, and at Soviet flirtation with Washington (in the SALT negotiations) and Iraq (a new friendship treaty), and realizing that Soviet connections weakened him with more moderate and wealthy Arab rulers, Sadat expelled most USSR military advisers in July 1972. He insisted they either turn over all military equipment in the country or remove it. Leaving with hardly a protest, Soviet personnel also removed their more sophisticated weapons, thus greatly diminishing Egypt's air-defense credibility (Evron, 1973, pp. 222–23).

Neither Egypt nor Israel was in a position to break free from its major arms patron. Egypt's domestic arms production, for example, was limited to small arms, ammunition, vehicles, aircraft, and missile parts, mostly of Soviet design (Katz, 1984, pp. 123–52). Israel had much more impressive military production capabilities, but still not enough to sustain a full-scale war against opponents receiving sophisticated weapons. Roughly twenty percent of Israel's military equipment was manufactured domestically, but this basically amounted to small arms and aircraft spare parts. This indigenous capability evolved mostly from collaborative relationships with foreign firms (Brzoska and Ohlson, 1986; SIPRI, 1971, pp. 768–69).

Despite, then, continued arms dependence and Israeli capabilities, Sadat's confidence in his newly imported weapons technology led him to order military planning for war with Israel. With a renewed Egyptian welcome, Soviet arms flowed again in October 1972, rising to even more generous levels by the following spring. The nature of this armament, entailing mainly advanced antiaircraft batteries but also including early versions of "Scud" short-range surface-to-surface missiles, fit well with Egyptian political and strategic needs. Cairo regained hope of a defensive umbrella that would neutralize Israel's jet fighter superiority; Egyptian forces could seize initial territory in a surprise raid, utilizing advanced Soviet bridging equipment quickly to cross the Suez Canal, and then revert to a defensive mode behind antiaircraft shields, absorbing Israeli counterstrikes, bleeding the attacking Israeli forces, and potentially striking back with Scuds. Presumably, this would lead to breakthrough negotiations and a diplomatic settlement of territorial questions.

Having suffered the recent loss of as many as thirteen jets in skirmishes with Israel, Syria seemed less confident of its weapons technology. Damascus also pressed for upgraded Soviet equipment in September 1973, just prior to the war. The USSR, however, had hardly left its Syrian clients defenseless, having agreed to supply several MiG fighters in May 1972 along with a full array of advanced SAM systems and "Osa class" missile patrol boats. This equipment was received from late 1972 through 1973, including approximately fifty SAM batteries arriving after April. Syria's subsequent progress in ground combat early in the war has indeed been attributed partly to superior night-vision equipment supplied by the USSR (Bailey, 1990, p. 311). Damascus nevertheless appeared less sanguine than Egypt about "bleeding Israel," and evidently hoped merely to seize Golan territories and rely on outside pressure to bring a prompt cease-fire (Mets, 1986, p. 95).

For its part, Israel was supremely confident of military superiority, a confidence that compounded a tendency to delay response to intelligence warnings. After the Nixon administration had reasserted Israel's strategic importance in 1971–72, the flow of advanced aircraft resumed in 1972–73, and US foreign military sales to Israel amounted to $300 million annually in those years. Tel Aviv had concentrated on preparing to overcome improved Arab air defenses, acquiring forty-two F-4 Phantoms and eighty A-4 Skyhawks (SIPRI, *Yearbook,* 1974). Thus, Israeli leaders anticipated continued air skirmishes with neighboring states, and worried about excessive superpower involvement (Evron, 1973, pp. 220–25; Nachmias, 1988, p. 59). Israeli intelligence had difficulty envisioning a viable Arab groundwar strategy, and initially appeared misled by Egyptian-Soviet frictions and visible Egyptian military preparations, interpreting the latter as rather routine war training (Mets, 1986, p. 93). Evidently a warming US-Egyptian relationship also was not well charted in Tel Aviv.[1]

Table 9

Arms Shipments to Israel, 1970–73

Major arms shipped to Israel, 1970–72

France	5 Saar-3 Class ships
US	8 S-65A helicopters; 17 A-4H Skyhawk fighters; 37A-4N Skyhawk-2 fighters; 120 M-48 Patton tanks; 25 M-114 155mm howitzers; 60 M-101-A1 105mm howitzers; 45 M-110 203mm howitzers; 5 Model 185 light planes; 330 AGM-12B Bullpup ASM; 105 M-107 175mm artillery; 546 AIM-7C Sparrow AAM; 6 RF-4E Phantom jets; 91 F-4E Phantom jets; 100 M-113-A1 APC; 100 M-60 tanks; 5 Model-180 aircraft; 45 T17E1 Staghound armored antiaircraft vehicles; 24 M-109 155mm howitzers; 300 AGM-45A Shrike antiradar missiles; 2 C-130 Hercules transports; 3 LSM type landing craft/mine layers; 20 Model-206B helicopters; 168 AIM-9D AAM; 1 Stratofreighter transport plane
UK	300 Centurion tanks

Major arms shipped to Israel, 1973

US	360 AIM 7-C Sparrow AAM; 30 M-107 175mm artillery; 110 AGM-12B Bullpup ASM; 200 M-60 tanks; 168 AIM-9D AAM; 32 A-4N Skyhawk-2 fighters; 60 F-4E Phantom jets; 8 TA-4H Skyhawk fighters; 2 Stratofreighter transports; 20 AN/PPS-15 radars; 12 M-730 Chaparral missile-armed antiaircraft vehicles;

(continued on next page)

Table 9 (*continued*)

	144 MIM-72A mobile SAM; 53 A-4E Skyhawk fighters; 500 BGM-71A TOW ATM; 200 AGM-65A ASM; 6 S-65A helicopters; 200 M-48 Patton tanks; 100 MIM-23B mobile Hawk SAM; 2000 AIM-9D AAM; 12 C-130E Hercules transports; 300 AGM-45A Shrike antiradar missiles
UK	100 Centurion tanks

Source: Estimates from SIPRI files; authors' files

Table 10
Arms Shipments to Egypt, 1970–73

Major arms shipped to Egypt, 1970–72

USSR	3 T-43 Class minesweepers; 12 P-6 Class attack craft; 4 SO-1 Class patrol craft; 100 D-20 152mm howitzer; 60 BM-21 122mm multiple rocket systems; 350 T-54 tanks; 50 ZSU-23-4 Shilka anti-aircraft vehicles; 400 T-55 tanks; 470 AA-2 ATOLL AAM; 55 SU-7 Fitter fighter/bombers; 60 Frog 7 SSM; 20 Frog SSM launchers; 750 Guideline SAM; 25 AS-5 Kelt SShM; 450 BTR-60P APC; 1200 SA-3 GOA mobile SAM; 100 SA-2 SAM launchers; 200 SA-3 SAM; 80 MI-8 HIP helicopters; 4 Yurka Class minesweepers; 20 MI-6 Hook helicopters; 5 Straight Flush fire-control radars; 25 MiG-21F fighters; 75 MiG-21MF fighters; 25 TU-16B Badger-B bombers; 20 SU-20 Fitter-C fighter/bombers; 800 SA-7 Grail SAM; 20 MiG-15 fighters; 35 MiG-17 fighters; 2 Whiskey Class submarines; 200 T-62 tanks; 250 SA-6 Gainful SAM; 25 SA-6 SAM; 150 AT-1 Snapper ATM; 200 AT-3 Sagger ATM; 1 Polnocny Class landing ship; 25 K-61 APC
Czechoslovakia	20 L-29 Delfin trainers; 100 OT-64 APC
Syria	4 P-4 Class fast-attack craft

Major arms shipped to Egypt, 1973

USSR	75 PT-76 light tanks; 100 T-55 tanks; 50 ZSU-23-4 Shilka anti-aircraft vehicles; 660 AA-2 ATOLL AAM; 200 BTR-60P APC; 800 SA-7 Grail SAM; 25 SAM-6 SAM; 300 T-62 tanks; 75 MiG 21MF fighters; 250 SA-6 Gainful SAM; 125 BMP-1 mechanized infantry combat vehicles; 200 AT-3 Sagger ATM; 150 AT-1 Snapper ATM; 1 Polnocny Class landing ship; 60 Scud-B SSM;

	50 T-54 tanks; 25 MI-8 HIP helicopters; 50 MiG-17 fighters; 30 MiG-19 fighters
France	6 Mirage 5 SD fighter-bombers

Source: Estimates from SIPRI files; authors' files.

Table 11

Arms Shipments to Syria, 1970–73

Major arms shipped to Syria, 1970–72

Czechoslovakia	20 L-29 Delfin trainers
USSR	40 MiG-21F fighters; 10 MiG-21 UTI fighters; 50 ZSU-57-2 anti-aircraft vehicles; 46 PT-76 light tanks; 50 M-1944 100mm artillery; 150 T-54 tanks; 270 AA-2 ATOLL AAM; 200 BTR-152 APC; 10 SU-Fitter fighter/bombers; 200 T-55 tanks; 2 SU-7U Moujik trainers; 20 MiG-17 fighters; 30 MI-8 HIP helicopters; 2 OSA-1 Class missile boats; 2 SSN-2 Styx-L ShSHM launchers; 24 SSN-2 Styx ShShM; 150 BTR-50 Pradass APC; 200 S-231 80mm artillery; 25 MiG-21 MF fighters; 2 MI-4 Hound helicopters; 100 BRDM-1 scout cars; 150 BTR 60P APC; 81 SA-2 Guideline SAM; 9 SA-2 SAM launchers; 9 SA-3 SAM; 250 SA-7 Grail SAM; 100 AT-1 Snapper ATM; 150 AT-3 Sagger ATM; 81 SA-3 GOA SAM; 100 BM-21 122mm multiple rocket system

Arms shipped to Syria, 1973

USSR	50 ZSU-57-2 anti-aircraft vehicles; 1050 AA-2 ATOLL AAM; 100 JSU-152 artillery; 100 JSU-122 artillery; 84 SSN-2 Styx ShShM; 7 OSA-1 Class missile boats; 7 SSN-2 Styx ShSHM launchers; 18 Frog SSM launchers; 30 Frog-7 SSM; 9 SA-2 SAM launchers; 81 SA-2 Guideline SAM; 250 SA-7 Grail SAM; 81 SA-3 GOA SAM; 9 SA-3 SAM; 40 PT-76; 100 AT-1 Snapper ATM; 150 AT-3 Sagger ATM; 100 D-30 122mm howitzers; 100 BM-21 122mm rocket systems; 4 YAK-40 Codling transports; 2 Vanya Class coastal minesweepers; 200 BTR-50P APC; 150 T-54 tanks; 20 SA-6 SAM; 15 MI-8 HIP helicopters; 50 T-34 tanks; 20 SU-7 Fitter fighter/bombers; 250 T-62 tanks; 40 MiG-17 fighters; 200 BTR-60P APC; 150 T-55 tanks; 175 MiG-21F fighters; 100 AT-2 Swatter ATM; 180 SA-6 Gainful SAM

Source: Estimates from SIPRI files; authors' files.

Israel's diplomatic jockeying with Washington led its leaders to forego any thoughts of a 1967-style preemptive attack as alarming intelligence warnings finally came in early October, heightened by the prewar departure of Soviet dependents from Egypt. The US government had long cautioned against preemption (Kissinger, 1979, pp. 459–67). Since Arab arms acquisition also meant that the prospects for an unusually long war were increased, Israel had to retain Washington's support and policy approval in order to assure ultimate arms resupply.

Israeli readings of Egypt's military capabilities also tended to give a false sense of security. It was assumed that a major attack across the Canal would require advanced medium and fighter bombers to knock out Israeli air fields. Egypt lacked such aircraft (Jaguars, Phantoms, and MiG 23s), and was not expected to receive any until 1975. In fact, however, Soviet tacticians had advised overcoming the Israeli air force with a defensive missile shield and the deterrent effects of Scuds, the first of which arrived in April 1973 (Herzog, 1982, pp. 227–28). The Soviets did not feel that the Scuds were sufficiently long range to destabilize the region through acute offensive threats to Israel. Improved Egyptian air defenses and a new tactic of sheltering aircraft also meant that an overall devastating Israeli preemptive blow would be much more difficult than in 1967 (Mets, 1986, pp. 94–95). Israel's greater territorial buffering, with Sinai, the Golan Heights, and Jordan's West Bank, allowed its leaders to countenance a delayed response to attack (Bar-Siman-Tov, 1987, pp. 188–90). Therefore, although most of the Israeli land, sea, and air forces had been alerted in advance of the attack on October 6, full land mobilization would take at least two more days.

Table 12

Israeli and Arab Force Balances in 1973

	Israel	Egypt	Syria	Iraq	Jordan
Army Manpower*	310	315	140	20†	5†
Naval Manpower*	4	17	2	—	—
Medium Tanks	2000	2200	1820	300	150
APCs	6000	2400	1300	300	200
Artillery	570	2280	675	54	36

	Israel	Egypt	Syria	Iraq	Jordan
Fighters	352	550	275	73	92
Bombers	8	48	0	0	0
Submarines	1	12	0	—	—
Missile Boats	14	17	9	—	—
Destroyer/Frigates	0	8	0	—	—
Small Combat Ships	18	17	13	—	—
Small Craft	10	38	2	—	—

Source: IISS, Military Balance, 1973–74
*In thousands.
†Jordanian and Iraqi totals are forces committed to the October war.

On the eve of war, as seen in Table 12, the overall military balance quantitatively favored the Arab forces. However, the ratios between Israel and any one of its major opponents was relatively close in combat personnel and tanks (mainly US M-60s and UK Centurions). Israeli Defense Forces (IDF) also enjoyed significant advantages in APCs (though not necessarily against combined Arab forces), and thus in troop mobility. The Israeli Air Force (IAF) relied on US-supplied A4 Skyhawks and F4 Phantoms, along with French Mirages; the Egyptian and Syrian air forces possessed less capable MiG-21, MiG-19, and MiG-17 fighters, at an estimated three-to-one combined numerical advantage. On the naval front, again the Arab side had overall numerical advantages, though Israeli forces were designed for fast mobility and compared quite favorably one-on-one in guided-missile ships and small combat vessels (Herzog, 1982, book 5; Cordesman, 1987).

THE COURSE OF WAR

As the fighting began, the Arabs for three days made significant initial progress against surprisingly lightly defended Israeli positions. By October 7, Israel was petitioning Washington urgently for immediate dispatch of Sidewinder missiles, three-hundred tanks, and the forty-eight Phantom jets already on order, citing losses of forty-four planes and over two-hundred tanks in the first two days. Items added to this list on the eighth included antitank weapons, Hawk antiaircraft missiles, helicopters, self-propelled guns, and ammunition. Thus, this is the first war we have considered in which the pressure of arms attrition was acute from the beginning.

Secretary of State Kissinger delayed and dissembled on these requests in order to enhance the US bargaining position and influence on a settlement (Kissinger, 1979, pp. 476–491). Washington was reluctant to dispatch arms in light of anticipated Israeli victories and possible territorial expansion. Yet the arms pipeline was opened by both superpowers to a degree on October 10, the day the battle tide began to turn in Israel's favor.

Once full Israeli mobilization came, and with US weapons airlifts, Israeli forces were able to push well into Golan and threaten Damascus; subsequently, and against strong resistance, they gained the upper hand on both sides of the Canal as well. By the end of the first week of war, Israel had destroyed more than fifty-five percent of Syria's armor and thirty percent of its air arm, although Israeli ground assaults had pulled up about thirty kilometers from Damascus. The intent of the general staff's October 10 plan for the northern front was to smash Syrian forces decisively but not to take Damascus, at least partly because of the unacceptable risks of Soviet involvement (Bar-Siman-Tov, 1987, p. 200). Syrian artillery, assisted by Iraqi, Moroccan, and Kuwaiti troops, kept up a relatively effective barrage with the assistance of Soviet airlifted equipment. American TOW antitank missiles came into play for Israel, on the other hand, on the fifteenth. This blunted Arab armor attacks.

After October 12, Syrian forces, finally pressed back toward their own capital, were unable to make very effective use of further Soviet supplies or of emergency Arab assistance. Once Syria's SAM network had been knocked out, Israel was undeterred by possible Soviet intervention in deciding to bomb widespread Syrian targets, including those near Damascus. Justifying the attacks on the basis of Syria's use of Frog surface-to-surface missiles against civilian targets on the seventh and eighth, Tel Aviv was confident in ultimate US support, in part because of Israel's early self-restraint. One side-effect of the bombing was the triggering of a large-scale Soviet arms airlift on the twelfth, to which Israel responded by bombing landing fields, steering clear of incoming Soviet planes (Bar-Siman-Tov, 1987, pp. 197–99). Syria, along with her Soviet benefactors, then desperately sought increased Egyptian offensives on the southern front to relieve the pressure.

Meanwhile, stalemate had set in on the Sinai front, as Egyptian forces reached the second Bar Lev line positions and paused from the tenth to the fourteenth to consolidate their gains. An attempted Israeli counteroffensive on the eighth had proved futile. Evidently geared to relieve pressure on Syria, Egypt's ultimate offensive effort to break through along a broad front on the fourteenth also failed over the next few days with great losses. Egypt's blockade of the Bab el-Mandeb straits was more successful, but Israel likewise employed hit and run naval tactics effectively to blockade Egyptian shipping. Israel also finally was able to reinforce its Sinai force with Golan-based troops, aircraft, and massive armor (even cutting Egypt's numerical tank advantage to less than two-to-one). US supplies were unloaded at El Arish airfield in the Sinai beginning on the tenth. Egyptian tank corps, extended beyond their SAM umbrella, suffered increasingly at the hands of the IAF, and IDF ground forces established a toehold on the west side of the Canal on the fourteenth, crossing in strength by the sixteenth, only to meet rather stiff and nearly overwhelming Egyptian opposition (Mets, 1986, p. 109; Bar-Siman-Tov, 1987, p. 196; Bailey, 1990, p. 322).

During the lull from the tenth to the thirteenth, Israel launched air strikes and counterattacks against Egyptian bridgeheads and force concentrations, but with mixed results. Finally, an Israeli infiltration force delivered a decisive blow to Egyptian antiaircraft missile positions on the sixteenth, allowing more effective control of the skies (El Badri, et al., 1987, pp. 87–88, 103–6). Even quite massive Soviet resupply of Arab forces after the twelfth, including a major sealift, did not prevent these mounting Israeli successes, though they did contribute to raising the cost.

Egypt and Syria clearly bore the brunt of the fighting throughout, although other Arab states sent forces. Jordan largely refrained from combat, at least partly due to its inadequate military equipment and preparation for air war against Israel. Syria and Egypt both accepted Amman's curtailed role, involving only segments of a division deployed mainly to preoccupy some Israeli units (Whetten, 1974, p. 271). In addition, over eighteen-thousand Iraqi troops and three-hundred Iraqi tanks were in Syria during the war but were not deployed at the front en masse, although Syrian forces were joined by parts of two Iraqi armored divisions, a special forces brigade, and three aircraft squadrons. Small Kuwaiti, Moroccan, Saudi, Algerian, Libyan, Yemeni, PLO, Sudanese, and Tunisian contingents helped on one or more of the fronts as well (Aker, 1985, pp. 163–65; *Keesings Contemporary Archives,* 1973, p. 26173; *Facts on File,* 1973, pp. 328,

834; *New York Times,* October 15, 1973, p. 16).[2] (See Appendix, Chronology 5, "The Yom Kippur-Ramadan War, 1973.")

DIPLOMATIC PRESSURE AND ARMS FLOW

In conversation after the war with noted Egyptian journalist Mohammed Heikal, Henry Kissinger delivered a telling statement of why the US reversed its efforts to coerce Israel through arms restraint at the beginning of the war and reopened the arms pipeline: "Do not deceive yourself, the United States could not—either today or tomorrow—allow Soviet arms to win a big victory, even if it was not decisive, against U.S. arms. This has nothing to do with Israel or with you" (quoted by Klinghofer and Apter, 1985, p. 123; see also, El Badri, et al., 1977, pp. 83–88; Bar-Siman-Tov, 1987, pp. 206–7; Nachmias, 1988, pp. 59–60; and *New York Times,* October 11, 1973). Other accounts mentioned Kissinger's and the administration's potential embarrassment at Israeli Prime Minister Golda Meir's intent to visit Washington and spur the arms deliveries (Kissinger, 1979, p. 493). Clearly, then, while reverse Israeli influence in Washington played some part, the issue of superpower technological competition had come to play an increasingly prominent role in arms-supply decisions for key Third World regions. While détente was framed as a tension reducing exercise in mutual cooperation, a contradictory zero-sum game for armaments supremacy and for regional hegemony was underway.

The first US air force flights arrived on October 14, as Washington decided to replace Israeli combat aircraft. The supplies, ultimately totalling over twenty-two-thousand tons, came to include forty replacement Phantom jets and a smaller contingent of A-4 Skyhawks, helicopters, spare aircraft parts, electronic interference equipment, M-60 and M-48 tanks, antitank missiles, radars, antiradar missiles, fuel trucks, munitions, and TV-guided bombs for use against air-defense emplacements. Forty percent of these supplies arrived before the cease-fire agreement in late October.

Meanwhile, with its cease-fire proposals rejected and Syrian forces slipping, Moscow was beginning its own airlift. Seven Soviet airborne divisions were alerted as early as October 8 for possible deployment to the Middle East, and the Soviet Mediterranean fleet was augmented. The Soviet arms airlift began on the tenth (some say the ninth) following the depletion of Syrian missile stocks (Frog surface-to-surface missiles had been launched against Israeli civilian targets) and during the Israeli bombing of Damascus. As the Arab positions deteriorated, the Soviet airlift activity increased. (Yugoslavia and even NATO member Turkey failed to object to the overflights.) In addition to fighter planes, the Soviets supplied Egypt with armored vehicles and T-62 tanks, while sending Syria fighters and tanks during the war (SIPRI, *Yearbook,* 1974). Thus, a competitive supply dynamic was set in motion, with the Israelis trying to stimulate Washington to greater efforts.

The American airlift's military significance is debated by some, since most of the heavy armament, i.e., tanks and planes, were not used in the fighting. Nevertheless, certain important new technologies, such as antitank missiles, as well as much needed spare parts, appeared crucial, and the overall impact was both political and psychological. The extent of the airlift certainly diminished both Syria's and Egypt's long- term prospects and may have softened their attitude about a cease-fire (See Bar-Siman-Tov, 1987, pp. 212–13; El-Badri et al., 1977, pp. 83–88; Whetten, 1974, p. 253; Mets, 1986, pp. 104–7). Moreover, the receipt of large quantities of US arms heartened Israel to go on the counteroffensive in the Sinai. Previously, both sides had suffered massive armor attrition, particularly during Egypt's ill-fated offensive of the October 14. Israel had long planned for the contingency of crossing the Canal to attack the rear of Egyptian forces, and had the bridging equipment and engineers standing by in Sinai.

From the war's outset, the superpowers had sought to exercise restraining diplomatic influence. Indeed, the Soviet ambassador visited Sadat on the first day to seek permission to begin negotiating a cease-fire, while Ambassador Anatoly Dobrynin in Washington stayed in close touch with American officials about such an eventuality. Secretary of State Kissinger also favored a very early cease-fire to bring on negotiations before Israel's battlefield losses would require massive US resupply, and to preserve influence with the Arabs before oil disruptions could occur. As early as October 7, contact with President Sadat was established (Kissinger, 1979, pp. 481-82). Given political cross-pressures, the Nixon administration highly favored a "peace without victory" outcome. At least initially, Kissinger preferred a withdrawal to ante-bellum positions over the Arab and Soviet demand for a return to pre-1967 borders; by the war's third week, however, both Washington and Moscow merely sought a cease-fire in place and subsequent disengagement (Mets, 1986, pp. 102–3).

Israel's first consideration of a cease-fire came as early as October 12 under US and Soviet prodding. Israeli leaders felt relief at their first air successes against Syria, but were still concerned about severe arms-supply shortages and difficulties in Sinai. Supposedly reliable intelligence reports warned of an impending Soviet airborne mobilization to relieve the Arabs. In view of vituperative Soviet warnings (Israel sank a Soviet ship during air raids on Syria), the cabinet decided to accept a cease-fire, at least on the Syrian front, if proposed. Washington also gave assurances of direct assistance if Soviet forces became involved, and reinforced its Mediterranean naval fleet to back up the promise (Bar-Siman-Tov, 1987, p. 202).

Egypt refused an early cease-fire, however, although Syria, as noted, apparently was ready to agree. Through the fourteenth Cairo continued to perceive successes against the IDF, with reports of forty-one planes downed in four days, and tank attrition for the war of over five-hundred Israeli vehicles. The last Bar-Lev positions surrendered on the thirteenth, and the Israeli navy continued to suffer reported losses. Thus Sadat wanted to keep up the pressure, but Israel still had not turned the full brunt of its forces to the Sinai front (El Badri, et al., 1977, pp. 88–91, 167; Mets, 1986, p. 100).

Sadat's refusals left Kissinger with the dilemma of the impending need to resupply Israel. Kissinger also knew of and feared Israel's nuclear option. Indeed, in the complex psychology of the crisis, Moscow knew of Kissinger's dilemma, and though favoring a cease-fire, given Syria's mounting setbacks, nevertheless could wait to see if Washington would carry through with arms supplies or put added pressure on Israel (Kissinger, 1979, pp. 575–99).

Despite its arms-airlift commitment, Washington continued to press for a cease-fire after the fourteenth. Kissinger indicated to Sadat that the airlift would cease immediately after such an agreement (Kissinger, 1982, pp. 522–23; Bar-Siman-Tov, 1987, p. 214). Nonetheless, the Egyptian leadership felt it was winning, and it took four days of intense talks with the Soviets, together with the dire warnings of Egyptian military commanders, to convince them otherwise. Moscow was especially concerned after the sixteenth that a crushing Israeli blow to the Egyptians could doom the Sadat regime and Soviet investments in it. Chairman Leonid Brezhnev sent Sadat the text of the proposed joint US-Soviet UN cease-fire proposal late on the October 20, reiterating pledges to guarantee the cease-fire unilaterally, and, as understood by the Egyptians, to commit Soviet troops to do so if necessary (Herzog, 1982, pp. 276–78).

As the Soviets saw Egypt join Syria's slide toward defeat, they became increasingly alarmed that tacit understandings with Washington about "peace without victory" might come unglued. This was perhaps the first war in which space-based and high altitude reconnaissance proved telling, particularly in alerting the superpower arms patrons of unfolding patterns even before their clients realized them. Arab forces especially did not fully appreciate the magnitude of their growing Sinai dilemma. Visiting Cairo as Israeli forces crossed the Canal on the sixteenth, Premier Aleksei Kosygin urged an immediate cease-fire. Still believing optimistic battlefield reports, Sadat resisted the Soviet pressure until the eighteenth, when, confronted by reconnaissance photos, he relented. Moscow immediately and urgently invited Secretary Kissinger for a visit that would develop the cease-fire terms.

Meanwhile, on the seventeenth Kissinger renewed efforts to move Israel toward a cease-fire linked to the 1967 UN Resolution 242, which called for the return of "occupied territories" in return for a peace settlement. Tel Aviv was counselled to assume that a cease-fire would become effective within forty-eight hours of its imposition (Kissinger, 1979, pp. 532–38). Thus the Israelis were on notice that only limited time was available to achieve their military goals of destroying Arab armies, and that these should not include substantial new territorial gains.

The Americans and Soviets had agreed privately on the cease-fire terms by the twenty-first, and both evidently then coupled their diplomatic blandishments with arms-supply pressures. Washington implied arms slowdowns to heighten the impact of President Nixon's request of Israel to accept the cease-fire (Bar-Siman-Tov, 1987, p. 215). Egypt agreed to terms on the nineteenth, and Moscow turned to the US to deliver Israel. Relieved by the shift of fighting to the Sinai front, Syria also remained relatively resistant to Soviet cease-fire pressure, only agreeing on the twenty-fourth after Moscow's ambassador in Damascus "not only threatened, but actually halted, the arms supply, sending a cargo ship away without unloading its arms, briefly ending the airlift and threatening to send Soviet SAM technicians home" (Krause, 1987, pp. 13–14; see also Ziring, 1984, pp. 363–64). Kissinger, continually balancing Israeli military and bargaining gains against losses in US-Arab diplomacy and against the limits of Soviet tolerance, was reluctant to impose severe terms on Tel Aviv. The US wanted to be seen as the main power broker by both the Arabs and Israelis, and would resist terms under which Moscow could claim credit for engineering Israeli territorial withdrawals. Even as Kissinger flew to Moscow on the twentieth, President Nixon, beleaguered by the Watergate scandal in Washington, evidently was more prepared than his secretary of state to pursue an overall Middle Eastern settlement with Moscow. Washington sweetened its proposals to the Israelis with promise of a $2.2-billion military aid package, but did not consult Tel Aviv on the terms of the cease-fire resolution finally drafted in Moscow on October 21 (Bar-Siman-Tov, 1987, pp. 215–20).

Despite severe misgivings at what was seen as a superpower-imposed timetable, Israel saw little alternative to accepting the terms, given continuing needs for US military supply and support. Yet Tel Aviv also sought to delay implementation past the October 22 deadline to finish its military operations on both sides of the Canal (Bar-Siman-Tov, 1987, pp. 223–25). By the twenty-fourth, however, with Egypt's Third Army surrounded, US pressures for a cease-fire became more explicit, along with warnings of more direct Soviet involvements, which, though not entirely clear at the time, realistically meant resupply of the stranded Third Army.

Under intense American pressure, then, Israel once again agreed to a cease-fire to commence on the twenty-fourth, but a desperate Egypt, having contacted Washington directly for assistance and threatening to abort its newly developing US relationship, tried to lift the siege of the Third Army. This fighting allowed Israel finally to attack Suez City. Citing potentially imminent Soviet intervention, and indicating its own uncertain support, Washington pushed Israel to cease hostilities on the twenty-fifth with the passage of an additional UN resolution calling for withdrawal to the October 22 lines. Indeed, it is reported that Washington itself was contemplating resupply of the Third Army (Bailey, 1990, p. 333).[3]

By this time, Tel Aviv had the opportunity to accomplish most of its strategic objectives, but still refused to lift the siege of Egypt's Third Army. Additional US pressure was employed, this time in the form of a deadline of October 27 to allow nonmilitary supplies through to the Egyptians; failing this the US would vote for Security Council cease-fire enforcement. Israel counter-threatened to mobilize US domestic opinion against the Nixon administration. Kissinger reportedly still opposed contingency plans to cut off the Israeli airlift and directly supply the Egyptians, and stuck instead to diplomatic pressures. Although these were insufficient to bring clear Israeli compliance, fortunately on the twenty-seventh Egypt offered direct talks among military officers on disengagement in the desert (Bar-Siman-

Tov, 1987, pp. 233–35). Egypt thus was allowed to emerge from the crisis with a new degree of pride in military accomplishment against Israel; the Israelis gained tacit Egyptian recognition and technically had not given in to superpower pressure; and any renewed US-Soviet confrontations over the issue were avoided.

In this context Tel Aviv undertook first to cease further attacks and to allow a relief column through to the Third Army; yet sporadic clashes reportedly continued until the twenty-eighth, when UN emergency forces began to arrive to separate the parties. At least for effect, Syria accepted the UN imposed cease-fire on October 29, after Moscow supposedly stipulated that Israel would withdraw from all occupied territory and recognize Palestinian rights (*New York Times,* October 30, 1973). Skirmishes along the Syrian cease-fire line reportedly continued through May of 1974, with Syria deriving added Soviet and Arab military assistance in the process (*Middle East Economic Digest,* March 15 and May 24, 1974; *New York Times,* April 17, 1974; *Foreign Broadcast Information Service,* March 8, 1974; *Jerusalem Post,* May 19 and June 11, 1974; *Arab World,* May 23, 1974).

In addition to the superpowers, many other states attempted to bring pressure on one side or the other during the war. Twenty-two African states severed political and economic relations with Israel; India and Pakistan both blamed Israel; and the Organization of Arab Petroleum Exporting Countries (OAPEC) implemented the decision to reduce oil production by five percent monthly and selectively embargo certain Western states seen as pro-Israeli (the relatively mild and largely uniform global supply and pricing effects of these moves have been well documented; see Pearson, 1979). In the arms arena, Algeria's President Houari Boumedienne flew to Moscow during the second week of fighting reportedly to offer $100 million to finance greater Soviet arms support for the Arab side (Mets, 1986, p. 110). Britain, fearing Arab alienation and oil sanctions, instituted an arms embargo against both warring sides, as did most of Western Europe; the embargo's main, but not very telling, effect was denial of spare parts for Israel's British Centurion tanks. France likewise refused to ship arms (Ovendale, 1984, p. 194; Bailey, 1990, pp. 316, 323).

CONCLUSIONS

Despite the appearance of successful arms-transfer diplomacy in the 1973 case, a closer look reveals room for doubt. Krause, for one, concludes that although promises of increased deliveries can work as inducements to cease-fire agreements, such as that which preserved Egypt's Third Army in the Sinai, threats to withhold supplies are relatively ineffective at stopping combat, at least when compared to other forms of diplomatic pressure (Krause, 1987). Indeed, none of the arms pressures in this case, nor in the earlier Arab-Israeli fighting, produced concessions that the parties took to be against their own basic interests. Battlefield attrition, war weariness, fears of escalation and achievement of battle objectives, rather than worries over inadequate arms supply, played prominent roles in conditioning the decisions to end the fighting. In 1973, formal Israeli agreements to cease fire were influenced by long-term military assistance needs, but the timing by which the guns actually were silenced had to do more with jockeying for territorial advantage and bargaining leverage before the superpowers intervened directly or the peacekeepers arrived.

Although it has been argued that first withholding arms and then promising resumption in return for desired policy shifts is a useful strategy, Krause (1987) concludes that for supply restrictions to be effective, prior shipments must have been abundant. This, of course, opens the way for wars to begin in the first place, and to be carried on for some time. Indeed, it is further argued that superpowers will be delayed in applying effective pressure on clients in such high-profile crises because it takes time for arms supplies to build to the point where they could meaningfully affect the pace of fighting or peace negotiations. Patrons must prove their reliability first to the clients, and in some cases we have seen that suppliers see benefits in proving their weapons in combat or in covering over weapon deficiencies.

In the 1973 case, "Prior arms shipments provided no residual influence in the early stages, and in fact the weakness of an ally's position provided it with bargaining power against its patron" (Krause, 1987, p. 15). Washington, for example, was quite anxious for a cease-fire and settlement at least partly to deflect attention from the domestic Watergate crisis and to relieve the oil "crisis" atmosphere (Nachmias, 1988).

The desire for long-term weapon resupply can be a more potent factor in promoting cease-fires and negotiations than acute battlefield needs. This is especially true if the war is relatively inconclusive but reveals pronounced arms deficiencies in what is likely to be an ongoing rivalry. One side may try to convince its patrons to provide higher-technology equipment. During the US airlift to Israel, for example, the latter's shopping list came to include many new items for which the war revealed needs, such as high quantities of armored personnel carriers and mobile long-range artillery for attacking missile sites, equipment that would come into play a decade later in Lebanon. Egypt already possessed mobile and hand-held antitank missiles, and Israel wanted these as well. Much of this equipment arrived only in the last days of the war. Still on Tel Aviv's shopping list were airborne missiles, naval equipment, Maverick TV-guided "smart bombs," electro-optical target consoles and avionics, missile decoy devices, and TOW antitank missiles.

Thus, a resourceful arms client, not hard-pressed at the war's conclusion, can use the endgame to acquire the next generation of equipment, and can even squeeze in extra days of fighting to achieve goals considered necessary while intending to comply with arms suppliers' ultimate demands for peace. In Israel's case, this of course had the concomitant and probably undesired effect of increasing dependence on one primary arms source and increasing debt levels, which had to be offset with massive aid from that arms supplier (Nachmias, 1988, pp. 61–63).

It has been argued that Israel and the US operated on different policy wavelengths during the 1973 war (Bar-Siman-Tov, 1987, pp. 235–37). The Israelis supposedly failed to realize new US priorities for influence with Egypt and other key Arab states. Thus, Tel Aviv assumed that familiar arms-supply relationships with Washington would prevail given relatively "good" Israeli behavior and military tactics. Washington's priorities, on the other hand, favored a stalemate-type outcome that would enhance US influence with both sides. At the same time, Israel's early military failures created an unexpectedly acute need for American arms and hence heightened both potential leverage and long-term dependence. As a result, it was left to resourceful and resistant Israeli diplomacy to stall for the best possible military outcome, and for the Soviets to turn up the heat on Washington to protect its clients.

The endgame maneuvering in this case is not entirely unfamiliar. In the 1965 India-Pakistan war a stalemate had been reached before either side appeared ready to collapse, and the effects of an arms embargo helped convince Pakistani leaders of their bleak battlefield prospects. In contrast to the 1973 Yom Kippur War, relatively little armament arrived during that war. Yet there was similar hedging on cease-fire timing and terms, amid considerable major-power diplomatic pressure. Indeed, in prior Arab-Israeli wars in 1956 and 1967, ceasefire was achieved with heavy Soviet diplomatic pressure on Washington and the West to restrain Israel and prevent the destruction of valued Arab client states, just as in South Asia in 1971 the US tried to assure Pakistan's basic survival.

It was hypothesized in chapter one that highly dependent recipients under severe battlefield pressure could be expected to accede more readily to supplier influence. Supplies to the defending state also were considered more crucial for peace than those to attackers. Indeed, Israel put off its response to prewar intelligence warnings and delayed going on the offensive once war began partly because of dependence on sophisticated US weapons. However, in the heat of battle, arms recipients on both sides effectively resisted supplier ceasefire pressure when their fighting prospects seemed bright. When prospects dimmed, each of the main combatants entertained these blandishments much more seriously, or in Egypt's case, undertook nearly suicidal counterattacks to attract superpower assistance. Thus, it is once again quite clear that the pacifying effects either of arms shipments or denials depend fundamentally on the combatants' assessment of the battlefield and diplomatic arena.

Ultimately, perhaps more than any war we have studied, the 1973 case involved massive military resupply to both sides. Military equipment attrition rates were extremely high, with first Soviet and then American supplies replenishing Egypt, Syria, and Israel. Efforts to manipulate the pace of fighting and prospects for negotiations followed from these arms transfers, but with only limited and imprecise effect on the parties.

Wartime arms supply cutoffs were discussed but not implemented, and certainly not bilaterally imposed by the superpowers, despite each combatant's clear dependence on a single patron. Instead, the arms-supply pattern tended to strengthen the weaker party at each turn in the fighting (first Israel, then Syria, then Egypt), as superpowers sought a stalemated ("peace without victory") outcome and vindication of their own weapons technologies and reputations. This type of management effort would be tried to an extent again during the Iran-Iraq fighting of the 1980s, though amid a far greater and more commercially minded array of suppliers. Indeed, the prospect of both superpowers aiding Egypt even emerged at the end of the 1973 fighting, but on the whole, arms diplomacy worked in only a rough way to discourage the parties about their long-term chances of crushing the opponent. Throughout the war, superpower arms-supply management efforts left wide room for fighting and the rejection of cease-fire deadlines. We turn now to the second Arab-Israeli case to determine whether these patterns continued.

CHAPTER 8

ISRAELI-ARAB WAR IN LEBANON, 1982

INTRODUCTION: THE BACKGROUND OF WAR

From 1976 onward, the fierce and seemingly endless Lebanese civil war drew the interest and intervention of Lebanon's powerful immediate neighbors, Israel and Syria. By the early 1980s, Syrian forces, under a basic Arab League mandate, occupied much of the Beqa'a Valley adjoining the key Beirut-Damascus road. In addition to their nominal League pacification mission, their self-interested role was to prevent Lebanon's takeover by factions powerful enough to undermine Syrian influence or to provoke massive Israeli counter-intervention. This meant a complex balancing act, first opposing Islamic and PLO groups, then Christian factions; in the process the civil war remained tragically unresolved. Israel's self-appointed role in the country was to guarantee the security of its own northern borders and settlements by maintaining the breakaway South Lebanese Army (SLA) under Christian command, and by intervening periodically, generally with air attacks against suspected PLO bases or Syrian forces.

With the Camp David Egyptian-Israeli peace accords of 1979, the Syrian front remained the main flash point; Lebanon extended that front and also became the only territory from which the PLO could mount serious attacks on Israel. In the early 1980s, the cycles of attack, reprisal, and temporary cease-fires gradually escalated (Cordesman, 1987, pp. 58–59). Nonetheless, Israel and Syria had developed their own tacit understandings about respective spheres of influence, acceptable military involvement levels and strategies, and lines of demarcation.

These nascent arrangements began to unravel, however, in 1981, after Syria's offensive against Israeli-backed Lebanese Christian Phalangist militia forces and mountain strongholds north and east of Beirut. Under Syrian helicopter siege in April, Phalangists appealed for Israeli rescue, and the IAF responded by downing two Soviet built

Syrian MI-8 helicopters, thus violating the tenuous Israeli-Syrian arrangements. For protection, Damascus then moved Soviet-supplied surface-to-air missile batteries for the first time into Lebanon, while Soviet and Syrian troops conducted joint training exercises (Klinghofer and Apter, 1985; Roberts, 1983). Mediation by US Special Envoy Philip Habib failed to resolve the missile emplacement issue.

In July 1981, Lebanese-based PLO units opened fire with rocket barrages against northern Israeli settlements, and the IAF undertook devastating retaliatory bombing attacks throughout Lebanon. This time Habib, with Saudi assistance, fostered relatively successful cease-fire agreements, but their scope was disputed—attacks along the Israeli-Lebanese border largely ceased, but attacks on Israeli targets abroad continued and Tel Aviv claimed these as violations. Israeli Defense Minister Ariel Sharon thus began to campaign for a massive cross-border Lebanon intervention to wipe out PLO strongholds and empower a new Phalangist Lebanese government under Bashir Gemayel, which would oust Syria and normalize relations with Israel. It was argued that the April 1982 deadline for Israeli withdrawal from Sinai under the Camp David Accords would mean that Egypt and the US would hardly object to such action in Lebanon (Herzog, 1982, p. 341).

Nevertheless, restraining US pressure, internal Israeli governmental opposition, and concern about completing the Sinai evacuation stymied these plans until June 3, 1982, when Israel's ambassador to the UK was shot in London. The attempted assassination, apparently spawned by the breakaway Iraqi-and-Syrian-supported Abu Nidal group (one attacker reportedly was a Syrian agent; see Cordesman, 1987a, p. 60) and not the mainline PLO, was seized as an opportunity to renew widespread air attacks on PLO targets in Lebanon even though Israel's northern border had remained relatively quiet. Israel launched its "Operation Peace for Galilee," a full-scale Lebanon invasion, on June 6. Despite the stated rationale at the time—to put Israel's northern settlements out of range of "terrorist artillery," a distance of some 40 km (*Keesings Contemporary Archives,* vol. 28, 1982, p. 31904)— the operation came to resemble the full Sharon invasion plan.[1]

ARMAMENT AND THE APPROACH OF WAR

Continued improvement in both Israeli and Syrian weapons technology, as well as PLO combat preparations, clearly contributed to the rising tension levels in 1982, as seen in a controversy over Syrian

SAM emplacements in the Beqa'a Valley (Roberts, 1983). Each side had boosted offensive, defensive, and retaliatory capabilities. Syrian forces in Lebanon numbered approximately thirty thousand, with large additional forces just over the border. Along with advanced Soviet-supplied SAM cover, they deployed in Lebanon two-hundred T-62 and T-55 tanks with an additional one hundred tanks on the Syrian border, more than three-hundred artillery pieces, one-hundred antiaircraft guns, approximately two-hundred antitank weapons, and three-hundred APCs. Syria possessed the most sophisticated Soviet armament allowed into the Third World: T-72 tanks, MiG-25s, Scud-B and Scud-C, FROG and SS-21 surface-to-surface missiles, as well as French Gazelle attack helicopters and French-German HOT missiles. Strategic priorities reflected increased antiaircraft and antitank capability to enable Syrian forces to remain in Lebanon despite Israeli overflights, as well as acquisition of missiles, tanks, and aircraft to hit back against Israeli forces. The ultimate threat of surface-to-surface missiles also was there, though not in very large numbers, as the Soviets sought to preserve control of crisis events (see Tables 13 and 14; Nachmias, 1988, p. 147).

Table 13

Arms Shipments to Israel, 1979–82

Major Arms Shipped to Israel, 1979–81

Australia	2 S-65A helicopters
US	40 F-15 fighters; 75 F-16A fighters; 30 Model 500 MD helicopters armed with TOW ATM; 4 RU-21E reconnaissance aircraft; 400 M-113-A2 APCs; 28 M-548 APCs; 49 M-577-A1 mobile command posts; 150 M-60-A3 tanks; 25 M-88-A1 armored recovery vehicles; 6 I-Hawk mobile SAM systems; 15 RGM-84A L ShSHM launchers; 400 AGM-65A ASM; 160 AIM-7 E Sparrows AAM for F-15s; 170 AIM-7 F Sparrow AAM; 100 AIM-9 J AAM for F-15s; 600 AIM 9L AAM; 5000 FGM-77A Dragon ATM; 100 MIM-23B Hawk land mobil SAM; 60 RGM-84A Harpoon SSM

Major Arms Shipped to Israel, 1982

US	Approx. 6 F-15A Eagle fighters; 25 F-16A fighters; 18 Model 209 helicopters armed with TOW ATM; 100 M-109-A1 155mm self-propelled howitzers; 400 M-113-A2 APCs; 28 M-548 APCs; 49 M-577-A1 mobil command posts; 50 M-60-A3 tanks; 25 M-88-A1 armored recovery vehicles; six I-Hawk SAM systems; 23 RGM-84A L ShSHM launchers; 200 AGM-65A ASM; 50 AIM-7-E Sparrow AAM; 144 BGM-71A TOW ATM for 18 Model 209 Cobra helicopters; 8 RGM-84A Harpoon SSM for 2 Flagstaff-2 Class fast attack craft; 1 Flagstaff-2 Class hydrofoil fast attack craft delivered prior to licensed production

Source: Estimates from SIPRI files; authors' files.

Table 14

Arms Shipments to Syria, 1979–82

Major Arms Shipped to Syria, 1979–81

Czechoslovakia	16 L-39 Albatross jet trainers; 100 OT-64 APCs
France	Approx. 30 SA-342K Gazelle helicopters; 16 SA 342L Gazelle helicopters armed with HOT ATM; 216 HOT ATM for Gazelle helicopters; 500 Milan ATM
Libya	500 T-62 tanks
USSR	4 AN-26 Curl light planes (in civilian markings); 15 Mi-8 Hip helicopters; 45 MiG-23 BN fighter-bombers; 20 MiG-25 fighters; 15 MiG-27 fighter-strike aircraft; 15 SU-22 Fitter-J fighter-bombers; 100 BM-21 122mm multiple rocket systems; 50 BMP-1 mechanized infantry combat vehicles; 20 BMP-1 Spigot-missile-armed tank destroyers; 12 BRDM-2 Gaskin-missile-armed antiaircraft vehicles; 100 BRDM-2 Sagger missile-armed tank destroyers; 1000 BRDM-2 Sagger ATM; 600 T-55 tanks; 350 T-72 tanks; 4 FROG L mobil SAM ; 30 SA-6 SAM systems; 24 SA-8 SAM systems; 10 SSN-2 Styx-L ShSHM launchers for OSA-2

(continued on next page)

Table 14 (*continued*)

fast attack boats; 180 AA-2 Atoll AAM for SU-22 fighters; 600 AA-2 Atoll AAM for MiG fighters; 80 AT-4 Spigot ATM; 20 FROG-7 Land mobile SAM; 270 SA-6 Gainful land-mobile SAM; 192 SA-8 Gecko land-mobile SAM; 96 SA-9 Gaskin land mobile SAM; 50 SSN-2 Styx SSM for OSA-2 fast attack boats; 10 OSA-2 Class fast attack craft armed with Styx ShSHM; 1-2 Yevgenia Class coastal mine sweepers

Major Arms Shipped to Syria, 1982

Czechoslovakia	Approx. 8 L-39 Albatross jet trainers
Libya	20 MiG-21F fighters; 15 MiG-23 fighters
USSR	2 IL-76 Candid transports; 5 Mi-8 Hip helicopters; 26 MiG-23M fighters; 6 MiG-27 fighter-strike aircraft; 30 SU-22 Fitter-J fighter-bombers; 50 BM-21 122mm multiple rocket systems; 100 BMP-1 Spigot-missile-armed tank destroyers; 6 BRDM-2 Gaskin-missile-armed antiaircraft vehicles; 100 BRDM-2 Sagger-missile-armed tank destroyers; 1000 BRDM-2 Sagger ATM; 50 M-1973 152mm self-propelled guns; 100 M-1974 122mm self-propelled howitzers; 100 T-62 tanks; 175 T-72 tanks; 25 ZSU-23-4 Shilka-gun-armed antiaircraft vehicles; 10 SA-3 mobile antiaircraft systems; 8 SA-8 mobile antiaircraft systems; 10 SSN-2 Styx L ShSHM launchers for Osa-2 fast attack boats; 60 AA-2 Atoll AAM for SU-22 fighters; 200 AA-2 Atoll AAM for MiG fighters; 100 AT-4 Spigot ATM; 90 SA-3 GOA land-mobile SAM; 35 SA-7 Grail-portable SAM; 64 SA-8 Gecko land-mobile SAM; 48 SA-9 Gaskin land-mobile SAM; 17 SSN-2 Styx SSM for Osa-2 fast attack boats; 10 Osa-2 Class fast attack craft

Source: Estimates from SIPRI files; authors' files.

Aside from their southern coastal enclaves and camps, the PLO also deployed forces behind Syrian lines in the southeast sector; total PLO forces numbered around fifteen thousand with an additional eighteen thousand reserve militia personnel. Their arsenal featured weapons similar to, though in many cases older and less advanced than, Syria's: multiple rocket launchers, over 350 artillery pieces (including many antiaircraft guns and long range 130 mm guns); 300 aging Soviet-built tanks; 200–300 large antitank devices (high velocity recoilless guns and "Sagger" antitank missiles); portable SA-7 Soviet antiaircraft missiles, and 150 APCs (Dupuy and Martell, 1986, pp. 86–90).

Israel planned its invasion, featuring major air bombardments, for some eight divisions (by mid-June totalling more than ninety-thousand troops) and twelve-hundred tanks, in a three-pronged attack: along the coastal plain up to the southern Beirut suburbs (and airport); in the central sector to cut the Beirut-Damascus road; and through Syrian and PLO forces in the east up to the southern Beqa'a (Herzog, 1982, p. 344; Nachmias, 1988, p. 133). Table 15 shows the relative forces and equipment finally engaged in the 1982 fighting, with reflection of Israel's increasing emphasis on air superiority and high mobility in order to spare their ground troops. In prior years, Syria's air force had been revitalized with Soviet MiG-23s, MiG-21s, and Sukhoi-22 fighters. As war approached in 1982, Israeli arms acquisitions increased markedly. The total dollar value of US supplies to Israel (including training and other assistance) had mounted sixfold between 1980 and 1981, with nearly another fifty-percent increase in 1982 (Yaniv, 1987, p. 138; SIPRI, *Yearbook,* 1983).

Table 15

Israeli and Arab Forces Engaged in the 1982 War

	Israel	Syria	PLO
Troops	76,000	22,000	15,000
Tanks	800	352	300
APCs	1,500	300	150
Large Crew Served Anti-Tank Weapons	200	—	200–300
Major Artillery	—	300	350+
AntiAircraft Guns	—	100	250+
Total Combat Aircraft	634	450	0
Total Aircraft Engaged	364	96	0
Attack Aircraft	275	225	0
Armed Helicopters	42	16	0
Major SAM Launchers	—	125	—

Source: Cordesman, 1987, p. 56.

Israel thus maintained significant air-war advantages, with its own steadily advancing aircraft industry and add-on capabilities (especially avionics for over-the-horizon combat; see Bavly and Salpeter, 1984, pp. 86–87). The IAF relied on advanced US F-16 Falcons, F-4E Phantoms (for ground attack), modified A-4 Skyhawks (with ECMs to counter Soviet heat-seeking missiles), and F-15 Eagles, and also featured its own Kfir Mach 2 fighter (with US engines) and converted Magister light attack and trainer jets. In addition, Grumman E-2C Hawkeyes provided early warning and airborne fighter control capabilities, and transport and attack helicopters, featuring TOW tank-killing capabilities, came to play an ever more prominent role (Hughes, 1982, pp. 413–14). Israeli weapon acquisitions after 1980 had emphasized missile systems for these and other weapon platforms, including air-to-air (AAM), SAM, antiship, and antitank capabilities, nearly all derived from the US (see Table 13). Additional US artillery pieces also would be used against entrenched Arab positions in Lebanon, and in the siege of Beirut.

The Reagan administration had pinned many strategic hopes on Israel in plans to bar Soviet influence in the region. This was part of, and in some sense conflicted with, a larger strategy engineered by Secretary of State Alexander Haig to create a regional "strategic consensus," a sort of mini-NATO reminiscent of the Dulles era, in which Israel, Egypt, Jordan, and Saudi Arabia would be enlisted as US allies against the Soviets. Arms transfers were a key to this strategy, as seen in growing military cooperation with Egypt and large sales (sixty F-15s and five AWACS planes) to Saudi Arabia and Jordan (Nachmias, 1988, p. 126).

Indeed, Secretary of Defense Caspar Weinberger and Israeli Defense Minister Sharon had worked out an unusual formal strategic cooperation agreement in September 1981 that formally designated the Soviet Union as the common opponent. In this way, Israel hoped to gain added economic and military assistance, while the US continued efforts to engineer its anti-Soviet pseudo-alliance among moderate Middle Eastern powers. Designating the USSR as the US-Israeli target was expected not to offend cooperative Arab states, although Tel Aviv still hoped to drive a wedge between Washington and the oil-rich Arabs. Israel played up its strategic importance to Washington in sharing intelligence data; providing data on battlefield performance of captured Soviet weapons; testing advanced US weapons; providing logistical facilities for the US Rapid Deployment Force;

and relaying US arms and providing assistance in controversial Third World conflicts. The new strategic partnership played on past relations but added dimensions such as the prepositioning of US arms in Israel to balance Soviet stockpiles in Libya. Evidently, however, Washington rejected Israeli offers of permanent bases and air cover for the Sixth Fleet, which would have inflamed US-Arab relations (Klinghofer and Apter, 1985, pp. 191-92).

It appears that with the heating of tensions and the need to match Israeli technology and US patronage, Syria utilized Saudi financial assistance to acquire further Soviet equipment in 1982 (from 1981 orders), both from the USSR and Libya, including five squadrons of MiG-23s and Mig-25s (some few of the latter delivered in April and May just prior to the war and after earlier Israeli attacks), four squadrons of SU-22 Fitter fighter/ground-attack aircraft, air-to-air and antitank missiles, naval corvettes, counter-electronic warfare aircraft, howitzers, T-72 and T-62 tanks, and newer SAM systems (see Table 14). In 1982, Moscow evidently also offered Syria the advanced MiG-27. (Countering US initiatives, in January the USSR also agreed to provide SAM-8s to Jordan; Klinghofer and Apter, 1985, p. 194; SIPRI, *Yearbook,* 1983.) Clearly, the Syrians and their arms patrons were worried about war and wanted to avoid being outgunned by the Israeli-US side; the Middle East continued as a competitive proving ground for major-power weaponry as well as diplomacy.

THE COURSE OF WAR

The war, which Nachmias describes as an Israeli military and Syrian political victory, had five phases: June 6-11, the major battles; June 11, first formal cease-fire; June 12-24, slow Israeli movement toward Beirut and Beirut-Damascus highway; June 25, second formal cease-fire, continued Beirut siege; September, Israeli West Beirut occupation and political maneuvering for outside peacekeeping and a pullback (See Nachmias, 1988, p. 137). The key to Israel's military dominance was a massive air battle, involving over one-hundred aircraft on June 9. Israeli jets destroyed seventeen out of nineteen Syrian SAM sites in the Beqa'a Valley, and shot down twenty-nine MiGs with no reported IAF losses (*Foreign Affairs Chronology,* 1990; Dupuy and Martell, 1986, p. 120). This cleared the way for IDF ground columns to penetrate, as planned, to the outskirts of Beirut and to the Damascus road. Furthermore, on June 10, IAF jets attacked Beirut

International Airport and ground forces battled Syrian troops in the Beqa'a as an additional twenty to twenty-five Syrian MiGs were downed. Tel Aviv demanded that Syrian troops withdraw from Beirut to spare the city an attack.

Yielding to heavy international pressure on the eleventh, however, Israel and Syria reached the first of a series of pauses or cease-fires; it followed more heavy tank, artillery, and air battles, with both sides using antitank helicopters (Cordesman, 1987a, pp. 68–70). Israel's pattern here was similar to prior wars in accepting formal cease-fires while continuing military action informally (Nachmias, 1988, p. 140). Just before the cease-fire took effect, Syria tried with some success to reinforce its Beqa'a tank forces, but suffered an ambush with antitank missiles, and the resultant loss of nine T-72s. Eighteen more MiGs were brought down as well (Gabriel, 1984, p. 105; Cordesman, 1987a, pp. 70–71).

Israel did not interpret the cease-fire as applying to the PLO fronts, and Israeli and Palestinian forces fought on in the Beirut suburbs amid extensive Israeli air and artillery attacks on West Beirut (*Middle East Journal,* Chronology, 1982; Gabriel, 1984, p. 105). When Israel's invasion plans and aborted attacks had been rumored in late 1981 and early 1982, the PLO adopted a very limited forward deployment strategy, calling for rapid retreat and conservation of forces and weapons after limited delaying tactics. This strategy was not well implemented, however, as PLO forces fell back on Beirut (Cordesman, 1987a, p. 60). An informal Israeli-PLO version of the cease-fire on June 12 soon broke down, and the PLO announced that about two-thousand Middle Eastern "volunteers" had arrived in Lebanon to assist in the war; four-hundred Iranian fighters reportedly arrived in Damascus as well.

Israel's basic objectives for a Lebanese peace settlement were drawn up by the cabinet on the June 13, including removal of all foreign troops (including Syria and PLO) from Lebanon; "iron-clad guarantees and safeguards" against the return of PLO forces within a forty- to fifty-mile km. demilitarized zone (DMZ) along Israel's northern border; a non-UN international peacekeeping force, preferably including US forces, deployed between Beirut and Israel; and reestablishment of a strong Lebanese government able to conclude a peace treaty with Tel Aviv (*Keesings Contemporary Archives,* vol. 28, 1982, p. 31917). An ancillary goal was to discredit and destroy the PLO so that Palestinians in the West Bank and Jordan would be obliged to come to terms with Israel (*Middle East Journal,* Chronology, 1982).

Ultimately the war provided none of these as lasting benefits, although several were implemented for short periods.

Fighting continued, as the IDF cut off West Beirut, trapping the PLO leadership and thousands of fighters and creating a grave international diplomatic dilemma. The specter of door-to-door fighting and the daily attrition of both civilians and soldiers confronted political leaders on all sides. Israeli armored forces pushed north of Beirut toward Syrian positions on June 14, resulting in the war's first direct Soviet warning to Israel about Moscow's interests (*Keesings Contemporary Archives,* vol. 28, 1982, p. 31916). Though the warnings were not very specific and failed to impress Israeli leadership, they seemed to buoy the Syrians enough that they refused Israel's demand for withdrawal from Beirut, citing the Arab League mandate. Syrian President Hafiz al-Assad further reinforced his forces near Beirut and along the Damascus highway (*Middle East Journal,* Chronology, 1982; Gabriel, 1984, p. 108; Klinghofer and Apter, 1985, p. 211). Israel moved in force against these positions, cutting off retreat routes and mounting a naval blockade against the port of Beirut (*Keesings Contemporary Archives,* vol. 28, 1982, p. 31916).

Major fighting erupted on June 21, with Israeli bombing and shelling of West Beirut (including at least eight direct hits on the Soviet embassy, with only mild counter protest) and offensives against Syria along the Damascus highway. The road was cut, trapping Syrian forces as well as those of the PLO in Beirut (Gabriel, 1984, p. 108; Klinghofer and Apter, 1985, p. 213). A one-day Israeli-Syrian cease-fire ended with renewed large scale clashes on the twenty-third, and Syrian forces showed signs of total breakdown. After the destruction of three SAM-8 and a SAM-6 battery on the twenty-fourth and twenty-fifth, Syrian positions were no longer tenable, and yet another cease-fire was announced (Gabriel, 1984, p. 112; *Middle East Journal,* Chronology, 1982; Cordesman, 1987a, p. 75). Thus the IDF campaign resulted in Israeli control of key positions on the main highway as well as many forward PLO bases in the south.

The remainder of the crisis involved Israel's continued stranglehold on Beirut, and competing demands for the PLO's ouster and Israeli withdrawal from Lebanon. These were punctuated with bombardments and supply restrictions against the city throughout July and into August, and pressure for a new Phalangist government and Israeli-Lebanese peace treaty as well. Resolution of the standoff was left to international diplomacy. Before it was over, however, "Operation

Peace for Galilee" would produce a total of 19,085 fatalities and 31,085 wounded, with battlefield casualties of 368 Israeli killed and 2383 wounded, at least 1200 Palestinian deaths and 3700 wounded, and an estimated 1000 Syrian fatalities with 4000 wounded. Syrian aircraft losses numbered approximately ninety-two, including several advanced MiG-23s and six Gazelle attack helicopters. Reported Israeli air losses were on the order of one Skyhawk, one attack helicopter, and one med-evac helicopter (Dupuy and Martell, 1986, pp. 141–45, 179; *Foreign Affairs Chronology,* 1990; *Middle East Journal,* Chronology, November 30, 1982; Klinghofer and Apter, 1985, p. 212). Despite the low Israeli weapons attrition, however, the war was to be the first to spawn major Israeli domestic opposition and human-rights concerns, since it involved cabinet deception, produced large numbers of civilian casualties in Lebanon, and was not clearly proportional to immediate perceived threats to the borders. (See Appendix, Chronology 6, "Israeli-Arab War in Lebanon.")

DIPLOMATIC PRESSURE AND ARMS FLOW

Frenzied and rather ineffective diplomatic efforts accompanied this crisis from the beginning, and arms diplomacy came to be included at least to a moderate degree. Last minute attempts were made at the UN on June 5 and June 6 to avert full-scale war. Hoping to avoid involvement, Soviet leaders initially styled the crisis as an Israeli-Palestinian, rather than Syrian, dispute; the Soviet news agency Tass asserted that Israel had attempted "physical extermination" of the Palestinian people, and accused the US of having had prior knowledge of the attack (*Keesings Contemporary Archives,* vol. 28, 1982, p. 31916; Klinghofer and Apter, 1985, pp. 210–11). At Lebanon's request, the UN Security Council convened and issued a cease-fire call. On the sixth leaders of nine European Community nations called for an immediate truce, and the UN followed with Resolution 509 demanding Israel's withdrawal and a multilateral cease-fire. Evidently, as of June 7 the Reagan administration was still being assured by Israeli Prime Minister Menachem Begin, and asked to reassure Damascus, that Israel would not engage the Syrians, but Reagan reportedly was feeling increasingly manipulated (Nachmias, 1988, pp. 138–39). Israeli leaders assumed that with the recent death of the Saudi King Khalid, and Washington's need for stable allies, there would be no withholding of US arms. Thus, they were not very concerned when, immediately following the invasion, the Reagan administration suspended required Congressional notification of a pending F-16 fighter shipment, which was supposed to follow the Sinai withdrawal (Nachmias, 1988, pp. 139–40).

With the simultaneous IDF advance on the Damascus highway and wholesale destruction of Syrian forces on June 9, Moscow was forced into some sort of commitment. Syria began to augment its troop deployments and SAM installations in the Beqa'a (Dupuy and Martell, 1986, p. 144) even as US Secretary of State Haig outlined a plan on the eighth for reduction of Syrian forces in Lebanon and strengthening of UN peacekeeping contingents (Haig, 1984, chapter 15). Finally, in reinforcing Syrian resolve, Soviet diplomacy and arms replenishment would lead to more fighting along the Damascus highway and to further Syrian setbacks, showing that rearming defenders is not always an effective strategy.

Conspicuously absent from these early diplomatic pressures was any clear threat or warning of arms-supply cutoffs to either side, or of forceful superpower intervention. This lent credence to charges that the US approved Israel's initial attack strategy to change the balance of forces in Lebanon, even though Haig repeatedly had warned the Israelis (as late as May) about the required level of "internationally recognized provocation" by the PLO or Syria that would make such an attack, with the risks of Syrian-Soviet involvement, acceptable. Tel Aviv and Washington apparently had misperceived each other's positions in these consultations (Haig, 1984, chapter 15; Nachmias, 1988, pp. 130–35). Nevertheless, on June 8, the US vetoed a UN condemnation of Israel and effort to enforce Resolution 509. It was not until the ninth, when serious Israeli-Syrian clashes ensued, that Washington, preoccupied with the Falklands crisis and responding to Soviet pleas and its own hopes of opening a PLO dialogue, began openly to express concern over the escalating hostilities. The Reagan administration soon requested a halt to the invasion (Klinghofer and Apter, 1985, pp. 210–11).

The European Communities (EC) joined these efforts with a stiff condemnation of the invasion on June 10; European aid to Israel was suspended for the duration of the war (*Middle East Journal,* Chronology, 1982, and March 25, 1983; Davis, 1987, p. 93). However, American aid would continue, with Israel and the US ultimately moving in 1983 toward establishment of a joint military-political committee, cooperation in the Lavi fighter project (a follow-on to the Israeli-built

Kfir utilizing more advanced US technology which was later to be ended when it threatened to compete with US F-16 sales), and a free-trade agreement. Thus the pressure on Israel was muted and presented only outside limits for IDF military action.

The PLO, shocked by the general lack of concrete support by the USSR and most Arab states, and unable to match the Israeli fighting units, sued for a cease-fire in West Beirut on June 14. However, PLO forces showed no intention of leaving the city voluntarily, especially, and to Israel's consternation, after Washington let it be known on the sixteenth that in exchange for Reagan's agreeing to see Prime Minister Begin on the twenty-first Israel had agreed not to invade Beirut (Haig, 1984, chapter 15; Davis, 1987, p. 97; Klinghofer and Apter, 1985, p. 210). Still, US leaders recognized that unconditional Israeli withdrawal no longer was a "realistic" means for resolving the Lebanese crisis. It would take the prospect of a politically costly war of attrition around Beirut, added US pressures and commitments, and the lingering hope of a separate peace with a new Lebanese government to change Israeli thinking.

June 16 brought news of the first Soviet arms resupplies to the hard-pressed Syrians, paid for by the Saudis, who ironically were receiving massive US arms themselves. Six-hundred tons of arms reportedly reached Syria within forty-eight hours. President Assad had made two secret consultative trips to Moscow, and senior Soviet air defense advisors were dispatched to Damascus. With fewer diplomatic cards and military hopes than in 1973, Moscow nevertheless worried about the conspicuous defeat and capture (thus opening to American inspection) of its front-line weapon systems—MiG-23s and MiG-25s, T-72 tanks, and SAM-6 and SAM-9 batteries.[2] However, the Soviet response was a short spurt of weapon transfers on a much smaller scale than in 1973; no further supplies came until the autumn, and then with Soviet personnel to operate them, presumably with greater skill and caution than the Syrians. Aid probably would have been greater if fighting had shifted to Syrian soil (engaging the Soviet friendship treaty), and reportedly this was signaled to the US and thereby Israel by the alert of two Soviet airborne divisions and requests for overflight permission from Turkey (Klinghofer and Apter, 1985, p. 212). Simultaneously, however, desperate PLO calls for Soviet assistance were met only with rather pro-forma letters of diplomatic support; it was left to Algeria to transfer $20-million worth of replacement supplies (Bavly and Salpeter, 1984, p. 114).[3]

Meanwhile on June 17, American cease-fire pressures came to include requests for Israel to supply information on possible violation of US arms-export restrictions on the use of cluster bombs in Lebanon (*Middle East Journal,* Chronology, 1982). American misgivings would be discussed during Prime Minister Begin's mid-June visit to Washington (*Keesings Contemporary Archives,* vol. 28, 1982, p. 31916), and a forty-eight-hour truce was declared to coincide with that trip. Although small-scale clashes continued, both Israel and Syria used the time for reinforcements. Washington stepped up its diplomatic efforts as Begin was preparing to visit and US envoy Habib continued negotiations with Lebanese leaders concerning restoration of governmental control over Palestinian and other militia (*Middle East Journal,* Chronology, 1982). Peace talks remained at an impasse, however, as Begin declared on the seventeenth that Israel would not accept a return to the status quo. While in Washington, Begin encountered rather unexpected Congressional opposition to the campaign and to the unauthorized use of certain US weapons (particularly cluster bombs).

Nevertheless, efforts to bring about the simultaneous disarming of the PLO, resumption of Lebanese sovereignty over West Beirut, and Israeli pullback faltered. On June 19 Saudi Arabia warned Israel against invading the city, while Syria called for attacks against US interests in the region. Syria too refused Lebanese requests to withdraw, and Reagan issued confusing signals by agreeing with Israel's objectives but not necessarily all its strategies during his meeting with Begin on the twenty-first. Evidently the Americans had not realized the full extent of Israeli battle plans, and the line was drawn against Israeli penetration of West Beirut (Haig, 1984, chapter 15). On the same day the EC attempted to boost the pressure as the foreign ministers discussed imposing sanctions on Tel Aviv (*Middle East Journal,* Chronology, 1982; *Keesings Contemporary Archives,* vol. 28, 1982, p. 31917.)

All of this activity had only a mild impact on the fighting, perhaps facilitating temporary cease-fires such as that on June 22 after Congressional criticism of Israeli arms policy. US, Arab, and European diplomacy turned as well toward the PLO, urging their safe evacuation from Beirut and displacing the Soviets as Palestinian confidants (*Middle East Journal,* Chronology, 1982). Meanwhile, on the twenty-fifth the Lebanese cabinet finally fell apart, and the South Atlantic war impinged on the Middle East as US Secretary of State Haig resigned.

This was seen to harden American opposition to Israeli policy, as George Schulz, who was known to favor strong Arab economic ties, became the new US Secretary of State. Despite its calls for sanctions against the US for its role in Israel's invasion, by the twenty-seventh the PLO had agreed to withdrawal from Lebanon pending satisfactory arrangements on timing and destination (*Keesings Contemporary Archives,* vol. 28, 1982, p. 31917; *Middle East Journal,* Chronology, 1982; to add pressure for agreement, Israeli planes dropped leaflets on Beirut on June 28 warning of an impending invasion).

With only slow diplomatic progress, Britain placed an embargo on arms sales to Israel on June 30, and by early July the Reagan administration was hinting about reporting Israeli Arms Export Control Act violations to Congress. Israel had rejected PLO proposals on July 4 for a partial mutual withdrawal and international peacekeeping, and three Arab League representatives requested Moscow's assistance. After a unanimous Security Council resolution calling for resumption of normal supplies to besieged Beirut, negotiating progress picked up noticeably on July 6; French Foreign Minister Claude Cheysson confirmed PLO agreement to a political solution, and the US agreed in principle to join its European allies in contributing "a small contingent" to a temporary multinational peacekeeping force (*Foreign Affairs Chronology,* 1990). However, in a letter to President Reagan, Soviet Premier Brezhnev raised concerns about a direct US military presence (*Keesings Contemporary Archives,* vol. 28, 1982, p. 31917).

Through the Saudis, Washington was still seeking a safe haven for the PLO, and on July 18, having become increasingly embarrassed by television reports of Israel's continued Beirut bombardment and denial of relief supplies to the city, the US temporarily suspended shipment of five-thousand cluster bombs to Israel (Bavly and Salpeter, 1984, p. 107; *Middle East Journal,* Chronology, July 19, 1982). Syria also threatened unofficially to introduce new weapons in Lebanon if Israel continued its attacks (*Middle East Journal,* Chronology, July 24, 1982). The British and limited American embargoes had negligible direct effects on Israeli fighting capability, but were political signals of displeasure.

In a pattern somewhat reminiscent of the 1973 war, the US further stepped up arms supply threats as Israel continued to ignore UN ceasefire calls regarding Beirut through early August. Soviet Premier Brezhnev again requested US pressure to halt Israeli bombing of West Beirut on August 2 (*Middle East Journal,* Chronology, August 1982).

Palestinian evacuation negotiations were temporarily suspended and US-Israeli relations deteriorated as Reagan sent Begin a message questioning the use of US arms and listing possible military, economic, and diplomatic sanctions. On the fourth Washington abstained as the UN Security Council censured Israel for its Lebanese invasion, but still the US vetoed a subsequent Soviet attempt to bar Israeli weapon resupplies, a clear signal that Tel Aviv would not be forced out of Lebanon (*Keesings Contemporary Archives,* vol. 28, 1982, p. 31918; *Middle East Journal,* Chronology, August 1-6, 1982).

Habib finally engineered agreement for PLO withdrawal on August 6–7, and on the tenth the Israeli cabinet conditionally accepted (Dupuy and Martell, 1986, p. 162; *Keesings Contemporary Archives,* vol. 28, 1982, p. 31918). Yet Israeli Defense Minister Sharon reportedly unilaterally authorized massive bombings of Beirut for eleven hours on August 11–12, which cinched PLO intentions to abandon the city after losing 130 dead and nearly 400 wounded (Dupuy and Martell, 1986, p. 162; Bavly and Salpeter, 1984, pp. 108–9). Both the US and the full Israeli cabinet strongly denounced the attacks, and a formal cease-fire with US-UK-French-Italian peacekeeping was achieved on August 12 after another US visit by Prime Minister Begin. Full Israeli, Lebanese, and PLO approval followed soon after, although Egypt tried to keep up pressure for Israeli troop withdrawals by suspending Palestinian autonomy talks (Dupuy and Martell, 1986, p. 163; *Keesings Contemporary Archives,* vol. 28, 1982, p. 31918; *Middle East Journal,* Chronology, August 22–27, 1982).

After the bulk of PLO and Syrian troops had been evacuated from Beirut in September (the Palestinians turned their heavy weapons over to a leftist Lebanese militia; see *Middle East Journal,* Chronology, August 26, 1982) and peacekeeping forces had begun their withdrawal, fighting between Israel and Syrian-PLO factions flared anew. Israel objected to alleged PLO attacks and cease-fire violations from Syrian-held territory and to the kidnapping or capture of Israeli soldiers in Lebanon. It was also clear that Syria's role in Lebanon had been sustained by Soviet support, and that Israel had failed to win its full political agenda.

This resumption also followed a September 1 statement outlining US Mideast policy—the so-called Reagan Plan, which called for a freeze on Israeli settlements in occupied territories and a "fully autonomous" Palestinian "entity" linked to Jordan (*Middle East Journal,* Chronology, 1982). Despite the plan's denial of a PLO state and failure to involve Syria, Israel quickly joined Syria and extremist Palestinian factions in rejecting the proposals. The PLO along with moderate Arab states expressed interest, and Jordan was heavily courted with offers of arms deals (Nachmias, 1988, p. 127). Tel Aviv reportedly was furious with Washington both for launching the plan and for preserving the weakened PLO presumably for a role in the ultimate West Bank negotiations (Klinghofer and Apter, 1985, p. 215).

On September 15, Israeli troops and tanks entered West Beirut in force following the assassination of President-elect Bashir Gemayel, who had met secretly with the Israeli leadership in northern Israel on September 3 (*Middle East Journal,* Chronology, 1982). In the wake of subsequent massacres at the Sabra and Shatilla Palestinian refugee camps by Lebanese Christian militia allowed into the camps by Israeli authorities, peacekeeping forces were returned to the city and Israeli forces pulled back. Saudi Arabia and other Arab governments also reportedly held back on aid commitments to Lebanon, promised in 1983 to encourage Lebanon's political rebuilding efforts, until Israel and other outside forces withdrew (*Middle East Journal,* Chronology, February 15, 1983).

In a key turning point in the war's balance of forces, Soviet authorities felt it necessary to supply Syria with additional SAM-5 batteries (manned exclusively by Soviet crews) as well as hundreds of tanks, trucks, and armored personnel carriers totalling some $2.5-billion in value (roughly double what was lost during the war) during the late fall and into January 1983; the total number of Soviet personnel in Syria thus increased from 3500 to over 5000 (Bavly and Salpeter, 1984, pp. 121–25; Nachmias, 1988, p. 145; *Middle East Journal,* Chronology, October 25, 1982). This commitment restored Syria to more respectable fighting form, as Israel did not yet have a proven counter to the SAM-5, which could hit aircraft at long distance. The move also injected Soviet forces more directly in a deterrent role reminiscent of 1970 along the Suez Canal. In so doing, Moscow brushed off Israeli diplomatic overtures, and the Fez Arab League regional security summit approached for consideration of the Reagan Plan. Indeed with the concomitant delivery of SAM-8s to Jordan in December, Moscow's objective seemed to be to stymie the Reagan Plan, undermine US influence with the Palestinians and Jordan, offset the increased US military presence in the area, and restore sagging Soviet credibility among the Arabs (Klinghofer and Apter, 1985, pp. 213–19).

Given a more assertive Soviet role, neither the US administration nor Congress were inclined to carry through with weapons sanctions against Israel, although a Senate appropriations subcommittee postponed consideration of Mideast aid proposals in view of the "fluid" situation in the region. Indeed, in a remarkable example of attempted reverse arms influence, in September 1982 Israel refused to share military intelligence acquired during the Lebanon war with Washington until all anti-Israeli arms restrictions were lifted. The CIA reportedly was keenly interested in data on the effectiveness of Israeli techniques for destroying Soviet missile sites (*Middle East Journal,* Chronology, September 4 and 23, 1982, and January 16, 1983; Nachmias, 1988, pp. 147–48). Agreement on intelligence data sharing was renewed in March 1983, although Washington still pressed for Israeli withdrawal from Lebanon by suspending the delivery of F-16 fighter jets (*Middle East Journal,* Chronology, March 31, 1983). Amid sporadic Syrian-Israeli clashes, in early May Tel Aviv agreed in principle to a phased withdrawal of its forces, and the US lifted the F-16 "embargo."

Arms diplomacy, then, seemed to move the Israelis, but as in other cases we have seen, the situation was diplomatically far more complicated than that. The F-16 delay probably had been prolonged through September of 1982 in an effort to obtain Israeli support for the Reagan Plan, and Israel's intelligence-data counter move was meant to break that pressure. Indeed, Israel insisted on its own terms for the war's political settlement: a bilateral peace treaty with Lebanon; negotiations in both Beirut and Jerusalem; no talks with the PLO on the future of the West Bank; no freeze of West Bank settlements; and a simultaneous withdrawal of all Syrian, PLO, and Israeli forces from Lebanon with retention of Israeli border patrols (Nachmias, 1988, pp. 148–49). By March 1983 the Reagan Plan was effectively dead, with Israeli, Syrian, and Jordanian-PLO rejection, despite US arms offers to Jordan. Washington nevertheless seemed intent on salvaging something diplomatically from Lebanon.

At this point, both the Israeli and the US leadership had mixed emotions about a separate Lebanese-Israeli peace treaty, since it clearly could not be implemented with continued Syrian presence in the country, and since US-Syrian talks probably would have opened the sensitive question of the Golan Heights (Klinghofer and Apter, 1985, pp. 223–25; Nachmias, 1988, pp. 150–51). Nevertheless, both the Phalangist dominated Lebanese leadership and the Israelis went through the motions of peacemaking; the go-ahead was given for F-16s, and the terms of the agreement (framed on May 17) were made very favorable to both Lebanon and Israel with promises of considerable US military and political support (including training and equipment for the Lebanese army).

Predictably, though, the agreement was rejected by Syria, and President Assad abruptly cut off talks with US envoy Habib. Washington had severely underestimated Syrian interest in controlling and brokering any and all Lebanese peace accords (*Middle East Journal*, Chronology, May 1983; Yaniv, 1987, pp. 170–71; Nachmias, 1988, p. 147; and Habib, personal interview, 1985). The Syrian rejection and pressure on Jordan and the PLO were reminiscent of Egyptian President Gamal Abdel Nasser's successful resistance to American alliance building in the 1950s. Therefore, while Israeli troops were pulled back south, terrorist attacks on US and Western forces in Beirut would mount, leading to the peacekeepers' ignominious departure, the Lebanese government's downfall, and the persistence of the civil war, amid plentiful arms supplies, for seven more years.

CONCLUSIONS

The pattern of arms diplomacy and deliveries and their effects on the 1982 war are by this time rather familiar from our previous Middle Eastern and Third World cases. Increased armament prior to the war clearly facilitated preparations for renewed combat, and particularly Israel's attempt to remake Lebanon through air- and quick-moving-armor assaults. Resupplies during the fighting, carefully managed and limited though they were, also bolstered at least one of the defending and weaker parties, Syria (if not the PLO), and kept them in the war. In this sense, arms supplies once again reflected rather than reshaped major-power and regional-actor political priorities. Washington evidently had approved of Israel's basic forceful initiative to redraw the Lebanese political scene and force the issue of the Palestinians' future. Somehow US and even some Israeli leaders appeared to believe this could be done without involving the Syrians. The USSR remained at least politically committed to its Syrian clients, if not so clearly to the PLO. Continued arms supplies were seen as necessary to these major-power strategies, and once again to the vindication of each power's military technology.

When the Israeli-Syrian confrontation threatened to get out of control, and when Israel's Beirut siege drew worldwide condemnation,

US leaders were moved to draw limits to the conflict and tried mild arms-limitation pressures on Israel to punctuate their diplomatic shuttles. As in 1973, the effects of these restrictions, as well as European sanctions, were minimal in bringing a lasting cease-fire; indeed even Israeli undertakings not to invade Beirut were breached in September.

Given the massive Israeli arsenal it would have taken a comprehensive supply and spare parts shutoff to produce a significant political effect. As one example, Israeli Defense Minister Sharon was able to authorize the most intensive air attacks of the war in early August immediately after the formal suspension of US deliveries of cluster munitions to Tel Aviv on July 15. These attacks were repudiated quickly and the cease-fire at least temporarily restored by Israel's cabinet after a very blunt US diplomatic demand (Davis, 1987, pp. 99–100). But the restraining effects of the arms restrictions themselves were not very great, as seen in the failure of the F-16 delays. Since more massive restrictions were seen as risking overall Israeli security, in the end as in other wars, arms diplomacy did not turn around Israeli policy. In fact, an October 1983 terror bombing of US marine barracks in Beirut clinched the closest US-Israeli security understanding yet seen, a strategic cooperation agreement that not only lifted the ban on cluster-bomb shipments but added new aid funds to finance Israeli weapon development (including Lavi fighter and other systems; see Nachmias, 1988, p. 153).

In view of Israel's sweeping initial battlefield success, the final withdrawal terms for West Beirut in fact reinforced Israeli policy under multinational auspices. The PLO at least temporarily was ousted, though through US intervention it was not destroyed as Tel Aviv would have liked, and a shaky new Lebanese government amenable to Israeli interests was empowered briefly. The fact that Syria was allowed to remain in Lebanon, however, with forces replenished by a more involved Soviet Union, ultimately upset these arrangements. US promises of arms for Jordan were insufficient to bring Amman aboard the Reagan Plan or peace process in the face of such pressures. Thus, although US leaders seized the opportunity to launch new and grandiose peace initiatives, they basically responded to pressures generated by other key actors—Israel, Syria, the USSR; in a sense US willingness to intervene as part of the multinational force upheld initial Israeli goals while relieving Tel Aviv of paying a higher battlefield price for them.

Indeed, one arms-transfer analyst has concluded that Washington was totally frustrated in this case through "lack of leverage and its total inability to influence the policies of either its friends or its foes" as well as through policy misunderstandings and reversals (Nachmias, 1988, pp. 125, 142–43). Although President Reagan was advised by senior Congressional leaders, mid-level bureaucrats, and certain political leaders to withhold arms supplies to Israel early in the campaign, his evident hope that somehow Israeli battlefield successes could be translated to political settlements prevented this. Though the USSR had remarkably little overall influence on an American administration bent on its own Middle Eastern diplomatic gambit, it was able to use strategic arms transfers to Syria as a wedge to frustrate US diplomacy.

The situation became stalemated for several months around Beirut, and Israel's basic position was at least moderately painful. Financial costs of the war mounted to some $2 billion, though losses of Israeli equipment were minimal; ammunition had to be replenished, casualties were relatively high, and domestic opposition was rather vociferous. Still, costs had not mounted to where outside arms-supply pressures alone were particularly telling in ending the siege, and the US Congress and administration showed little lasting inclination to punish Tel Aviv and strengthen Soviet backed Syria by reducing levels of assistance (Bavly and Salpeter, 1984, pp. 209–15). A combination of political and security arrangements, alarm at the quagmire of Lebanese politics, implication in atrocities, and long-term US security commitments brought about Israel's withdrawal and sporadic repeated interventions.

As demonstrated by Moscow's endgame diplomacy, arms transfers can further political priorities, especially in creating deterrent effects and signaling commitments. Syria was supplied with advanced weapons (the most sophisticated of which were defensive in function and kept under Soviet control) in order that Moscow might regain its role in a larger regional diplomatic game until then completely dominated by Washington. The battlefield fate of Lebanon, the PLO, Israel, or even Syria seemed secondary to a continued viable Soviet role in the region and among Arab clients. This was especially true with Brezhnev's death and uncertainties about who would be his successor. In the process, though, Syria, under a more effective antiaircraft missile shield, was able to maintain forces in Lebanon and thus was sustained as the dominant intervening power for many years.

The bolstering of the Syrian side meant that Israel's political negotiation agenda could not be realized. There was little point in delaying arrangements for a pullback from the embarrassing Beirut morass as long as foreign forces could be substituted. Indirectly, then, arms supplies influenced the terms of settlement, though their manipulation was next to useless in determining the pace of concessions. Although the two regional protagonists were highly dependent on single arms suppliers, those suppliers did not propose to apply strong arms restrictions or sanctions, and in Israel's case the rate of weapons attrition was acceptably low.

As predicted by the hypotheses of chapter one, in this case arms supply by the USSR tended to equalize the combatants' military capabilities, promoting stalemate and diminishing the search for a broad negotiated settlement, especially as attrition for the militarily dominant party remained low. The cease-fire and disengagement agreements of 1982–83 were rather minimal compared to the earlier hopes of both the US and Israel, and were soon tragically broken. Soviet supplies to Syria, then, in some sense set the tone for the war's end, even though they probably prolonged the fighting. Syria was allowed to remain dominant in the crumbling Lebanon but not equipped to carry on warfare successfully in counterattacks on Israel. Moscow, preoccupied with its own succession problems, then could sit back and watch the US struggle vainly, and with inglorious losses, to control the unfolding Lebanese political turmoil. With the example of this reinforced stalemate in mind, we turn to perhaps the most notorious long-term Middle Eastern war of attrition, the decade long Iran-Iraq conflict of the 1980s.

CHAPTER 9

THE IRAQ-IRAN WAR, 1980–88

INTRODUCTION: THE BACKGROUND OF WAR

In late September 1980 one of the bloodiest wars of the second half of the twentieth century began as Iraq attacked Iran. This was to be different from other wars during the post–World War II period in that the East-West conflict was of minor importance. Indeed the superpowers badly misjudged the issues and forces involved in the conflict in this economically and geopolitically pivotal world region. Resultant arms transfers were an important element in the war's length and carnage; more than in prior wars, arms suppliers sent weapons simultaneously to both sides, and for the first time many of the new Third World arms exporters played a significant role.

It was a war in which Iraq sought to use the unstable political and military situation in revolutionary Iran to its own advantage. Iraqi leader Saddam Hussein pursued territorial claims along the Shatt-al-Arab; the Iraqi leadership grudgingly had been forced to cede territory to the better-armed Shah of Iran under the Algiers Accord of 1975 in return for an easing of the Kurdish rebellion. In initiating the war, Saddam Hussein probably also hoped to gain part or all of the oil-rich Southwestern Iranian region of Khuzestan, mostly inhabited by ethnic Arabs, and to prevent the spillover of an Islamic revolution into Arab lands, including his own. It was for this cause that he received the wholehearted diplomatic and financial support of previously suspicious conservative Arab states in the Gulf, and particularly that of Saudi Arabia, as well as the more distant Jordan.

The military balance and prior arms transfers are generally acknowledged to have heavily influenced Iraqi decisions to initiate the war. During the 1970s, Iraq and Iran were in a competitive arms race, with Iran having the upper hand, not only because of its higher oil income but also because the Americans were a more reliable and resourceful supplier to Iran under the Shah than the Soviets were to Iraq. However, the cancellation of almost all arms contracts in the wake of the Iranian revolution, and the withdrawal of the tens of thousands of Western military advisers, technicians, and experts, drastically changed the equation. Western suppliers became reluctant to send military goods to Iran, and when radicals took hostages in the US embassy in Teheran most Western states declared formal arms embargoes. US interests in defending Teheran also melted. Because of its reliance on Western high technology, the Iranian military seemed to be rapidly losing its fighting ability, and the leadership was destabilized by repeated purges. Thus, Iran's political structure was in disarray, with conflicts between the moderate President Abdolhassan Bani-Sadr and the more radical Islamic clerics. Iraq's armed forces now seemed overwhelmingly superior—a strong temptation for Saddam Hussein and his advisors.

Between 1982 and 1986 the Iraq-Iran war indeed became the mainstay of the international arms trade. Demand from both sides helped arms industries to expand, virtually around the globe. The US government, while ostensibly committed to an Iranian arms embargo—"Operation Staunch"—ultimately let itself be politically seduced into dealing weapons to Teheran, resulting in the Iran-Contra scandal, and did not object when close clients such as Israel filled the breech with important resupplies of American equipment. Some of Washington's other close associates, such as Saudi Arabia, were major financiers of the Iraqi efforts. Despite their conflicting bloc memberships, the Soviet Union and France also emerged as mainstays of Iraqi armament. China rather blatantly supplied both sides for profit. The mixture of motives for arms supplies made strange bedfellows and provided both belligerents with the potential for one of the century's longest wars.

Prewar deliveries to Iraq were much larger than those to the relatively isolated Iran. Iranian equipment, parts, and ammunition shortages gradually grew to become a significant problem, ultimately one factor in Teheran's decision in the summer of 1988 to terminate the war, as Iranian forces had to withdraw almost totally from Iraqi territory. When the war ended, the front line was nearly identical to the prewar international boundary.

Regardless of their actual importance for the war's course, arms supplies have loomed large in Western perceptions and analyses of the dispute. Arms demand from both sides, but especially Iran, nourished the rise of a large grey and black market that put some dealers in jail, made others rich, and provided stories for scores of journalists

(Adams, 1990, pp. 127–36; Bock and Deniau, 1988; Dietl, 1986; Koppe and Koch, 1990; Leyendecker and Rickelmann, 1990; Lifshultz et al, 1991; Roth, 1986; Timmerman, 1988; Timmerman 1991). Washington's Iran-Contra scandal, in which the Reagan administration tried to sell arms to Teheran in return for help in freeing western hostages in Beirut (including the US CIA station chief), while using the funds received to finance illegal arms assistance to the Nicaraguan "Contra" rebels, added to the image of the war as fueled by shady weapons deals.

Table 16

Arms Shipments to Iraq, 1977–79

Czechoslovakia	24 L-39 Albatross jet trainers
France	44 SA-316B helicopters armed with AS-12 missiles; 10 SA-342K Gazelle helicopters armed with HOT ATM; 6 Super Frelon helicopters armed with AM-39 Exocet AShMs; 100 AMX-30B;30 VCR-6 APC armed with HOT ATM
FRG	4 Bo-105 helicopters
Sudan	10 MiG-21MF fighters (for spares)
Switzerland	16 AS-202 Bravo trainers
USSR	4 An-12 Cub-A transports; 2 An-24 Coke transports; 2 An-26 Curl light planes; 20 Mi-24 Hind-D helicopters; 66 Mil-8 Hip helicopters; 70 MiG-23BN fighter-bomber; 2 Tu-134 transports; 50 BM-21 122mm MRS; 450 T-62 tanks; 50 T-72 tanks; 135 SA-6 Gainful land-mobile SAM; 24 SSN-2 Styx ShSHM for 2 OSA-2 Class FAC; 4 Polnocny Class landing ships

Source: Estimates from SIPRI files; authors' files. Major weapons.

Table 17

Arms Shipments to Iran, 1977–79

France	90 AS-12 AShM; 9 Combattante Class FAC
Italy	15 AB-212 ASW helicopter; 13 CH-47C Chinook helicopter (additionally 23 ordered, of which 20 cancelled in 1979 and 4

	delivered later); 9 SH-3D Sea King helicopters; 40 Seakiller-Marte ShSHMs
Netherlands	5 F-27 transports
UK	250 FV-101 Skorpion light tanks; 20 Sultan FV-105 command vehicles
US	8 B-707-320C transports; 10 B-747-100B transports; 24 CH-47C Chinook helicopters; 54 F-14A Tomcat strike-fighter aircraft; 7 F-33C Bonanza trainers; 36 F-4E Phantom fighters; 14 F-5F jet fighter trainers; 40 Model-209 AH-IJ helicopters; 156 Model-214A helicopters; 2 Model-214B helicopters; 26 Model-214CV helicopters; 3 RH-53D naval helicopters; 100 M-113A1 APCs; 2 RGM-84AL ShSHMs; 472 AGM-65A ASMs (arming F-4s); 282 AIM-54A Phoenix AAMs (arming F-14s); 683 AIM-9J AAMs (arming F-14s, F-4s and F-5s); 720 BGM-71A TOW ATMs (arming helicopters); 10,000 FGM-77A Dragon ATMs; 9 RGM-84 Harpoon ShSHMs; 2 Gearing Class destroyers
USSR	100 ZSU-23-4 Shilka antiaircraft gun vehicles; 2000 SA-7 Grail Portable SAMs; 1000 SA-9 Gaskin land-mobile SAM vehicles

Source: Estimates from SIPRI files; authors' files. Major weapons.

ARMAMENT AND THE APPROACH OF WAR

By the late 1970s, both Iraq and Iran were among the most heavily armed nations in the Third World (see tables 16 and 17). Both were preferred customers because of their oil wealth, and also were able to exploit the East-West conflict to attract suppliers from the socialist and capitalist worlds. Iran had ordered weapons predominantly from the US, but also a number of other Western states and, in 1967 and 1976, the Soviet Union (Krause, 1985, pp. 145–52; Bennett, 1985, pp. 762–63). The Shah, Mohammad Reza Pahlavi, who personally managed the wholesale weapons procurement of the 1970s, had benefitted from massive oil revenues but also from the Nixon Doctrine's aim of helping Iran to become America's "policeman" in the Gulf area. In 1972, President Nixon opened the US conventional arms arsenal to the Shah (Kissinger, 1979, pp. 1263–64; Kissinger, 1982, pp. 667–70, 675–6). The Shah ordered a larger stock of the most advanced US weapons than any other customer in the world, including NATO allies (Sorley, 1983; Klare, 1984). In some cases Iran cofinanced the development of armament systems, such as US F-14 Tomcat fighter aircraft and British Centurion tanks, and thus jumped the queue to receive them in advance of US or UK forces.

The Shah also wanted to build up a domestic arms industry as part of Iranian technological and industrial development. Western companies contracted to construct turnkey factories and train large numbers of Iranian workers and engineers. Thousands of foreign contract workers, advisers, and instructors arrived in the late 1970s (Shultz, 1989). The Iranian armed forces were in a rapid transformation process, but still could not cope with all the new equipment, and ultimately failed to preserve the regime against a revolutionary challenge (Huyser, 1986). The dramatic growth of Iranian military might in the decade of the 1970s, which on paper brought Teheran near the level of West Germany or the UK in sheer numbers, remained illusory. Still, the enormous costs to achieve such growth were real. Indeed, it is not unreasonable to conclude that the high priority of military spending ironically resulted in a misallocation of resources that undermined the Shah's power (Moran, 1978).

With the creeping radicalization of the Iranian leadership between early 1979, when the Shah finally turned over power to his protégé Shahpour Bakhtiar, and the beginning of the war, the armed forces were purged and further transformed. In waves of purges, scores of officers were retired or imprisoned. Others left the country voluntarily (Zabih, 1988). Most hard hit among the services was the air force, in which most pilots had been American educated and therefore were suspected of disloyalty. While the armed forces were weakened, parallel military organizations were set up, such as the Revolutionary Guards and the Basiji.

The regular military was further disrupted by the severance of ties with traditional arms suppliers. Initially, it was the new Iranian leadership and not the arms suppliers who wanted to cancel purchases. In the spring of 1979, arms contracts valued at more than $20 billion were canceled, mostly in the US, but also in the UK, Germany, the Netherlands, and Italy (SIPRI, *Yearbook,* 1980, pp. 98–100). In some cases, such as the F-14 fighter and the AIM-54A Phoenix AAM, suppliers wanted weapons returned. The Iranian leadership generally refused, but departing American technicians took some sensitive electronics with them. Relations between Iran and its suppliers were further strained when the US embassy in Teheran was stormed in early 1980; Washington and its European allies decided to embargo all Iranian arms deliveries.

Thus, on the eve of war, the readiness of the Iranian armed forces was shattered, a fact not lost on Saddam Hussein. Many weapon systems had to be removed from service for lack of parts; some were cannibalized to provide parts for others. Again the air force was hardest hit because of its prior orientation toward very sophisticated American systems. Few technicians remained to repair the available weapons. Most domestic arms production programs had come to a standstill, the major exceptions being a German supplied small-arms complex and a Swedish supplied explosive plant that continued production, though evidently at lower levels (Schultz, 1989, pp. 56-69; *Jane's Defence Weekly*, February 4, 1989, p. 163).[1]

For its part, between the mid 1950s and early 1970s, Iraq had become almost totally dependent on Soviet arms (Krause, 1985, pp. 152-68). These close ties were documented in a treaty of friendship and cooperation signed in 1972. The Soviet Union delivered large quantities of fighter aircraft, tanks, and artillery, including the most modern types available. In line with standard superpower practice, however, Moscow did not transfer much more ammunition or spare parts than the minimum needed for continued operation. Some of the material was used in the early 1970s in an internal Iraqi campaign against Kurdish insurgents, but most went into the buildup of a growing war machine.

The Iraqi-Soviet relationship was not trouble free, however. The Ba'ath party, in power since 1962, was strongly anti-Communist. While at times it had accepted coalitions with the Iraqi Communist Party (ICP), after a failed 1978 coup attempt by military commanders supported by the Communists, the ICP was crushed. Ba'athist leadership suspected Soviet support for the coup and relations cooled for some time. Other issues of contention were the treatment of Kurds in Iraq, the support of differing Palestinian factions, and Soviet military support for Syria, arch rival of the Ba'athist Iraqi leadership. Despite these tensions, though, Iraq remained, along with Syria and Libya, among the best customers for Soviet arms, receiving an estimated volume of $7 billion of weapons between 1955 and 1980 (Hosmer and Wolf, 1983, p. 74).

Mounting oil revenues from the early 1970s also made it possible for the Iraqis to diversify their arms sources. In 1973, Baghdad began to make contact with French suppliers as Paris sought to cultivate special relations with oil-rich Arab states. In 1975, Saddam Hussein visited France, and although nominally only the vice-president at the time, he was received as a head of state (Timmerman, 1991, pp. 24-38).

A number of arms-for-oil deals were concluded. The French government agreed to supply various types of helicopters, such as SA-330 Pumas and Super Frelons, armed with advanced ASMs, including French-German coproduced Milans. In 1977, thirty-six Mirage F-1 fighter aircraft were ordered, followed by twenty-four more of the same type in 1979, all armed with Magic AAMs. No other Western supplier received similarly large orders; the Iraqi leadership deliberately cultivated the French connection while UK and US dealers, the predominant Iranian suppliers, had little chance.

THE COURSE OF WAR

The beginning of the Iraq-Iran war is often dated September 22, 1980, although Iraqi-initiated border skirmishing had occurred through much of the year and large Iraqi troop concentrations had massed since early summer. Full-scale fighting erupted on September 21, and the next day Iraqi French-supplied Mirages F-1s and Soviet-supplied MiG-23s flew preemptive air strikes against a number of Iranian airfields, including those at Teheran, in order to destroy those aircraft still airworthy (Cordesman and Wagner, 1990a, pp. 81–83). Within days, Abadan and Khorramshahr, the main oil cities in Iranian Khuzestan, were cut off and the front moved slowly northward and eastward; Iranian regular troops and Revolutionary Guards gave heavy resistance.

In the first months of fighting, Iranian troops suffered setbacks mostly due to faulty coordination. A central command under President Bani-Sadr was not created until mid-October. The troops, and especially the Revolutionary Guards and other volunteer militia, also were only lightly armed. Many of the modern Western weapon systems were either in disrepair or unavailable, and many of the troops also had not received proper training to use the available weapons. From the war's very early phases, Iranian commanders therefore used tactics reminiscent of the World War I; they sought to augment firepower with sacrifices from their massive infantry. It was hoped that sending large numbers of inadequately armed troops into battle would overwhelm the enemy, outnumbering the guns available to kill them.

The Iraqi side also had its command and control difficulties (Staudenmaier, 1985, p. 220). As supply lines were stretched, Iraqi troops ran into logistical difficulties. Tanks, the main weapon used on the ground, were not well supported with fuel or repair crews; frustrated commanders ordered their soldiers to dig the tanks in and use them as artillery pieces. This further slowed advances and created an unexpectedly large demand for more armor. The Iraqi air force's numerical advantages over Iran also were not rapidly translated into clear-cut air superiority. Iraqi commanders seemed fearful of losing planes to ground fire, and the Iranians made skillful use of their remaining operable fighters (Cordesman and Wagner, 1990a, pp. 98–102). F-14s, for instance, devoid of their AAMs, were used for short-radar warning, guiding other planes such as F-5s.

The first winter brought a "sitzkrieg" reminiscent of the dug-in infantry skirmishes of World War I (Staudenmaier, 1985, p. 221); it became clear that the Iraqi leadership had violated the major postulate of warfare according to Clausewitz: it had no clear political objective. By December 1980, as the weather made warfare difficult, Iraqi forces had occupied about half of the Iranian Khuzestan province, including the major oil installations but excluding the supply routes from the Iranian heartland. When the Arab population in Khuzestan failed to rise in response, however, Saddam Hussein and his advisers grew confused. Advantages were not pressed; the army was ordered to hold the ground it had occupied; more tanks were dug in; positions were fortified and troops were told to expect a longer war than initially anticipated. There were no attempts to beat the Iranians decisively, a feat that may or may not have been feasible given Iran's ultimate population advantage. Baghdad's strategy seems to have been to hope for an internal breakdown of the Iranian resistance.

Iran, on the other hand, took the opportunity to coordinate its military actions and prepare for counteroffensives. This proved very difficult for a number of reasons, including the ongoing political struggle for power in Teheran. Finally, however, President Bani-Sadr was ousted in the summer of 1981 and a clerical government took over. Although the various troop contingents were not easy to combine, groups of volunteer forces slowly began to conduct joint operations. Regular forces, purged again, this time of pro–Bani-Sadr elements, were reinforced in the summer of 1981 with officers previously ousted or jailed. With nationalism overcoming ideological division, coordination improved. Volunteers provided the initial brunt of the offensive; artillery and mechanized regular troops supported the attack and followed.

From May 1981 onward, the Iranian forces began to retake significant ground. The yearlong siege of Abadan was broken in late September 1981. In November, Iranians neared Khorramshahr, and after the winter pause, reoccupied the town in May 1982. By the summer,

Iraqi troops had been driven from almost all of Iranian territory, but Iranian forces did not stop there. They began a series of offensives to conquer Iraqi territory and Teheran began to insist on the downfall of Saddam Hussein. However, these attacks proved very costly in human terms, as Iraq's defense of home territory was more effective than its previous offensives. Iraqi commanders learned to make more deadly use of their superior firepower both on the ground and from the air. Iranian commanders ordered larger and larger infantry contingents into battle to gain planned objectives, resulting in the deaths of tens of thousands of Iranian foot soldiers. The first Iranian charges of Iraq's use of poison gas stemmed from these battles, a claim substantiated in later battles by international experts.

To offset Iranian success on the ground, the Iraqi leadership widened the war, ordering intensified air attacks against Iranian oil installations and ships in the Persian (also called Arabian) Gulf. In August 1983, Iraq declared the northern part of the Gulf an "exclusion zone" (Cordesman and Wagner, 1990a, p. 171), and Iraqi French- and Soviet-supplied aircraft and FROG-7 missiles were used to attack Iranian cities. This static war of attrition, marked by few changes in the front line, heavy casualties, and attacks on cities and ships continued until early 1986, punctuated by frequent artillery assaults from both sides. A number of local offenses were conducted, mostly by Iran, which dictated the pace of activity on the ground. But Iraqi infantry and artillery were dug in and the Iraqi air force came to enjoy largely uncontested control of the skies.

At the same time, Iraq set the pace in the tanker and air wars. Fixed-wing aircraft, including Mirage F-1s and Super Etendards, and helicopters, all equipped with the French supplied eighty-kilometer-range AM-39 Exocet AShM, hit a large number of tankers trying to reach Iranian oil installations in the Northern Gulf as well as the installations themselves from February 1984 onward. These attacks, meant in part to gain the attention of oil-dependent major powers, led to a further, though not fatal, decline in Iranian oil exports. From the spring of 1984, Iran too began regularly to attack oil tankers further south in the Gulf, but at a significantly lower rate of sorties.

During the second half of 1984 and all of 1985, the Iraqis also increasingly used their air superiority to attack Iranian civilian targets. Scud missiles and derivatives with ranges of up to eight-hundred kilometers were employed, though with mixed results. Although the Iraqis had fewer Scuds than aircraft, and the missiles had smaller payloads than warplanes, because of their high incoming velocity and short warning times they had jarring psychological impacts on the population. Again, Iran responded in kind but had significantly fewer aircraft and missiles available (McNaugher, 1990; Carus, 1991).

The deadlock began to change significantly in early 1986. During the prior fall, Iranian forces again massed for their annual winter offensive on the southern-most front, but on a larger scale than before. More than 200,000 men were assembled by early February 1986, opposite Iraq's second-largest city, Basra. Tehran decided to attack Basra because of its supposed strategic value, notwithstanding the several miles of wetlands, waterways, and marshes that would have to be crossed in the process. The fall of Basra would deprive Baghdad of its southern supply and oil-export lines. Initially, Iraqi firepower drove back Iranian forces, but due to bad weather and Iraqi tactical problems, the Iranians took the Iraqi Faw peninsula, blocking the waterway between Basra and the Gulf in mid-February. When the weather cleared, Iraqi air, artillery, and infantry forces counterattacked, using poison gas. Iranian troops held the peninsula, but could not take Basra. By mid-March, both sides were exhausted and had dug once more into fortified positions. Iran had suffered 27,000–30,000, and Iraq at least 5000, casualties (Cordesman and Wagner, 1990a, p. 224).

Following this costly territorial gain, the Iranian leadership tried to mobilize the country during 1986 for what was called the final offensive. Civil servants were drawn into the forces, universities closed, and women were employed in logistical posts. Although some spare parts for Western supplied weapons had been obtained, there was still a lack of heavy equipment, only partly offset by deliveries from North Korea and China. The "final attack," therefore, was planned as a larger version of earlier ones: World-War-I-style infantry "human waves" by irregular volunteers under heavy artillery protection, followed by mechanized regular troops. During the fall of 1986, a number of smaller offensives, called "Kerbala," after the Shi'ite holy city in Iraq, were initiated to prepare for the great winter campaign. The large-scale "Kerbala-5" offensive began in early January 1987; despite heavy Iraqi fortification and superior firepower, Iranian troops scored some early successes, establishing bridgeheads on the Iraqi side of the Tigris river and coming within ten kilometers of Basra. By mid-month, however, Iraqi aircraft and artillery had stopped the Iranian offensive. The Iranian attempt to take Basra in early 1987 (more than 50,000 Iranian and up to 15,000 Iraqi soldiers killed) was the bloodiest sequence in a war that ultimately would cost more than one-million lives (Cordesman and Wagner, 1990a, pp. 178–83, 261).

By mid-February 1987, the Iranian leadership realized that Iraqi defenses could not be broken with available troops. They instead began a siege of Basra. As had been the rule in this war, Iraq responded to pressure on the ground by intensifying attacks upon civilian targets, the "War of the Cities," as well as Gulf tankers. From April 1987, these two "fronts" received much more international attention. Already in 1986, Kuwait had asked the US and the Soviet Union to protect its tankers from Iranian attacks. The Soviet Union offered to "re-flag" some Kuwaiti tankers, and, probably as a response, Washington quickly agreed to do the same in April 1987 (Saivetz, 1989a, pp. 90–93; Cordesman and Wagner, 1990a, p. 279).

In contrast to Iraq, Iran had few aircraft available for the tanker war. Instead, small craft, such as Swedish-supplied fast sports boats were employed. Tankers were attacked with Italian Sea Killer ShSHMs, and, from early 1987, Chinese supplied HY-2 "Silkworm" SShMs. The latter weapon in particular came to be regarded as an additional threat to shipping in the Gulf, as some Silkworms were stationed near the Strait of Hormuz, a potential "choke point" for the entire Gulf. When on May 17, 1987, the *USS Stark* was hit by two Iraqi Exocets, the US decided to provide extensive naval protection for Gulf shipping, ironically, in order to stop primarily Iranian attacks.

After a calm period in the summer of 1987 to cool reactions to the *Stark* incident, Iraq resumed heavy attacks on shipping. But it was Iranian activity that received most international attention. In addition to air and naval attacks, the Iranian navy began to lay mines in the southern Gulf as Teheran threatened at various times to close off the Straits of Hormuz. US naval forces sent to the Gulf to protect tankers were inadequately prepared for mine warfare. Minesweepers from Western European countries, coordinated by the Western European Union, arrived in late 1987 to clear the shipping lanes. This further internationalized the conflict.

Contrary to annual practice since 1981, Iranian forces did not prepare for a large offensive in the fall of 1987. The main reason seems to have been a lack of volunteers and an unwillingness to press more people into the war effort. Also, the latest rounds of offensives had shown that Iraqi defenses were stronger than ever. Iraq continued to receive large quantities of weapons, while for Iran resupply was a growing problem.

Instead, buoyed by major-power support, in April 1988 the Iraqis launched their greatest land attack since the early phase of the war, scoring a major tactical victory with the recapture of the Faw peninsula. By mid-1988, Iran had lost virtually all the territorial gains made since 1982 (Cordesman and Wagner, 1990a, p. 395). Concomitantly, attacks on civilian targets reached their peak in March and April 1988. Each side launched hundreds of attacks against the other's residential and economic centers. Iraq launched more than three-hundred Scud missiles, mostly of improved range, while Iran countered with about eighty launches (Cordesman and Wagner, 1990, p, 363-368). Although Iraq had one-hundred such missiles and Iran none when the war began, by the time it was over, in August 1988, a total of more than four hundred had been used (Carus, 1991, p. 37). (See Appendix, Chronology 7, "The Iran-Iraq War, 1980–88.")

DIPLOMATIC PRESSURE AND ARMS FLOW

The Iraq-Iran war provided one of the most dynamic demand factors of the international arms trade during the 1980s. US government estimates put the cost of arms purchases at more than $15 billion for Iran and $50 billion for Iraq (United States Arms Control and Disarmament Agency, *World Military Expenditures and Arms Transfers,* 1989; Grimmett, 1989). SIPRI has estimated major weapon purchases at more than $3 billion for Iran and $24 billion for Iraq (SIPRI, *Fact Sheets,* 1988 and 1990; estimates, particularly for Iranian arms during the war, are very rough and must be used with caution). During the period of war, about twenty percent of all arms transferred internationally were sold to these two states, evidently partly for profit and partly because the major powers could not decide which side, if any, they wanted to win. Iraq received substantially more weapons than Iran (Tables 18 and 19) but had difficulties utilizing them, while Iran had urgent needs that could not be entirely met despite a multitude of sources on black and grey markets (SIPRI, *Yearbook,* 1984, pp. 194–201; and 1987, pp. 203–7; Medalia, 1986; Cordesman, 1987c; Grimmett, 1989; Timmerman, 1988; Brzoska, 1987; Cordesman and Wagner, 1990a, pp. 48–53).

While Iraq received most of its weaponry from countries that were its predominant prewar suppliers, most Iranian weapons came from nontraditional sources. Only a few states, such as Libya and Syria, were prepared openly to support Iran. Crucial supplies had to be bought

Table 18

Values of Major Weapon Deliveries to Iraq, 1980–88*

Year	Country	Value	Year	Country	Value
1980	Brazil	100	1983	Brazil	138
	Czechoslovakia	20		China	397
	Egypt	21		Czechoslovakia	78
	France	188		Denmark	189
	Iran	0		Egypt	314
	Switzerland	4		France	777
	USSR	1356		FRG	3
1981	Brazil	100		Iran	5
	Czechoslovakia	107		Italy	18
	Egypt	32		Jordan	201
	France	951		Romania	85
	GDR	13		Spain	37
	Hungary	36		Switzerland	38
	Iran	55		UK	14
	Jordan	12		USSR	1096
	Poland	204	1984	Brazil	107
	Romania	34		China	397
	Switzerland	16		Czechoslovakia	78
	USSR	965		Egypt	94
	Yugoslavia	50		France	864
1982	Brazil	100		FRG	3
	China	80		Italy	39
	Czechoslovakia	97		Jordan	94
	Egypt	44		Kuwait	36
	France	189		Romania	72
	FRG	12		Spain	25
	Iran	5		USSR	2365
	Italy	38	1985	Brazil	68
	Jordan	42		China	397
	Poland	68		Czechoslovakia	78
	Romania	85		Egypt	118
	Spain	37		France	722
	Switzerland	9		FRG	6
	UK	2		Italy	22
	USSR	1102		Poland	20

	South Africa	40		France	233
	Spain	25		Italy	3
	USSR	1714		South Africa	40
1986	Brazil	17		Switzerland	20
	China	397		US	45
	Czechoslovakia	37		USSR	3271
	Egypt	149	1988	Brazil	159
	France	756		Canada	6
	Jordan	16		China	156
	Poland	20		Czechoslovakia	37
	South Africa	40		Egypt	100
	Saudi Arabia	3		France	271
	USSR	1044		FRG	12
1987	Brazil	162		Italy	6
	China	433		South Africa	40
	Czechoslovakia	37		Switzerland	5
	Egypt	189		US	191
				USSR	1166

Source: Estimates from SIPRI files; authors' files.
*Estimates in US million dollars.

Table 19

Values of Major Weapon Deliveries to Iran, 1980–88*

1980	Italy	6		North Korea	50
	Libya	26		Libya	30
1981	France	132		Switzerland	8
	Italy	30		Syria	16
	Libya	59	1984	China	111
	Netherlands	11		Ethiopia	22
1982	China	121		North Korea	34
	Italy	35		Libya	<.5
	North Korea	30		Netherlands	5
	Switzerland	<.5		Switzerland	39
	Syria	89		UK	40
1983	China	131	1985	Austria	112
	Iraq	46		China	309

(*continued on next page*)

Table 19 (*continued*)

	Israel	3		Libya	30
	North Korea	94		US	102
	Libya	26		USSR	14
	Netherlands	5	1987	Afghanistan	<.5
	UK	140		China	544
	US	19		Czechoslovakia	43
1986	China	430		North Korea	100
	Czechoslovakia	43		Libya	14
	Israel	3	1988	China	400
	North Korea	47		Czechoslovakia	43
	South Korea	66		North Korea	113

Source: Estimates from SIPRI files; authors' files.
*Estimates in million US dollars.

on the black market or clandestinely shipped by states such as Israel. Iraq also tapped clandestine and "dual-use" (suitable for either civilian or military use) technologies in certain areas, such as production of missiles and poison gas. All in all, documents indicate that Iraq received military equipment exclusively from nineteen countries and Iran exclusively from sixteen countries, with twenty-eight countries on the list for both recipients (SIPRI, *Yearbook,* 1987, pp. 204–5). In many cases, these were illegal transactions. or transactions that bordered on illegality.

A number of governments were involved in clandestine arms transfers to the belligerents: the US supplied Hawk missile parts to Iran; North Korea supplied Scuds to both Iraq and Iran. Other governments, such as Germany, chose not to control the delivery of certain militarily useful goods, including ingredients for poison gas or helicopters, also used for civilian purposes (Brzoska, 1987).

While Iraq was favored with much larger and more stable wartime arms supply, the one difficult period for Baghdad was the early phase from 1980 to mid-1982. The main reason was a reluctance by the Soviet Union to support the Iraqi invasion. Indeed, immediately upon the invasion, Iraqi Foreign Minister Tariq Aziz flew to Moscow officially to brief the Soviet leadership, but probably also to talk about arms shipments as well. The Soviets, already estranged because of the treatment of Iraqi communists and Iraqi overtures to the West, were not impressed. They condemned the invasion, declared their neutrality, and halted arms deliveries, evidently even recalling some supply ships already en route (Saivetz, 1989a, pp. 35–41; Cordesman and Wagner, 1990a, p. 103).

Although some weapons and spare parts were delivered later in 1980 and during 1981, Moscow only began to sell weapons to Iraq on a large scale again in September 1982, when Baghdad was in turn defending its territory against Iranian counterthrusts (Saivetz, 1989a, pp. 40–41; Krause, 1985, pp. 164–68; Cordesman and Wagner, 1990a, p. 104). By that time, the Soviet leadership had begun to view Iraq's improved ties with the West as a threat to its influence. As we saw in the last chapter, Soviet worries that its Middle Eastern position was on the decline became acute during the 1982 Lebanon war. Clearly, Iraq's increasing ability to diversify its arms supply meant that any concerted opposition to its war effort by one power was weakened.

The Iranian political situation also was turning to Moscow's disadvantage. The communist Tudeh party, whose majority had supported the revolution and its initial radicalization, was losing power. It was finally outlawed in February 1983, and many of its members were imprisoned or exiled. Sometime in the summer of 1982, the Soviet leadership, still headed by Leonid Brezhnev, must have decided to set neutrality aside and back Iraq. It was only during Mikhail Gorbachev's subsequent policy of disentangling from Third World conflicts in 1985 that this stand began to change again and the Soviet Union tried to regain a more balanced position (Saivetz, 1989b).

Yet even during the cool period in Iraqi-Soviet relations, Iraqi armed forces were able to receive Soviet-type weapons and, possibly more important, ammunition and spare parts. Much of it came from socialist countries in Eastern Europe, such as East Germany (which delivered fifty T-55 tanks), Bulgaria (small arms and ammunition), Romania (ammunition), Poland (three-hundred T-55 tanks), Yugoslavia (ammunition, spare parts) and Czechoslovakia (ammunition, jet trainers, and spare parts) (Saivetz, 1989a, pp. 35–36). It is still unclear whether these deliveries were instigated by Moscow or whether they represented independent activities of East Bloc states interested in earning foreign exchange. Either way, they enabled Iraq to overcome the immediate effects of the Soviet arms boycott. In addition, Iraq was able to tap Third World sources, such as Egypt, China, Somalia, and North Yemen, for Soviet ammunition and spare parts. For these suppliers, the shipments were a badly needed source of foreign exchange and a chance to improve relations with the Arab League. Egypt especially enjoyed the opportunity to reenter the League after the period of alienation following the 1978 Camp David accords.[2]

Iraq's initial supply problems led Baghdad to intensify and diversify its search for logistical support. As noted, the French connection was strengthened with a number of new orders for aircraft, missiles, tanks, and electronic equipment. Government and industry officials in Paris were eager to sell as much as possible, even when Iraq was unable to pay directly (Timmerman, 1991; Kolodziej, 1989). In 1983, the French government even agreed to lease Iraq five of its own Super Etendard fighters when the firm Dassault was late in delivering Mirage F-1s.[3] These aircraft and Exocet antiship missiles were of great importance in Iraq's "tanker war." French-supplied weapons also enabled Baghdad to attack Iranian oil installations outside Khuzestan.

Among other important contributions to the Iraqi war effort were deliveries from Austria (howitzers), Brazil (armored vehicles, training aircraft), Chile (bombs, ammunition), China (fighter aircraft, ammunition), South Africa (howitzers, ammunition), Spain (helicopters, trucks, ammunition), Switzerland (training aircraft), and West Germany (tank transporters and helicopters), as well as satellite information from the US. Baghdad received substantial financial support (indeed, up to $50 billion, according to reliable estimates) from the conservative Arab Gulf states alarmed at the prospect of a victorious Iran. This aid tended to dry up, however, with declining oil revenues beginning in 1986 (Cordesman and Wagner, 1990a, p. 5; Neuman, 1988, p. 1048). The conservative Arab states, as well as Jordan, also sometimes bought weapons in their own name and later shipped them to Iraq.

Another long-term strategy to increase supply stability was the build-up of a domestic arms industry. When the war began, hardly any Iraqi production capability existed (Brzoska and Ohlson, 1986, p. 272). When the war ended, however, Iraqi factories were able to turn out ammunition, modifications of armored vehicles, missiles, and, most notoriously, large amounts of poison gas (*Jane's Defence Weekly*, 13 May 1989, pp. 836–37; *International Defense Review*, vol. 22, no. 6, 1989, pp. 835–44). Technical expertise came from a number of countries in the East and the West, with a preference shown for German suppliers and technicians (Leyendecker and Rickelmann, 1990; Koppe and Koch, 1990; Timmerman, 1991; Brzoska, 1991).

Iraq's diversification strategies took time to work. Deliveries began to come pouring in from about the fall of 1982, but it sometimes took as long as several months or years for the armed forces properly to integrate the newly available equipment. As noted, when new sources became plentiful, the Soviet Union also started to increase its deliveries again. Thus beginning in the second half of 1982, Baghdad enjoyed an oversupply of modern weaponry stimulated by various suppliers' interest in trade, in Iraq's and the Gulf's defense against Iran, or in superpower weapons competition in the region.

On the other side, Western supply embargoes of Iran largely were maintained (Cordesman, 1987c, pp. 25–26); for Teheran, weapon diversification proved difficult though ultimately also quite possible. During the war's initial two years, when weapons in the Iranian arsenal were predominantly Western-made, the main direct outside acquisitions were spare parts. Some were delivered from the US in a deal freeing the US embassy hostages; more came from Israel.[4] Other suppliers included Portugal, Greece, Spain, Singapore, and South Korea. Iran's major regional allies, Libya and, to a lesser extent, Syria, retransferred some equipment and spare parts originally supplied by Western countries. For instance, Iran's forces received more than 130 Brazilian armored cars via Libya (Brzoska and Ohlson, 1987, p. 188). After 1984, for combinations of economic and political reasons, limited US, British, and French supplies were to come in as well, despite lip service to the embargo.

The Iranians also procured Soviet military equipment during the embargo period, albeit on a low level. Reports of Soviet assistance (trucks, electronic equipment, and satellite information) differ; probably, some specific Soviet offers were refused (see Chubin, 1983b, p. 934; Saivetz, 1989a, p. 36; and Wilbur, 1990, p. 114). Syria and Libya, both major Soviet clients, did ship several hundred tanks, artillery pieces, and missiles to Iran (Cordesman and Wagner, 1990a, p. 104). It is another sign of Moscow's pro-Iranian tilt during the war's first two years that deliveries to these two Iranian allies were not curtailed. In fact, within two weeks of Iraq's initial attack, the Soviet Union signed a treaty of friendship and cooperation with Syria, Baghdad's regional arch rival. Additionally, even early in the war Chinese and North Korean weapon transfers to Iran were reported (Möller, 1988). Most of the Soviet-style equipment received from the outside or captured from Iraq was given to irregular forces, while Iran's regular forces continued to rely mainly on Western equipment.

The deteriorating Iranian supply situation improved somewhat, at least for a time, from about 1984. Chinese and North Korean deliveries increased markedly, and came to include aircraft, armored vehicles, missiles, and artillery pieces as well as ammunition (Gill, 1991, p. 37). In June 1985, Prime Minister Hashem Rafsanjani travelled to Beijing, reportedly clinching a major deal for F-6 fighter aircraft, T-59 tanks, and various types of artillery and missiles, including the soon-to-be notorious HY-2 Silkworm (Saivetz, 1989a, p. 56). The aircraft had little impact on the war, but the missiles, which were delivered starting in the summer of 1986 and became operational in February 1987, and artillery were of major importance (Cordesman and Wagner, 1990a, p. 274). North Korean deliveries, mostly after the mid-1980s, also comprised artillery and armor, plus missiles similar to the Soviet Scuds. These, plus similar equipment provided by Libya and Syria, enabled Iran to retaliate in kind against Iraqi missile attacks and, to some degree, to menace the Straits.[5]

Another improvement of the Iranian supply situation resulted from an opportunity to produce large amounts of ammunition, as well as certain weapon systems, domestically. Production of explosives and casings was increased early in the war when chemical precursors and components became abundantly available via Belgium, East Germany, and Yugoslavia, from a cartel of West European powder producers managed from Sweden.[6] Iran also came to modify Scud missiles and claimed to have embarked on aircraft production by the end of the war.

As indicated, the Iranians tapped the black and gray (illegal or semi-legal) arms markets in a number of countries. In addition to suppliers mentioned earlier, some new sources emerged: trucks and tank transporters from the FRG and Sweden; 13-meter Boghammer speed boats and RBS-70 laser guided antiaircraft missiles from Sweden; and training aircraft from Switzerland,[7]. The French company Luchaire sold ammunition, possibly with the connivance of some officials in the French Ministry of Defense (Brzoska, 1987; Cordesman, 1987c).

During this phase of improved Iranian logistics, the tangle of US-Israeli deliveries in the context of the "Iran-Contra" scandal also emerged. While investigations into this affair provided one of the few instances when exact information about Iranian arms supply became available, there is no agreement about its importance to the war effort. Some observers have argued that spare parts for Hawk air defense missiles were crucial in providing better air cover during Teheran's offensives of early 1986 and 1987.[8]

Improved supplies were only a temporary phenomenon. Indeed, public disclosure of US weapon deliveries to Iran had the counter effect of bolstering American and Western embargoes. "Operation Staunch" was revived with much more vigor. Iranian black- and gray-market buyers found fewer sellers after 1986 because of heightened public awareness of the problem and better government and customs enforcement. Spare parts for Western weapons became very scarce, and China came under Western pressure to review its arms-transfer policy (Gill, 1991, pp. 32–36). Western governments also tightened controls over dual-use goods. "Thus Iran's access to arms was being curtailed at precisely the moment when its strategy called for more resources and when existing stocks could no longer be raided to serve as improvised replacements" (Chubin, 1989, p. 6).

As indicated by the plethora of arms transfers during the war, the international community was hardly prepared either to condemn or counter Iraq for its military assault in 1980, nor to bring quick effective pressure for a halt to the fighting. Hostility towards the Iranian revolutionary regime was too deep and widespread. The first relevant UN Security Council resolution, 479, of September 28, 1980, simply called for a cease-fire in place (which would have benefitted Iraq; see Urquhart, 1988, pp. 508–9). Olof Palme, former Swedish prime minister, was named as the UN special envoy to mediate the crisis. Several other parties, such as the PLO, Algeria, the Islamic Conference Organization, the Arab League, and Soviet leader Leonid Brezhnev also tried at various times to mediate (Cordesman and Wagner, 1990a, p. 106).

Perhaps predictably, international efforts to stop the war increased somewhat in 1982, when Iran began to take the initiative. Iraq now was prepared to go back to the Algiers Accord and prewar boundaries. The Security Council adopted Resolution 514 on July 12, which, in contrast to Resolution 479, called for a cease-fire along recognized boundaries. Iran considered this a pro-Iraqi position, and for some years Teheran regarded the UN as hostile, making further peacemaking attempts difficult (Urquhart, 1988, pp. 512–14). The Iranian government announced extreme demands for a cessation of hostilities, including large reparations and the fall of the Saddam Hussein regime. The conservative Arab states, already financially involved on the side of Iraq, offered to pay several tens of billions of dollars to Iran in compensation (Alnasrawi, 1986). While this did not satisfy the Iranians, negotiations did not falter because of money but because of Iran's tenacious insistence on Hussein's downfall.

Between 1982 and late 1986, therefore, the focus of the UN debate turned to "side-issues," such as the attacks on civilian targets and tankers. The UN called for a halt to urban bombing on June 12, 1984. This was observed until March 1985 (Staudenmaier, 1985, p. 223; Urquhart, 1988, p. 509). Iran proposed another truce on ship attacks in the Gulf, which was rejected by Iraq, and Teheran continued trying, largely unsuccessfully, to make Iraq's use of poison gas an international issue. It was not until March 1984 that the UN agreed to investigate Iranian allegations. When the expert team reported that poison gas had been used on Iranian soldiers in violation of the Geneva Convention (which Iraq had ratified), the UN still did not agree to condemn Iraq until early 1986.

It took the revelation of the Iran-Contra affair and its widespread media impact to revive serious peacemaking efforts. An embarrassed Reagan administration, which had been caught playing both sides, became the most important proponent of a settlement. The USSR, wary of the festering war on its southern periphery and trying to improve its relations with the US on a number of issues, supported the initiative. The main stumbling block was China, whose leaders were unwilling to commit themselves to any strong sanctions (Gill, 1991). Negotiations in the UN and in bilateral talks among US envoys and individual governments concentrated on two issues: how to arrange for a cease-fire and an arms embargo. After more than six years of large-scale deliveries and booming black- and grey-markets, a consensus finally was developing in the West that arms suppliers and traders bore significant responsibility for political embarrassments as well as the mounting casualties.

On July 20, 1987, the UN Security Council unanimously adopted resolution 598, after long deliberations and intensive diplomatic activity by the US and the secretary general (Chubin, 1989; Wilbur, 1990). The resolution, after repeating earlier calls to stop the fighting and deploring the costs in monetary and human terms, demanded that Iraq and Iran observe an immediate cease-fire and authorize the secretary general to dispatch a UN observer team. The secretary general also was requested to assign an expert team to study the question of reconstruction.

Shaped by US proposals, the resolution generally was seen as favoring Iraq. Washington, now directly involved militarily by escorting tankers in the Gulf, failed in its effort to bolster the resolution with a UN enforced, or threatened, arms embargo. The Soviet Union rejected such sanctions in order not to lose leverage over the ceasefire negotiations. Moscow and other Security Council members had been in favor of a more pro-Iranian resolution, for instance, one acknowledging some of Teheran's claims. Behind this reasoning was a strong sense that at least portions of Iran's leadership had become weary of the war and might drop the demand for Saddam Hussein's demise in return for an international guarantee that questions of reparation and war guilt would be settled.

Initially, Resolution 598 had little effect. Iraq accepted it and Iran, without formally rejecting, complained that is was inadequate. The situation was further aggravated by several incidents involving Iranian and US ships in the Gulf in the fall of 1987. Still, the resolution and the discussions preceding it firmly engaged the UN Secretariat and Security Council members in peacemaking efforts (Urquhart, 1988, pp. 510–13). These continued throughout the winter and into 1988, even as the war on the ground and against civilian targets intensified.

In July 1988, in view of heightened foreign pressure, logistical and economic difficulties, battlefield setbacks, and US assistance to Iraq's cause, Iranian President Ali Khameini finally contacted Secretary General Perez de Cuellar requesting a cease-fire and accepting Resolution 598. As another tragic corollary so familiar in major wars, the Iranian leadership thereby accepted terms not much different from those offered in 1982, and, given the uncertainty of reparations from conservative Arab states, worse in financial terms (Chubin, 1989, pp. 5–14; Wilbur, 1990, pp. 119–24).

The war's internationalization, begun in 1987, had increased with several encounters between Western navies and Iranian forces. On the morning of July 3, 1988, the *USS Vincennes* shot down the commercial flight Iran Air 655 en route from Bandar Abbas to Dubai. At UN headquarters, the major powers in the Security Council, the US, the Soviet Union, and China, were hectically negotiating an arms embargo to enforce a resolution along the lines of 598. Even if it had been balanced rather than ostensibly aimed at Iran, such an embargo would have hurt Iranian logistics more, given the material advantage Iraq had accumulated earlier. Iran, in a deteriorating stalemate position, also was near the financial limit. Not only had the war effort, including arms imports, diminished foreign reserves, it had also progressively crippled the domestic economy.[9]

With the Iranian leadership wanting peace, the Iraqi leadership began to reconsider. In late July and early August, Saddam Hussein and his advisers seemed to hesitate about accepting a cease-fire along the original borders while Iraqi troops were on the offensive again. For a few weeks, Baghdad delayed as low-level fighting continued. But strong international pressure, from the US, the Soviet Union, the Arab states, and Western Europe, induced Saddam Hussein to go along with the cease-fire on August 6. A pure military calculation might have shown that the Iraqis could have gained additional territory by continuing the fight, but the same miscalculation had been made in 1980. It seemed also unlikely that the international community was prepared to sit still as it had done earlier. Iraq's major financiers and arms suppliers at least threatened that they would not be willing to support a renewed offensive.

The cease-fire held, although several of its terms, such as determining reconstruction costs and investigating war guilt, did not materialize. The United Nations Iraq-Iran Military Observer Group (UNIIMOG) was successful in keeping combatants apart, settling minor incidents, and promoting prisoner exchanges. In November 1990, following Iraq's invasion of Kuwait, a peace accord between the two countries was signed, formally ending the war.

CONCLUSIONS

Arms-transfer relationships, a key factor in prolonging the war, also were among several factors facilitating its end. For example, Israeli, Libyan, and US supplies to Iran in July 1981 were crucial in keeping Teheran in the war and ultimately lifting the siege of Abadan in September. On the other hand, by the end of the war the lack of adequate resupply had finally caught up with Iran. This problem was compounded by serious UN negotiations for an arms embargo from early 1987. Iran would have been without its major supplier if China had agreed to such a measure. If the embargo would have included effective enforcement measures, Iran's logistical position would rapidly have deteriorated. Similarly, while deliveries of sophisticated weaponry had helped Iraq overcome Iranian numerical advantages, pressure from its suppliers, especially France and the Soviet Union, as well as its financiers, such as Kuwait and Saudi Arabia, also helped secure Baghdad's agreement to a settlement on terms not fully reflecting existing battlefield advantages.

Looking back on the long and largely deadlocked expanse of the war, the Soviet arms boycott during the first two years contributed to Iraq's failure to hold conquered territory and thus to Iraq's tactical and strategic confusion. Subsequently, massive deliveries from the USSR and many other states allowed Iraq to hold its position during the long period of attrition, as well as to widen the scope of the war by attacking civilian targets, including ships in the Gulf. Without these deliveries, and the financing for them, Iraq's position would have been very difficult in view of repeated Iranian offensives. It is doubtful whether Iraq could have substituted manpower for firepower the way the Iranians did. Iran's difficulties in replenishing military arsenals were partly overcome through the adoption of such a tactical approach. But in the end, logistical as well as economic problems became decisive in shaping the decision to finish the war.

An important pattern emerged in this decade-long struggle (see chronology), namely the tendency for major arms shipments to follow rather than precede battlefield offensives. In a war of fast movement (as in the war's early phase) or of attrition, vast amounts of weaponry are expended whenever one side tries to break through for a crucial advantage, and this equipment then must be replaced. For example, Iraqi arms negotiations and acquisitions seemed to occur immediately following the initiation of major engagements, particularly in the early part of the war. Similar patterns were seen for Iran, especially later in the conflict as the Shah's prewar arms inventory deteriorated. Thus, arms replenishment in prolonged warfare tends to keep parties viable rather than inspiring them to new attacks, especially since it takes weeks or months for new arms shipments to become operationally effective.

Occasionally, though, specific arms deliveries set the stage for specific offensives or operations, and sometimes crucial equipment was pressed into service immediately upon receipt. Iraq's midwar acquisition of "smart bomb" and laser-guided missile technology from France, and Swedish deliveries of RBS-70 SAM systems to Iran both proved to be of almost immediate use. Iran's advance purchase of British and Dutch transport ships, delivered in June and October 1985, also was well timed for the Faw Peninsula offensive of February 1986.

One further notable and disturbing effect of conventional arms supply was noted. While supply difficulties ultimately helped choke off the war, at times during the fighting they may have contributed to atrocities. Massive orders for replacement arms generally could not be filled immediately, except in relatively small quantities from suppliers' own weapon stocks. Most major powers were unwilling to deplete their own readiness unless the situation were desperate. Thus, for example, while waiting for new deliveries and confronting severe manpower disadvantages, Baghdad devised such strategies as the use of chemical weapons to stem Iranian offensives (later for use against its own Kurdish population as well). Both sides also sought to improve their weapon-production capabilities, as in Teheran's technology-transfer demands in arms deals with China, leading to the production of an Iranian version of the Scud-B missile.

Without massive resupplies it seems that the war could have ended earlier; yet the war's halfhearted supply restrictions and delays also led to the resurgence of unconventional mass-destructive weaponry. Despite grandiose claims, neither of the two belligerents had domestic capabilities sufficient to supply their own forces, but they were able to produce certain horrific products, such as chemical weapons in the case of Iraq and modified missiles in the case of Iran, along with small arms and ammunition. The war could have ended even as early as 1981 had there been an effective embargo against Iraq, provided the terms would have sufficiently penalized Baghdad or compensated Teheran. It could have ended in 1982 or 1983 had the Iranian side not been able to receive substantial amounts of weaponry, spare parts, and components for its ammunition industry. Yet, remarkably little diplomatic activity in pursuit of an early settlement or cease-fire occurred, in stark contrast to earlier wars we have reviewed.

The war's endgame ultimately demonstrated that the belligerents were not invulnerable to focused outside leverage—by arms suppliers in the case of Iraq and through threatened embargo in the case of Iran. But the diversity and complexity of the arms-supply network, which was the most significant international aspect of the Iraq-Iran war, also meant that such vulnerability was limited and effective only in conjunction with battlefield setbacks, economic dislocation or sanctions, and exhaustion. For most of the war the parties were able to find new arms suppliers and routes to receive spare parts and ammunition compatible with equipment already on hand.

On the whole, efforts to stop arms deliveries to the belligerents were much less effective than major-power political leaders tried to make the world believe. Indeed, one suspects a desire on the part of the superpowers to preserve the Iran-Iraq stalemate and continued heavy attrition in order to weaken and preoccupy both sides. Both Soviet and US leaders appeared to encourage proxy suppliers, sometimes to both sides simultaneously. The Soviet boycott of Iraq in 1980–82 was leaky, and unaccompanied by pressures on Soviet allies to follow suit. The US, as the main proponent of a ban on deliveries to Iran, also followed an incoherent policy, ostensibly pressing allies for restraint while making side deals of its own. Israeli and French deliveries of US equipment and parts to Iran, and the Iran-Contra affair were the most visible indicators of Washington's duplicity. Interested in making sure that neither side won the war, the major powers failed to use their available influence for an early settlement, for instance, through arms-sales restrictions on Iraq or oil-import bans on both sides.

Other states adopted similar policies; indeed it was in the interest of wealthy conservative Arab Gulf states to keep both revolutionary Iran and secular socialist Ba'athist Iraq at bay. Thus, both sides, but especially the Iraqis, were allowed to run up huge debts in trying to pay for imported weaponry. Despite the mounting debt load, credits continued to be offered, sometimes even by the arms suppliers themselves. France was particularly willing to guarantee Iraqi supplies in order to assure Baghdad's survival and ultimate ability to repay the debts already owed. The end result was a war well financed by oil money and fuelled with weapons, which cost lives and property throughout the Gulf and filled the coffers of arms producers and dealers worldwide while setting the stage for the subsequent rape of Kuwait and Gulf war of 1990–91.

In addition, the Iran-Iraq war demonstrated that the international arms market of the 1980s was different from the market of prior decades. A multitude of suppliers and commercial interests gained in importance. On the whole, the situation seemed comparable to the 1920s, when political considerations had only limited influence on arms flows.

Political concerns increased, though, in 1986, as the threat to tankers turned into a serious nuisance. Worries of dangerous potential escalation increased with the war's internationalization. Improved East-West relations made it possible in Moscow and Washington, as well as Tokyo, London, Bonn, and Paris, to think beyond zero-sum game solutions. And the inconsistency between public pronouncements and actual export policies did not go unnoticed in a number of countries. Arms-export policies were more frequently discussed and debated, and as a result export laws were changed, for instance in Sweden, Italy, and Belgium (Anthony, 1991). The Iran-Contra scandal provided further such impetus in Washington, so that effective international action for peacemaking finally began late in 1987.

With these sobering conclusions from the first of our "long wars," we turn now to Africa, the scene of others in the strange series of seemingly endless international conflicts that characterized much of the 1980s—until Mikhail Gorbachev's post–cold war initiatives. We will find perhaps greater major-power investments in choosing sides in the African wars, but an equally telling set of arms-transfer effects.

CHAPTER 10

THE WAR IN THE WESTERN SAHARA, 1976–91

INTRODUCTION: THE BACKGROUND OF WAR

With the end of Portuguese colonialism, the Spanish Sahara, a strip of desert between Morocco and Mauritania on the Atlantic Coast, became the last sizeable European colony in Africa. In 1974, when the Spanish government decided to end colonial status, a bitter international dispute arose over the territory's future; the dispute was heightened by the presence of valuable phosphate deposits in this otherwise largely barren land. A mainly indigenous political group, the "Frente Popular para la Liberación de la Saghia el Hambra y del Rio de Oro" (Polisario), which had waged an ongoing insurgency against Spanish forces, claimed the territory, but so did neighboring Morocco and Mauritania. Morocco considered the northern sectors (about two-thirds) of the Western Sahara, where the phosphates were situated, to be a part of precolonial "Greater Morocco," but was prepared to cede the largely unoccupied southern third to Mauritania.

The Spanish government and the UN General Assembly put the case before the International Court of Justice at the Hague, which decided that the population of the former colony, the Sahrawis, should determine its future by referendum. However, the Moroccan government, led by King Hassan II, ignored this decision and moved to "establish facts" of occupation as fast as possible. In October 1975, as an expression of Moroccan claims on the territory, the king announced the organization of the "Green March," a trek into the Sahara by several-hundred-thousand Moroccans. By early November some 350,000 marchers, including about 35,000 troops, were on the move south. Morocco's almost universal public joy over the announced annexation would help the monarch overcome internal unrest in scenes quite similar to those to be seen in Argentina seven years later (see chapter 7).

Still officially in charge of the territory but interested in getting rid of it without further entanglement, Spain gave in to Moroccan pressure. Instead of enforcing the International Court's decision, it agreed in the Madrid Accord, signed on November 14, 1975, to hand sovereignty over to Morocco and Mauritania by the end of February 1976 (Dougherty, 1980, pp. 96–100). Civilian "Green Marchers" were called home, and Moroccan troops began to infiltrate the territory and to man military posts left by Spanish troops. As agreed, all Spanish forces and officials vacated the former colony before March 1. Polisario responded by stepping up its military activities, as large segments of the Sahrawi population fled over the border into Algeria.

Algerian leadership under President Houari Boumedienne was disturbed about this turn of events. They were opposed to the extension of Mauritanian and, especially, Moroccan territory and power (fears of a "Greater Morocco" movement had lingered since the Algerian-Moroccan war of 1963). A Sahrawi state friendly to Algeria might make it easier to transport Algerian natural resources to the Atlantic Coast. Algeria also was closer to the "radical" Arab camp, while Morocco was an important conservative state. Until the late 1980s, this conflict badly polarized the North African region.

During this initial phase of the war, Morocco (and, to a lesser degree, Mauritania) easily had the upper hand. But between 1977 and 1981, Polisario, utilizing neighboring sanctuaries and assistance, conducted a number of very successful military operations, ultimately knocking Mauritania out of the war. From 1981, with considerable foreign assistance, Morocco was able slowly to regain the advantage, and beginning about 1985 a stalemate quite advantageous to Rabat set in, with only sporadic further military activity. Diplomatic activity, ongoing from the beginning of the war, finally culminated in an agreement in 1991 calling for an armistice and a UN supervised referendum.

At least in the 1970s, changes in the military situation were closely related to arms transfers. The early Moroccan successes depended on large quantities of modern military equipment supplied mostly by France, the US, and Spain. Morocco increasingly played up its stance as an Arab League moderate useful to the major powers in stabilizing Middle Eastern, and particularly Arab-Israeli, politics. Polisario's counteroffensives were fuelled by relatively abundant arms deliveries and ammunition from Algeria and Libya. However, the link between arms and war success was weakened from about 1980 as a result of a radical US-inspired change in Moroccan tactics. Sand walls were built around the major economic centers of the Western Sahara with outposts along the wall connected by modern communication devices.

In the late 1970s, both sides' great reliance on imported weaponry should have afforded suppliers a good opportunity to manipulate the warring parties. At least in one supplying country, the US, the link between arms transfers and war was intensely debated. The question of whether to supply Morocco became a test case for the Carter administration's professed determination to limit foreign arms transfers. Other suppliers also became uneasy with supporting Morocco. In parallel, first Libyan and then Algerian support for Polisario eventually was reduced under diplomatic inducements and pressure. While, in the early 1980s, Morocco was winning the military war, Polisario was winning the diplomatic war. More and more countries, and from 1982 the Organization of African Unity (OAU), recognized the Democratic Republic of Sahara (SADR).

In the end it was both parties' exhaustion that opened the way for a negotiated settlement. What about the role of arms transfers as instruments in ending the conflict? For example, were those in Washington during the Carter administration correct in arguing that a ban on deliveries would force Morocco to the negotiating table? Or were their opponents correct in noting that Morocco would only negotiate from a position of strength? How much influence was exercised through US arms or those of other suppliers? Was Polisario strategy effectively controlled by its patrons (or its patrons' patron, i.e., the USSR which supplied both Algeria and Libya)? The relationship between fighting, arms transfers, and diplomacy became an issue both for participants and outsiders.[1]

ARMAMENT AND THE APPROACH OF WAR

Morocco's armed forces were supplied with weaponry from many sources after independence in 1956, including the US, France, Italy, and the Soviet Union, with which King Hassan II had established cordial relations in the early 1960s. However, armament levels remained fairly low; in the late 1960s and early 1970s, most equipment came from the US, often in the form of military aid (SIPRI, 1971, pp. 591–94). Morocco hosted a number of strategic bases and was, after Ethiopia, the second-largest American military aid recipient in Africa between the 1950s and the mid-1970s. However, as Table 20 shows, Morocco had not conspicuously prepared for a major military campaign as 1975 approached; indeed, the Saharan war followed far less prewar arms buildup than did the other wars we have reviewed.

Table 20

Arms Shipments to Morocco, 1972–74

Canada	Five C-119 Packet transports (secondhand)
France	1 Sirius Class mine sweeper and coastal patrol boat
Italy	12 AB-205 Helicopters; six C-119 Packet transports (secondhand)
US	25 M-48 Patton tanks; 6 King Air A-100 transports; six C-130 H Hercules transports

Source: Estimates from SIPRI files; authors' files. Major weapons.

In the early 1970s, a reorganization and modernization of the armed forces had gotten underway, with the cost of modern-weapon imports eased by the increase in world-oil and natural-resource prices, including phosphate ore found in large quantities in Morocco. In late 1973, a group of Pentagon planners came to assist in the establishment of two armored brigades equipped with M-60 tanks and supported by AH-1 antitank helicopters (Clément, 1986, pp. 92–93; Hodges, 1983, p. 356). French companies were approached to deliver artillery and aircraft, and a deal struck in early 1975 called for delivery of twenty-four Mirage F-1s and an option on fifty more at a cost of 1.4-billion French francs (Clément, 1986, p. 93). When the war began, the Moroccan armed forces were just beginning to introduce this advanced equipment, which was of substantially greater technical complexity than the material received earlier.

Thus, while Morocco's improving armed forces numbered about sixty thousand at the time of the "Green March" (with Mauritania fielding six-thousand more, equipped with outdated Soviet and French equipment), Polisario's two-thousand-man guerrilla force remained poorly equipped with small arms, mortars, radios, and about twenty trucks, mostly captured from the Spanish (Dougherty, 1980, pp. 110–11; Clément, 1986, p. 95). In early November 1975 they received their first substantial outside support, light arms from Algeria, including Soviet rifles, French mortars, and Chinese mines (Clément, 1986, p. 96). Algeria's armed forces were in a good position to provide armaments since they had earlier received large consignments mostly from the USSR and other socialist bloc states.

THE COURSE OF THE WAR

Despite some Polisario armed opposition, Moroccan and Mauritanian troops had little initial difficulty occupying large parts of the territory still nominally under Spanish authority. Polisario guerrillas, although growing fast in strength and numbering about five thousand by the end of 1975 (Seddon, 1988, p. 100; Clément 1986, pp. 96–97), were not equipped to counter Moroccan tank columns and fighter aircraft.

When Morocco tried to eliminate the resistance early in 1976, the conflict nearly escalated into a full-fledged regional war. Moroccan F-5 aircraft, reportedly using napalm, repeatedly bombed Polisario and refugee camps inside Algeria officially in pursuit of guerrillas. Polisario was given a Soviet supplied SAM-6 antiaircraft battery, manned with Algerian personnel (Clément, 1986, p. 97), and shot down a number of Moroccan planes. In battles near Amgala on January 27 and February 14, Algerian forces participated in the fighting, and Libya offered its support to Algeria (Clément, 1986, p. 98). But Algiers was hesitant to widen the war, and instead of further direct intervention limited its involvement to logistical support and arms transfers.

Those who assumed that the war was over in the spring of 1976, including King Hassan II, were mistaken. In the course of that year Polisario began to take the initiative against the weaker foe, Mauritania. Utilizing fast cross-country vehicles armed with guns or short-range missiles, Polisario undertook long-range incursions from Algerian territory. In June, the Mauritanian capital Nouakchott was attacked, and though Polisario lost a large number of vehicles and about 450 men (Seddon, 1988, p. 101), it demonstrated the weakness of the Mauritanian defenses.[2]

The Mauritanian government requested Moroccan and French assistance; along with six-thousand additional Moroccan troops, the French garrison in Senegal was strengthened, and in late 1977 and early 1978 French Jaguar jet fighters attacked Polisario columns in Mauritania. This outside support had little effect. Finally, during the night of July 9–10, 1978, the armed forces seized power in Nouakchott and announced an end to the fighting with Polisario. A formal separate peace accord was signed thirteen months later. Moroccan troops were withdrawn from Mauritania and instead occupied Saharan territory nearby.

However, this deployment stretched Moroccan forces thinly over a large region. In addition, it boosted Polisario's case in the eyes of the Algerian government, which increased its support. Polisario troops, now operating in larger bands, assembled and disassembled quickly in the desert to concentrate attacks on bases and settlements, both in the Western Sahara and in Southern Morocco. While often sustaining heavy losses, they inflicted painful Moroccan casualties in turn. The possession of SAM-7 missiles from early 1978 (Seddon, 1988, p. 103) enabled Polisario to shoot down a number of modern F-5s and Mirage F-1s in addition to older aircraft. These setbacks, plus lack of military intelligence and difficulty in using its air superiority, induced Moroccan commanders to give up a number of small bases and to concentrate troops in the larger settlements and areas of economic importance.

The war entered its most intense and bloody phase during late 1979 and 1980. Polisario controlled large stretches of territory and increasingly employed heavier armament, such as tanks. The Moroccans attempted to counter with superior firepower (see Table 21). Moroccan tanks usually outgunned Polisario's older captured or Algerian-Libyan supplied armor.[3] Morocco could field advanced Austrian Kürassier, French AMX-13, and South African Ratel tanks, in addition to its older Soviet T-54s and American M-48 Pattons.

Table 21

Arms Shipments to Morocco, 1975–91

1975	US	12 Beech T-34C Turbo-Mentor Training aircraft
	France	25 Mirage F-1 Fighter Aircraft ordered in December
1976	France	Deliveries of 40 SA-330 Puma and SA-342 Gazelle helicopters; 6 SA-342L Gazelle helicopters
	Jordan	36 106mm recoilless guns transferred on Mar. 26; 20 F-5A Fighter aircraft transferred on May 13; 6 F-5A transferred on May 21; 16 155mm mortars transferred on Oct. 12.
	Switzerland	4 AS-202/18 Bravo Training aircraft sold in early 1976.

(*continued on next page*)

166   Arms and Warfare

Table 21 (*continued*)

Year	Country	Details
	US	9 C-130 Hercules Transport aircraft ordered late 1976; delivery to start early in 1977; about 100 tanks; AAMs, ATMs, trucks, troop carriers delivered; sale of 24 F-5E and F-5F in Feb.; 20 Rockwell T-2D advanced trainers delivered in Sep.
1977	France	Sale of 24 Alpha Jet advanced trainers and light strike aircraft
	US	Negotiations over air-defence radar and control system. (Cost: $200m); Sidewinder AAMs ordered to arm F-5s; 6 C-130 Hercules delivered early 1977
	Switzerland	10 AS-202/18 Bravo delivered in December
1978	France	Crotale AAM-batteries delivered; additional batch of 50 Mirage F-1 jet fighters ordered
	Israel	240 RAM V-1 armoured vehicles delivered between 1978 and 1980
	Italy	6 CH-47C Chinook helicopters ordered for delivery in 1980
	South Africa	Several dozens of Ratel and Eland APC delivered 1978–80
	US	Order of 24 OV-10A Bronco, 24 Bell Huey Cobra helicopters from Jan. deferred for an indefinite period
1979	France	First 10 Mirage F-1s delivered
	FRG	Sale of 2 DO 28D-2 Skyservant light aircraft
	US	Ammunition for F-5s, spare parts for F-5s and C-130 Hercules delivered in Mar.; 70 M-113 Vulcan, 40 M-163 Vulcan air-defence guns ordered; sale of "integrated intrusion detection system" from Northrop Page Communications approved by State Department in March; 2 Super King Air 200 Beechcraft delivered in September; sale of 20 F-5E/F Fighters to replace Northrop F-5As and F-5Bs; 24 Hughes 500MD defender helicopters; deliveries of 6 OV-10A Bronco aircraft
1980	France	108 AMX 10 Reconnaissance Cars ordered (delivered between 1982 and 1988)
	Italy	Sale of 19 AB-206 Jet Ranger, 5 AB-212 and 6 additional CH-47 helicopters
	Spain	Sale of 1 frigate and 4 patrol boats
1981	Italy	5 CH-47C Chinook, 5 AB-212 helicopters, 19 Jet Ranger 206B helicopters ordered
	France	24 Gazelle helicopters delivered in Mar.
	US	OV-10A Bronco arrive in Morocco between Jan. and Mar.; F-5E/Fs in July and Aug.; Sales of 108 M-60-A3 tanks in Mar. and 7 C-130 Hercules transport aircraft in June
1982	France	Suspension of all deliveries because of $1bn plus arms debts of Morocco to France.
	US	Air-defence radar and control system in operation by Sept.; 252 cluster bombs delivered
1983	France	Deliveries of 24 SA-342L Gazelle helicopters completed

1984	Egypt	Sakr-30 122mm Multiple Rocket Launchers (about 50 delivered between 1984 and 1988)
	South Africa	About 80 Ratel-20 APC delivered
	Spain	Armoured fighting vehicles, mortars, ammunition delivered
	US	1 King Air 200 Super King Air transport aircraft delivered
1985	Austria	Proposed sale of additional Cuirassier tanks to Morocco not licensed
	Spain	Contract for 3 patrol boats signed on Oct. 2
1986	Spain	Military vehicles, electronic equipment and ammunition delivered
	US	Discussions of sale of F-16 fighters between King Hassan and Secretary of Defense Weinberger in early Dec.
1987	France	Negotiations about sale of 24 Mirage 2000 fighters; HOT-2 anti-tank missiles ordered (delivered between 1988 and 1990)
	US	100 M-48-A5 Patton tanks ordered, delivery 1988–89
1988	Denmark	2 Osprey Class Offshore Patrol Vessels delivered
	France	Atlas Commando Scout Cars with HOT ATM delivered
1989	Denmark	2 additional Osprey Class Offshore Patrol Vessels delivered
	Spain	Sales of 6 Lazaga Class Patrol Craft; 7 CN-235 transport aircraft
	US	2 F-5E Tiger fighter delivered
1990	France	28 AMX-10R Scout Cars ordered
1991	US	20 F-16A fighter ordered

Source: Estimates from SIPRI files; authors' files. Major weapons.

The war took a new turn in late August 1980 when Moroccan forces began to extend local fortifications into the first of a number of "walls." The first of these was designed to shield against attacks in Morocco from neighboring Algeria. Soon the barrier was extended to the south, including the settlements of Smara and the phosphate mines at Bou-Craa and back westward to the coast, enclosing the Western Sahara's resource-rich "useful triangle." This wall, finished in May 1982, consisted of sandbanks, mines, regularly staged observation posts, and artillery positions. Electronic devices were interlinked to monitor all crossings over the wall and mobile forces were available for pursuit. Although Polisario frequently disturbed the construction and sometimes got inside the wall, these attacks proved unacceptably costly in terms of equipment and personnel. Gradually, Moroccan troops built several more such fortifications, so that by 1986 about two-thirds of the territory was enclosed. Though Polisario was free to roam outside the walls, by the mid-1980s military activity had diminished, until the summer of 1991, when Moroccan forces tried, largely unsuccessfully, to destroy Polisario positions outside the walls as well. (See Appendix, Chronology 8, "The War in the Western Sahara, 1975–91.")

DIPLOMATIC PRESSURE AND ARMS FLOW

Morocco's 1975–76 West Saharan offensive did little damage to its diplomatic and arms-supply relations. Though it violated the tenor of the International Court's rulings concerning the territory, few states were prepared to challenge Morocco (and Mauritania) openly, especially after the Spanish government agreed to the partition. Although Algeria, Libya, and other "radical" Arab regimes were strongly opposed, their largest arms supplier, the Soviet Union, was reluctant to offend an old friend, Morocco's King Hassan. The UN Security Council appealed to all parties for utmost restraint, and the General Assembly adopted two contradictory resolutions, one effectively supporting Morocco, and the other proclaiming the Sahwaris' right to self-determination (Moynihan, 1979, p. 247).

Morocco's main arms suppliers, the US and France, officially declared neutrality but in practice upheld Rabat with large arms deliveries. In December 1975, the Ford administration informed Congress of its intent to sell equipment and ammunition, including 24 F-5E aircraft, to Morocco. However, the deal did not go through because the Moroccan Air Force preferred longer-range French F-1s. The F-1 purchase was only one of a number concluded with French suppliers. A major reason for Franco-American support was that in Paris and Washington few observers conceived of Polisario as a legitimate or viable force. Algeria was a different issue, but both the French and Americans hoped that a strong Moroccan army would help deter Algiers from entering the war. As reported, Algeria did refrain from escalation, but Polisario proved to be a quite formidable enemy in its own right.

It was first in the US, and especially with the change of administrations in 1977, that doubts about material support of Morocco set in. From early in the war there were reports that US weapons were used in the Western Sahara in violation of a 1960 agreement. In congressional hearings, commencing in October 1977, administration officials initially tried to play down the issue (Hodges, 1985, p. 266; Kamil, 1987, pp. 27–29). In a letter to President Jimmy Carter on February 8, 1978, Senator Dick Clark, chair of the Sub-Committee on

Africa, wrote that arms deliveries in support of a questionable claim risked "escalating the war far beyond the local conflict it is at the moment, possibly triggering a greater Soviet response in support of Algeria" (quoted in Hodges, 1985, p. 266; see also United States Congress, 1980). Increasing congressional pressure pushed President Carter to order a ban on ammunition and weapons deliveries. A planned sale of twenty-four OV-10 Broncos, low-flying aircraft developed specifically for counterinsurgency purposes, and twenty-four Cobra helicopters was cancelled, and Morocco was officially told not to use its F-5s over West Saharan territory. The embargo was not complete, however, as spare parts for the F-5s, which continued to fly missions over the disputed terrain, as well as six Chinook CH-47 helicopters, were not included. In May 1979, the State Department approved the export of a highly sophisticated tactical electronic battlefield system, Northrop Page's Intrusion Detection and Communication System, valued at $200 million, which was later installed along the wall (United States Congress, 1980, 1981a, 1983).

After these conflicting decisions, the National Security Council was ordered to rationalize and streamline policy. Three options were presented on October 16, 1979: to provide Morocco with weapons to win the Saharan war (favored by the Defense Department, the Joint Chiefs, and National Security Advisor Zbigniew Brzezinski);[4] to increase deliveries but continue the existing policy of supplying only equipment not deemed especially useful in the war (favored by Secretary of State Cyrus Vance); and to continue the official partial embargo, an option not favored by any participant. Sensitive to charges of weakness on Iran and Central America, and shocked by the Soviet invasion of Afghanistan, President Carter adopted option one, deciding to allow the sale of helicopters and counterinsurgency aircraft, which he had stopped in 1978. He also decided not to insist on the strict enforcement of customary clauses in US military-aid agreements barring use of weapons for nondefensive purposes outside the recipient's territory. National Security Advisor Brzezinski and Under Secretary of State Warren Christopher were sent to Morocco and Algeria to explain the new US policy.

An official announcement about the delivery of weapons worth $232.5 million was made on January 24, 1980. In the words of Assistant Secretary of State Harold Saunders, the package, containing twelve helicopters, twenty F-5E fighters, and six Bronco OV-10 aircraft, was designed not to bring about a change in the military situation but to safeguard the throne of King Hassan II, "an avowed friend and supporter" of the US (Hodges, 1980, p. 42). The arms, paid for by Saudi Arabia, were a "political signal" to the parties concerned, especially Algeria. They also reflected the Moroccan stand on a number of issues considered more important in Washington than the Western Sahara, such as base rights for the US Sixth fleet, support for the newly developed US Rapid Deployment Force, assistance in the Camp David peace process, and material help in propping up pro-Western regimes in Africa (Brzezinski, 1983, p. 447).[5]

Not unexpectedly, there was strong congressional opposition, especially to the revocation of the 1960 agreement. In both Senate Foreign Relations Committee and House Foreign Affairs Committee hearings, negative views on the proposed sales were dominant. Opponents, such as Chairman of the House Subcommittee on Africa Stephen Solarz and UN Ambassador Andrew Young, argued that the costs of war were a greater threat to Hassan II's throne than Polisario, and that his refusal to negotiate was actually strengthened by unconditional deliveries (United States Congress, 1980; Solarz, 1980; Wright, 1983b; Hodges, 1985, p. 367). In an effort to find some middle ground, Representatives Clement Zablocki and Solarz wrote President Carter, suggesting that the weapons should be delivered under the condition that King Hassan "demonstrate good faith efforts to reach a negotiated settlement solution in the Western Sahara" (Kamil, 1987, p. 54). Assistant Secretary Saunders, leading administration efforts in Congress, countered with the argument than King Hassan could not be forced to negotiate and that it made more sense to support than to punish him (Hodges, 1980, p. 47).

Shortly after taking office, Ronald Reagan moved to further increase support for Morocco. Secretary of State Alexander Haig quickly proposed the sale of 108 M-60 A-3 tanks. Numerous US officials, including Special Ambassador Vernon Walters and Secretary Haig himself, visited Morocco in 1981–82. A joint military commission was created to discuss base rights and military-aid issues. US advisers arrived to train Moroccan personnel in the use of US weaponry, and in November 1982 the first of a number of joint exercises were held (Hodges, 1985, pp. 268–69). During all this time, Washington was officially neutral on the question of self-determination for the Sahara, supporting UN resolutions calling for negotiations but voting against condemnations of Morocco. Some mild diplomatic pressure was applied to Hassan, but he was shrewd enough to make his strategic support and friendship more important to Washington than his compliance.

France, both cooperating and in some sense competing with the US for North African influence, also supplied large weapons shipments to Morocco in the war's first years despite an officially neutral position. In addition to the Mirage F-1s, in early 1976 Paris agreed to deliver helicopters, Stentor radars, Panhard and SAVIEM armored cars, AMX-30 tanks, and other items worth nearly 3.5-million francs, again paid for by the Saudis (Clément, 1986, p. 103). Code-named Marrakech, deliveries were made an urgent priority, and continued on a high level throughout 1976 and 1977.

As noted, Paris's anti-Polisario involvement peaked in December 1977 with the direct intervention of French Jaguar jets. After the Mauritanian capitulation and an improvement in political relations with Algeria in 1978, however, the French government, headed by Valéry Giscard d'Estaing, adopted a lower profile. This did not preclude further weapon deliveries, including Mirages and Alpha Jet fighters that had been ordered earlier. But deliveries were scaled back (see Chronology and Table 21), and Paris downplayed its diplomatic efforts on behalf of Rabat in francophone Africa.

The government of François Mitterand, which came to power in 1981, and like the Carter Administration initially looked into limiting the arms trade, took further steps to improve relations with Algeria and Polisario. While it pledged to honor all previous Moroccan arms contracts, it refused to authorize new deals in 1981 and 1982 (Hodges, 1983, pp. 348–50). This was justified by Morocco's failure to pay promptly, but was also widely understood as a political signal of preference for Algeria. Beginning in 1983, new sales again were authorized, but Morocco ordered very little new French equipment. Clearly, then, on the whole France was hardly prepared to press Rabat to negotiate with Polisario. While good relations with Algiers were in the French government's interest, support for King Hassan was valued at least partly because of his government's large standing debts to France. Nevertheless, Paris's reduced role beginning in the late 1970s helped Polisario to build a following among some French-oriented African states.

Avowedly another neutral on the Saharan issue, Madrid also continued and even increased arms deliveries to Rabat, mainly including warships, but also small-caliber artillery, ammunition, and trucks during 1976 and 1977 (Clément, 1986, p. 104). This contradictory position caused trouble from various quarters: the left parties in Spain opposed it on principle; Algeria applied pressure by supporting anti-Spanish groups in the Canary Islands and discriminating against Spanish exports to Algeria; and armed Polisario groups began to raid fishing boats off the West-Saharan coast, holding some fishermen hostage. On December 14, 1977, the conservative Spanish Minister of Foreign Affairs, Marcelino Oreja, announced a halt in arms shipments to Morocco and Mauritania (Hodges, 1983, p. 352). As with US and French restraints, though, this was partially lifted the following summer; nevertheless, Spanish deliveries remained at a low level until 1982.

Ironically, it was under the Socialist government of Felipe Gonzáles, who had earlier attacked the Spanish deliveries to Morocco, that arms sales again increased. Soon after coming to power in October 1982, he declared a desire to "create a relationship of confidence" (Hodges, 1983, p. 354) with Morocco, which included the increased arms transfers. Indeed, beginning 1983 Spain became Rabat's most important arms supplier.

In the end, then, traditionally important suppliers, though with some intermittent slowdowns and despite lip service to arms restraint, filled the bulk of Morocco's weapons needs. In addition, Rabat approached a number of other potential sources, reportedly obtaining small arms, ammunition, and spare parts from Iran, Taiwan, Egypt, Romania, and South Korea; secondhand US planes from Jordan (Clément, 1986, pp. 103–5; Kamil, 1987, p. 31); and six CH-47C large transport helicopters, produced under US license, from Italy. For some of this equipment US approval was needed and obtained, even during the period of Washington's own sales restrictions. In fact, the extent of third-party deliveries was used by pro-Moroccan lobbyists as an argument for renewing direct American deliveries (Kamil, 1987, p. 32).

Though not as extensively as in the Persian Gulf (see chapter 9) war, material also was delivered by an array of other countries, including West Germany (small planes), Austria (tanks), and Belgium (trucks and others vehicles, small arms, ammunition). From Egypt came Soviet-type weapons, such as 23-mm antiaircraft guns and SAM-7s, some secondhand and some newly produced on license. South Africa also delivered a few dozen Eland and Ratel armored personnel carriers between 1978 and 1980.

This long list shows that Moroccan buyers flashing Saudi funds could tap a broad supply network. By the same token, it was the gradual reduction of Arab financial support that greatly reduced the size and number of Moroccan orders for new weaponry after 1979. Oil prices began to decline, and fear of a Moroccan-Algerian war for supremacy in the Maghreb had subsided. The Arab Gulf states turned attention and checkbooks to other trouble spots, such as Afghanistan and the Iraq-Iran war. Morocco, already under strong economic pressure because of war costs and debts, could hardly increase the burden by financing further large weapon purchases. US military aid programs and Spanish supplies on credit came to form the backbone of Moroccan fighting capabilities.

While a good deal is known, then, about arms deliveries to Morocco, there is little detailed information about Polisario's wartime supplies. As with many guerrilla forces, a primary arms source were the garrisons and warehouses of their opponents. As just one example, when the base at Lebouirate in Southern Morocco was taken in 1980, Polisario reportedly captured fifty-four ex-Soviet T-54 tanks.

Certainly Polisario's most consistent foreign support came from Algeria. Small arms, ammunition, mortars, Land Rovers, and some surface-to-air missile (SAMs) were available from Algerian stocks to Polisario from late 1975 to the late 1980s. Excepting SAMs, however, the Algerians did not provide their latest Soviet weaponry. They hoped that a limited guerrilla war would, along with high costs, constitute enough of a security nuisance in the south to bring the Moroccans to the negotiating table.

After about 1980, though, the new Algerian leadership under President Chadli Benjedid seems to have reduced deliveries of weapons and ammunition, fearing a regional war that most likely would have become the focus of East-West contention, especially in the wake of Iranian and Afghani developments. The Algerian government also tried to assuage Western European concerns over the war as it attempted to sell large quantities of oil products and natural gas to EC consumers (Dougherty, 1980, pp. 108–110). Algeria was quite content with diplomatic success in winning international recognition for SADR, and with its new positive Western image as a mediator and go-between during the Iran hostage negotiations. Finally, later in the decade, the prospect of a Maghreb economic union among the five North African states overshadowed the benefits of Western Saharan liberation.

Polisario's other important supplier was Libya. While low-level deliveries began in 1976, the most important phase of Libyan support was between early 1979 and mid-1980. With Algerian connivance, a number of heavy trucks ferried weapons and ammunition on a road dubbed "piste Khaddafi" through the desert to the Sahwari camps in Algeria. Among useful items received were Toyota Land Cruisers, new Land Rovers, ex-Soviet Multiple Rocket Launchers, some SAM-9s, a large number of SAM-7s, some Soviet 23-mm antiaircraft guns, as well as armored vehicles of Brazilian, Soviet, and Czech origin (Clément, 1986, pp. 116–17). During this phase of abundant deliveries, Polisario forces changed their strategy, moving from what was internally termed the "Vietnamese period" to the "Cuban period," trying to win the war with conventional engagements (Hodges, 1980, p. 42; Clément, 1986, p. 116).

From about mid-1980, Algeria began to interfere in the flow of weapons from Libya. The details of the Algerian-Libyan relationship during this time remain to be clarified, but the most likely explanations include Algeria's fear of international war escalation and resentment over Libyan adventurism in other African countries, such as Mali and Chad. In early 1982, Libyan arms deliveries ceased totally (Clément, 1986, p. 128), as Morocco and Libya surprisingly developed more cordial diplomatic relations, culminating in the August 1984 declaration of intent to unify the two states (the Treaty of Oujda).[6]

It is not clear to what extent the Soviet Union authorized or planned any of the deliveries to Polisario.[7] Obviously, most of Polisario's weapons were of Soviet origin, but Moscow considered both Algeria and Libya rich enough to pay for deliveries and may not have insisted on clearing the retransfers.[8] The Soviet Union had good reason not to be caught red-handed supplying Polisario in light of its good economic and political relations with Morocco. In 1978, a multi-billion dollar deal was sealed to assure long term phosphate supplies.

Polisario's arms procurers, like those of Morocco, also tried to obtain weapons from other sources. But unlike their Moroccan counterparts in the late 1970s, they had little money to offer. Polisario therefore remained heavily dependent on its two "radical" North African patrons. Since in practice all materiel had to come through Algerian territory—Polisario never held significant segments of the Saharan coast—Algeria enjoyed additional leverage over Polisario's arms pipeline.

During the first few years of the war, a number of parties tried to push the combatants toward the conference table. In the UN General Assembly, Morocco (and Mauritania) were condemned for their actions in several resolutions, but with no agreement on concrete countermeasures. The OAU also attempted a peacemaking role; at its 1978 summit a committee of five was set up to help solve the crisis. The committee was unsuccessful, but its report to the 1979 summit, reiterating Saharawan rights of self-determination, helped increase African states' support for the Polisario position. Morocco refused further cooperation with the OAU committee in October 1979 (Seddon, 1988, p. 110). By 1980, a majority of OAU member states had diplomatically recognized SADR. In order to avoid SADR's OAU membership, Morocco then offered to hold a controlled referendum. The OAU established an implementation committee for this task, but proved unable to achieve progress through 1982. In February 1983 the OAU officially recognized SADR as its fifty-first member. Negotiations continued, but in the fall of 1983 Morocco refused further participation and withdrew from the OAU itself in November 1985.

At this point, when the number of states recognizing SADR had grown to more than sixty and international organizations were consistently adopting cease-fire resolutions supporting a referendum, Morocco agreed to indirect proximity talks under the aegis of the UN Secretary General and the OAU Chairman. From then on, it became less a question of whether but rather when and how the conflict would be solved. There was early agreement that a popular referendum should decide, but which people would vote? And who should administer and control the referendum? Repeatedly, negotiations stalled on these questions (Osterud, 1989).

On August 11, 1988, Morocco and Polisario agreed upon a proposed UN cease-fire plan and referendum, but it was June 1990 before the UN Secretary General could report to the Security Council on formulae acceptable to the parties. In April 1991, the Security Council, in Resolution 690, established the United Nations Mission for the Referendum in Western Sahara (MINURSO). But by the summer, the peace plan seemed in danger again; instead of diminishing its armed forces in the region Morocco increased them, and conducted large-scale operations outside the wall. The referendum had to be postponed because Morocco and Polisario did not agree on a voters' list (differences concerned the role of Moroccans who had moved into the territory).

It was certainly not military power that brought Morocco to the negotiation table and led it to accept a settlement on terms it had rejected in the late 1970s and early 1980s. Morocco had military control when negotiations began to become fruitful. It was rather a combination of economic exhaustion—partly caused by the war, including the costs of armaments—and the hope that fifteen years of occupation, control of natural resources, and the large influx of Moroccans would secure a majority of pro-Moroccan voters, allowing for the satisfactory resolution of the conflict.

Another important factor was that the conflict, which at times had threatened to erupt into major regional warfare, was increasingly judged by North African states as an anachronistic burden to their relationships. While some tensions between Morocco and Algeria remained, their relations gradually improved in the second half of the 1980s. In 1988, North African heads of state announced their intention to cooperate to solve existing differences. Many Polisario leaders privately were shocked by this turn of events, and an internal leadership struggle ensued. But because of their dependence on Algeria, they had little choice but to cooperate.

CONCLUSIONS

In the Saharan war, large consignment of arms were sent to the combatants, most prominently to Morocco. They contributed to heavy casualties and cost large sums of money. Ultimately, they profoundly affected the fighting, but apart from pressures on Polisario, had little effect on the peacemaking process. The major weapons suppliers, including the US, chose not to test their leverage over Morocco. Certainly, there were discontinuities in supply, and there was talk that these were signals to King Hassan to alter his stand and to negotiate. But, in fact, it was easy for the king and his advisers to overlook these arguments and manipulate other interests affecting the flow of weapons. Restrictions depended mostly on US internal politics during the Carter administration, foreign policy considerations such as French-Algerian and Libyan relations, debt levels, and security consideration, as in the case of Spain. The East-West conflict was a background factor, and there was also a good deal of competition between the US and France. French policymakers judged that US influence in Morocco was "disproportionate to its interests" (Jouve, 1985, p. 317). In the end, Morocco's regional strategic role became the king's greatest asset, and there were no credible attempts to force Hassan's hand.

Arms deliveries were plentiful in the late 1970s when Hassan effectively refused to negotiate, but for various reasons they declined in the early 1980s as he still refused to negotiate. One thing had changed between the two periods, however: Polisario had grown from a seemingly irrelevant guerrilla movement into a recognized player on the international diplomatic scene. In 1976 and 1977, decision makers in Washington, Paris, and Madrid had doubts about the legitimacy of Moroccan territorial claims, but no doubts over its military capability to control the Western Sahara. By the decade's end, when this assumption was proved wrong, arms deliveries still could be justified by Algerian support for Polisario and the possibility that the Soviet Union was behind it all. But this argument soon lost credibility both because of Algerian restraint and because Moscow refused to leave its neutral stance in the conflict. Polisario had to be recognized as a force in African politics, even as Morocco solidified its role as a friend of Western interests.

Another change over time had to do with funding. By 1980, oil money to fuel the war became more scarce. In the 1970s, Morocco had been able to broaden its arms-acquisition network somewhat to resist any focussed diplomatic pressure, but in the 1980s Rabat lacked the means to substitute suppliers. Early in the decade, one of the most diligent observers of the conflict, British journalist Tony Hodges, wrote that, "A joint Franco-American decision to halt the flow of arms to Morocco would leave King Hassan with little option but to accept the OAU's calls for talks with Polisario" (Hodges, 1985, p. 272). It seems likely that Hassan was aware of this vulnerability and styled Moroccan foreign policy to minimize it; after 1981 he possessed sufficient armor to be less dependent on outside support, and more important, he enjoyed political influence on key regional issues to preclude the likelihood of sanctions even in the face of heavy debts.

Algeria retained considerable leverage over Polisario. This was a direct result of the latter's use of Algerian sanctuaries, but also because Algeria kept close control of arms supplies, subordinating the pace of war to its own foreign policy interests. When this control was threatened by Libyan deliveries, they were blocked. Allowing for sketchy information on arms flows, Polisario did not appear to be in a position to act against their patron's wishes. It should not be surprising that arms leverage is potentially greater on a nonstate actor involved in a war than on an independent government.

This leverage was especially crucial in 1980–81 when, just as Polisario successes in the field were the greatest, Algiers decided to deescalate the conflict. The decision was easily enforced by cutting into the weapon pipeline; its timing gives an East-West perspective to this conflict that it otherwise lacks. One of the factors leading to the Algerian decision was the fear that local fighting might become another focus in the rapidly cooling East-West atmosphere. Algeria instead decided to put its weight behind diplomatic efforts in the hope that in the long run Morocco would have to acquiesce. Shortly thereafter, though, US strategic advice and technological assistance to Morocco on wall building helped postpone that acquiescence for at least a decade.

Different from many other cases at the time, and more similar to the situation in the early 1990s, the superpower context was less important for the pattern of warfare than were North African interests. Yet the background of superpower involvement in African conflicts in the Horn, Zaire, and Angola, as well as Middle Eastern disputes, heightened Morocco's prominence. This relatively weak East-West linkage to the Sahara did not particularly enhance suppliers' potential to influence recipient behavior, however, since reverse influence by the regional actors was quite effective.

On a much different level, arms transfers to Morocco influenced the war's outcome in an indirect way. During the 1980s, aid givers, including the International Monetary Fund, demanded stringent fiscal austerity, reportedly including a reduction of military expenditures. At times, for instance in 1979, 1981, and 1984, austerity led to Moroccan food riots. Still, the king survived these threats, contrary to predictions by some observers in the late 1970s. Ironically, this may have been due partly to the army's prolonged Saharan preoccupation, forestalling the most likely threat to the throne, a coup—several of which had been attempted in the early 1970s. In addition, as long as the costs seemed tolerable, the war was a source of popularity for the king.

From the mid-1980s, when peaceful conflict resolution got underway in earnest, arms deliveries were rare and did not change the situation either on the battlefield or at the negotiating table. Polisario received fewer and fewer weapons even before it had essentially lost the war in 1982, just enough to make its continued presence clear to the Moroccans and the world. Morocco had no means and no real need for many more weapons. In the end, Algeria's deescalation strategy yielded results. While Polisario lost the war militarily, it won face-saving victories on the diplomatic and economic fronts. Morocco accepted previously unpalatable terms of settlement, though the military stalemate remained comfortable enough to stall the outcome. A war that had reportedly cost more than $1 billion a year and up to ten-thousand lives (Ruf, 1992) had been in vain. Arms suppliers, sharing responsibility in this, had done little to prevent or deescalate it. Embargoes had been too leaky for much effect, and the war remained essentially enough restricted to forestall much alarm in foreign capitals.

Since this war was related to and in a sense subsumed in larger African conflicts, we understand more fully its connection to international interests by turning to the somewhat related situation in the Horn. The Ethiopian-Somali fighting did not last as long, but coincided with much of the early Saharan struggle and involved some of the same actors, patrons, and North African-Middle Eastern political aspirations.

CHAPTER 11

THE OGADEN WAR, 1977–78

INTRODUCTION: THE BACKGROUND OF WAR

Few regions in the world have been as war and poverty ravaged as the valleys and plateaus of Ethiopia (Matthies, 1977 and 1990). Among the many wars, with their untold sufferings, the one fought in the Ogaden in 1977–78 by far drew the most international attention and involvement. In this case the Soviet Union and Cuba intervened on an unprecedented scale to save the Ethiopian government. Zbigniew Brzezinski, at the time deeply involved in US decision-making as Presidential Assistant for National Security Affairs (NSA), later observed of the US-Soviet negotiations to limit strategic nuclear arms that "SALT lies buried in the sands of the Ogaden" (Brzezinski, 1983, p. 189). This stark assessment reflects a widespread feeling in the West at the time that the Soviet Union ruthlessly used the war to expand its position in what was regarded as the geostrategic hinge between Africa and the Middle East.

Ethiopia was in turmoil when the war began. The military committee, the Dergue, which had seized power from Emperor Haile Selassie in 1974, had not succeeded in pulling the fragmented state together. Instead, the adoption of a social and economic reform program, with accompanying socialist ideology, had intensified long-standing ethnic divisions. Regional insurgency activity increased in various parts of the country, including Eritrea and the Ogaden, a large region in the east where about 1.5-million people of Somali ethnic origin formed the majority population. The Ethiopian military was enlarged through draft programs but was largely unsuccessful in bringing the dissidents to heel. Step by step the Dergue, often after bloody internal showdowns, hardened its ideological stand and increasingly ruled through terror. On February 3, 1977, the official head of state, General Tafari-Banti, and a number of his colleagues on the ruling military council

The Ogaden War, 1977–78   181

were killed by council rivals at the Grand Palace in Addis Ababa (*Keesings Contemporary Archives,* vol. 23, March 4, 1977, p. 28221).

From the outside, Ethiopia seemed set to dissolve into anarchy. Foreign affairs were in corresponding disarray. The US, Western European states, and conservative regional governments, which had been Haile Selassi's traditional supporters and military suppliers, grew increasingly nervous and disillusioned. In the spring of 1977, Ethiopia and Washington, its most important arms supplier, cut their links.

At the same time, the Dergue's closer ideological associates, such as the Soviet Union, remained skeptical of the new government's credibility and longevity. While an arms-transfer relationship had been established with Moscow in late 1976, it was not until midwar that massive deliveries to the Ethiopian armed forces began.

The Somali leadership, military officers espousing an ideology similar to that of the Dergue, tried to take advantage of this disruption, much as Iraq later sought to redress grievances when Iran underwent its revolutionary upheaval (see chapter 9). They revived the claim to unite all Somali ethnic groups under one state, symbolized in the five stars of the republic's flag. This claim already had led to previous border clashes with both Ethiopia and Kenya; Somalis in the Ogaden region had formed the Western Somali Liberation Front (WSLF), which fought the Ethiopian central government with quiet, but substantial, Somali support.

Ethiopia, with its much larger population and economic resources, had seemed an overwhelming enemy until 1977. But during the 1970s the Somalis received substantial Soviet military aid and gradually built up an army that seemed better trained and equipped than the nominally larger Ethiopian forces. Thus, when the impression of chaos next door combined with the loss of Ethiopia's predominant arms supplier in 1977, the temptation for Siad Barré's government became too great to resist. A window of opportunity seemed open as long as the Soviet Union had not fully embraced the Dergue.

The Ogaden war, as it has often come to be called, entailed a classic reversal in superpower arms-delivery relationships. While a large body of literature on the war treats the East-West dimension, our focus again is on the narrower question of the impact of weapon deliveries and the denial of such deliveries, especially as they affected battlefield and diplomatic outcomes.

ARMAMENT AND THE APPROACH OF WAR

During the early part of the 1970s, both Ethiopia and Somalia were firmly locked into superpower arms-supply relations—the US and allies backing Ethiopia and the Soviet bloc serving Somalia. Since the 1950s, Washington had fostered the emperor's armed forces under a mutual defense assistance agreement (signed March 22, 1953). Between 1953 and 1977, US military aid to Ethiopia amounted to almost $183 million. In addition, weapons valued at more than $90 million had been sold, and 3,552 Ethiopian officers and soldiers trained in the US (US Department of Defense, 1986, pp. 234–35). Washington had obtained certain advantages from this close relationship; a secret treaty, also dated March 22, 1953, gave the US access to the former Italian "Kagnew" communication station near Asmara in Eritrea. With the advent of satellite technology in the late 1960s, however, Kagnew began to lose importance as an intelligence outpost.[1]

Ethiopia's privileged-client status also had to do with US perceptions of the country and its ruler as stable and reliable pro-US factors in African politics. But this image of Haile Selassie waned in the early 1970s, with widely reported human-rights violations. In 1973, after the October Arab-Israeli war (see chapter 5), diplomatic relations with Israel were broken. The emperor tried to conceal the 1972–73 famine, which led to worldwide condemnation when it was discovered—too late for hundreds of thousands of victims. Therefore, when in 1974 a group of young officers, calling itself the Dergue, overthrew the traditional monarchy, Washington remained cautious but not particularly hostile. Military assistance was continued, though on terms slowly changing from grant to credit and cash programs.[2] By 1976, military aid was below $3 million, and was expected to be phased out in 1977.

Ethiopian weapon purchases, mostly authorized under the Foreign Military Sales (FMS) program, increased substantially, draining off considerable scarce foreign exchange. In 1976, FMS agreements reached an absolute peak of almost $63 million, $25 million of which was financed by the US government at commercial rates. Most of the materiel ordered was delivered in 1977, which became the record year, with more than $61 million in American arms deliveries (US Department of Defense, 1986, pp. 234–35).

Table 22

Arms Shipments to Ethiopia, 1974–78

Major Weapons Delivered to Ethiopia, 1974–76

US	72 M-60-A1 tanks; 90 M-113-A1 APC; 12 M-109-A1 155mm howitzers; 4 DHC-3 Otter transports; 6 F-5E Tiger-2 fighters; 12 V-150 Commando APCs
FRG	2 DO-28D-1 transport
Iran	36 AGM-12B Bullpup AShMs, arming former Iranian F-5 fighters
Yugoslavia	1 Kraljevica CL patrol craft
France	4 SS-12 SSM

Major Weapons Delivered to Ethiopia, 1977–78

France	1 EDIC/EDA type landing craft
US	4 Swift-type patrol craft
USSR	6 AN-26 CURL light planes; 85 T-34 tanks; 40 BRDM-1 scout cars; 1500 SA-7 Grail SAMs; 20 T-62 tanks; 100 BMP-1 mechanized infantry combat vehicles; 300 SA-3 GOA SAMs; 100 T-54 tanks; 20 MiG-23 fighters; 2 AN-12 CUB-A transports; 50 MiG-21MF fighters; 50 BRDM-2 scout cars; 40 BTR-152 APCs; 6 MiG-17F fighters; 40 T-55 tanks; 100 BTR-60P APCs; 1000 AT-3 Sagger ATMs; 100 D-20 152mm howitzers; 15 SA-3 SAM anti-aircraft systems; 150 D-30 122mm howitzers; 100 S-23 180mm artillery; 30 M-47 Patton tanks
Yugoslavia	50 M-47 Patton tanks

Source: Estimates from authors' files; SIPRI files

Table 23

Arms Shipments to Somalia, 1974-78

Major Weapons Delivered to Somalia, 1974-76

USSR	50 T-54 tanks; 6 MiG-19 fighters; 60 M-1938 122mm artillery; 30 SA-2 Guideline SAMs; 7 MiG-21F fighters; 7 MiG-15 UTI fighter-trainers; 50 T-55 tanks; 30 BM-13-16 132mm multiple rocket systems; 10 SA-3 GOA antiaircraft systems; 13 MiG-17 fighters; 3 SA-2 SAM launchers; 25 M-1955 100mm artillery; 10 BRDM-2 Gaskin antiaircraft vehicles; 25 M-1944 100mm artillery; 60 SA-9 Gaskin SAMs; 2 OSA-2 Class patrol boats; 60 AT-3 Sagger ATMs; 48 SSN-2 Styx SSMs; 10 BRDM-2 Sagger tank destroyers; 4 SSN-2 Styx L ShSHM launchers; 1 MOL Class fast-attack craft; 10 BTR-60P APCs; 10 ZSU-23-4 Shilka antiaircraft vehicles

Major Weapons Delivered to Somalia, 1977-78

Egypt	35 T-54 tanks
USSR	3 MOL Class fast attack craft

Source: Estimates from authors' files; SIPRI files

However, the numbers hide serious political frictions that were developing between the two governments. Problems for Washington grew when the Dergue, many of whom had been trained in the US and other Western countries, started to sound and act increasingly like an orthodox Marxist-Leninist government. Ethiopians, on the other hand, grew more and more suspicious of US intentions. Actions that had little or nothing to do with Ethiopia, such as an increase in FMS credit rates, were interpreted as hostile.

US policy toward Ethiopia dramatically changed in early 1977 with the advent of the Carter administration and its emphasis on human-rights concerns. In February, reports surfaced that the new US leaders would discontinue both military assistance and arms sales because of the Dergue's human rights violations. A diplomatic crisis emerged as the more radical Mengistu Haile Mariam came to power in Addis Ababa. The break was initiated by the Ethiopian side, which on April 23 ordered the US out of their military-assistance mission and the Kagnew station. President Carter then decided not to authorize new military aid or sales programs, and "temporarily" halted weapon deliveries in the pipeline, including 14 M-60 tanks and 480 TOW missiles (United States Congress, 1977c, p. 173). On May 7, the Dergue abrogated the 1953 assistance treaty, though insignificant quantities of "nonlethal" American military items continued to flow into Ethiopia until well after the eruption of the Somali war in July 1977 (Lewis, 1985b, p. 106).

Alongside the US, other Western powers had supplied the Ethiopian armed forces. Iran under the Shah, for instance, had delivered used F-5 fighter aircraft. West Germany had sold small airplanes and helped to train the police (Albrecht and Sommer, 1974). Since the early 1960s, a special relationship had existed with Israel, generally involving advice and training missions more than weapons per se. Despite the break of diplomatic relations in October 1973, and based on Israel's suspicion of Somali-Arab ties, Israeli-Ethiopian military connections remained close (Ayoob, 1980b, pp. 160–62). But compared with US deliveries, all these relationships were minor until 1977.

This was also true for East Bloc states. Long before Ethiopia's falling out with the West, the Dergue had tried to diversify arms supplies and, if necessary, substitute for US arms. As early as September 1974, Foreign Minister Gebre-Selassie Zewde threatened to turn to China or the Soviet Union (Agyeman-Duah, 1986, pp. 287–307). While Soviet Ambassador Anatoly Ratanov promised military materiel, Moscow remained cautious at that time (Patman, 1989, p. 172). Several times during 1975, as well, the Dergue sent representatives to Moscow for military assistance (Porter, 1984, pp. 192–93; Lewis, 1985b, p. 104). The Soviet leadership still doubted the Dergue's stability, and under Somali pressure was slow to establish a competing arms-supply relationship in the Horn (Patman, 1989, pp. 172–90).

When Ethiopian radicalism increased, however, the Soviets experienced increasing political pressure to change their stand. It seemed irreconcilable with revolutionary rhetoric not to support a declared Marxist-Leninist state; the Dergue increasingly demanded a clear decision.

An additional factor in Soviet decision making were the Chinese. Some in the Ethiopian leadership were considered to be pro-Maoist, and though Chinese assistance to Addis Ababa remained largely economic, in January 1977 it came to include the delivery of two-hundred tons of small arms and ammunition (Patman, 1989, p. 179; Porter, 1984, p. 211). Therefore, finally recognizing Ethiopia's importance and estrangement from Washington, on December 14, 1976, Moscow concluded a fateful military-assistance agreement for the delivery of supplies valued at some $100 million.[3]

Deliveries began to reach Ethiopia from South Yemen in late March 1977. Another larger agreement (reportedly amounting to deliveries in the range of $350–500 million) was concluded in Moscow on May 6 of that year, alongside a "Declaration on the Foundations of Friendly Relations and Co-operation" (Patman, 1989, p. 204), which was said to have laid out further deliveries up to 1981 (Porter, 1984, p. 196).[4] Reportedly, therefore, increasing supplies of outdated T-34 tanks, but also newer T-54s and T-55s, were reaching Ethiopia by June–July 1977 (Ayoob, 1980b, p. 150).

The Soviet Union had, of course, been Somalia's nearly exclusive patron since 1963. In the early 1960s, because of its irredentist claims, the pro-Western Somali government had not succeeded in finding Western arms; Mogadishu finally accepted a large Soviet offer. Somali-Soviet relations improved in 1969 when the avowedly socialist Siad Barré took power in a military coup. Somalia's geostrategic importance for Moscow further increased when the latter's relations with Egypt and Sudan soured in the early 1970s. The harbor at Berbera became a major Soviet naval and intelligence base. Together with South Yemen, Somalia thus emerged as the pivot of USSR military planning both in the southern part of the Middle East and for Sub-Saharan Africa. The relationship was formalized in a 1974 treaty of friendship and cooperation.

The Barré regime used its increased leverage to secure large quantities of East Bloc weapons, including several hundred tanks and squadrons of fighter aircraft. Most of the weapons were quite dated by Soviet standards, but they made Somalia one of the best-armed states in Africa. Reportedly, Somali arms imports from Moscow amounted to $300 million between 1974 and 1977.[5] It has been claimed, though not fully documented, that in secret agreements the Soviets received Somali assurances to use these weapons only for defensive purposes (Remnek, 1981, p. 74). In order to preserve

Moscow's leverage over the deployment of its client's armed forces, only a bare minimum of spare parts were delivered alongside the weapons—in line with general Soviet arms transfer praxis. In addition, maintenance remained mainly in Soviet and East European hands, since the Somalis did not have sufficient technicians. Other Warsaw Pact members provided considerable military assistance, including many advisers from East Germany, who were assigned mostly to train internal security forces. With these weapons and training, Somali forces grew from about twelve thousand in 1970 to about thirty thousand in 1977–78 (Ottaway, 1982, p. 67).

Somali-Soviet relations, which had become increasingly strained after the Ethiopian revolution, hit bottom after the Soviet-Ethiopian deal of December 1976. The Somalis lobbied hard against the agreement and sharply protested its conclusion. Moscow, in the spring of 1977, voiced strict opposition to further Somali military moves against Ethiopia.[6] The Soviets threatened to stop weapons deliveries in the event of Somali aggression, and did so shortly after Somali troops crossed the border in 1977.

Sensing this drift, Somalia also had begun looking for alternative arms sources well before the break with its superpower patron. Its obvious starting point was the Arab League, of which Mogadishu had become a member in 1974. The Saudis appeared interested, both out of concern about the Soviet build-up in the Red Sea area, and a desire to substitute Arab influence along the African Red Sea coast. While the Saudis themselves could only deliver used weapons of various origins, they could provide good offices to bring the Somalis together with Western suppliers. Private and semiofficial contacts with the Carter administration led to the US president's acknowledgment in the spring of 1977 that relations with Somalia were improving fast.

But the US position remained ultimately vague. While Washington was tempted to wrest the Somali government from the Soviet hold, the US was wary because of continuing Somali socialist rhetoric and irredentist claims. Military assistance and arms supplies were offered unofficially, but on condition that Somalia renounce its claims on Kenya and Ethiopia.[7] In June 1977, President Carter mentioned the possibility of supplying "defensive weapons" should the Somali government be prepared to terminate its dependence on the Soviet Union for military equipment (Lewis, 1985b, p. 106). The Somalis answered with a specific request for arms (Vance, 1983, p. 73), and after considerable discussion, Washington decided that it would "in principle" help other countries to meet Somalia's needs for defensive weapons. The Somali side was so informed in mid-July 1977, in time to bolster their resolve to take advantage of Ethiopian dislocations (Vance, 1983, p. 73).[8]

Meanwhile, Mogadishu also continued to approach other Western suppliers. On April 5 and 6 1977, President Barré hosted Saudi Foreign Minister Prince Saud as-Faisal, and on July 13 he visited Saudi Arabia. The Saudis were willing to grant substantial aid to buy Western weapons but on condition of a total break with the USSR (Ayoob, 1980b, p. 152; Patman, 1989, p. 211). Intensive contacts also proceeded with Egypt, France, and Britain; the last two, acting in coordination with Washington, assured Somalia of their willingness to supply defensive weapons if irredentist claims were dropped. The Chinese were another possibility, though in early 1977 they reportedly limited their offer to some spare parts for older Soviet equipment (Patman, 1989, p. 211). In the end, then, Somali efforts for arms diversification met only with limited, mostly verbal, success. This did not stop them from launching into war, but the uncertain supply situation grew even worse once the fighting commenced.

THE COURSE OF WAR

It is difficult to say exactly when hostilities began. WSLF guerrillas in the Ogaden had been active since the end of 1975 (Matthies, 1987, p. 241). They were supported by Somali deliveries of small arms and ammunition, and also through disguised Somali troop units. The scenario somewhat resembled India's support of Bengali rebels in 1971 (see chapter 4), and by the end of 1976, the countryside, mostly dry savannah and semidesert with few roads, predominantly inhabited by Somali nomads, was largely under WSLF control. The main Ethiopian force in the Ogaden, the Third Division, was confined to a few towns and urban centers. It was short of aerial reconnaissance capacity, and many of its trucks and armored vehicles lacked maintenance and spare parts. Because of intense fighting in the region of Eritrea and elsewhere, and the need for the military to control Addis Ababa, there were no obvious reinforcements in sight. In fact, a brigade from the Third Division was redeployed to the northern province of Begemder in May 1977, and considering the lack of transportation, they would have a hard time returning if needed.

The opportunity ripened for a direct Somali assault. In early July guerrillas, reinforced by Somali troops, besieged the major towns of

Diredawa and Harrar. Ethiopian troops were immediately hard pressed, and those in Mogadishu arguing for a full-scale attack before the discontinuation of Soviet supplies prevailed. The means to achieve the strategic objective of annexing the Ogaden was to be a quick multicolumn armored assault. Such a frontal approach had certain advantages from Somalia's point of view. Logistical problems would be minimized and international opinion presented with a fait accompli. In addition, it conformed to Soviet style training and tactics inherited from central Europe. The offensive began with regular Somali armored columns crossing the Ethiopian border on July 23.

Somali operations did not proceed quite as planned, but initially achieved most of their aims. Secondhand and outdated Soviet equipment, inadequately adapted to the Ogaden's scorching heat, presented continuous operational problems. Engine overheating and burnout was frequent both for trucks and armored vehicles, hampering the assault and limiting resupply. The Somali air force could do little to support land operations because Ethiopian F-5s were superior to its own limited-range MiG-21s. Later, a lack of spare parts and very limited Somali maintenance capacities further hampered the air force in much the same way the Central American air forces fizzled during the Football War (see chapter 5).[9]

While successful on most of the various battlefields, the Somali position weakened the longer the war lasted. The thrust of the initial attack already was lost in August 1977. While the armored columns in the south of the Ogaden had reached their objectives, i.e., the perimeter of the Ethiopian heartland, to the north the advance slowed with the accumulation of logistical difficulties. Still, in late November only the two main urban centers of Harar and Diredawa were still in Ethiopian hands, though Somali troops had difficulty sustaining the siege of the two garrisons.

With the intensification of hostilities, not only in the Ogaden but also in Eritrea, the Ethiopian government had begun a crash effort to augment its military forces. Large contingents of men were recruited into people's militias. Cuban advisers, arriving en masse, trained many of these forces. The number of men under arms grew from sixty thousand in June 1977 to more than a quarter million in October. Positions in the Ogaden were reinforced by additional Ethiopian troops, numbering more than fifty thousand by December. Soviet weapons began to reach the front line in substantial numbers in early December. At about the same time, Soviet advisers, under the leadership of

Army General Vasily I. Petrov, began to coordinate military activity. Soviet, Cuban, and Ethiopian pilots, the latter trained in crash courses, attacked Somali positions and ferried supplies to the beleaguered garrisons. Finally, Cuban infantry troops arrived from the Caribbean during January and February 1978.[10]

Amid the Cubans' arrival, the counteroffensive began on February 2, and, though this time on the Ethiopian side, classical Soviet tactics again were used, with heavy air attacks and artillery fire preparing for a massive and direct armored offensive against strategic points. The battered but reinforced Third Division, parts of the First Division, and the newly established Fifth and Sixth Divisions were united under a central theater command. About 120,000 Ethiopian troops (including militia), 3000 Cubans, and 1000–1500 Soviet advisers were massed near Harrar and Diredawa (*Österreichische Militärische Zeitschrift,* vol. 16, no. 2, 1978, p. 150). Ethiopia's objective was to recapture the northern part of the Ogaden, in turn threatening Northern Somali territory. Regular Somali armored units had great difficulty repelling this thrust; in addition to maintenance and logistical problems, increasingly they were outgunned and outmaneuvered by superior attacking forces.

Thus, in conjunction with East Bloc troop support and advice, superior weaponry and supplies had become a key factor in Ethiopia's political survival. For example, masses of BMP-1 infantry carriers greatly enhanced mobility, while Sagger antitank missiles proved a deadly threat to Somali armor. Although Ethiopian troops had received little training, and though tactical leadership remained a problem, Cuban support and superior mobility and firepower drove the Somalis back. The Ethiopian advance began slowly, with some initial setbacks in early February, but soon gained momentum, culminating in the decisive battle at the Babile Gap on the road from Harrar to Jijiga late in the month. Jijiga was the major Somali logistical base in the Ogaden, where the only Somali radar was located. Though defenders had dug themselves in on high positions surrounding the Kara-Marda Pass, Jijiga fell to the Ethiopians on March 6 after mobile forces surrounded the compound, killing an estimated four thousand Somalis (*Österreichische Militärische Zeitschrift,* vol. 16, no. 3, 1978, p. 242).[11]

The rest of the Somali forces in the area, about 20,000 men, soon left Ethiopian territory. While it took the Ethiopian military several more years to regain control over most of the Ogaden (eventually, of course, Eritrea was lost and the government fell), the war was effectively over by late March 1978. It left about 26,000 Ethiopians and 8000 Somalis killed (Matthies, 1987, p. 244). In addition, about 650,000 Ogaden-Somalis fled from the draconian measures of Ethiopian reoccupation and administration during this period.[12] (See Appendix, Chronology 9, "The Ogaden War, 1977–78.")

DIPLOMATIC PRESSURE AND ARMS FLOW

Diplomatic efforts to halt the fighting began before its actual outbreak. An obvious potential crisis mediator was the Organization of African Unity (OAU), of which both states were active members. In May 1973, an eight-nation committee had been established to settle the Ogaden conflict. It met in emergency session on August 5, 1977, but Somalia, which officially denied that any regular troops were in the Ogaden, refused to participate unless there was an in-depth investigation of Ethiopian rule, to include WSLF participation. Ethiopia rejected both demands.[13] Later efforts to mediate, for instance by Nigerian Foreign Minister General Joseph N. Garba in September and again in early February, failed (*Africa Research Bulletin,* vol. 14, September 15, 1977, pp. 4525–26).

The Soviet Union, with ties to both states, also was a logical outside mediator. Both governments espoused socialism and were seeking good relations with Moscow, and it was clearly in the Soviet interest not to lose Somalia (and the Berbera naval station) while winning Ethiopia as an ally. In early 1977, the Soviets proposed a "socialist federation" in the Horn, including Somalia, Ethiopia, South Yemen, and possibly Djibuti (which still was a French colony destined to become independent in June 1977). Eritrea and Ogaden would receive a degree of autonomy within Ethiopia. Both Ethiopians and Somalis were offered sufficient weapons to defend themselves, along with guarantees that the other side would not be overly armed. This combination of federation and classical balance-of-power strategy was reportedly first offered in March by Cuban President Fidel Castro, who visited Mogadishu from the twelfth to the fourteenth and Addis Ababa on the fifteenth, and participated in a secret summit meeting in Aden on March 16. It also was the subject of a visit to Mogadishu by Soviet President Nikolai Podgorny on April 2, 1977. However, the Somalis rejected discussion of the Soviet proposals before their national aspirations were satisfied (Patman, 1989, p. 151, pp. 202–3).

The Soviet plan pleased the Ethiopian side much more than the Somalis. From this it might be concluded that Ethiopia had begun to assume a greater importance in Soviet eyes, a view that Castro, who judged that the Ethiopians had more revolutionary zeal, might have promoted. But we know too little about Soviet decision making in this case to make sound judgments. Soviet diplomatic activity increased again starting in July 1977, as military experts were called back from Somalia or transferred directly to Ethiopia. Moscow punctuated this pressure by stopping authorization for new Somali arms deals in late July; weapon deliveries from earlier agreements were turned off and on again between August and October in order to pressure the Somalis to withdraw from the Ogaden. Siad Barré tried and failed during a Moscow visit in August 1977 to convince the Soviet leadership to change its position. Addis Ababa sharply protested that Soviet weapons continued to reach Somalia, and the Somali weapons pipeline was finally closed on October 19 (Matthies, 1987, p. 243), without much evident effect on Somalia's willingness to fight. On November 13, the Somali government broke relations by renouncing the 1974 treaty of cooperation and friendship. The last of the two-to-four-thousand Cuban, Soviet, and East European advisers had to leave the country (*Österreichische Militärische Zeitschrift,* vol. 16, no. 2, 1978, p. 150).

Nevertheless, the Soviet Union continued to send signals to Mogadishu that it was interested in cooperation. For instance, Libya's Muammar al-Qaddafi, who along with most Arab leaders politically supported Somalia, met with President Siad Barré in late February 1978 to offer a resumption of Soviet supplies on the condition of respect for existing Ethiopian borders. The Somali president was uninterested (Porter, 1984, p. 199).

With the loss of its one major ally, however, the Somalis struggled to strengthen links with other possible arms suppliers. This proved difficult because their interference inside Ethiopia, a violation of the OAU charter, was taken more seriously than the Somalis had anticipated. Their success in securing additional weapons was very limited.

When Somalia attacked in July 1977, Washington withdrew its offer to help Mogadishu obtain "defensive" arms. This was communicated to the Somalis on August 4 by Assistant Secretary of State for African Affairs Richard Moose. A fortnight later, this restriction was extended to cover the retransfer of US-manufactured arms in the hands of third countries (Vance, 1983, pp. 73–74). On September 1, a State

Department spokesman explained that in the current crisis, arms to Somalia "would add fuel to the fire we are more interested in putting out" (quoted in Ayoob, 1980b, p. 155; and Porter, 1984, p. 209). The Somalis again tried to obtain American weapons in October and November, after the break with Moscow. On November 17, a US congressional and military delegation arrived to take stock of Somali arms requirements, but the Somalis were told that there could be no deliveries before a withdrawal from Ethiopia (*Österreichische Militärische Zeitschrift,* vol. 16, no. 2, 1978, p. 150). In addition, Somali leaders were counseled to accept OAU mediation, but stubbornly, as in resistance to Soviet offers, they refused.

On November 10, US, British, French, and West German officials met to discuss the problems in the Horn. They agreed that Somalia had little chance to retain the Ogaden. But support of Somalia was deemed impossible as long as its forces were fighting outside of their territory. It was decided that little could be done and that mediation efforts were fruitless for the time being. Channels would be held open to Ethiopia and diplomatic pressure continued on Somalia so that Western or UN Security Council mediation could be started as soon as feasible (Vance, 1983, p. 74). The group met again at the end of January, this time with Italy involved as well. There was agreement to step up pressures on the two combatants for negotiations, and also to approach the Soviet Union (Vance, 1983, p. 85).

The Somalis were somewhat more successful in securing diplomatic support and military materiel in the region, including from a number of former Ethiopian allies. Egypt sold domestically manufactured Soviet-type equipment. Iran and Saudi Arabia helped financially so that Somalia could buy some ammunition and spare parts on the international black markets. It seems, however, that rumors of US arms shipments, in contravention of American "end-use" regulations, were false.[14] Yet, even if such weapons had been delivered, they most likely would not have helped much. The Somalis desperately needed transport vehicles, spare parts, and maintenance personnel for Soviet-style equipment. These could only have been supplied by regional allies, and only Egypt's help was of major relevance to the Somali war effort.[15]

While Mogadishu was nearly shut out of weapons resupply, the Ethiopians received an unprecedented flow of Soviet arms. The airlift began in earnest in late October 1977, with the heaviest activity after November 26 (*Washington Post,* 20 January 1978, p. 30). Most of the many tanks, aircraft, and artillery pieces were flown by large Soviet Antonov An-22 (maximum payload: eighty tons) and Ilyushin Il-76 (maximum payload: forty tons) transports, both from the air force and Aeroflot. At the height of the activity, about fifteen percent of total Soviet air transport capacity was employed to fly resupplies from airfields near the Black Sea, Moscow, Tblisi, and from the Russian Far East (*Österreichische Militärische Zeitschrift,* vol. 16, no. 3, 1978, p. 242). Some aircraft refueled in Libya, others in Baghdad and Aden. A number of East European countries, but also Turkey, Greece, Saudi Arabia, and Sudan originally granted overflight rights. Pakistan, Iran, Sudan, and Egypt later canceled permission, once it became apparent that a large anti-Somali airlift was going on (Porter, 1984, pp. 201–2). Because of an overload of Ethiopian airports, some flights ended in South Yemen, with ships shuttling the military equipment to Ethiopian ports. In addition, between July 1977 and June 1978 more than thirty-five Soviet supply ships sailed from Black Sea ports via the Suez Canal to the Ethiopian-Eritrean ports of Assab and Massawa. About three-fourths of all military supplies came by sea (Porter, 1984, p. 202).

Many of these weapons were taken from Soviet military stocks, for instance, near the Chinese border; much was of older vintage. According to official US estimates, about sixty-one-thousand tons of military equipment were transported to Ethiopia in early 1978 alone (Porter, 1984, p. 200), and between October and January, this totalled approximately $1 billion in value.

Washington viewed these Soviet shipments with growing alarm, but diplomatic protests were rebuffed with references to Ethiopia's right to self-defense. When Cuban advisers and, later, troops showed up in large numbers, the Carter administration increased its hostile tone. At the same time, however, the Americans and Soviets tried jointly to manage the crisis (Napper, 1983, pp. 235–48). Washington argued in a number of private contacts that Moscow should convince the Ethiopians to give autonomy to the Ogaden while the US would try to get the Somalis to withdraw. The Soviets sent a counteroffer of a joint statement on the situation to be followed by a US-Soviet mediation effort, which the Americans rejected so as not to "legitimize" the Soviet role in Ethiopia (Brzezinski, 1983, p. 181; Napper, 1983, p. 236).

With the advance of the Ethiopian and Cuban troops in February 1978, US concern shifted to a counterinvasion of Somalia that would have extended Soviet influence over the whole Horn. Washington warned that this would be unacceptable. In the National Security Council (NSC) staff, there was talk of some kind of "military option," including a large-scale naval deployment (Vance, 1983, p. 86).[16] Meanwhile, however, the State Department continued to work for cooperation with the USSR. A private suggestion was made that the crisis be referred to the UN Security Council, which the Soviets rejected (Napper, 1983, p. 237). Instead, Secretary of State Cyrus Vance received confirmation from Soviet Ambassador Anatoly Dobrynin that the Ethiopians had assured the Soviets they would not move into Somalia. A US delegation to Addis Ababa on February 17–19, headed by deputy NSC chief David Aaron, received the same assurance (Napper, 1983, p. 237), and Cuban Defense Minister Raul Castro gave similar undertakings regarding Cuban troops (Vance, 1983, p. 87). After that, Brzezinski's plans to counter the Soviets had no chance of adoption as US policy.

One channel between the US government and the Ethiopian leadership was Israel. Ironically, given the state of Soviet-Israeli relations at the time, Tel Aviv maintained arms supplies to Ethiopia during the conflict, sending spare parts and ammunition. More important for the Ethiopian military effort, though, was Israeli technical and personnel assistance, for instance, in maintaining US supplied F-5 fighter aircraft. In violation of US arms-export law, some of the Israeli supplied equipment had originated in the US, and Washington protested diplomatically. Yet, there is reason to assume that, as in the Iran-Iraq war, these Israeli actions, taken in Tel Aviv's interest to weaken an Arab League member (Somalia), had tacit American support (Ayoob, 1980b, p. 162).

As noted, by early March the situation for the Somali forces in the Ogaden had become desperate. The Somali government, which had resisted diverse countries' pressures to withdraw, finally told Washington that it would yield. This communication was relayed to Moscow, again linked with demands for allowing an orderly retreat without threat to Somali borders (Napper, 1983, pp. 237–38). With the Soviets repeating earlier assurances, President Carter announced on March 9 that President Barré had ordered the withdrawal of Somali forces from Ethiopian territory. This was completed on the fifteenth. The most dangerous part of the war was over. It had not escalated into a superpower confrontation, but it severely affected US attitudes toward the Soviet Union, which were to be further jarred in the immediate future by the Soviet intervention in the Afghan civil war.

CONCLUSIONS

Ethiopia's victory—with much credit due to Soviet advisers and Cuban forces—was a result of mass, mobility, and firepower, classical attributes of military strategy. All three had only recently been added to the Ethiopian armed forces from East Bloc patrons and advisers.

But this is not the only way in which Soviet weapon deliveries were decisive for this war; by extensively arming Somalia between 1963 and 1977, Moscow had provided the means to carry out the attack in the first place. Then the Soviet turn toward Ethiopia heightened Somalia's resentments and threatened an erosion of the favorable Somali-Soviet linkage. "The Somali decision to escalate the fighting in the Ogaden seems to have resulted directly from this shift in Soviet strategy in the Horn, since it worked to the detriment of Somali interests." (Ayoob, 1980b, p. 151) By threatening to change alliance, Moscow introduced into Somali decision making the consideration of "now or never." In this context, the prior and continued delivery of weapons and military materiel had a heightened effect intensifying the conflict.

US policy also reinforced Somali misperceptions. As in other cases, such as Pakistan (see chapters 3 and 4), the vacillations of supplier policy led the prospective recipient to play the "client game" of trying to trap the superpower into a commitment of support. Prewar arms transfers and promises strengthened the will and capability to find a violent solution of the conflict, hardening conflict positions, increasing the probability of escalation, and reducing the chances of peaceful resolution.

On the other hand, Soviet calculations that Somali behavior could be steered by withholding weapons were proved wrong. Mogadishu did not deviate from their political and military strategy to capture the Ogaden once the decision had been made, despite the gradual withdrawal of Soviet support. As the events on the battlefield soon proved, Somalia was dependent on the Soviet Union militarily—but President Barré refused to accept the dependence politically, even when it became clear that there was no substitute arms-transfer patron available. Superpower reactions were not the Somalis' only miscalculation; fairly soon after the initiation of hostilities, Somali troops ran into various logistical problems in difficult terrain. Yet all this did not impress the Somali leadership.

Soviet arms diplomacy and balance of power maneuvers provided only weak leverage in efforts to limit the war during its initial stages. Moscow could not translate its supply relationships to both countries into a political settlement. Clearly, though, in conjunction with Cuban intervention, its subsequent massive arms resupply enabled Ethiopia to reestablish the status-quo ante in the Ogaden. Acting in concert—and using promises of future arms transfers as one instrument—the two superpowers could constrain the Ethiopians from crossing into Somalia, if the Ethiopians had in fact intended to do so, and could finally convince Somalia to capitulate.

The Carter administration's arms-supply restraint helped to limit the war. Had Washington allowed or encouraged allies such as Iran and Saudi Arabia to arm Somalia more extensively, the war might have lasted longer, might have been even bloodier, and might have spilled into Somalia thus further engaging the superpowers. Given the massive Soviet-Cuban involvement, the Ethiopians would most probably have prevailed on the battlefield anyway.

Without this East Bloc intervention, the Somalis would have stood a good chance to capture the Ogaden. The Ethiopian army, and with it the central state, might have disintegrated. Of course, the Ethiopian-Soviet relationship flourished for a period after the war. In 1978 a treaty of friendship and cooperation was signed. Moscow continued to pour in weapons, but while the Ethiopian armed forces grew ever larger, they remained unable to squelch regional turmoil, as the overall situation finally degenerated into an economic and social nightmare that might have been avoided without Soviet arms transfers. Thus, the USSR essentially "inherited the wind."

After the war, the Somalis at first had difficulties finding alternate arms suppliers; a further erosion of US-Soviet relations was required before Somali-US negotiations were successful. The first shipment of US military aid was authorized in August 1980, with deliveries beginning in late 1980. At the same time, the US received the right to use the former Soviet base at Berbera.

Negotiations about a diplomatic settlement of the Ethiopian-Somali conflict only began in earnest in 1986. Both governments were in serious trouble by then, with antigovernment guerrilla forces in Somalia and the renewed Eritrean insurrection, respectively, threatening governmental survival. In spring 1988 a deal was struck, including autonomy for the Ogaden within Ethiopia and a pledge not to support insurgents in the other country. This settlement, along the lines earlier suggested by the US, did not afford more than a breathing space, however. Both governments fell to rebel groups in 1991, with Somalia sinking into bloody civil war fought with the plentitude of weapons supplied over the last three decades.

Thus, in this case arms-supply policies were crucial both to the origin and outcome of the war. The losing party, unable to restore its forces, as predicated in our earlier theory, ultimately sued for peace. The "victor" itself might have lost except for a massive outside infusion of arms and armed forces, and did lose politically and economically in the long run. Ethiopia's ability to struggle was prolonged, Somalia's was foreshortened. Both of these states, though, among the most destitute and conflict prone in Africa, suffered long-term dislocation and continued misery directly related to the arms received.

We turn now to our final case study, again one in which two poverty-stricken African adversaries turned a long-standing political dispute into a nearly mutually fatal military confrontation. In the Ugandan-Tanzanian struggle of 1977, we will again be confronted with a decisive war outcome fostered by arms policies that ultimately led to the downfall of one, and possibly both, regimes.

CHAPTER 12

THE TANZANIA-UGANDA WAR, 1978–79

INTRODUCTION: THE BACKGROUND OF WAR

Our final case study took place soon after the Ethiopia-Somalia fighting, and also involved two destitute states, this time two that lacked major-power patrons. Therefore, the level of weaponry in the confrontation between Uganda and Tanzania remained relatively rudimentary, though not quite as primitive as in another such confrontation, the Central American football war (see chapter 5). Yet, despite the rather weak nature of the combatants, principles of high international importance were at stake.

Idi Amin and his clan, ruling Uganda since 1971, had one of worst human rights records in recent history, reportedly killing up to six per cent of the population.[1] Ethnic and tribal relations, already difficult before Amin, worsened after he came to power. The Tanzanian government was one of the few African states to draw political consequences from this tragic fact. In the same manner as dissidents in the second India-Pakistan war (see chapter 4) and the Morocco-Polisario confrontation (see chapter 10), Ugandan guerrillas were allowed to operate from Tanzanian territory.[2] Many other states were prepared to tolerate the Amin regime, and a good number also supplied it weapons and military equipment. It was only in 1977–78 that many such supporters, including Uganda's most important arms supplier, the Soviet Union, withdrew their assistance. By mid-1978, Uganda was crumbling and increasingly isolated.

When the Tanzanians finally invaded in early 1979, they violated the international, and particularly African, principle of nonintervention. They had some compelling excuses—the human-rights violations, concern for Ugandan exile revolutionary groups, and, perhaps most pertinently, an earlier border violation by the Ugandans—but technically this still could have been judged an illegal war of aggression. Again, though, the international community largely stood by. Neither the OAU, the UN, nor the superpowers showed much inclination to become involved. An exception to the international restraint was Libya's Colonel Muammar Quaddafi. Libya not only was Amin's sole arms supplier during the fighting, but sent troops to bail him out. Although it was massive and included heavy military equipment, this intervention did little to stop the Tanzanians and Ugandan opposition. In the end, it turned out to be a complete disaster for the Libyans, indicating that not all third-party interventions work as effectively as Cuba's efforts did in Ethiopia (see chapter 11).

The war also set a precedent for Africa, with one regime toppling another. The victim was no ordinary government, however. Internal violence had embittered and outraged large segments of the Ugandan population (excepting in the north, Amin's home base), which helped the invading forces. Frequent foreign-policy turnabouts had left Amin with few foreign friends as well. In the end, almost all governments were happy to see him go, and were prepared to rationalize Tanzania's technical breach of international law. It is less clear, though, how international arms supplies affected either the outbreak or course of the fighting.

ARMAMENT AND THE APPROACH OF WAR

Measured in terms of conventional firepower, the Ugandan forces should have been superior to those of Tanzania, especially with Libyan help. Amin, a ruthless British-educated military dictator, invested a large share of available resources in both the armed forces and the newly expanded internal security apparatus after seizing power in 1971. Amin's early support came mainly from Western countries, with Britain taking the lead as the former colonial power. Rumors in fact persisted that the British secret service had orchestrated the overthrow of the self-proclaimed socialist president, Milton Obote.[3]

However, for a number of reasons Ugandan-British relations began to sour in 1971. In July, Amin travelled to London to demand a substantial increase in military aid. The British in turn demanded payment for the sophisticated equipment he requested (Avirgan and Honey, 1982, p. 10). Shortly thereafter, human-rights abuses mounted against resident Asians holding British passports, and in August 1972 Amin demanded that Britain remove all of them within ninety days. London then promptly stopped all military aid, and later declared an economic embargo. These sanctions lost effect, though, as Kenyan businessmen continued to act as conduits for British goods in return for Ugandan coffee.

Amin also was turned down by the Israeli government, another previous benefactor. Israel had provided small arms and training aircraft in the 1960s; now Amin wanted major weapons. Tel Aviv refused and instead provided only a personal Israel Aircraft Industries Commodore VIP aircraft (Avirgan and Honey, 1982, p. 11). All Israeli advisers were expelled in the spring of 1972.

Table 24

Arms Shipments to Uganda, 1975–78

Major Arms Shipped to Uganda, 1975–77

USSR	100 AA-2 Atoll AAMs; 20 MiG-21F fighters; 200 AT-3 Sagger ATMs; 100 BRDM scout cars; 16 T-54 tanks; K-61 APC; 15 T-55 tanks
Libya	20 Soviet M-1938 122-mm artillery; 10 Soviet T-34 tanks; 10 British Saladin FV-601 APCs; 10 British Saracen FV-603 APCs; 40 French Mirage-5 fighters
US	1 Model-212 helicopter; 1 Gulfstream-2 transport
Iraq	6 Soviet MiG-17 fighters; 6 MiG-19 fighters
Switzerland	6 AS-202 Bravo trainers

Major Arms Shipped to Uganda, 1978

Libya	Mainly artillery, including BM-21 multiple rocket launchers for Libyan troops.

Source: Estimates from authors' files; SIPRI files

By that time, Amin had realized that he had to look for new arms sources (to assess his success, see Table 24). In a complete foreign-policy turnaround, he approached the Arabs and the Soviet Union. The first Arab state to assist Amin militarily was Libya, beginning in early 1972. Other Arab League members, such as Saudi Arabia, followed somewhat later, with a shipment of former German G-3 rifles. Kampala received comparatively large sums from the Arab world, officially for religious and development purposes, and a good part of that money was used to buy weapons and other military equipment in Western countries and on the black market. For instance, an American C-130 Hercules transport aircraft with full ground-support equipment was obtained in 1974.[4] This aircraft later was used in regular flights to Britain's Stansted airport in Essex, with a stopover at Benaghazi, Libya, to obtain other illegal goods, including dual-use communication equipment and military spare parts.[5] Yugoslavia also reportedly represented another important commercial source of small arms and ammunition (Avirgan and Honey, 1982, pp. 17–19).

Detecting a chance to boost their African influence, the Soviets sent their first military mission in November 1973 and began to transfer fairly modern equipment in 1974, including small quantities of MiG fighter aircraft and tanks of 1950s vintage. By 1975, Moscow had supplied an estimated $48-million worth of military hardware (Avirgan and Honey, 1982, pp. 11–12). While these deliveries were small compared to those bound for Middle Eastern countries, or to Somalia and Ethiopia, they were massive by East African standards. The USSR also provided military training through advisers, aided in this task by East European and Libyan experts. Several thousand Ugandans were sent to Eastern Europe and the Soviet Union for military and technical training.

Amin used this assistance to threaten neighboring countries, including Tanzania. A number of exercises involving newly acquired Soviet arms, such as the MiGs, were staged close to the Tanzanian border. Amin let the Tanzanians know that his MiGs would only need twenty minutes to reach Dar es Salaam (*Africa South of the Sahara, 1978–79*, p. 999). By then, however, for a variety of reasons the Soviet Union had become disenchanted with their Ugandan client. In November 1975, diplomatic relations were interrupted when Amin, as the head of the OAU, refused to recognize the Soviet-supported MPLA as the sole Angolan liberation movement. He personally favored the Zairean-backed FNLA headed by Holden Roberto, but remained officially neutral. Stalled payments for USSR deliveries were another irritant. The Soviets, knowing of Amin's large incomes from Arab states and noticing Ugandan black market purchases, demanded full payment but received practically nothing. In the final analysis, Moscow probably lost all hope of controlling or steering Amin in view of his instability, his brutality, and his unfettered personal ambitions. Also, the demise of Portuguese colonialism had offered Moscow better opportunities in the southern part of Africa, over which the Ugandan government had little influence in comparison to Tanzania's president, Julius Nyerere.

The last major Soviet deliveries were related to the Israeli raid on Entebbe on July, 4, 1976. In the course of the rescue of 243 hostages held by terrorists claiming to represent the radical Popular Front for the Liberation of Palestine (PFLP), a good part of the Ugandan air force was destroyed. This included about thirty MiG-17s and Mig-21s. Less than half of the aircraft destroyed were replaced by the Soviets during 1976 and 1977, with more aircraft coming from Iraq and Libya (see Table 24).

During 1977 some deliveries of major Soviet weapons continued from earlier sales, but the pipeline gradually was closed and the last advisers left in late 1978. Since the Ugandan armed forces, and especially the air force, had by then been built around such support, the suspension of arms deliveries was a hard blow. It was only partly offset by Libyan, Iraqi, and possibly Eastern European supplies and technical support. As in the Somali case (chapter 11), however, supply uncertainties hardly seemed to chasten the aggressive Amin.

For a number of reasons, Uganda's comparatively massive military build-up was not translated into a corresponding increase in fighting power, however. This was partly due to irrationality of planning, overseen by Amin personally. It was also the result of ethnic realignment. Soldiers and officers from the Acholi, Lugbara, and Langi groups, which were supposed to be loyal to Obote, were killed or driven from the armed forces and replaced with northerners such as Nubians, people from the West Nile district, and former AnyaNya rebels from Sudan (*Africa South of the Sahara,* 1978–79, p. 1047). Mercenaries arrived from a number of countries, and the professional quality of the army suffered; loyalties were mainly along personal and ethnic lines. The Soviet and Libyan advisers also contributed to the problem, teaching the Ugandans East Bloc military tactics with emphasis on armor and attack. Without actual East Bloc reinforcements, however, this approach would prove far less effective than it did in Ethiopia (see chapter 11).

Tanzania's army also was an offspring of the British East African colonial forces. Indeed, some weapons stocks, including artillery pieces, were still left from that time. Immediately after independence, President Nyerere had speculated about the need for a military force. The army, however, soon revolted and Nyerere's government had to be bailed out by British forces in 1964. He then settled for the Tanzanian People's Defence Forces (TPDF), largely organized along militia lines. The TPDF had few heavy weapons and lacked battle experience. A number of soldiers and officers had served as instructors to guerrilla forces in Mozambique and Zimbabwe, and a few fought in Rhodesia alongside Zimbabwe African National Union (ZANU) forces.

Since the late 1960s, China had been the main Tanzanian arms supplier (SIPRI, 1971, pp. 637–38; Bailey, 1975). As seen partially in Table 25, in addition to small arms (not "major weapons") this included fairly large quantities of mortars and larger artillery, as well as several patrol boats, about twenty T-59 medium tanks and fourteen T-62 light tanks, some armored vehicles, and a squadron of Chinese-built MiG-17s delivered in 1974. Dependence on China was the result of the growing hostilities in southern Africa. The Tanzanians would have preferred a more diversified supply, and indeed the Tanzanian army bought equipment on the commercial market; the air force flew a small number of dual-purpose Canadian, American, and West-German aircraft. But given budgetary constraints, Dar es Salaam decision makers saw no real alternative to the low-cost Chinese connection (Bailey 1975, p. 45).[6]

THE COURSE OF WAR

Repeatedly after 1971, guerrillas operating from Tanzania crossed the border into Uganda in the area west of Lake Victoria. These incursions were small-scale, but one in October 1978 coincided with a severe split in the Ugandan armed forces, as the Simba (Lion) battalion, stationed in Mbarara with primary anti-insurgency responsibilities in Western Uganda close to the Tanzanian border, remained loyal to Vice President General Mustafa Adrisi. Adrisi had recently fallen from Amin's favor and was hospitalized in Cairo after a mysterious "car accident." Instead of driving the invaders off, many soldiers at

Table 25

Arms Shipments to Tanzania, 1975–1978

Major Weapons Shipped to Tanzania, 1975–77

China	10 M-1931 122mm artillery; 20 Type-531 APCs; 10 Type-56 APCs; 10 Type-55 APCs; 4 Huchuan Class hydrofoil FACs
UK	2 HS-748M transports
USSR	25 BM-21 multiple rocket throwers
US	6 Model-310 light planes

Major Weapons Shipped to Tanzania, 1978

UK	2 HS-748M transports
USSR	25 BM-21 multiple rocket throwers; 20 T-54 tanks; 20 BRDM-2 scout cars

Source: Estimates from authors' files; SIPRI files

Mbarara joined forces with them and staged a mutiny. About three-thousand troops loyal to Amin were rushed south from the area around Kampala (Smith, 1980, p. 178). Much better armed and supported by aerial bombardments, they met with little resistance from the two-hundred or so mutineers and the guerrillas, who fled over the border to Tanzania. Ugandan troops followed them, repeatedly crossing the frontier.

By October 30, about two-thousand Ugandan motorized and infantry troops, supported from the air, had invaded the 710-square mile Tanzanian Kagera Salient. They met with little military opposition; the few Tanzanian border troops in the area possessed at most 122-mm mortars (Avirgan and Honey, 1982, p. 54). Amin declared the Salient's annexation to Uganda, as his troops looted the region, reportedly killing fifteen-hundred people (Avirgan and Honey, 1982, p. 62).

At the same time, Ugandan radio and diplomats tried to create the impression that Tanzanians were invading Uganda. Unfooled, many governments worldwide began to pressure Amin to withdraw from the Salient. On November 13, Radio Uganda announced a voluntary pullback from Tanzanian territory.

Tanzania had begun moving troops and equipment, mostly from central and eastern Tanzania, within days of the Ugandan invasion. Because of a lack of suitable transport equipment and poor infrastructure, however, the relocation was slow and costly. Trucks, buses, boats, and cars were confiscated for transport over several thousand kilometers during the rainy season. About four-thousand soldiers, equipped with small arms, mortars, and artillery, as well as some armored vehicles of Chinese origin, were in position south of the Kagera river by early November, with more on the way. Nyerere ordered "Operation Attrition" to encircle the Ugandan troops in the Kagera. These troops retreated hastily, destroying and looting on the way. Using a Chinese-supplied pontoon bridge, Tanzanian forces crossed the Kagera on November 19. They encountered few Ugandan soldiers, and by November 24, Tanzanian forces stood at Uganda's border.

As in many wars in which the tide turns, pressure mounted on Tanzanian leaders to do more, to crush Amin while he was in a weak position. The leadership, including President Nyerere, finally agreed to an invasion in early January 1979, but reportedly only up to the barracks of Mbabara and Masaka, close to the border (Smith, 1980, p. 182). Nyerere felt that he had tried hard enough for OAU condemnation of Amin, and that unilateral action was needed even if it violated the letter or spirit of the OAU and UN charters. Ugandan exiles, clamoring for action, were encouraged to assemble their men under arms. In a pattern similar to the 1971 India-Pakistan affair (see chapter 4), a new organization, the Uganda National Liberation Army (UNLA) was set up with active Tanzanian support. The men were given mostly Chinese-supplied small arms. Meanwhile, Tanzanian troop strength was further increased, so that reportedly up to twenty-thousand soldiers were assembled in the border region. During the night of January 21–22, the advance of about twelve-hundred Ugandan exiles and five-thousand regular Tanzanian troops began.

Initially, the fighting, involving infantry and artillery, was fairly heavy and confined to the area just beyond the frontier. But by January 26, Ugandan resistance near the border began to crumble, and Tanzanian and UNLA troops pursued withdrawing Ugandan forces, moving gradually deeper into Uganda. The Tanzanian tactic, a classic one, was to bombard presumed Ugandan positions with artillery and to advance when it was fairly certain that little resistance would be met. Thus, the advance was slow, but comparatively safe. The joint Tanzanian and UNLA troops reached their original operative aims on February 25 (Smith, 1980, p. 182; Avirgan and Honey, 1982, pp. 85–88), and only in late February did the Tanzanian government decide to let its troops go on to topple Amin.[7]

The Tanzanian advance now began to create large logistical problems. Not only did most of the soldiers have to walk, but they also had to carry ammunition and other equipment. Because of transport problems, few artillery pieces were taken along; however, with the hasty retreat of Ugandan and Libyan forces, UNLA and TPDF troops were able to capture large stocks of Soviet supplied weapons, including T-55 tanks, BM-21 armored vehicles, D-30 130-mm howitzers, small arms, and ammunition. Since there was a high degree of compatibility between these weapons and Chinese equipment, the Tanzanians could make good use of it.

It helped the campaign that the Ugandan and later Libyan resistance was neither well planned nor executed. Often, the Tanzanians succeeded probably more because of Ugandan and Libyan disarray than because of their own superior capabilities. Tanzanians lacked good military intelligence; they continued to put great emphasis on artillery used to clear positions, more than once shelling strongholds already abandoned by opposing forces. Morale on the Ugandan side was low, as evidenced by several mutinies and many desertions. The long-suffering local population in the area south of Kampala, mostly from the Buganda tribe, made life difficult for Ugandan and Libyan defenders. Regular troops answered with several massacres against the local residents, who retaliated with support for commandos infiltrating behind Ugandan lines and sabotaging infrastructure facilities. The number of UNLA forces grew steadily because of new recruitment in freshly occupied territory.

Tanzanian strategy also benefitted from the Ugandan air force's decline; once by far the largest in the region, because of losses to Tanzanian fire, lack of spare parts, and pilot desertions, it was out of existence by mid-February 1979. Briefly, in the later half of March, Tanzanian forces again had to cope with enemy air activity, as Libyan Mig-21s were deployed. In one of the strangest incidents of the war, a large Libyan Tu-22 bomber made at least two sorties over Tanzania without doing much damage.

Although the Tanzanian air force also was not much in evidence, due mainly to poor communications and the resultant inability of its Chinese supplied MiG squadrons to mount more than a few sorties to support battlefield operations,[8] Ugandans suffered more heavily from the lack of weapons and spare parts than did Tanzania. For Uganda's British- and Soviet-supplied weapons, such as tanks, aircraft, and armored vehicles, spare parts were very scarce, even early in the war.

Libyan advisers and troops—up to one thousand were in the country in late 1977—did not participate in the early fighting, though this changed drastically after the end of February 1979, when more supplies, including heavy arms, and more Libyan troops arrived.[9] Between early March and early April, in fact, Libyans took over much of the fighting. Quaddafi's late intrusion into the conflict is difficult to understand unless one sees it as an emotional reaction. The Libyan leadership had tried to mediate between Tanzania and Uganda in February. When Nyerere showed disinterest, Quaddafi warned Tanzania immediately to withdraw. Not only did Tanzanian forces continue their advance, they even used the Libyan involvement as justification for their violation of the OAU charter. Quaddafi, reportedly without consultation at home, then ordered an airlift of about fifteen-hundred additional Libyan soldiers to Entebbe. They arrived between early and mid-March by air, armed with their personal weapons. They took over some of the Libyan equipment sent earlier, and received additional artillery, also airlifted in early March. Still, the troops were not adequately trained or equipped. They were unfamiliar with the terrain; their motivation to fight was low; and after some bloody encounters they withdrew to the north of Kampala. Those that had not been killed or captured were airlifted out in early April (Avirgan and Honey, 1982, pp. 120–23).

Thus, shortages of weaponry and spare parts and the economic boycott were factors eroding Ugandan military power. But the main factors were the disintegration of the Ugandan armed forces and the northern soldiers' and officers' distaste for fighting in the hostile southern Buganda territory. Tanzanian and UNLA troops captured a partly destroyed Kampala, deserted by Ugandan and Libyan forces, on April 11, 1979. The invaders had not suffered large losses in personnel and equipment; their weak logistical chain had held, partly because of the inventiveness of soldiers and officers, partly because of the support of the local population. Sparse stocks of weapons, spare parts, and ammunition had been sufficient, mostly because fighting had been at such a low level and also because of the capture of Ugandan equipment.

Upon their arrival in Kampala, the UNLA and Tanzanians were greeted as liberators. This changed when these troops, now predominantly Ugandan, moved northward into regions inhabited by ethnic groups that had supported Amin. Still, the troops captured Arua in Amin's native West Nile Province at the end of May 1979. On June 3, Tanzanian troops reached the Sudanese border, and the war seemed over.

Tanzania had lost some four-hundred soldiers, but only about one hundred in actual combat. About one-thousand Ugandan and up to six-hundred Libyan soldiers had lost their lives. The number of civilian deaths, first in the Kagery Salient and then in Uganda, was at least five thousand. In financial terms the war cost Tanzania $250–$500 million (*Keesings Contemporary Archives,* vol. 25, September 21, 1979, p. 29838; Avirgan and Honey, 1982, p. 196). The Tanzanian economy remained in great difficulty, probably contributing to the ultimate replacement of the Nyerere regime (handing over power in 1985); the government urgently appealed, largely in vain, to Western economic aid donors. Uganda was even worse off, but retained great optimism that things would soon improve. Instead, the internal squabbles over power and ethnic balances that had been suppressed during the military campaign broke open. The war was reenacted several times over as a civil conflict costing more lives than the 1978–79 interstate war, though not as much as Amin's deadly rule. Tanzanian forces stayed much longer than had been intended. They withdrew hastily, amid bloody confrontations, in 1980 (Rupesinghe, 1989). (See Appendix, Chronology 10, "Tanzanian-Ugandan War, 1978–79.")

DIPLOMATIC PRESSURE AND THE FLOW OF ARMS

As noted, when Ugandan emissaries began to shop for missing items in late 1978, the conservative Arab states and the USSR refused to send materiel. (*Africa Research Bulletin,* vol. 16, Feb. 1–28, 1979, p. 5155).[10] These patrons judged that Amin's time was probably short and that it made little sense to support the losing side. An acquisition team sent to several other possible arms suppliers, reportedly including Iraq, Spain, and Portugal, came back empty-handed, mostly because the emissaries could not prepay for deliveries. An economic boycott staged by the British and supported by the US since the summer of 1978 now showed some effect, mostly because the Kenyans began to enforce it, depriving Amin of the necessary cash to purchase ammunition and arms on the black market. The Kenyan government and Western oil companies united in stopping oil supply to Uganda, which added to the military's discomfiture. Finally, the Kenyans banned at least some overland arms deliveries.[11] Thus, as in other wars, the effect of an arms embargo was heightened by a more general boycott.

Libya, although alone among former patrons still willing to aid Amin, wavered. Between the Ugandan invasion of the Kagera Salient in October 1978 and late February 1979 they airlifted only small amounts of weapons and parts for Soviet equipment. Later, shipments were comparatively larger and included artillery and aircraft.

Tanzania received small-scale outside weapon support during the war. Because of the large number of Chinese weapons in their arsenal, the Tanzanians approached Beijing early for additional supplies. Chinese leaders, more conservative than in Mao's day, wanted to avoid any undue African exposure, however, and refused to send more than token consignments of weapons. Tanzanians also approached the Soviets, but had difficulty in obtaining arms from Uganda's former patron; neither combatant carried the perceived strategic importance for Moscow of the earlier Ethiopia-Somalia tradeoff. President Nyerere had additional success garnering "nonlethal" equipment, such as "Buffalo" transport aircraft from Canada and pontoon bridges from Britain (Avirgan and Honey, 1982, p. 76). Only a few African states were prepared openly to send military supplies. The southern frontline states, as well as Algeria and Ethiopia, dispatched token shipments (Okoth, 1984, p. 22), and during Nyerere's visit to Beira, Mozambique, in early November 1978, President Samoro Machel promised to send a contingent of troops to the Kagera by mid-November (Avirgan and Honey, 1982, pp. 66–67). None of these outside deliveries or promises had much effect on the war, though.

The commitments did, however, demonstrate the split in the OAU, the natural party to foster negotiations between the Ugandan and Tanzanian governments. Not only is it the OAU's proclaimed aim to solve African disputes, but there also was a particular history of OAU trouble-shooting in East Africa. After the unsuccessful attempt by troops loyal to former president Obote to overthrow Amin in September 1972, and amid sporadic infiltration from Tanzania, the OAU stepped in to mediate. On October 5, 1972, at Mogadishu, Somalia, the two sides agreed not to undertake future military operations against each other (*Africa Contemporary Record,* 1972–73, p. C87; Okoth, 1984, p. 4).

Later, shortly after Amin's troops had crossed into Tanzania in 1978, President Nyerere alarmed the OAU by demanding a condemnation of Ugandan aggression. Instead, the organization, led at the time by Sudanese President Gafar al-Numeiry, offered to mediate. Nyerere rejected mediation in principle, and between October and December held a series of talks with OAU governmental representatives, including President Numeiry. However, Nyerere could not win a majority of states for his position. The former French colonies, the North Africans, but also Zaire and Nigeria, opposed Tanzanian demands. The OAU continued to recommend a cease-fire, and was not prepared officially to condemn Amin, especially after the announced withdrawal of Ugandan forces on November 13.

When Tanzanian troops in turn violated the border in late January 1979, the OAU mediation committee met once more, aiming to negotiate a cease-fire. Envoys were sent to Kampala and Dar es Salaam during February. While Amin readily agreed to terms and mutual troop withdrawal, Nyerere continued to insist on the condemnation of Amin's earlier invasions, which he posited as the beginning of the war. On March 2, the OAU mediation committee declared that it had failed (*Keesings Contemporary Archives,* vol. 25, June 22, 1979, p. 29670; Okoth, 1984, p. 12). Libya also had offered its good offices for mediation in February. While Amin readily accepted this offer as well, Libyan Foreign Minister Ali Adbessalam was turned down in Dar es Salaam with the argument that the OAU was already dealing with the matter (*Keesings Contemporary Archives,* vol. 25, June 22, 1979, p. 29670).

CONCLUSIONS

Neither of the two sides received much outside military support, except for Libya's last-ditch effort. One might assume that such isolation must have influenced the course of the war. But in fact, the absence of arms resupply was only one factor in the war's outcome, and probably less important than others. One important contributing factor to the Ugandan shortage of spares and equipment was the economic embargo, whose efficiency increased greatly through Kenyan wartime cooperation. Ugandan middlemen were unable to procure weapons on the black and gray markets. Of course, the embargo had additional effects in the economic sphere by limiting Amin's ability to hand out favors. As in other cases, such as the Central American football war and, to some extent, the Iraq-Iran war, economic boycotts were more important than specific denials of weapon supplies. Sellers on the black and grey markets are willing to supply any buyer—but required the necessary cash.

Equipment advantages also were not decisive. Judging from the equipment alone, the Ugandans should have prevailed, even with their spare parts problems. Indeed just as the admittedly belated and poorly executed Libyan intervention failed to help, more spare parts probably would not have helped either. Uganda's basic problem was the regime's internal collapse. Only a major foreign intervention, on the order of the Soviet-Cuban involvements in Ethiopia and Angola, might have saved the regime; for a number of reasons, of course, the Soviets had no such interest. At the low level of sophistication of fighting by both forces, as in Central America, weapons played a subordinate role to morale, tactical coordination, and support from the local population. In these respects, the Tanzanians and their Ugandan friends had a clear edge.

Tanzania won the war despite disadvantages in weaponry. All in all, the Tanzanians were not in a much better situation with respect to arms resupply than the Ugandans. Considering Libya's last-minute effort, they received even less support. To a degree, though, it helped that Tanzanian forces relied less on armor and motorized transport than the Ugandans. Nevertheless, their cautious tactical approach required fairly large amounts of artillery and ammunition, much of which was carried manually, thus further slowing the advance. It was not calculable beforehand that they would be able to capture so much of that type of equipment on the battlefield. Had the Ugandans fought harder, Tanzania might have run into greater supply problems.

The lack of outside supplies probably helped to limit the military damage, though not necessarily the economic costs, of the war. Considering the size of the forces and the proclaimed issues at stake, the number of Ugandan and Tanzanian soldiers killed was low. Many civilians suffered, though tragically that was not uniquely specific to the time of the war. Uganda showed diplomatic willingness to retreat given the incentive of OAU mediation, but Tanzania had reached the end of patience with the Ugandan strongman, and pushed unrelentingly to topple him once the counterinvasion began. Success in capturing weapons along the way, and the relatively friendly reception by the local population probably reinforced that resolve, despite the ultimately high economic and political price.

CHAPTER 13

RECENT TRENDS, ANALYSIS, AND PROJECTION

INTRODUCTION

We have reviewed tumultuous events in various parts of the world, seeking the effects of arms transferred during warfare—long wars and short, wars involving major powers as intervenors or patrons and those involving only smaller powers, wars over territory or status, wars in which arms were lavished or withheld. Our narratives indicate that these effects are not as clear-cut as one might suspect. Indeed, frequently we have found this question of "fuel on the fire" less pertinent to the outcome of fighting than other factors, such as the viability of the combatting governments, battlefield fortunes, the extent of overall sanctions, and the ability to stall peace accords while taking extra advantage of an opponent. On some occasions, though, the availability or scarcity of arms had telling effects on parties' fates, strategies, and terms of conflict settlement. One of the tasks of this chapter will be to put these circumstances into a useful framework.

The other task is to look forward, to assess whether the patterns detected in the case studies appear valid now that the cold war has ended and the international system supposedly has entered a new era. Developments in Europe, for example, are changing the map literally more drastically than in any period since 1960, when so many new Afro-Asian nations emerged. Power realignments, including the downfall of one "superpower" and the economic malaise of the other, together with the rise of ethnic tension and growing concern for regional and global trade, portend fundamental structural shifts reminiscent of the nineteenth century, when the full impact of the industrial revolution and the emergence of nationalism were felt.

In order to accomplish the dual objectives of this analysis, we will first review and classify the findings from our historical cases. Then, to project patterns to the coming period, we shall focus on the effects of armament in a cross section of three of the ongoing conflicts in

1991. The 1991 analysis will reflect wars in the post–cold war era in each region where substantial information on arms shipments was available. As in the previous case studies, we will describe the war, the arrival, if any, of arms resupply, and effects on the processes of escalation, de-escalation, and negotiation.

FINDINGS OF HISTORICAL CASE STUDIES

Our historical analysis drew upon wars of the past three decades in which belligerents were dependent on external arms supplies to varying degrees. These ranged from cases of high dependency on single arms patrons, often with weapons advantages for one side in the fighting (e.g., India-Pakistan; El Salvador-Honduras), to cases of polarized and nearly equal access to arms from a few major-power suppliers (Israel-Arabs), to later cases of highly diversified and multiple arms suppliers (Iran-Iraq). In Table 26, we classify the structure of the war and the pattern of outcomes, according to: whether resupply occurred for one or both sides (symmetry); whether or not a formal or informal arms embargo applied to one or both sides; whether the outcome was stalemated or decisively favored one side; prewar arms advantage; and whether negotiations of various types occurred in the context of arms supplies.

On the whole, we found that arms suppliers have relatively little leverage over the outcome of hostilities. However, the effect of arms supply on the level of hostility and the occurrence of negotiated settlement varied across cases. Seven of the wars saw some sort of formal arms embargo or supply restriction, while two more had informal restraints, and another, the 1973 Arab-Israeli war, saw only threatened restrictions or delays.

Arms deliveries clearly were a factor in decisions to go to war, because of considerations about military superiority, perceptions of changes in the balance of power, and interest in establishing links with supporting states. Arms transfers also condition decision-makers' perceptions about external recognition of their "just causes." In our study, only Morocco, El Salvador, and Tanzania launched into wars without considerable prior arms buildup. All three had accomplished at least some modernization of forces, though.

Table 26

Impact of Arms Resupply on Military and Diplomatic Outcomes of War

War	Resupply	Embargo	Outcome	Prewar advantage	Negotiations during war
1965 India-Pakistan	Symmetric*	Symmetric	Stalemate	Pakistan (qualitative)	Growing major power restraints
1969 El Salvador-Honduras	None	Symmetric	Stalemate	El Salvador (qualitative)	High pressure (OAS) and diverse/delayed effect
1971 India-Pakistan	Symmetric	Asymmetric	India	India (qualitative)	Major power pressure/delayed effect/expected third party aid
1973 Arab states-Israel	Symmetric	Threat	Israel	Israel (qualitative)/Arab states (quantitative)	Pressed by major powers/delayed effect
1976–91 Morocco-Polisario	Asymmetric	Insignificant	Stalemate	Morocco	Major and regional power pressure/delayed effect/UN mediation
1977–78 Ethiopia-Somalia	Asymmetric	Informal/Asymmetric	Ethiopia (Cuba, USSR)	Somalia	Insignificant (OAU)/military intervention
1978–79 Tanzania-Uganda	Asymmetric†	Informal/Symmetric	Tanzania	Uganda (Libya)	Insignificant (OAU)/military intervention
1980–88 Iraq-Iran	Asymmetric	Asymmetric/Partial	Stalemate	Iraq	Failed attempts (Gulf states, UN)/delayed effect
1982 Argentina-UK	Asymmetric	Asymmetric	UK	UK (qualitative)/Argentina (geographical)	Failed attempts (US, Peru UN)
1982 Israel-Arab (Lebanon)	Symmetric	Partial/Sporadic	Israel (military)/Syria (political)	Israel	Multilateral/bilateral pressures; delayed effects; Western intervention

*US had set Pakistani capability within limits. †Late in the war, Uganda received substantial supplies from Libya.

216   Arms and Warfare

Arms deliveries during wars generally prolonged and intensified the fighting. In long wars they often resulted in costly stalemates and sometimes contributed to the end of hostilities either by enabling one side to win or survive, or by exhausting one side's resources. Arms supplies or their denial apparently affected the rate of attrition and the ability of combatants to forego negotiations for a period.

Embargoes, whether partial or total, had little chance of compelling warring parties to stop wars or come to the negotiation table when it was not in their perceived interest to do so. Embargo effects were undermined by arms consumers' diversification strategies, domestic production, decision-makers' unwillingness to submit to external pressures, and the dynamics of "the heat of battle." Embargo effectiveness improved with high war-attrition rates, high-technology warfare, and the inability of arms recipients to diversify weapons sources; when combined with other forms of sanctions (e.g., economic restrictions or threats of direct military intervention or assistance to an enemy) embargoes did tend gradually to bring combatants to heel. In general, arms embargoes tended to have stronger effects on short wars and those fought with more sophisticated equipment (Arab-Israeli; India-Pakistan) while economic embargoes ultimately had more effect in longer wars (Iraq-Iran) and those among very poor recipients (Tanzania-Uganda; El Salvador-Honduras). Warring parties generally were able to find new, albeit probably inferior, arms sources in time to keep most wars going despite efforts to stop the fighting.

The case studies provide support for the position that it is best not to deliver any weapons during conflict, unless the supplier favors one side to win. This is not because a halt in deliveries can necessarily stop fighting, but because more weapons tend to make conflicts longer and bloodier, and lead to severe political dislocations in the aftermath.

Chapter one's extended hypotheses posited that arms resupply, which tends to equalize the military capabilities in two-party wars, would facilitate negotiations by promoting stalemates. As seen in Table 26, four cases ended in relative stalemate: the India-Pakistan wars of 1965; the Central American Football War (at very low operational arms levels and with El Salvador still occupying Honduran territory); the Saharan war (a political standoff with Moroccan territorial and military advantage); and the Iran-Iraq war (with Iraqi territorial advantage). Superpower efforts to promote stalemate in the Middle East just missed the mark in 1973, though for parts of the war stalemate looked likely at least in the Sinai. The 1982 Lebanon fighting ended in separate political and military victories for Syria and Israel, but the situation between these two states also resembled a stalemate since no overall winner was apparent.

When fighting and attrition levels are high in a stalemate, we expected a determined search either for arms or negotiations, or both. In 1965 we saw roughly this pattern in the endgame of the India-Pakistan war as envoys first surveyed the possibility of resupply, and then capitulated to strong international pressures and inducements for talks. Despite primitive weapons, attrition was also relatively high in Central America, but El Salvador, in a superior territorial position, held out for the best possible political terms before being forced by economic embargo to desist. Morocco could afford to sit behind its desert walls, with multinational arms resupply, and wait out Polisario until bitter economic conditions set in late in the 1980s. Then its leaders hoped that population shifts would assure a desirable plebiscite outcome. In the Gulf during the 1980s, Iraq utilized disruptive attacks on shipping to pressure outside powers to restrain Iran and bring a satisfactory close to their war; only the added weight of direct US intervention and again massive economic dislocation ultimately turned this trick with Teheran. Of course, Iraq, like Morocco, continued to obtain significant arms supplies during the stalemate while Iran had a much more difficult, though ultimately adequate, search. The plug finally was pulled on Polisario's external arms support (from Algeria and Libya) in the Sahara. Thus, the nexus between arms-induced stalemate and serious peace talks is not as straightforward as hypothesized.

The role of outside powers in promoting negotiations appears enhanced in stalemate situations as compared to decisive victories, though such peacemaking initiatives were not invariably successful in either case. In 1971, a decisive Indian victory on the eastern front still left impetus for hectic major-power pressure to preserve a western-front stalemate. Several South Asian, Latin American, and Arab-Israeli cases, either involving stalemates of decisive battlefield outcomes, also involved heavy major-power diplomatic pressure, because of the perceived strategic importance of these regions. However, effects of the pressure were often delayed and arms per se were seldom the sole key to settlement.

Symmetrical resupply, i.e., situations in which both sides have or neither side has access to arms replenishment during war, appears associated with the promotion of stalemated outcomes (India-Pakistan;

Central America; and nearly so in the Arab-Israeli wars of 1973 and 1982). In the Iran-Iraq war, both sides had access to multiple arms sources, though Iraq enjoyed an advantage, and again stalemate was the general outcome. Again, though the hypotheses are correct in positing a link between resupply and stalemate, and in assuming that stalemates involve greater diplomatic activity, the crucial further link to more successful and timely peace negotiations is not proven. Asymmetrical resupply, i.e., clearly favoring one side, in most cases, with the exception of Uganda, led to quite decisive military outcomes favoring the better-armed side and less diplomatic haggling, although the human and material costs of such wars also were quite high. Arms supplies also did not preclude the perceived need for direct military intervention.

Looking more specifically at individual cases, we first note outcomes in cases of minimal supply restraint. In the 1973 Arab-Israeli fighting, for example, massive arms resupply from basically two sources, one for each side, proved crucial in keeping the war going amid an extremely high military attrition rate. In this and other crises we studied, particularly in Africa, supplies tended to strengthen the weaker party and keep it in the war at every turn, though without direct intervention, further superpower efforts to manage the fighting through arms supply generally fell short. Similar effects were seen in the arms supply free-for-all surrounding the Iran-Iraq war. Clearly the major-arms patrons had great interests in assuring the survival of their favored clients, in proving their weapons' quality in battlefield tests, and in precluding a decisive war outcome that might threaten their individual or joint interests. These concerns generally outweighed desire for quick peace settlements. Pressure for cease-fires or settlements only mounted when one side seemed fatally threatened by the fighting.

In the Yom Kippur-Ramadan war and others in the Third World, major powers with strategic political interests tended to limit the amount of back-up ammunition and spare parts that came with weapons in order to assure some potential control over the pace of fighting. In 1973, Washington's implied threat to withhold further supplies, coupled with indications of possible support for Egypt, compelled Israel to accept a cease-fire, though not against Tel Aviv's own battlefield interests.

Thus, diplomacy surrounding supplies to the defending parties had much more telling effects on war outcomes than supplies to attackers; conversely, embargoes or restrictions on attackers' arms also had greater effects than sanctions against defenders or than bilateral sanctions (one side was generally in an advantaged position through bilateral embargoes anyway). In the Ethiopia-Somali and Tanzania-Uganda wars, which saw no formal arms embargo, the inability of war initiators to keep up their pace of armament proved critical for the outcome and negotiations. Yet both aggressors, Somalia and Uganda, collapsed as much because of internal and organizational deficiencies (and in Somalia's case because of third-party intervention) as because of arms scarcity; not even Libya's poorly executed last-ditch intervention could save Idi Amin.

Similarly, the 1965 India-Pakistan war, which did see a formal symmetric Anglo-American embargo (with more telling effects on Western-oriented Pakistan, which also technically had attacked first), ended as much because of Pakistani tactical disadvantages and overall major-power pressure (more effectively concerted than in any other case) as because of effective arms sanctions. In the 1971 round of South Asian fighting, Pakistan, once more technically the war initiator (though highly provoked), again was officially embargoed by the US, though some equipment continued to get through. Uncertain supply significantly restrained Pakistani strategy, especially in air warfare, but its disastrous Bengali policies seemed to preordain the outcome. Thus, both the 1965 and 1971 embargoes and ammunition and parts restrictions de-escalated the fighting, but other factors, including relatively congruent major-power diplomacy, the losing side's domestic political errors, and the winning side's achievement of basic war aims, brought on the actual cease-fire accords.

Similar arms embargo effects were seen during the El Salvador-Honduras war; Washington's timely supply cutoff to both poorly armed and highly dependent clients had telling effects, hastening their mutual exhaustion. In addition, cease-fire pressures were heightened by implied threats to arm one side if the other did not agree; similar threats finally worked on Israel in 1973 as well, though not until Tel Aviv's war aims basically were achieved. In both cases, though, one side was able effectively to hold out for relatively long periods against concerted international pressure despite high arms dependency. The duration of our other Latin case, the 1982 Falklands-Malvinas war, was too short for the EC embargo against the attacker to have had a telling effect. Britain's more diversified arms resources and superior military capability (augmented by the US) brought a swift though costly end to the fighting. British resupplies had the twin effects of intensifying and shortening the conflict, though, contrary to our predictions, Argentina did not quickly sue for peace even in view of its obvious disadvantages.

Not unexpectedly, then, embargoes had their greatest effect on highly dependent arms clients, and particularly against attackers overextended by prolonged warfare. Of course, the ability to find alternate weapons sources increased with the economic means available to warring parties—El Salvador, Honduras, Polisario, Uganda, and Somalia were more vulnerable to supply restrictions than were India, Pakistan, Argentina, Israel, Iran, or the Arab states. In addition, long-term arms-supply relations and interests generally appeared more important in promoting peace talks than acute battlefield needs and shortages, especially in ongoing disputes that produced repeated wars. States such as Israel, Egypt, Syria, Pakistan, and India did not want to risk their long term relations with sources of sophisticated armament, so ultimately they gave in to cease-fire pressures but tended to stall and delay the inevitable as long as possible to gain maximum tactical advantages; El Salvador and Morocco did so as well.

The two superpowers also were more prone to use arms transfers as a means to influence warring parties than were other suppliers, even considering the US-Soviet quantitative lead in the arms market. It is, therefore, not surprising that during wars the share of superpower deliveries generally declined, a central finding in Stephanie Neuman's studies (1986a). However, our Middle Eastern cases proved an exception to this rule; these wars evidently were so central to the superpowers' perceived interests that weapons deliveries were stepped up during periods of heavy combat. Contrary to Neuman's claim that diversification to minor suppliers did not diminish superpower control over local wars (Neuman, 1988, pp. 1064–65), it appears that in many wars reviewed here, including those in South Asia, the Arab-Persian Gulf, and the Middle East, resort to more economically motivated suppliers, such as France, China, or Korea, increasingly undercut great-power leverage via arms supplies. The most that major powers appeared able to achieve by outside arms pressure, such as threatened or actual embargoes, asymmetric resupply, or withholding of security protection, was the limitation of escalation during war and the general agreement to cease hostilities.

As predicted in the hypotheses as well, peace negotiations are proposed sooner by parties suffering battlefield setbacks and supply problems. This was clearly seen in the pattern of Indian-Pakistani, Arab-Israeli, and Ugandan-Tanzanian fighting. When in trouble, even the Israelis were ready to sue for peace on at least one front. Yet, cease-fires often are used only to delay and regroup, with a renewed search for arms patronage and battlefield advantage. In the end, both Pakistan and Egypt generally made the greater concessions in negotiated cease-fire outcomes, as reflective of their weaker battlefield positions.[1] The illusion, harbored by governments such as Pakistan, Argentina, and Somalia, that major-power patrons might ultimately rescue them also retarded negotiations.

Arms resupply appeared most important in three wars: Arab-Israel, 1973; Ethiopia-Somalia; and Iran-Iraq. In two of these cases, the role of outside suppliers and diplomatic pressures exerted by them had at least the delayed effect of helping bring the belligerents to negotiations. A similar effect is discernible in four out of five cases of formal arms embargo, and in two out of four additional cases of threatened, informal, or sporadic embargoes. In effect, then, arms supply or embargo decisions are intricately woven in the larger pattern of diplomatic efforts to halt wars, though they are seldom decisive in themselves. In five wars, resupplies flowed, or were promised to one side while the other found it difficult to obtain arms. Here the deficient side tended to lose, although tactical, political, and organizational factors also explained much of the outcome.

Thus of the basic rival hypotheses, it certainly does not appear that the arrival of new arms averts or abates violence, nor obviates the need for third party intervention. Indeed, it may enhance such perceived needs, as in Ethiopia. Depending upon the type of stalemate produced, however, the prospects for negotiated settlements may ultimately be improved, but the process is likely to be long and difficult, and require other forms of diplomatic pressure. Supplies, embargoes, or supply restrictions affording distinct advantages to one side, particularly the defending side, tend to promote decisive war outcomes, and multilateral multifaceted embargoes against dependent, overextended, and ultimately poorly organized attackers stand the greatest chance of success in halting violence.

EVIDENCE FROM RECENT WARS

In order to determine whether these findings appear to be holding up in the post–cold war period, we have gone on to sample wars of

222 Arms and Warfare

the early 1990s, choosing those similar in circumstance and regional representation to the historical cases just reviewed. Several 1991 wars were civil wars and internal ethnic rebellions; these included Sri Lankan, East Timorese, and Sudanese violence, among others. While a number of these represented interesting arms-transfer phenomena, we will not examine them here because they do not correspond to our historical cases of international or internationalized civil wars (in none of the three, for example, did formal outside military intervention take place in 1991). Instead, as seen in Table 27, we will focus on three more comparable cases that concerned issues ranging from international territorial to cross-border ethnic disputes; we will discuss them each briefly in turn before presenting conclusions.

Table 27

Impact of Arms Resupply on Military and Diplomatic Outcomes of Selected Wars Ongoing in 1991

War/Conflict	Resupply	Embargo	Outcome	Prewar advantage	Negotiations during war
Iraq-Coalition	Asymmetric	Asymmetric	Coalition victory	Iraq (prior invasion)	Failed UN, French, USSR efforts; Iraqi, Kuwaiti, and US search for support
Yugoslavia	Asymmetric (domestic arms production in Serbia)	Symmetric	Serbian advantage	Serbian advantage	EC, USSR, UN mediation, largely ineffective
India-Pakistan	Symmetric (uncertain)	Asymmetric/ partial	Open/ deterrence	India	Limited US and USSR pressure, mostly because of nuclear option and cold-war end

Gulf War (Iraq-Kuwait Coalition, 1990–91)

Arms Transfers. In the period 1986–90, Iraq was the world's fourth largest weapons importer, totalling $10.2 billion. The prior war with Iran, ending in 1988, fuelled Iraq's demand for arms and military supplies. By 1990, these imports had declined to a quarter of the 1989 level, but Baghdad's military resources were no longer depleted, so that its capacity for action appeared to have improved. During the Iran-Iraq war, Baghdad took deliveries from some thirty supplier states, with one-third of its major weapons purchases between 1980 and 1990 coming from countries ultimately joining the military alliance against it in 1991 (SIPRI, *Fact Sheet, 1990,* mimeo; SIPRI, *Yearbook,* 1991, p. 201). In the two years before the Kuwait invasion, major European powers, Brazil, and the US supplied Iraq with additional weaponry that would prove appropriate for the war. The USSR also sent twenty-five SA-16 portable SAMs and 24 Su-24 Fencer fighter-bombers, while France provided land-mobile SAMs, antitank missiles, and point defense radars.

The 1988 cease-fire with Iran enabled the Iraqi military to consolidate. Ambitious arms-manufacturing projects were launched to emulate major-power and Israeli capabilities, including a three-stage intermediate-range ballistic missile (IRBM) and an airborne early warning system (AEW) developed with Indian assistance on a Soviet airframe. UN inspectors ultimately verified that one "supergun" with 350-mm diameter had been built prior to June 1990, while two 1000-mm guns were in prototype stage (*Jane's Defence Weekly,* September 14, 1991, pp. 458–59). Analysts judged Iraq within less than half a decade of attaining nuclear status, and in the months preceding the Kuwait war, press reports cited alleged transfers of nuclear-related items, including triggers; German firms were especially implicated in supplying uranium enrichment equipment and technical assistance (*Der Spiegel,* April 1990, p. 14).

Kuwaiti defense capabilities could not have been considered a match, nor a deterrent, for Iraq's war machine. Kuwait's arms policy, in conjunction with political neutrality, aimed for deterrent effect, threatening high costs to invaders. Yet the reality of deployable military force was quite deficient. The moderate defensive stance of Kuwait's leadership was illustrated in January 1990 by the cancellation of a deal to acquire thirty Mirage 2000s; Deputy Chief of Staff Jabar Khaled al Sabah explained that instead, the "purchase of F-18 is sufficient to meet [our] air force needs" (*Defense Electronics,* January 1990, p. 14).

Saudi Arabia presented a somewhat more formidable military machine, though still not a match for the Iraqis in available experienced personnel. The Saudis received steady deliveries of both attack and defensive weapons including, in 1991, 350 French portable Mistral

SAMs and 3400 Shahine-2 land-mobile SAMs; 62 British Tornado fighters; and 22 F-15C American fighters, 150 M-60-A3 main battle tanks, and 28 helicopters (SIPRI, *Yearbook,* 1991, p. 286). Saddam Hussein and the Revolutionary Council might have considered the possibility of a Saudi response raising the cost of his Kuwaiti invasion, although he could hardly have envisaged such a broad-based response as the US-led and UN-sanctioned coalition.

Armament and the Course of War. Early on August 2, 1990, on the pretext of oil and debt disputes, Iraqi tanks and thirty-thousand troops crossed into Kuwait, encountering little resistance from fifteen-thousand defenders and reaching Kuwait City within hours. The following day, US Secretary of Defense Dick Cheney announced the dispatch of ground units and combat aircraft, including F-15s and AWACS radar planes, to Saudi Arabia as the first step in building a multinational force to deter a wider Iraqi attack (the aim of restoring Kuwaiti sovereignty was at this point left to an economic blockade). Washington also accelerated a requested Saudi shipment of forty-eight F-18s, and Congress was notified of the administration's intent to sell $919-million worth of spare parts and engineering support to the Saudis (*Aviation Week and Space Technology,* August 13, 1990; *Keesings Contemporary Archives,* vol. 36, August 1990, p. 37638). In addition to an embargo of Iraq, the Americans also halted scheduled shipments of $4.9 million in the military pipeline for Baghdad (*Defense News,* August 20, 1990, p. 27).

On August 6, the UN imposed a further sweeping trade embargo (Resolution 661), with Soviet support. Thus, Iraq lost its major arms supplier, the Soviet Union, and other open arms shipments were halted. Moscow's denunciation may have taken Saddam Hussein by surprise, but with large weapons stockpiles built since the end of the Iran war, and low arms attrition in overrunning Kuwait, Iraq still was seemingly in a strong military position in the autumn of 1990.

While the embargo held quite well, some arms probably leaked through via clandestine sources. One such route might have taken Chinese munitions to Iraq via Pakistan; while vowing to abide by UN sanctions, Chinese officials acknowledged discussions about arms shipments (*Far Eastern Economic Review,* no. 149, September 13, 1990, p. 6).[2] Israeli sources claimed that five ships carried Soviet and Polish arms to Iraq within a fortnight of the invasion, while the US and Britain scrambled to intercept such goods. Turkish authorities interdicted food and other cargo, while Armscor, the South African state-owned arms manufacturer, circumvented the embargo via Jordan (*International Herald Tribune,* August 16, 1990, p. 1).[3] In addition, many German firms were accused of association with Iraqi arms projects during the second half of 1990.[4]

In the various diplomatic attempts to avoid the outbreak of large-scale hostilities, Iraq's two major weapon suppliers, France and the USSR, implemented the embargo but appeared more conciliatory than her major opponent, the US. There are no detailed reports on how either used their prior arms relationship to influence Iraqi behavior, but it seems fair to assume that they tried to capitalize on it as a token of good faith; ostensibly, both failed. Throughout the autumn of 1990, French President François Mitterand openly favored a nonconfrontational stance and peace negotiations by the UN coalition. While his eleventh hour January 1991 proposal, calling for Iraq's withdrawal from Kuwait and a subsequent Middle East peace conference, won Soviet, German, and Italian backing, it was vigorously opposed by London and Washington, which rejected any apparent "linkage" to the Arab-Israeli dispute. More importantly, Iraq ignored this proposal and Moscow's subsequent similar one (also opposed by Washington). Thus, having voted for Security Council Resolution 678 authorizing the use of "all necessary means" to enforce the earlier peace resolution (January 15), the French and Soviet governments stood by the coalition. Given Iraqi intransigence, it seems unlikely that their power brokering would have worked even if they had not implemented the earlier arms embargo.[5]

Two days after the UN deadline, the US-led "Operation Desert Storm" offensive began. This first phase of war was fought from the air, with the allies seizing the initiative. US commanders directed the conduct of the war with high-technology weapons and an electronic battlefield capability developed over the years in preparation for war against the Soviet Union. These were appropriate to counter the largely Soviet-equipped Iraqi army, with its Soviet-style command and control structure (*Facts on File,* vol. 51, January 17, 1991, p. 26). The allies flew more than thirty-thousand sorties during January, softening up Iraqi defenses and targeting nearly every aspect of Iraq's infrastructure. Later in the month, the bombing was shifted to troop concentrations—particularly the elite Republican Guard—and supply lines in both Iraq and Kuwait. Efforts to knock out Iraq's politically troublesome Scuds also were stepped up. Carrier-based and land-based aircraft were employed, including B-52 bombers, ship-launched

Tomahawk cruise missiles, and Royal Air Force Tornados (*Keesings Contemporary Archives,* vol. 37, January 1991, p. 37936). The super-sophisticated F-117A Stealth fighter successfully evaded Iraqi radar and hit ground targets during night missions (*Facts on File,* vol. 51, January 17, 1991, p. 27). Patriot antimissile missiles, converted from their intended antiaircraft mode, had their first operational use on January 18, and though credited with a number of Scud "kills" during the war, the subsequent debate about their actual effectiveness raged long and loud.

The one-sided character of the air war was a stark demonstration of the effectiveness of high-tech weapons, with one side enjoying a monopoly of satellite and airborne surveillance. Despite experience in the long Iranian war, Iraqi forces also suffered training, morale, and tactical disadvantages. Together, these factors rendered the Iraqi air force impotent; it turned from any notion of counterattack simply to preserving its aircraft, a pattern reminiscent of the India-Pakistan and, in naval terms, the South Atlantic case.[6] Baghdad's modern weapons, which would have been effective in local wars, proved inadequate in the night skies against the bulk of coalition forces.

Allied air supremacy paved the way for the ensuing (February 23) ground assault against Iraqi forces. US General Norman Schwartzkopf declared on January 30 that the flow of supplies to Iraqi forces in Kuwait had been cut from the twenty-thousand tons per day needed for sustenance to only two-thousand (*Keesings Contemporary Archives,* vol. 37, January 1991, p. 37938). Within four days of their ground offensive, allied troops had liberated Kuwait, and went on to rout the Iraqi army.

Arms and Diplomacy. As noted, some arms leaked through the embargo, but were of only minor importance to the war effort. Any additional supply would have been superfluous, especially since the Iraqi military did not even employ all the weapons they had. Possibly with a larger inventory of fighters the air force would have been willing to risk more in battle, but the fleet as such was not small, at seven-hundred planes. Because of the war's brevity, the overall sanctions did not appear to affect supplies and ammunition to Iraqi forces; distribution was a greater logistical problem than shortage.

Resupplies had an important political impact, though, in relation to noncombatant Israel. As Scuds rained down in January 1991, US deliveries of Patriots, F-15s, and cargo helicopters won Tel Aviv's renewed pledge to stay out of the war. American personnel also were dispatched to operate the Patriots, and satellite reconnaissance and battle reports were provided (*Keesings Contemporary Archives,* vol. 37, January 1991, p. 37939). In addition, Germany delivered a Patriot battery to Israel with eight launchers, and promised nuclear-biological-chemical (NBC) tracking vehicles, and two submarines.[7]

The coalition ended in a position to dictate cease-fire terms. President George Bush had set a February 23 deadline for Iraq's unconditional withdrawal from Kuwait. Baghdad defiantly delayed until the 26th, but after the US pledged to continue the war, Baghdad informed the UN of its intention to comply fully with all resolutions. Iraq had been brought to this position by the superiority of allied arms and continued prosecution of the war. Any hopes for lifting of sanctions and renewed oil revenue were contingent upon full implementation of the resolutions. Unprecedented international regimes were implemented to examine Iraqi armaments potential, raising hopes, at least temporarily, of significant new agreements on arms-trade controls. The resounding victory also may have subtly shifted Washington's strategic calculations about the need for Israeli power, a shift reflected in subsequent friction and bickering over Arab-Israeli peace talks and US loan guarantees.

India vs. Pakistan—Kashmir Crisis

Arms Transfers. The Indo-Pakistani dispute over Kashmir/Jammu Kashmir, largely latent since the 1965 war, has never lost its combat potential. Tension levels have mounted and subsided, at times modulated by commitments on both sides to resolve the dispute peacefully. After a mini-crisis in April 1990, tension rose anew in 1991, as the population of the mainly Muslim northern section of Kashmir became more vociferous in favor of Pakistan, and the Indian army was accused of heavy-handed efforts to suppress such sentiments. Pakistan denied Indian accusations that it trained and armed guerrillas, a charge and a pattern going back to 1948.[8]

Low-level artillery shelling across the cease-fire line intensified in the summer of 1991 and continued sporadically, with each side blaming the other (*Economist,* September 7, 1991, p. 34, and November 23, 1991, p. 21). Border fatalities were estimated at one hundred for the year, though skirmishes were poorly reported as the press appeared to grow accustomed to the sporadic flare-ups and casualties.

Since they are each other's principal perceived threats, India and Pakistan largely set their military expenditures by their projected needs in a mutual war. Their peoples appear to harbor persistent expectations of a fourth such war (*Economist,* November 23, 1991, p. 21; *Keesings Contemporary Archives,* vol. 36, April 1990, p. 37377). India's defense budget for 1991–92 was increased nominally by seven percent, a cut in real terms when inflation is considered (*Asia-Pacific Defence Reporter,* April 1991). In the face of mounting economic problems, the budget was further reduced in order to qualify for loans from the International Monetary Fund (IMF) (*Economist,* July 27, 1991, p. 36). Pakistan's corresponding arms budget was increased by 11.6 percent, which also was not a rise in real terms. During 1990–91, however, Pakistani politicians, including the Finance Minister, had declared that in light of increased Kashmir conflict, it was impossible to cut the armed forces (*Defence,* July 1991). Nevertheless, there was strong outside pressure to do so, for instance from IMF negotiators and in view of the settling Afghani situation. Since Kashmiri border clashes are characterized by low-intensity shelling, they generally do not occasion large weapons acquisitions. Meanwhile, though, Indian officials were becoming uncertain of continued Soviet viability and support; spare parts problems for the air force were beginning to mount even in 1991.[9]

Pakistan's arms acquisition pattern was shaped by the US decision in October 1990 to suspend military assistance. For the first time, President Bush failed to certify that Pakistan did not possess "a nuclear explosive device." The arms suspension affected several weapons deliveries under contract: 77 F-16A fighters; 10 helicopters; 40 howitzers; 44 antiship missiles; 200 Sparrow air-to-air missiles (AAMS), and 2,476 TOW antitank missiles. However, seven months before the embargo, Pakistan had acquired the advanced US low altitude air defense radar system (LAADS), and Pakistani assembly of Swedish laser-guided RBS-70 missiles, locally named Anza, had begun; it was claimed that the missiles could hit any flying object within a five-kilometer radius with one-hundred percent accuracy (*Asia-Pacific Defence Reporter,* March 1990, p. 21). At about the same time, Islamabad also bought fifty used Mirage III Dassault fighters from the Australian air force. Subsequently, in July 1991, Islamabad secured delivery of the first prototype MBT 2000 Al-Khalid main battle tank from China; the tank was to be produced, beginning in 1993, under a license first granted in 1989 (SIPRI, *Yearbook,* 1991, p. 284). Chinese sources also acknowledged sale of short-range missiles, which

Washington protested as likely to exacerbate border tensions (*International Herald Tribune,* June 21, 1991, p. 5).

The Indian government called in Australia's ambassador to express "deep regret and disappointment" as news of Pakistan's pending Mirage fighter order broke in April; the deal was considered especially unfortunate in light of the rising Kashmiri clashes. The strong Indian protests extracted an Australian promise to reconsider the sale in the event of further Indian-Pakistani disruption (*Milavnews,* May 1990, pp. 2, 20), but the first thirty-two of the fifty Mirages arrived by sea in late December, with another sixteen set to follow in January (*World Weapons Review,* December 26, 1990, p. 6; *Defense and Armament International,* January 1991, p. 9). The planes had to be overhauled upon arrival, though, entailing a delay in their deployment. To compensate for them, India ordered two-hundred SA-16 portable SAMs from Moscow, which arrived during the same period (SIPRI, *Yearbook,* 1992, p. 337).

With the suspension of US-Pakistani arms deliveries and economic aid in October, the arms-acquisition balance shifted in New Delhi's favor. Although India had long since (1974) exploded a nuclear device (for "peaceful" purposes), it was not the target of any embargo, and Washington became somewhat friendlier even as Soviet backing became problematic with USSR disintegration. New Delhi negotiated with US firms for flight-control systems and considered Soviet and other undisclosed aircraft in relation to a planned 1992 air force upgrade (*Defense News,* August 12, 1991, p. 1). India could also consider upgrading MiGs with modern US avionics while Pakistan had to make do with outmoded, second-hand Mirages. With the end of the cold war and the Afghan war, Pakistan, like Israel, had lost some of its strategic appeal (by mid-1992, in fact, the US and India were conducting their first tentative small-scale joint naval exercises). On the whole, however, neither India nor Pakistan could be confident of spare parts and ammunition from their traditional suppliers in case of war.

Armament and the Course of War. As tensions over Kashmir mounted in April 1990, concern grew at the prospect of full-scale war. The Jammu and Kashmir Liberation Front (JKLF) seized prominent administrators as hostages (they were later killed), demanding the release of militants. India alleged Pakistani conspiracy in the crisis, as Kashmiris extended their campaign beyond the state, planting bombs in New Delhi and Bombay. The Hindu nationalist Bhahartiya

Janata Party (BJP) called on the government to engage in "hot pursuit" of terrorists and to strike dissident training camps in Pakistan. Prime Minister V.P. Singh, rather insecure in office, warned that Pakistan could not take Kashmir without a war. Exchanges of fire across the cease-fire lines ensued, and the Jammu and Kashmir state government imposed a curfew in the valley, banning eight political groups and closing three daily newspapers (*Keesings Contemporary Archives,* vol. 36, April 1990, p. 37377).

Political kidnapping recurred in February 1991, and violent clashes between Muslim separatists and Indian security forces resulted in twenty-seven deaths and one-thousand arrests in one week of March. After three days of clashes and charges of Indian human-rights abuses at the end of March, both sides reportedly reinforced their border troops (*Keesings Contemporary Archives,* vol. 37, March 1991, p. 38102). The continuing crisis led to India's extension of presidential rule in Jammu and Kashmir for another six months, through August, along with the state's exclusion from the May national elections (*Keesings Contemporary Archives,* vol. 37, April 1991, pp. 38151, 38161). However, the subcontinent was spared full-scale open warfare.

Arms and Diplomacy. Various diplomatic efforts were made to defuse the crisis after it intensified in April 1990. Indian Foreign Minister I. K. Gujral immediately met his Pakistani counterpart, Sahibzada Khan, at the UN and in New Delhi, mutually agreeing to restraint, though the Indians seemed to put the onus on Pakistan for easing the situation (*Keesings Contemporary Archives,* vol. 36, April 1990, p. 37377). Months of negotiation followed, concerning both the crisis and nuclear-arms issues. By the summer of 1990, the US and USSR were expressing increased concern that the Kashmir tensions might lead to a nuclear exchange between India and Pakistan. US satellite reconnaissance allegedly had observed transport convoys leaving the Pakistani nuclear complex near Islamabad, headed for military airfields. Reports also cited special weapons racks fitted to F-16s, which presumably could carry nuclear payloads. Indeed, on August 31, opposition leader Benazir Bhutto proclaimed Pakistan's capability to make nuclear weapons, even as China acknowledged that it had sold short-range missiles to Pakistan (*Milavnews,* July 1990, p. 20). Both sides had worked on missile delivery programs in 1990, test-firing IRBMs (India, Agni; Pakistan, Hatf-II).

Nevertheless, in October the Indian Prime Minister reaffirmed his belief in dialogue, asserting that bilateral negotiations could solve all outstanding issues (*All India Radio,* October 19, 1991). On January 27, 1991, in fact, the two sides concluded a nuclear nonintervention treaty, agreeing not to attack each other's nuclear facilities; they went on to agree to weekly exchanges of information about troop movements.

The outcome of three previous Indo-Pakistani wars has indicated how crucial the role of arms patrons was both to war planning and diplomatic initiatives. Putting aside the question of Indo-Pakistani nuclear deterrence for the moment, the end of the cold war and domestic political disruptions appear to have added just enough uncertainty to mitigate against full-scale war in the subcontinent. As noted, old patrons' support for each side had weakened, and in some cases nearly reversed; indeed at the UN in November 1991, Moscow voted with Pakistan, and so against its old Indian friends, on its proposal to make South Asia a nuclear free zone. Washington, in turn, came to support India's preference for bilateral talks in resolving the Kashmir dispute, as against Pakistan's choice of a UN-sponsored plebiscite.

The US aid suspension, basically related to the nuclear controversy, had a further telling effect in creating shortages of spare parts for Pakistan's F-16s, so grounding much of the fleet. India developed similar parts-supply problems for Soviet equipment, also putting much of the Indian air force out of action for long periods during the Kashmir conflict (*Economist,* November 30, 1991, p. 33). Along with each government's political weakness (Ms. Bhutto's rise to and fall from power; India's search for strong leadership and a return of the ill-fated Rajiv Gandhi),[10] these concurrent supply problems probably rendered them ill-prepared for war, especially since aircraft would be crucial for fighting in and around Kashmir. Notably in the past, supply problems on the subcontinent generally have been asymmetric, both in the historical cases we have reviewed (which generally favored India even in cases of bilateral embargo), and as late as 1985 and late-1987, when India lacked the main systems for its forty-nine Mirage 2000s due to lags in contracts (*Milavnews,* June 1990, p. 17). Judging by historical standards, a supply imbalance between the two air forces in 1991 would have made war more likely.

Thus, direct confrontations were minimized, which in the context of political and arms-transfer uncertainties, indicates that several factors in addition to nuclear deterrence were dampening the conflict. The Indians may not have been eager to incorporate areas north of the 1948 cease-fire line since they contain the hard core of Islamic militants, while Pakistan may only have been genuinely interested in the portion of Jammu and Kashmir where the majority population is Muslim (*Economist,* September 7, 1991, p. 34). Furthermore, Pakistan appeared to have a vested interest in containing the conflict since failure to do so could have resulted in the loss of Australia's Mirage shipments.

War in Europe: Yugoslavia's Disintegration

Arms Transfers. In the post–cold war restructuring of Europe, states are being dismembered and reconstituted by old nationalisms and antagonisms, often in tragically bloody confrontations. Simultaneously, in other parts of the continent, the twin processes of economic and political integration are proceeding, though it seems with second thoughts. The former trend represents a challenge and obstacle to the latter. While the Balkan fighting at least began as a civil war, the external supply of arms and widespread recognition of newly independent nation-states made the scene seem familiar to any observer of interstate conflict and highly unusual for post–1945 Europe.

Flows of arms clearly fuelled the Yugoslavian fighting. Before armed hostilities broke out, the central authorities and the Yugoslav National Army (JNA) had a near monopoly on battle weapons and quite a sizeable domestic arms industry predominantly located in Serbia. However, as the Yugoslav state disintegrated and the fighting intensified, the army progressively resembled an army of Serbia. JNA defections and arms flows from external sources would allow Slovenia and Croatia to sustain a moderate level of fighting. The Slovenes especially owed their fighting capability initially to equipment, including infantry and air defense weapons, retained as the JNA failed to disarm the territorials. While the Slovenes kept forty percent of their weapons, the Croats held considerably less, but still enough to mount campaigns against the JNA.

Slovenia declared independence on June 26, 1991, but had prepared for the occasion for two years. Within weeks of independence, the Slovene Territorial Defense Force (STDF) clashed with the JNA. The Slovenenes, the most economically advanced of Yugoslav republics, used Yugoslav-produced M56 sub-machine guns, derived from the German MP 40, as basic equipment. They also carried Romanian AK-47 and Hungarian AMD-65 assault rifles. Their farthest traveled weapon was the Armbrust, a short-range antiarmor device designed in Germany and marketed from Singapore, with which the Slovenes claimed to have destroyed eight federal tanks in the summer of 1991 (*Jane's Defence Weekly,* July 13, 1991, p. 49). Before independence they had no armored personnel carriers (APCs), but with post-independence fighting they quickly captured several from deserting federal troops; indeed, officials asserted that they had captured more federal weapons than they could possibly use.

Croatia proclaimed its independence on June 25, a declaration greeted by an escalation of the existing Serbo-Croatian clashes. Unlike the Slovenian Defense Force, however, the Croatian National Resistance (CNR) had not long prepared for possible military action. Numbering 150,000 former federal conscripts, Croatian forces were strengthened in June and July by federal army deserters, many bringing their personal weapons (*Jane's Defence Weekly,* August 24, 1991, p. 311). Raids on government stores netted additional arms.

A number of external arms sources were said to have supplied both breakaway republics. The recently stilled Lebanese civil war had released artillery, rocket launchers, machine guns, and ammunition for the clandestine market. The Lebanese Forces, the largest Christian group, reportedly sold most of its $100-million arsenal in secret during the spring of 1991 (*International Herald Tribune,* July 2, 1991, p. 3). Much of the weaponry and ammunition bound for Yugoslavia reportedly also came from the Soviet Union, where in common with Lebanon, not all arms were under central control. The US was an important source of small arms, which could be bought openly because of permissive gun laws; American guns and rifles were found in large numbers in arms seizures by German and Austrian border control units (*Frankfurter Rundschau,* November 16, 1991, p. 2; November 19 and 20, 1991, p. 4). US customs stopped additional attempts to export $12-million worth of infantry weapons. The Croats were interested in more expensive items as well, including the US Stinger low altitude SAM system (*Jane's Defence Weekly,* August 24, 1991, p. 311).

Croat and Slovene officials talked openly of buying weapons from several sources, including German, Austrian, and Singaporean dealers. Slovenia reportedly spent $50 million on imports from these countries, and from the Soviet Union and Eastern Europe (*International Herald Tribune,* July 9, 1991, p. 1).[11] Arms also were shipped from South Africa, using a Boeing 707 chartered from Uganda Airlines flying from Bophuthatswana via Entebbe to Zagreb (*New African,* November 1991, p. 31).

On the other hand, the most recent major arms purchased by the debt ridden Yugoslav central government had been the AA-11 infrared-guided Soviet Archer AAM, acquired in 1990 for MiG-29 fighters. These were inappropriate for civil war, however, since neither Slovenia nor Croatia possessed an air force. Somewhat more useful would have been the three Hercules transports that were contracted from the US in 1989 but not delivered. As noted, though, Serbian forces could rely on a diversified arms industry producing a wide range of ammunition and equipment, including light planes and tanks. Prior to the hostilities, this industry had been a major export earner (Brzoska and Ohlson, 1987, pp. 110–12). Of course, Serbia's opponents also picked up some of this equipment on the battlefield. The JNA arsenal featured 350 T-74 main battle tanks, obtained from the Soviet Union from 1983 to 1989, and 24 MiG-29s, received from 1988–89 (SIPRI, *Yearbook,* 1991, p. 268; *World Weapon Review,* June 27, 1990, p. 10).

Armament and the Course of War. Ethnic tensions rose steadily after the Slovenian and Croatian independence referenda in December 1990 and May 1991, respectively. Serbian separatists had engaged Croatian police in gun battles, and after one such incident in April 1991, as Serbs proclaimed a "Serbian Autonomous Region of Krajina" in Croatia, the JNA moved in to "reduce tensions." Intercommunal violence nevertheless continued, with shootings and bombings, and the JNA brought additional armored units to Croatia. Despite assurances to the contrary, their numbers heightened Croatian fears of a creeping military takeover. These misgivings prompted the formation of a de facto republican army, the Croatian National Guard Corps. The JNA faced increasing attacks and demonstrations, relying in turn on its tank units (*Keesings Contemporary Archives,* vol. 37, April 1991, pp. 38163–64).

By early May, Croats and Serbs were engaged in their bloodiest clashes since World War II. The JNA moved tanks into Borovo Selo and occupied villages near Knin, the main town in the "Autonomous Region." Croatia's President Franjo Tudjman blamed Serbian nationalists and fascists for trying to provoke military intervention in order to set up a Greater Serbia. The eight-member Yugoslav Collective State Presidency met on May 4, condemning the Borovo Selo incidents but ordering a reinforcement of the JNA's role. On May 6, the Defence Secretariat placed the army on full combat alert, ordered the Croat authorities to desist from further attacks, and threatened to settle accounts with those who inspired the uprisings. The Collective Presidency afforded the JNA even wider powers in Croatia on May 9, but stopped short of invoking a state of emergency; all along, the JNA presence contributed to the heightened tensions (*Keesings Contemporary Archives,* May 1991, p. 38203).

Croat and Slovene declarations of independence then further intensified the crisis. The federal parliament called for JNA intervention to protect "Yugoslavia's borders." As Ljubljana radio reported troop movements and military overflights, on June 27, 1991, members of the JNA were mobilized and dispatched to Slovenia's three borders. They met heavy resistance; fighting and air bombardments continued until the next afternoon. Both sides claimed control of the border crossings after battles that claimed one-hundred lives (*Keesings Contemporary Archives,* vol. 37, June 1991, p. 38275).

Slovene forces had successfully resisted the army's attacks, benefitting from nearly unanimous popular support in what had been Yugoslavia's most ethnically homogeneous republic. To prevail, the bulk of the JNA would have had to cross through hostile Croatian territory; thus, Yugoslav and JNA leaders showed discretion by not pressing the point too far.

Nevertheless, responding to a more proximate challenge, the army repeatedly bombarded the Croatian town of Vukovar, beginning on August 25. Despite Croat claims to have knocked out thirty tanks, bits of Croatia began to fall to Serbian forces. In a pattern of massive attacks against civilian centers designed to clear out ethnic opponents, the Serbs and their allies would gain at least one-fifth of the republic (the pattern would be repeated a year later in Bosnia-Herzegovina) (*Economist,* August 31, 1991, p. 44).

By the autumn, inadequate supplies appeared to be a key factor as the Croats were outgunned. Retreating, they tried to organize a defense; Croatian troops were ordered to surround federal bases in Zagreb. Oil lines to Serbia had been cut and atrocities on both sides mounted (*Economist,* September 21, 1991, p. 57). In the disastrous siege of Dubrovnik in October, however, lack of arms clearly hampered Croat defenders, further deflating morale. Their only potent weapons to fend off a Montenegrin (Serb ally) troop encirclement of the city were one heavy machine gun and two forty-year-old artillery pieces. Clandestine blockade running proved insufficient (*Economist,* November 2, 1991, p. 45). The fall of Vukovar, Serbia's first set-piece victory, followed late in November.

Arms and Diplomacy. Representing as it did Europe's first major warfare in forty-five years, the Yugoslav war proved highly disquieting to the European Community and NATO. With the US still largely preoccupied in the Middle East and seeing few strategic interests in the Balkans, Brussels seemed the logical focus for attempts to dampen the conflict; indeed, influential EC members appeared anxious to take on the role. There were indications, as well, that Washington and its allies did not see entirely eye-to-eye on the crisis; it appears that EC members, and particularly Germany, gradually became considerably more anxious to recognize the breakaway republics than the US.

On June 24, 1991, the EC offered $850 million to Yugoslavia if it were to remain united (*Economist,* June 29, 1991, p. 41). With this carrot, though, came the stick of threatened sanctions against Belgrade if force were used to achieve this outcome. Nevertheless, at that point Slovenian and Croatian independence appeared to be unavoidable. Secret talks reportedly took place in July between Serbia and Croatia about carving up Bosnia and Herzegovina between them, with a Muslim buffer in between (*Economist,* July 20, 1991, p. 49). The fact of these talks suggests that both sides were adequately equipped and motivated to make a fight for territory. But the Serbs were stronger, as the subsequent Croat retreat indicates, and as the Croat offer of "political autonomy" for Serbian areas also suggests. Thus, Belgrade had little incentive to accept negotiated terms as long as they were still gaining territory and as long as no one was enforcing cease-fire demands.

Of course, widespread diplomatic activity was underway to contain the war and find a political settlement. Under EC auspices, a number of cease-fires were negotiated during the summer and fall. Indeed, the Yugoslav fighting provided for the multination Conference on Security and Cooperation in Europe (CSCE) its first test of crisis management mechanisms. Unfortunately, it proved wanting, as one cease-fire after another broke down; from the fall of 1991, therefore, the UN Security Council also became involved.

Arms-transfer policies played a prominent role in these diplomatic maneuvers. The EC decided to ban all weapon deliveries to Yugoslavia in early July. By early August the community had approached more than twenty governments suspected of delivering arms, asking their support for the embargo; favorable answers reportedly were received from most (*Frankfurter Rundschau,* August 14, 1991, p. 2). In Resolution 713, passed on September 25, the Security Council backed this effort, calling for a voluntary arms embargo. However, these measures were judged mainly symbolic, aimed at showing the significance the major powers attributed to the fighting. Ironically, if they had any effects at all, the restrictions reduced the flow of arms to the Slovenian and Croatian forces at a time when public opinion in several European states had swung toward their side. As in other wars, in ex-Yugoslavia arms-resupply problems might have motivated many of the aborted cease-fires. Reportedly, the combatants used these pauses to obtain more food and ammunition (*Economist,* August 10, 1991, p. 38).

At its Hague conference on November 8, the EC finally imposed economic sanctions, after having debated and threatened to do so for much of the conflict. These sanctions were to be symmetrical on all combatants, as selective sanctions are difficult if not impossible to administer. But since the aim was basically to punish Serbia, means were drawn up to compensate friendly republics. In January 1991, UN mediator Cyrus Vance succeeded in negotiating a cease-fire involving the stationing of seventeen-thousand "blue helmet" troops.

The pattern of effective resupply of weaker or defending parties, seen in our historical review, was broken in this case, and the war did not have a prompt solution. Nevertheless, the Slovenes fared better in armament terms against the Serbs and terminated hostilities sooner than the Croats managed to do. Because of their domestic arms industrial base, Serbian forces were not very vulnerable to an embargo per se, though an additional cut off of fuel as well as trade and industrial components might have had a more telling effect at that time (it would be attempted a year later, perhaps too late, in relation to Bosnia). Again, it appears that once fighting breaks out, if embargoes favor the attacking side, they have little pacifying effect, and in any case, unless they proportionately penalize their attacker, their effectiveness may depend on other accompanying sanctions.[12]

CONCLUSIONS

As shown in Table 27, in the one recent confrontation that reached a conclusion, the Iran-Coalition Gulf war, arms-technology levels ultimately were crucial to that outcome, reversing an initial Iraqi regional advantage. With the formation of a massive countervailing coalition, a development that Iraqi leaders probably had not anticipated, the advantage swung to the allies; their satellite surveillance and more advanced weapons arsenal allowed a quick and decisive victory. The threat of armed attack and the stringent crisis economic and arms embargoes had done little to impress a basically impervious or incredulous Baghdad, though many held out hope that in the long run Iraqi leaders would need to avoid total economic collapse and accept terms. Once the fighting itself began and proved decisive, Iraq capitulated first in Kuwait and then on its home territory, but acceptance of settlement terms was still stalled and debated as long as possible.

The 1990–91 Indo-Pakistani conflict was unusual in that both parties were thought to possess nuclear capabilities. Mutual deterrence possibly helped shape their relations, but the uncertainties of effective arms resupplies may, along with domestic concerns, have done more to preclude a shooting war. With the end of the cold war, traditional arms-supply relations dried up on both sides, though not quite as acutely for the Indians. China, nevertheless, still offered some alternative for Pakistan, as it also has come to do for a number of debt-ridden LDCs. The symmetric supply problems, particularly for both air forces, probably made war less likely, although perceptions and intelligence reports can always sway a decision to launch an attack.

In what was left of Yugoslavia, arms supply was a determinant of levels of confrontation, as well as outcomes. The Slovenians retained a considerably larger share of former federal army weapons, and, given geographical advantages and ethnic homogeneity, fared much better in the fighting against central authorities than did the Croats, who appeared to run out of arms and parts. Indeed, secret talks of accommodation between Serbia and Croatia were broken off by the former just as the latter forces were beginning to have resupply problems. Arms from external sources did not arrive in sufficient quantities to halt the Croat retreat. As in previous wars of the cold war era, economic and supply embargoes appeared to have somewhat greater impact on negotiations than arms embargoes per se, especially in view of the availability of strategic fuel and clandestine arms sources.

These findings verify several conclusions of the prior case studies, and add some new insights. Wars again tend to be preceded by major arms acquisitions. Arms embargoes' weak impact on the course and outcome of hostilities is magnified when combined with other forms of sanctions. Truly symmetrical embargo effects tend to dampen conflict and prevent violent flare-ups. Arms advantages for those initiating combat, if sustained without relief for the defenders, tend to lengthen and increase the violence. Decisive arms advantages for defenders tend, on the other hand, to lead to quicker and more conclusive outcomes. Arms suppliers' diplomatic leverage is eroded by the availability of new, even inferior, weapons sources. Arms supply affects both the level of hostilities and combatants' willingness or ability to forego negotiations, as in Yugoslavia. The Gulf war demonstrated the importance of the quality of arms supplied; access to high-technology exporters may continue to prove crucial in future conflicts, though higher technology also can result in higher costs as well as greater dependency and vulnerability to outside supply and fuel cutoffs.

In the end, the potential effectiveness of arms-transfer relationships and arms transfers in containing wars is limited to specific circumstances involving attrition rates and dependency, military sophistication of the belligerents, technological level of fighting, viability of defenders, alternatives in supply, symmetry of impacts, and combinations of sanctions. On balance over time, the diplomatic impact of arms transfers themselves seems to have weakened.

Seen from this perspective, multilateral efforts to control the arms trade, which at least rhetorically increased after the Gulf war in 1991, while crucial, so far can only be judged a modest step in the right direction. While it certainly makes sense to focus on weapons of mass destruction and their delivery systems, as the major powers did at the behest of presidents Bush and Mitterand, efforts should not stop there. Efforts must include consideration of the differential impact of supplies and supply restrictions on attackers and defenders. They must come to grips with the evidence that resupply and embargo both tend to favor one side in a conflict. People suffering from wars usually are victims of conventional arms. Thus, an important element in alleviating such dangers could be a regulated supply favoring victims, along with the elimination of the arms black market.

An idea floated during the Football War may thus bear further consideration, i.e., the possibility of supplying arms or supplies to defenders on a controlled basis through multilateral or regional organizations. As such ideas were debated during the Bosnian crisis of 1992–93, however, complications arose in fears of escalated fighting, spillover attacks on UN peacekeeepers, and stimulation of competitive local arms races. Even more important than arming defenders is the determined effort to limit capabilities of the attacker. Arms embargoes can have effect, especially if the technological level of weaponry employed is high. Economic embargoes take a longer time to "bite"—depending on the economic resources of the target—but the subsequent impact, and even the anticipated effect appear greater than arms embargoes alone, especially in a world with multiple arms-supply sources. Creative diplomacy will be especially critical in the coming years as the collapse of the East Bloc, along with global trade and employment problems, threaten both to undermine effective export restrictions and release vast quantities of weapons on the market.

In the longer run, arms transfers should be subject to more open ("transparent") reporting—as in the new UN arms trade Registry—as well as regional multilateral supplier-client negotiations and security guarantees, to restrict the de-stabilizing build-ups that generally precede wars and drain treasuries. Stoppage of arms deliveries to combatants during warfare also would be more effective if coordinated so that shortages were generated simultaneously on both sides or so that aggressors were effectively discouraged. In any such regime, the participation of new suppliers (and particularly China), as well as recipients, will be imperative for successful arms transfer controls.

Our case analyses have shown that for much of the last half-century, suppliers have been fairly restrictive of arms during warfare, attempting to apply pressures for cease-fires and pacing resupply to preserve some measure of control. Of course, the control has been less than impressive and reliable, and some recipients have proven very adept at circumvention, indeed at reverse influence, to open the arms channels wider. In the end, it remains to suppliers to resist such temptation, along with the attendant desire to see one's arms prevail on the battlefield; with the decline of superpower competition, such resistance to fuelling the fires of war may be at least marginally easier.

Appendix

Short Chronologies of the Wars

Chronology 1

INDIA-PAKISTAN KASHMIR WAR, 1965

Date	Warfare	Diplomacy	Arms
Jan.–Mar. 1965	Increasing clashes at India-Pak. border at Rann of Kutch		
Apr.–June 1965	Continued conflict in Rann of Kutch and Kashmir	UK-USSR achieve negotiated settlement on Rann; US presses for Indian withdrawal from Pak. positions in Kashmir	
Aug. 1965	India retakes positions across Kashmir	UN-US-USSR advise India-Pak. to avoid full-scale war	Indians request Soviet subs and seize Pak. arms and equipment
Sept. 1–9, 1965	Pak. assault into Kashmir; major Indian assault into West Pak.	UN-UK-USSR request cease-fire. US warns both of aid cutoff; Chinese veiled threats to India	US-UK arms embargo of India and Pak.
Sept. 10–17, 1965	Tank battles in West Pak. peak	India accepts UN ceasefire; US warns PRC against involvement; China delivers ultimatum; USSR vows response to Chinese ultimatum	Pak. promised arms from Turkey & Iran, aircraft from China; India receives Soviet arms and MiG factory

Chronology 1 243

Date	Warfare	Diplomacy	Arms
Sept. 18–22, 1965		UK diplomatic mission; UN Security Council demands cease-fire by Sept. 22; China drops demands	UK indicates possible resumption of Indian military aid if China intervenes
Sept. 23, 1965	Sporadic clashes continue until Tashkent agreement in Jan. 1966.	Cease-fire mutually accepted by India and Pak.	

Chronology 2

INDIA-PAKISTAN BANGLADESH WAR, 1971

Date	Warfare	Diplomacy	Arms
March–June 1971	East-West Pak. civil war begins; border skirmishes with India	East Pak. claims independence; China offers Pak. interest free loan	US arms sent to Pak.; exports banned after civil war begins; arms agreed to prior are shipped
July–August 1971	Indian shelling of East Pak.; incursions reported	India-USSR sign treaty of friendship	France annnounces ban on weapon sales to Pak.; Canada refuses to allow Pak. to pick up jet engines
Sept.–October 1971	Shelling between India and Pak. becomes frequent	India proposes settlement after US announcement; changes to threat after arms shipments; Pak. proposes mutual withdrawal	US announces possible arms delivery to Pak.; N. Korea reportedly delivers arms to Pak.
November 1971	Major border fights and escalation of tensions	UN attempts to mediate dispute; US and India meet	Soviet arms shipments to India begin; Pak. requests arms from China; US suspends arms to India
Dec. 1–7, 1971	Full-scale war begins; India advances in East Pak.	USSR vetoes two UN cease-fire resolutions; US protests Indian attack on US merchant ship and cuts aid; China condemns Indian policy	India seizes Pak. weapons in East Pak.; US halts Indian arms licenses

Date	Warfare	Diplomacy	Arms
Dec. 9–13, 1971	Pak. retreating in East Pak.; India continues to advance	US urges India to comply with UN cease-fire resolution; India refuses; US moves fleet and advises Pak.	
Dec. 14–16, 1971	Indian troops outside Dacca; Pak. surrender in East Pak.; India orders cease-fire	Pak. and India exchange terms of surrender	China delivers ammunition to Pak.

Note: During war Jordan delivers US planes to Pak.

Chronology 3

THE CENTRAL AMERICAN FOOTBALL WAR, 1969

Date	Warfare	Diplomacy	Arms
April 1969		Honduras enforces Agrarian Reform Law and orders Salvadorans to vacate	
July 3–13, 1969	Troops clash along border; exchange mortar fire	Honduras and El Salvador sever relations after football rioting and seek OAS help; OAS calls for restraint and offers mediation	
July 14–17, 1969	Salvadoran forces invade and bomb Honduras; Honduras retaliates by bombing near San Salvador	OAS passes cease-fire resolution; UN appeals to both sides to stop fighting; Honduras willing to accept cease-fire	Honduras requests arms from OAS; request deferred; US stops military aid to both counries
July 18–20, 1969	Fighting slows due to lack of ammunition; El Salvador accepts cease-fire; OAS monitors for reported violations	Bishops in both countries as well as the Pope appeal for peace; OAS to impose sanctions against El Salvador if troops are not withdrawn	*New York Times* reports that El Salvador has purchased arms from West Germany and that Nicaragua has delivered supplies to Honduras
July 21–25, 1969	Cease-fire holds; El Salvador continues to occupy Honduran territory; both sides move troops toward border	El Salvador refuses to withdraw in noncompliance with OAS resolution; sanctions are again threatened	Honduras reportedly receiving supplies from Nicaragua (Nicaragua denies); El Salvador is shopping for arms

Date	Warfare	Diplomacy	Arms
July 27–30, 1969	Continued accusations of cease-fire violations; El Salvador agrees to withdraw from Honduras	OAS considers sanctions until withdrawal announcement; calls on members to aid war refugees	
Aug. 3, 1969	El Salvador withdraws from Honduras		

Note: US delivers one small plane to El Salvador in 1969.

Chronology 4

THE SOUTH ATLANTIC WAR, 1982

DATE	WARFARE	DIPLOMACY	ARMS
March 1982	Arg. lands a crew on S. Georgia Island	Arg. considers itself free to choose its own procedure to settle the Malvinas dispute	
April 1–15, 1982	Arg. troops land on East Falkland Island; British navy sails southward; UK announces 200-mile military exclusion zone (MEZ)	Arg. claims sovereignty over Falklands; UK breaks diplomatic and trade relations; Canada and Australia ban Arg. imports; Latin states back Arg.; US supplies intelligence to UK and holds talks with Arg.; UN adopts cease-fire	Austria suspends tank shipment to Arg.; Canada begins military embargo on Arg.; EC declares arms embargo on future sales to Arg.
April 16–30, 1982	UK task force recaptures S. Georgia; UK and Arg. both announce exclusion zone around the Falklands	Brazil closes ports to UK; Arg. rejects US proposals; UK agrees; OAS appeals to stop fighting; US suspends new EX/IM Bank credits to Arg.	Peruvian attack planes reportedly delivered to Arg.; US bans military sales to Arg. and offers UK material support
May 1–7, 1982	UK attacks Port Stanley, sinks Arg. cruiser *Belgrano,* and bombs air fields in Falklands; Arg. fighters bomb UK ships	Japan imposes sanctions on Arg.; UN attempt mediation; UN cease-fire receives initial support from both sides	Spare parts reportedly delivered to Arg. from Venezuela
May 9–17, 1982	Attacks on Port Stanley continue; Arg. attacks UK ships, loses fighter planes and supply ships; UK forces land on Falklands	Brazil denounces UK attacks; UK suspends UN talks for 48 hours	Brazil sells small planes and arms to Arg.

248

Date	Warfare	Diplomacy	Arms
May 19–31, 1982	Each side incurs damage to and losses of aircraft and ships; UK bombs Arg. land forces	Arg. and UK withdraw from UN negotiations; Arg. appeals to UK for negotiations; UK announces cease-fire must be linked to withdrawal	US delivers aerial tanker, ammunition, and missiles to UK; Arg. reportedly received ammunition and parts from S. Africa
June 2–14, 1982	UK continues bombing Port Stanley; Arg. repels a UK offensive; Arg. surrenders	Arg. makes a cease-fire proposal; Britain offers to agree if Arg. troops withdraw; cease-fire resolution in UN is vetoed by UK and US	Arms deliveries to Arg. are reported from Libya and other private sources

Chronology 5

THE YOM KIPPUR-RAMADAN WAR, 1973

Date	Warfare	Diplomacy	Arms
Spring–Oct. 5, 1973	Egypt intensifies ground preparations; Syria and Egypt continue build-up along Golan Hts., Suez Canal; Israel reinforces defenses near Golan Hts.	Arab Summit is held in Cairo (Sept.)	Egypt receives Scuds and launcher vehicles from USSR
Oct. 6–9, 1973	Israeli units mobilize; Egypt and Syria begin assault on Israeli forces; major tank and air battles on both fronts; Israel repels Syrian offensives	UN appeals to both sides to stop fighting; Security Council meets with no cease-fire resolution; US sends elements of 6th fleet to Medit; US-USSR indicate a consensus on limiting the conflict	Israel requests arms from US; Algeria sends planes to Eqypt; Iraq flies MiGs to Syria; Libya threatens to send Mirage fighters to Egypt
Oct. 10–15, 1973	Syria begins to retreat; Egypt consolidates its positions across the Suez Canal; Israel begins offensive into Syria; Egypt loses 200–300 tanks; Jordan and Saudis promise troops	UNSC remains deadlocked; US confers with Soviets and China, augments Medit. fleet; Syria and Egypt, backed by USSR, claim they will accept cease-fire only if Israel withdraws to pre-1967 war lines; China attacks US and Soviet policy	UK announces arms embargo against both sides; USSR and US increase their shipments to their clients
Oct. 16–20, 1973	Israel extends position at Suez Canal; heavy loses are reported on both sides; clashes along Syrian front, where a Jordanian-Iraqi attack fails; cease-fire agreed but does not hold	Sadat calls for cease-fire; OPEC announces reduction in oil flow to countries supporting Israel; Israel rejects Sadat's proposal; Saudi Arabia cuts oil to the US; Kuwait provides war funds to Arabs; Kissinger visits Moscow	US announces shipment of Phantoms to Israel; More Soviet arms deliveries are reported; US offers Isarel arms package for a cease-fire; North Korea offers arms to Arabs

DATE	WARFARE	DIPLOMACY	ARMS
Oct. 21–24, 1973	Israel moves toward the Gulf of Suez, encircling Egypt's 3rd Army and violating UN cease-fire; sporadic clashes continue until Oct. 31	US-USSR present joint resolution to the UNSC for a cease-fire; cease-fire adopted and peacekeeping forces are offered; Egypt accepts; Kissinger confers with Meir; Egypt appeals for US-USSR intervention; US refuses	US and USSR reportedly continue to make daily deliveries; Syrians agree to cease-fire after Soviets delay arms shipments
Oct. 25–Nov. 1973	Israel agrees to allow resupply to Egyptian 3rd Army	UN force to supervise the cease-fire; US puts troops on alert; Egypt and Israel to negotiate directly; Syria accepts cease-fire agreement after Soviet reassurance	Germany refuses US arms shipments from its territory

Chronology 6

ISRAELI-ARAB WAR IN LEBANON, 1982

DATE	WARFARE	DIPLOMACY	ARMS
Apr.–June 1982	IAF attacks PLO positions in Leb.; Israel invades Leb.; Israeli and Syrian troops clash, later announce cease-fire; Israel and PLO make short-lived truce	UNSC passes cease-fire resolution; US vetoes UN sanctions against Israel; EC and many Arab states condemn invasion; US seeks settlement; 400 Iranian "volunteers" to Syria	Soviets reportedly supplying Syria; UK embargoes arms to Israel; US explores possible violation of Arms Export Control Act
July–Sept. 1982	IAF bombs W. Beirut and PLO heavily; Syrian and PLO forces begin withdrawal from Beirut; Israel takes over most of W. Beirut, later withdraws; French, Italian, and US forces arrive; refugee-camp massacres occur; Israel begins withdrawal under pressure; peacekeepers leave, then return	US and France agree to peacekeeping force; Soviets oppose use of US forces; UNSC calls for Israel to halt advances; US objects to Israeli bombing; Syria willing to withdraw; Israel rejects Reagan peace plan; US aid to Leb. increases with attempts to find haven for PLO	US suspends cluster bombs and delays F-15 delivery to Israel; Israel asserts cluster bombs are consistent with US agreements; Israel seizes PLO weapons
Oct.–Dec. 1982	Leb. troops positioned between Christian and Druze militias; Syria fires on Israeli warplane; US forces begin patrols in E. Beirut; UNIFIL clash with militias; IDF and Leb. forces in brief clash; UK joins peacekeeping forces; Israel reduces forces in Leb.	Israel and Leb. agree to negotiate terms of withdrawal; Israel seeks normalized relations with Leb.; Leb. requests more MNF troops; US makes proposal to break the deadlock; Leb. demands withdrawal of foreign forces by Feb. 15, 1983	DOD plans to sell tanks to Leb.; USSR supplies Syria with missiles; US agrees to equip and train Leb. troops during 1983

Date	Warfare	Diplomacy	Arms
Jan.–June 1983	Low-level fighting between various groups in Leb.; minor standoff between Israel and US forces; Leb. Army takes control of Beirut; Israel and MNF troops wounded patrolling Beirut; Israel and Syrian forces clash	Leb. demands Israel withdraw; US calls on PLO, Syria, and Israel all to withdraw; USSR says it would intervene if there is a direct Israel-Syria conflict; in May Israel and Leb. reach tentative agreement; Syria rejects the plan	US suspends F-16 delivery to Israel; France grants Leb. loan to purchase military supplies; US releases F-16s to Israel in May
July–Dec. 1983	Israel fires on Syrian position and redeploys troops in Leb.; Druze shell MNF positions; US sends 2,000 Marines to Leb.; Syria forces withdrawal of PLO troops; US, French, and Israeli headquarters are destroyed; US troops under heavy fire; Israeli jets attack Syrian positions; Syria shells US forces in Beirut	USSR refuses to restrain Syrian involvement; Syria and Leb. agree to cease-fire on Sept. 25; US threatens to withdraw from UN if Israel is ousted from Gen. Assembly; Israel says it will reduce military presence in Leb.; PLO factions agree to a cease-fire; US says it may pull out of Leb.	US resumes delivery of cluster bombs and increases military aid to Israel in Nov.; US plans $1.4 billion in military grants to Israel in Dec.
Jan.–Mar. 1984	US warships fire on Druze positions in Beirut; Israel jets bomb suspected PLO and Druze positions in Leb.; US forces withdraw; British, Italian, and French MNF contingents withdraw from Leb.	US denies Leb. request to deploy troops to reestablish government control; Syria announces it will not withdraw until other foreign troops do; Leb. accepts reconcilation plan that abrogates May agreement with Israel; UN delays vote on peacekeeping forces	

Chronology 7

THE IRAQ-IRAN WAR, 1980–1988

DATE	WARFARE	DIPLOMACY	ARMS
Oct. 1979– 1980	Border clashes begin; Iraq damages refinery; Iran's forces on alert; Iraqi forces occupy region north of Basra; Iran uses ground-to-ground missiles to repel Iraqis; full-scale fighting in Sept.; Iraq bombs inside Iran; Iran retaliates; in Dec., third front opens in Kurdistan	Iraqi demands for Iran's evacuation of Tumbs Island and minority-groups autonomy are rejected; Khomeni calls for overthrow of Hussein; US remains neutral in the conflict; USSR follows suit; Saudis and Jordanians express support for Iraq; UN passes cease-fire resolution Sept. 28; Iran rejects Iraqi cease-fire offer	US arms embargo of Iran due to hostage crisis; Iraq is supplied by W. Germany, France, and Italy; after prewar deliveries, USSR stops military shipments to Iraq as war begins; USSR sells fuel to Iran; Iran receives supplies from Syria, N. Korea, and secretly from Israel; Iraq captures weapons from Iran
1981	Iranian counteroffensive claimed to be repelled by Iraq; Iran claims to destroy three Iraqi battalions; warfronts remain the same; Iran bombs Iraqi oil installations and power plants	Iran and Jordan sever relations; Kuwait makes interest-free loans to Iraq; USSR and Iran agree on Soviet advisers; Iran rejects offer of Ramadan cease-fire	US maintains Iran's arms embargo after hostage release; Iraq receives Mirages from France, ammunition from Egypt, ships from Italy; Iraq contracts with Spain for warships; Iran's request for US spare parts is denied; US supplies come via Israel; Algeria and Syria supply SAMs and mortars to Iran
1982	Fighting escalates after Iraqi attack in Feb.; Iran's offensive causes Iraqi retreat; Iraq is willing to withdraw if Iran assures end to war; Iraq declares unilateral cease-	Jordan sends "volunteers" for Iraq; Iran and Turkey sign economic agreement; Syria severs relations and oil pipeline with Iraq; Iraq seeks Egypt's support; UNSC	USSR and Iraq sign Jan. agreement for MiGs and missiles; deliveries of MiGs begin in Feb.; Iraq orders tanks, guns, artillery from France; Egypt offers arms; Syria and

Date	Warfare	Diplomacy	Arms
	fire and withdrawal on June 9; Iranian offensive moves into Iraq; Iran maintains threat throughout the year	adopts a cease-fire resolution on July 12; Iran rejects cease-fire; Egypt considers sending troops to Iraq	N. Korea supply Iran arms; China delivers planes to Iran; UK offers tank repairs to both sides
1983	Iran launches unsuccessful offensive in Feb. and heavy fighting ensues; Iran launches new attacks using "human wave" tactic in fall; Iran claims to retake Iranian villages; Iraqi missile attacks on Iranian towns	French and Iraqi officials meet; Iran rejects offer to end the shelling of civilian targets and denies using this tactic; Iran asks UNSC to investigate chemical weapons use by Iraq; Iraq seeks Turkish financial aid	USSR and Egypt deliver more fighters and tanks to Iraq; France and Iraq agree to offset weapons debt with oil shipments; France delivers Mirages, bombs, and missiles to Iraq; Swiss send PC-6s and PC-7s to Iran; Chinese tanks to Iraq in April; Brazilian vehicles to Iran for oil
1984	Iraq destroys Iranian naval targets; Iraq recaptures some lost positions; US begins to escort Gulf tankers in May; Saudis down Iranian jet; attacks on Gulf shipping by both sides continue; sporadic ground engagements; Iran launches offensive and dislodges some Iraqi troops; forces concentrated in southern sectors	UN agrees to investigate use of poison gas; Iraqi delegation visits USSR; Iran and Syria sign an oil purchase agreement; Iran and Soviets expel each other's diplomats; Iran presses for halt of Soviet arms to Iraq; UN calls for halt to "war of cities"; Iran and Egypt sign economic agreement; US expresses interest in reestablishing diplomatic ties with Iraq in Dec.	Soviets deliver tanks, bombers, and missiles to Iraq; UK supplies Iran spare parts for missiles and jets; Iraq receives armored vehicles from Brazil, cluster bombs from Chile, as does Iran; Arg. to supply Iran; US and W. Germany sell Iraq helicopters; Iraq receives French antiship missile equipment toward end of year; UK bans chemicals to Iraq; Iran to get equipment from Czechoslovakia, Spain, Japan, Brazil
1985	Fierce air raids on civilian targets by both sides; Iran begins major, mainly unsuccessful, offensive on Mar. 12;	Relations between Iran and Syria falter; India sends envoy for talks; US condemns Iraqi use of chemical weapons; Iran	Brazil, S. Africa, and Chile resupply Iraq; China ($1.5 billion), Libya, and Austria sell arms to Iran; US deli-

Date	Warfare	Diplomacy	Arms
	Iraqi air raids intensify to force Iran to end the war; Iran blocks Iraqi supply ships; Industrial targets in Iran are attacked	and Libya sign military agreement; Iraq breaks ties with Libya; Saddam Hussein visits Moscow to request arms; UN Secretary General aids in Iraq agreement to end "war of cities"	vers helicopters to Iraq and missiles to Iran; UK, France, and Arg. sell arms to both sides; USSR sends MiGs and SAMs to Iraq; UK and N. Korea supply Iranian navy
1986	Iraq continually attacks Iranian oil facilities; Iran captures Fao; Iraq attempts to regain Fao; Iran launches major offensive with little effect.	Soviets establish economic cooperation with Iran; UN confirms Iraqi use of poison gas; Iran seeks to persuade the Soviets to resume natural-gas purchases; US arms-for-hostage story begins to surface	Iran receives US helicopters and TOWs, French artillery shells, Spanish arms; China and Iran agree on Silkworm missiles; Iraq receives French "smart bombs," Soviet aircraft; emergency Egyptian resupply after fall of Fao; Saudis supply US bombs to Iraq; US agrees to provide logistic support to Iraq in Nov.; US seeks to stop Iranian arms shipments
1987–1988	Air attacks continue on both sides; US Gulf presence increased; USS *Stark* is struck by Iraqi missile; tanker war resumes; Iranian Silkworms deployed on July 4, 1987; Iraq attacks using chemical weapons and air raids; UN teams arrive to supervise cease-fire in July 1988; Iran and Iraq respect cease-fire on Aug. 20, 1988	Iran assures Arab nations it wants no wider war; Iran agrees to an Iraqi proposal to stop attacks on civilian targets; UNSC passes cease-fire resolution in July 1987; talks continue through Nov.; Iran tries to win Kuwait away from US; Iraq offers to end war of the cities; Iran expresses willingness to accept cease-fire on July 18, 1988; Iraq seeks direct negotiations	USSR delivers MiGs to Iraq; China delivers Silkworm missiles to both sides; N. Korea supplies Iran; Soviets resist US, UK attempt to embargo Iran; Swiss deliver arms to Iran and planes to Iraq; Iran receives weapons from Arg., Israel, UK, China, Libya, and Syria; possible Afghan Stingers to Iran; France, W. Germany, and Italy deliver chemicals to Iraq via Turkey; Egypt delivers aircraft to Iraq; USSR and China resist arms embargo provisions in cease-fire

Chronology 8

THE WAR IN THE WESTERN SAHARA, 1975–91

DATE	WARFARE	DIPLOMACY	ARMS
1975–1976	Moroccans march into Western Sahara as Spain withdraws; clashes with Polisario guerrillas begin; fighting between Moroccan and Algerian forces begins in 1976; Cubans reportedly fighting with Polisario; Morocco uses napalm in air attacks	Spain, Morocco, and Mauritania agree on power transfer; Polisario predicts war; Arab League tries mediation in 1976; Polisario forms government (SADR); Algeria recognizes SADR; Morocco breaks relations with Algeria; Castro visits Algeria and Polisario	Morocco receives US aircraft, tanks, troop carriers, and armored vehicles; French send helicopters and authorize sale of Mirages; Jordan sends guns, mortars, and F-5As in May 1976; Polisario reportedly receiving Libyan arms (since 1973)
1977–1978	Reacting to kidnappings of its citizens, France increases presence in Mauritania and strikes against Polisario; war turns to Morocco in 1978; US evacuates its military facilities	France expels Polisario members over kidnapping; captives are released to UN in Dec.; Polisario orders cease-fire in Mauritania in 1978; Morocco and Polisario hold talks; OAU works toward solution of conflict	Polisario reportedly receives equipment from Algeria; Morocco receives support aircraft and jets from France, missiles and helicopters from US; Morocco orders Italian helicopters
1979–1980	In large-scale fighting each side claims to inflict heavy losses on the other; Moroccan offensive in Nov.; Polisario downs jet and captures town; Morocco begins constructing fortification wall and arms civilians along Algerian border	Spanish PM meets with Polisario members; OAU calls for cease-fire; Mauritania recognizes Polisario and renounces claims to land; Morocco states it will occupy lands; Egypt expresses full support for Morocco	Morocco receives sonar, ammunition, spare parts, and jets from US, armored vehicles from Israel, Mirage jets from France, various weapons from Egypt, helicopters and jets from Italy; Polisario claims to seize tanks, arms, fuel, other vehicles and equipment from attacks on Moroccan troops

Date	Warfare	Diplomacy	Arms
1981–1983	Polisario stages many attacks on Moroccan forces; Moroccan infantry engages guerrillas; early in 1982 fighting slows due to hopes of resolution; US increases military role in Morocco; Polisario stages attack in 1983; Morocco launches sucessful offensive to secure territory for defensive wall	US officials visit Morocco; SADR and Libya agree to coordinate information; France attempts mediation; USSR denies providing weapons to Polisario; France reduces arms to Morocco in 1982; Morocco gives US forces transit facilities; Spain meets with both sides in 1983; Morocco refuses direct negotiations with Polisario	France sends helicopters to Morocco but suspends deliveries in 1982 due to debt; US sends planes, tanks, bombs, air defense radar and military instructors to Morocco; Italy sends helicopters; Polisario reportedly captures S. African arms from Morocco in 1982, along with other stocks of equipment
1984–1986	Polisario makes numerous claims of attacks during the year; Algerians and Moroccans skirmish inside Algeria; Morocco builds two defensive walls in 1985 and seeks cease-fire from Polisario; sporadic fighting continues; Polisario attacks Spanish merchant ships to reduce trade	Algeria to continue support for Polisario; Morocco signs treaty with Libya and withdraws from OAU after SADR delegation joins conference; Spanish government closes Polisario information office in 1985; UN resolves to mediate the dispute; UN talks fail and US Defense Secretary visits Morocco in 1986	Morocco orders rocket launchers from Egypt and receives vehicles, mortars, patrol boats from Spain, tanks from Austria, aircraft, tankers, and fighters from US; Polisario seizes mortars, machine guns, and ammunition during attacks on Moroccan forces; USSR reportedly supplies Polisario with equipment in 1985
1987–1988	Polisario launches major offensive against walled defenses, then withdraws; this is repeated later; in 1988, Polisario claims to break through wall; during continued attacks, US DC-7 is shot down	UN Secretary General meets with Polisario; Saudis and French attempt to mediate conflict; UN-OAU technical mission visits Western Sahara. 1988: UN and OAU reps meet with both sides to devise peace plan; Morocco and Polisario agree with peace plan	Morocco receives Mirage jet, Howitzers, and vehicles from France, tanks, guns, and missiles from the US; US discusses reducing Moroccan military debt; Polisario captures large quantity of arms, ammunition, and hardware from Morocco

DATE	WARFARE	DIPLOMACY	ARMS
1989–1991	In Sept., Polisario stages first offensive since the truce; Morocco maintains it crushed later attacks. 1991: the first fighting since Nov. 1989; Moroccan air attacks against Polisario positions. Sept. 1991: troops withdraw to arranged zones; UN observers enter the area	King Hassan of Morocco holds talks with Polisario officials. SADR plans to implement unilateral cease-fire. UN Secretary General holds talks with both sides. 1990: UN supervised talks in Geneva; Morocco rejects the proposal. 1991: UN supervised cease-fire to take effect in Sept.; UN formalizes peace plan, including plebiscite	Arms supplies are sharply reduced; Morocco receives scout cars and Commando missiles from France, F-5E aircraft from the US, and transport aircraft from Spain; no arms shipments recorded for 1991

Chronology 9

THE OGADEN WAR, 1977–78

DATE	WARFARE	DIPLOMACY	ARMS
Dec. 1976– June 1977	WSLF followers fight in Eth. in May; Somali guerrillas blow up five Eth. bridges	USSR reaffirms support for Eth. in Apr.; Somalia threatens war in May if Eth. invades; Somalia and China forge closer relations in June	Eth. and USSR conclude secret arms agreement; Eth. seeks military aid from Cuba
July– Aug. 1977	Each side claims to have destroyed many aircraft and tanks; Eth. mobilizes on Aug. 18, and reportedly repels Somali attacks	Arab nations offer support to Somalia	USSR agrees to supply Eth. with arms and Cuban and Soviet technicians; US reportedly offers Somalia defensive equipment
Sept.– Nov. 1977	Eth. suffers ground losses, begin successful air strikes; Arab troops reportedly fighting with Somalia; Eth. denies Cubans are fighting; Somalis suffer lack of spare parts	Eth. declares war on Somalia; OAU fails to negotiate a settlement; Eth. obtains Soviet and Cuban support in Oct.; Somalia expels all Cuban and Soviet experts	US, Britain, and France defer arms sales to Somalia; USSR delivers weapons to Eth. and halts deliveries to Somalia
Dec. 1977– Jan. 1978	Eth. conducts its first counteroffensive; sources claim Somali forces have withdrawn from Harer; Eth. conducts air raids in Somalia	Iran and Saudi Arabia claim they will aid Somalia if its borders are violated; Somalia offers direct negotiations with Eth.	Somalia seeks Iranian arms, aid, and appeals to the West for help to fend off Soviet invasion
Feb. 1978	Second Eth. offensive begins; Eth. aircraft bombing in Somalia continues; Somali air force virtually ceases to operate; fighting for	US bolsters naval force, calls for a cease-fire; Eth. rejects cease-fire, but reassures US it will not invade Somalia; OAU initative; Eth. threatens to	Israel discloses it has sold arms to Eth.; US turns down Somali request for arms; USSR brings in more Cuban per-

Date	Warfare	Diplomacy	Arms
	control of Addis Ababa-Djibouti railroad continues; WSLF claims to rout Eth.; Cuban paratroopers dropped behind Somali lines	sever relations with US, UK, and Germany if they fail to change their attitude toward the Somali invasion	sonnel; Egypt reportedly delivers tanks and missiles to Somalia
March 1978	Eth. penetrates Somali defenses at Jijiga; Somali resistance wanes; Somalia officially withdraws troops from the Ogaden; WSLF says it will continue to fight	Pres. Carter proposes a cease-fire; Saudi Arabia and Iran help persuade Somalia to leave; Eth. declares that Somalia must renounce territorial claims before any cease-fire is implemented	

Chronology 10

THE TANZANIA-UGANDA WAR, 1978–79

DATE	WARFARE	DIPLOMACY	ARMS
Sept. 1978	Ugandan planes violate Tanz. airspace		
Oct. 1978	Ugandan troops move into Tanz.; Ugandan planes bomb Tanz.	In Saudi Arabia, Amin appeals for aid; Kenya offers to mediate the dispute	
Nov.– Dec. 1978	Tanz. begins a counteroffensive; Ugandan troops withdraw; sporadic clashes continue	Uganda announces annexation; OAU and USSR appeal to both sides to stop fighting; Tanz. rejects Kenyan mediation offer; Nigeria presses Uganda to withdraw; US expresses support for Tanz., which seeks overthrow of Amin; Nyerere denounces OAU	
Jan.– Feb. 1979	Tanz. repels Ugandan invasion and advances troops inside Uganda; Tanz. obtains original objective and now seeks to oust Amin	Libya attempts to mediate; Amin accepts, Tanz. rejects proposal; OAU meets; Tanz. imposes conditions for a cease-fire	Uganda seeks new source of weapons but lacks cash; daily Libyan supplies reported; Soviets and Saudis refuse deliveries to Uganda; Tanz. recovers weapons of fleeing Ugandans
March 1979	Tanz. forces, facing heavy fighting, approach Kampala; Libyan plane bombs inside of Tanz.	UK halts aid to Uganda; OAU cease-fire fails; UK reportedly pressures oil companies to stop supplying Amin; Libya	Libyan, PLO troops, arms, and ammunition in Uganda; Tanz. fails to obtain arms from USSR;

262

Date	Warfare	Diplomacy	Arms
		threatens war if Tanz. does not withdraw; Kenya denies Libyan arms are entering its ports	Libya steps up its arms supplies to Amin prior to his fall
April 1979	Bombing continues in Uganda; Libyans now man critical positions; after heavy losses, Libyan troops retreat; Kampala is captured; new government secures the borders	Uganda asks Syria and Iraq for help; UNLF forms a provisional government; US pledges normal relations with the new government; Tanz. recognizes new government	

Notes

Chapter 1. Defining the Questions

1. The exceptions are often countries from which arms exports are just beginning to emerge. It takes at least a scandal or two before arms-export restraint of some kind is established. Examples of late-comer arms-exporting nations during the early 1980s that became sources of weapons before any restraint was enacted are South Korea and Singapore, from East Asia, and Bulgaria and Rumania, in Eastern Europe.
2. The original terms of the law of neutrality allowed private commercial transactions to continue while government sponsored activity was considered to be a breach of neutrality. Since it is now customary in all established arms-exporting states to have governments oversee and regulate transfers, the distinction between private and government sponsored transactions is no longer viable. Restraint in the export of weapons to countries at war is therefore extended, at least theoretically, to transfers from all types of suppliers.
3. Generally known as the "Nixon Doctrine" after a 1969 speech by President Nixon in Guam, this policy intended to substitute for direct military intervention through the support of regional powers that would help the US to secure its interests (Litwak, 1984; Sorley, 1983). Iran under the Shah was the main beneficiary of the Nixon Doctrine.
4. Reflecting ambiguity of motives, including the temptations of a lucrative arms-trade business, Britain's reformulated policy guidelines for arms supplies in the Iran-Iraq war in 1985 included a continued refusal to supply lethal equipment to either side, an attempt to fulfill existing arms-supply contracts, and a ban on future orders which would "significantly enhance the capability of either side to prolong or exacerbate the conflict." Sir Geoffrey Howe, 1985.
5. Some evidence of independent arms-transfer activity has come forward with the dissolution of the Soviet empire. Thus, for example, it is now evident that the "Kommerzielle Koordination," a GDR government bureau charged with acquiring foreign exchange, sold Soviet-type weapons in large quantities to numerous customers, including the CIA and private Western dealers.

6. The decision, made at the central government level, was reversed because of pressure from Slovakia, with its large arms industry. The contentious issue of arms exports contributed to the eventual separation of the Czech and Slovak Republics in late 1992.

Chapter 2. Research Tools: Controversies about Arms-Transfer Data and Methodology

1. There are few, but important, discussions of problems with arms-transfer data in the literature, which unfortunately are often ignored in arms-transfer studies. For overviews see Laurance, 1992; Catrina, 1988, Appendix I. Early critical assessments include Laurance and Sherwin, 1978; Kolodziej, 1979; Brzoska, 1982. The major institutions publishing arms-transfer data, ACDA and SIPRI (see below), inform the reader about the methods and sources used in their respective annual publications. For broader statements see Fei, 1979, and Brzoska and Ohlson, 1987, appendix.
2. Aircraft, missiles, ships above one-hundred tons, armored vehicles, electronic equipment such as radars and guidance equipment.
3. For condensed versions of these chronologies, see the Appendix.

Chapter 3: India-Pakistan Kashmir War, 1965

1. In fact, Pakistan's armed services were more alarmed than the president, according to the former air-force commander; see Khan, 1973, pp. 8–9.
2. Indeed the entire pattern of foreign economic assistance during the mid-1960s tended to favor India in freeing resources for defense preparations. Funds going to India from multilateral development banks more than doubled between 1964 and 1965, while similar assistance to Pakistan declined by over a quarter. US economic assistance declined to both states (by over twenty percent) during those years, though food aid to India rose by forty-five percent and to Pakistan by two percent. From 1954 to 1965, US military assistance to Pakistan amounted to an estimated $1.5 billion, while India received $84.5 million, mostly after 1962. US assistance to India was primarily transport aircraft, air defense radar and control, light weapons for mountain warfare, and road-building equipment (World Bank, *Annual Reports*; US government documents; Dupuy and Blanchard, 1972; *Facts on File*, vol. 25, 1965).
3. Pakistan, having mobilized more tanks, suffered comparatively higher losses (India had more total tanks in 1965), presumably from poorer tactics (Brines, 1968, pp. 344–45). In the entire war, India lost 65–70

aircraft, 175–90 tanks, 300 square miles of territory, and 3000 casualties. Pakistani losses amounted to approximately 20 planes, 200 tanks, 3800 casualties, and 720 square miles of territory, much of it near the key city of Lahore (Ganguly, 1986, p. 59; Kahn, 1979, p. 118).
4. Britain proclaimed an embargo only on India since she supposedly had no arms agreements with Pakistan, although four UK "Ton Class" naval vessels had been sold to Pakistan in 1965.
5. Numbers (4, 8, or more) and types of aircraft (MiG-19, MiG-21) differ in the various sources.
6. By September 18, reportedly under US pressure, Britain indicated willingness to resume Indian military aid if China implemented its ultimatum (Gupta, 1967, vol. 2, p. 165) and the results on the battlefield presented enough of an Indian showing that New Delhi was ready to accept a cease-fire. Pakistan was burned relatively more badly than India, had lost her major arms supplier, and could not fully compensate for this loss through Beijing, but at least she had fought gamely.
7. Indeed, Thayer (1969, p. 228) mentions a loophole in both US and UK military-aid agreements to India at that time that did not specify sole use of India's equipment against Chinese aggression, as Washington and London desired. Indian sources further charged that the UK clandestinely supplied small arms and ammunition to Pakistan throughout the war period (Gupta, 1967, vol. 2, p. 130). It is not clear whether these were government or private shipments, or whether they indeed existed.

Chapter 4: India-Pakistan Bangladesh War, 1971

1. See Siddiq, 1979, p. 98. In resisting pressure immediately to recognize the new state, Mrs. Gandhi went on record as promising a return of the refugees by year's end. See Singh, 1988, ch. 5, who also argues that Mujib was slow to opt for a declaration of independence because he was really only interested in regional autonomy.
2. Henry Kissinger had harsh warnings as well as reassurances about China for the Indians, though it was falsely reported by India that he had refused the type of defense cooperation against China seen in 1962 (Kissinger, 1979, p. 860; see also Sisson and Rose, 1990, p. 199; Ganguly, 1988, p. 124).
3. An estimated $40 million of "nonlethal" supplies were sold to Pakistan between 1967 and early 1971, which included $4 to $6 million for ammunition. See *New York Times,* October 9, 1970, p. 13; April 10, 1971, p. 1; April 14, 1971, p. 13; and April 16, 1971, p. 4.

4. The negotiations were carried out directly from the White House. The State Department, which was charged with exercising control over arms sales, was not consulted and later objected to the agreement. This case was later cited as one of the reasons for improved congressional oversight over US arms-export policy (Anthony, 1992).
5. Some charged that additional US arms were dispatched from overseas depots (see Wilcox, 1973, p. 31; Ayoob and Subrahmanyam, 1972, p. 227). There were further reports of Pakistani-US arms negotiations, mainly for parts and ammunition, as late as September 25 (*New York Times,* June 22, 1971, p. 1; June 23, 1971, p. 8). During the winter of 1971, Pakistani forces also reportedly seized fifty US "military boats" and transport vehicles sent to distribute relief supplies in East Pakistan (*New York Times,* June 3, 1971, p. 16; July 24, 1971, p. 1).
6. Economic assistance of about $75 million for fiscal 1971 also was suspended, but $90 million in food aid went through. World Bank President Robert McNamara pressed successfully for revocation of Pakistani lending as well (see Wilcox, 1973, p. 31; *New York Times,* June 24, 1971, p. 19; July 24, 1971, p. 1; *Keesings Contemporary Archives,* vol. 17, 1971, p. 24993; Sisson and Rose, 1990, pp. 255–65; Chowdhury, 1972, pp. 265–75; and Choudhury, 1975, pp. 202, 209.
7. Anthony (1992, p. 107) reports that up to 250 tanks of Czech origin were supplied.
8. According to Henry Kissinger, there was consensus within the administration that west Pakistan would lose its hold by early March (Kissinger, 1979, pp. 851–52; see also *New York Times,* November 9, 1971, p. 1).
9. Pakistan lost a reported 6000 men, losses roughly equal to 1965, and nearly one-third of its air force, one-fifth of its armor, 2 submarines, and 16 gunboats. Indian losses amounted to over 2500 killed (see Sethi, 1972, pp. 140–45).
10. Others saw it as an attempt to intimidate India (see Ziring, 1984, p. 388). While the official rationale was possible evacuation of Americans from the war zone (which irritated India), there appears to have been no intent to employ the *Enterprise* task force as long as the US and Soviets more-or-less agreed on west Pakistan's survival (Ganguly, 1986, p. 134).

Chapter 5: The Central American Football War, 1969

1. Ammunition and additional rifles may have been bought immediately before the fighting from international arms dealers (see *New York Times,* July 24, 1969, p. 3).

Chapter 6: The South Atlantic War, 1982

1. The Argentine invasion evidently caught London by surprise, as the Tory government had ceased sending regular naval patrols to the area while beginning to contract with Argentina to provide basic economic services. All of this seemingly was taken by Buenos Aires as an indication that if pushed, Britain would acquiesce in the islands' reversion to Argentine sovereignty.
2. In the end, some of the programs still in the pipeline in 1982 were later canceled for cost reasons. But that was after the war had been lost, and it is difficult to say what would have happened without the war.
3. In an attack on May 9, three torpedoes were fired from the *San Louis*. There are conflicting reports as to what happened and why. The most probable account is that they failed to hit their targets due to the combined failure of the Dutch-supplied fire-control system and the German-supplied torpedoes. A long, unsuccessful chase of the submarines followed, after which the two submarines were withdrawn because of a combination of maintenance problems and a fear of British antisubmarine warfare capabilities (*Der Spiegel,* no. 42, 1982, pp. 118–21; Scheina, 1984; Ruhe, 1984, pp. 7–12).
4. It was greatly feared by Argentinean pilots. They also had Sidewinders, but only AIM-9Bs, a version first produced in 1956 and later exported in great numbers from the US. Delivery of AIM-9Ls to the US Air Force and Navy had begun in 1977. The British task force was the first foreign customer of this much-improved version of the Sidewinder (Blake, 1988, p. 704). Fear of AIM-9L was one reason why Argentinean aircraft pilots avoided dogfights with Harrier pilots.
5. Goldblat and Milan (1983b, p. 36) claim that the Israeli government had only embargoed new deals, but not ongoing deliveries. The Israeli Gabriel missile is similar to the Exocet. As a ship-to-ship missile, though, the Gabriel would not have substituted for the AM-39 Exocet.
6. The story was originally reported by the *Johannesburg Star,* May 24, based on reports from the harbor of Durban. It was denied by South African officials. No missile of this type was in production in South Africa at the time. The South African navy had Gabriel missiles, though, and might have acted as conduit for Israeli supplies.
7. The Soviet offer was reported in news stories at the time. It was publicly denied by Argentine decision-makers, but used to pressure US Secretary of State Alexander Haig in private conversations as reported in his memoirs. Haig later recalled that General Galtieri once mentioned a Soviet offer to sink the British aircraft carrier *HMS Invincible* and let the Argentines claim credit, but later acknowledged that it had been a bluff (Haig, 1984, pp. 274–75, 294–95).

8. A curious division of labor followed from the dispute over US policy in this conflict. While Secretary Haig negotiated, the Defense Department under Secretary Weinberger delivered. Both acted with support from President Reagan. He even called General Galtieri on April 15 to support Haig's mediation effort and at the same time agreed to Weinberger's gradual increase in military supplies to Britain. A special central clearing house was set up in the Pentagon to provide twenty-four-hour response for release of such goods. Long before the official public US commitment to Britain, US supply had become critical. After committing itself fully on April 30, Washington offered to behave as an ally, to put its full logistical force behind the British fighting forces. By the end of the war, the aid bill, excluding the latest version of Sidewinder missiles and fuel, was $60 million (Freedman and Gamba-Stonehouse, p. 190). The Defense Department also drafted contingency plans to transfer warships to the British task force should that prove necessary (Cordesman and Wagner, 1990b, p. 263).

9. In the discussion of Resolution 502, other states' reactions to the war were clarified. Latin American states, with the exception of Argentine rivals Chile and Brazil, supported the anticolonial cause. The East Bloc likewise supported Argentina's grievance, but not the invasion. Most African and Asian states, including permanent Security Council member China, as well as Spain, took the same position. The British side received support from Western Europe and some Commonwealth states, including those in the Caribbean. Only Panama voted against the resolution, with China, Poland, Spain, and the Soviet Union abstaining.

10. The Falkland-Malvinas case has become a major object of conflict-resolution literature. Useful summaries are provided in three case studies, numbered 127, 406, 406A&B, and 431, prepared for the Pew Program in international affairs and written by Gunnar P. Nielsson; Gregory F. Treverton, Don Lippincott, and Stephen Flanagan; and Chaim D. Kaufmann, respectively. One of the participants from the US Department of State, Douglas Kinney, has written a comprehensive account. A useful overview is the collection of essays edited by Alberto R. Coll and Anthony C. Arend. Especially interesting is the joint Argentinean-British account by Laurence Freedman and Virginia Gamba-Stonehouse. The Argentinean Junta thought of Secretary Haig as a fellow military man. Special envoy Vernon Walters, also a former US Army general, enjoyed special fame as a protector of Latin American military men from the time when he was military attaché in Brazil in the early 1960s. He had been to Argentina several times in 1981 to discuss common interests and became personally friendly with General Galtieri. Another strong supporter of a strategic link

between Washington and Buenos Aires was Thomas Enders, Under Secretary of State for Latin America. Together with UN Ambassador Kirkpatrick, he was among the chief proponents of a close alliance between the United States and authoritarian governments in Latin America in order to combat left-wing forces, especially in Central America.

11. In the various accounts of the Haig mission there is no evidence of pressure applied to either side. It seems that the secretary saw his role more in terms of "good offices" rather than as a superpower agent pressing smaller powers into a settlement. Haig seems to have used only arguments: about the nonsense of war between nations basically belonging to the same side; about sparsely inhabited islands; and about the proximity of positions. At least some within the British Foreign Office seem to have feared that the US might make its level of military assistance conditional on British concessions, and advised placating the Americans. But such thinking did not get very far since it clashed with the tough stance adopted and maintained throughout the crisis by Prime Minister Thatcher, who assumed that the United States had to support its British ally in rebuking a blatant breach of international law (Freedman and Gamba-Storehouse, 1990, pp. 216–17, 304). She also reportedly felt that President Reagan owed her a reward for loyal foreign policy support. One argument made by Haig in London was the danger of the Argentineans turning to the Soviets for weapons. This was not taken very seriously by the British side. Even in Washington there was evidently only limited concern about such risks (Treverton and Flanagan, 1988, p. 17; Haig 1984, p. 276).

12. This began to change only when the White House staff recorded a drop in President Reagan's popularity linked to his low profile in the crisis from mid-April. The Argentineans were clearly concerned throughout about US help for the British military effort. Possibly their cooperation in mediation was premised on the assumption that such assistance would remain limited given a neutral US role. They were reassured in this hope by UN Ambassador Jeane Kirkpatrick, who stated in a number of interviews that the US would not abandon Argentina. When it was reported in various media that Washington was giving London more than a helping hand, Haig told Galtieri at his next stop in Buenos Aires, on April 15, that support was limited to normal peacetime cooperation. It is not clear whether Haig really was unaware of the extent of, or merely understated the support being given to the British. He, for instance, unsuccessfully tried to stop news stories about the support, saying that they would destroy his mediation effort (Haig, 1984, chapter 13). On the other hand, it was not the Department of State but rather the Pentagon that was in charge of arms and logistical assistance. In many accounts of American decision-making at this time, the lack of cabinet coordination in foreign policy is stressed.

Notes to Pages 95 to 124   271

Chapter 7: The Yom Kippur-Ramadan War, 1973

1. The deception of Israeli leadership was furthered by the fact that although Egyptian forces along the Canal were strengthened in May 1973, no Arab attack was forthcoming, having been postponed until the fall because of a June US-Soviet summit. Israeli Defense Force (IDF) planning assumed that intelligence would guarantee at least forty-eight hours of warning, so that Israel's extensive mobilization schemes could begin. Combat readiness was to be expected within seventy-two hours, while standing Israeli forces were designed to hold off the enemy only for a short time. In this case, though, the IDF ultimately received only about ten hours warning. The Israeli air force, at least, was on full alert due to its prior weeks of skirmishing against Syria (Mets, 1986, p. 94).
2. It was estimated that casualties in the war amounted to 15,000 Egyptian dead, compared to 7,000 Syrians and 2,400 Israelis; Iraqi casualties were 125 and Jordan lost 27 soldiers. An additional 66,000 Arabs and 5,500 Israelis were wounded (Bailey, 1990, p. 335).
3. With the difficulty of implementing the UN approved cease-fire accord of October 21, and the reiteration of UN demands along with plans to send observers on the twenty-third, arms diplomacy entered the picture again amid increasingly frightening US-Soviet tension. Sadat, fearing the decimation of his army in Sinai and the loss of Suez City, appealed on the twenty-fourth for joint superpower military intervention to impose a cease-fire accord. The US immediately refused, citing a tradition of opposition to such moves. The longer the fighting lasted, however, the more Moscow signaled support for the idea, and possible willingness to act unilaterally, augmenting its already alerted airborne forces. Kissinger, in consultation with President Nixon, responded on the twenty-fifth with a worldwide high "status three" alert of forces, including nuclear forces, while attempting to reassure Moscow and apply significant arms-embargo threats against Israel at the same time. Indeed, Israel also was warned that the IDF might be left alone to face Soviet intervention, however improbable that scenario might have been (Kissinger, 1982, pp. 575–99).

Chapter 8: Israeli-Arab War in Lebanon, 1982

1. The full plan never had been approved by the entire Israeli cabinet, and was withheld in consultations with the opposition Labor Party as well; see Nachmias, 1988, pp. 135–36 and Herzog, 1982, p. 342.
2. To show the stakes of such concerns about technological security, several Soviet advisers reportedly were killed when Israel attacked

one of its own downed aircraft to keep its electronic equipment out of enemy hands. (*Middle East Journal*, Chronology, 1982; Bavly and Salpeter, 1984, p. 116; Klinghofer and Apter, 1985, p. 213)

3. Among the PLO weapons captured by Israel during its sweeps were (by October) over 1,300 armored vehicles, including 80 Soviet T-34, T-55, and T-62 tanks, 82 field artillery pieces, 62 Katyusha rocket launchers, 215 mortars, 196 antiaircraft weapons, 1,352 antitank weapons, and more than 33,000 small arms. (Bavly and Salpeter, 1984, p. 93; Cordesman, 1987a, p. 63)

Chapter 9: The Iraq-Iran War, 1980–88

1. Supply problems affected almost exclusively the regular armed forces. The various militia were mostly equipped only with small arms, which remained plentiful. The weakening of the armed forces was not unwelcome by the political leadership because it removed its most important internal threat. But when Saddam Hussein ordered his attack, Tehran quickly put ideology aside in moving to strengthen its defenses.
2. A number of factories had been built in Egypt during the 1960s and early 1970s that produced Soviet-type ammunition and weapons. These had continued production even after the Soviet-Egyptian rift in the mid-1970s and were now well positioned to supply Iraq. In the early 1980s, annual exports of weapons and ammunition from Egypt to Iraq reportedly amounted to $1 billion (*Wehrtechnik,* no. 1, 1991, p. 104), a figure that probably also includes the retransfer of older equipment originally sent by the Soviets to Egypt.
3. The Super Etendards were returned to France in September 1985—undamaged.
4. The role of the US as arms supplier to Iran is still unclear, despite many investigations. Washington openly delivered military equipment valued at $480 million as part of the deal to free US American hostages in Teheran in January 1981 (Cordesman and Wagner, 1990a, p. 115). There are allegations that additional equipment worth several billion dollars was given unofficially. Some of these allegations are linked to the claim that there was a deal by the Reagan team prior to elections in the US not to release hostages before the elections (see Hersh, 1991, pp. 1–2.)While there were reports that Israel delivered spare parts even during the hostage crisis (Brzezinski, 1983), later deliveries were reportedly much larger. Some were linked with US policy, others done on Israeli initiatives alone (Azid, 1987; Cordesman 1987c, pp. 22–23). In 1991, there were reports that Israeli deliveries had amounted to several billion dollars, using a number of

European countries, as well as Pakistan, as conduits (*Far Eastern Economic Review*, no. 154, December 19, 1991, pp. 23–25; Hersh, 1991, pp. 1–2; Lifshultz, Ali, and Galster, 1991). On possible Israeli reasons to supply Iran and the history of Iranian-Israeli military relations, see Kliemann, 1984; and Beit-Hallahmi, 1987.
5. Reportedly, Vietnam also sold weapons—mostly ex-US equipment (Cordesman, 1987c, p. 24).
6. After Swedish customs had unveiled the extensive network in 1985, criminal proceedings began in Belgium, Sweden, West Germany, and France. Only in Belgium and Sweden were companies indicted, because in other countries the goods transferred had not been on the control lists (Westander, 1988). Still, deliveries to Iran decreased sharply after the fall of 1985, a serious blow to the domestic ammunition industry that affected stocks a year later.
7. In one of his rare slips in accuracy, Anthony Cordesman, the most prolific author on the war, writes that six Pontius PC-7 military training aircraft were sold in August 1984 (Cordesman, 1987c, p. 24). The correct name of the aircraft is Pilatus PC-7.
8. While Cordesman and Wagner judge the spare parts as indecisive (1990a, p. 242), Gary Sick sees them as important elements in facilitating the Kerbala offensives (1990, p. 223).
9. Still, Iranian acceptance of Resolution 598 came as a surprise to many. It was only when spiritual leader Ayatollah Ruholla Khomeini, concerned about the survival of the revolution, announced his consent over the radio on July 20 that the shift in the Iranian position was believed to be genuine.

Chapter 10: The War in the Western Sahara, 1976–91

1. Since Mauritania was only a minor participant, which withdrew early from the war, Mauritania's armament pattern will not be discussed in this chapter. The focus is on Morocco and, as far as the availability of information allows, Polisario.
2. With the profusion of refugees there was no shortage of Sahwari fighters. On the other hand, Mauritania's military and economic situation deteriorated rapidly as the war effort absorbed about sixty percent of the national budget despite large subsidies from Saudi Arabia and Kuwait (see Clément, 1986, p. 111).
3. Libya had also reportedly sent some modern Brazilian-made Cascavel armored cars (see Clément, 1986, p. 116).
4. They argued, backed by an alarmist CIA report, that Hassan II's throne was in danger and that the US was on its way to creating another Iran (see Hodges, 1985, p. 167; and Kamil, 1987, p. 47).

5. Moroccan troops had intervened twice in Zaire against insurgencies in the Southern region of Katanga bordering Angola in early 1977 and early 1978. The US had provided logistical support on both occasions. On their way back from Zaire, Moroccan troops attempted a coup d'état in socialist Benin, but failed. To round out his series of "cooperative initiatives," King Hassan also was helping pro-Western forces in Chad.
6. Both sides had interests in such rapprochement; Morocco had been supporting anti-Libyan forces in Chad, while Tripoli supported Polisario. Both also were unhappy with Algeria's new fraternity treaties with Tunisia and Mauritania in 1983.
7. In closed hearings in 1980, the US government evidently indicated that there was evidence of direct Soviet support, but was unwilling to repeat these charges in public (see Kamil, 1987, pp. 56–57).
8. Hodges (1983, p. 354) flatly declares that "none of the Eastern European countries supplied military equipment to Polisario directly." Clément (1986, p. 94), on the other hand, states that on July 4, 1975, a secret Algerian-Soviet treaty was signed, including arrangements for the delivery of light arms and ammunition to Polisario. He also states (p. 111) that the Soviet Union in 1978 did not allow the Algerians to provide SAM-6 and SAM-7 antiaircraft missiles. Since Polisario used both types in battle, either there was no such order or the Algerians (or Libyans) disregarded it (see also Hubel, 1988).

Chapter 11: The Ogaden War, 1977–78

1. Its use was further curtailed in the early 1970s because of Washington's reluctance, reinforced during the Vietnam war, to rely too heavily on military assets in potentially hostile countries. As a replacement, facilities were constructed on the Indian Ocean island of Diego Garcia.
2. The two main reasons for this policy as given in the testimony of Assistant Secretary of State William E. Schauffele, Jr., before the Senate Subcommittee on African Affairs on August 6, 1976, were "not only [to] contribute to the stability of this second most populous country in Black Africa but also [to] assist black African states in maintaining the principle of territorial integrity, a cardinal principle of the Organization of African Unity" (Lewis, 1985b, p. 103).
3. See Porter, 1984, p. 194. These were US estimates at the time using some unknown method to arrive at dollar values. They must therefore be treated with caution. Not surprisingly, other authors later gave divergent figures; see for instance, Agyeman-Duah, 1986, p. 303, and Ottaway, 1982, p. 103, who quotes a figure of $200 million.

4. Porter, 1984, p. 194, claims that in fact agreements had a much higher value and that deliveries made later during the course of the war were more or less included in the May contract.
5. See Henze, 1982, p. 6. Henze, among other posts, served as a diplomat in Ethiopia in the early 1970s and was the officer in charge of the Horn at the US National Security Council at the time of the war; see Brzezinski, 1983, p. 572; Ottaway, 1982, p. 67, gives a Soviet supply figure of $300 million to $1 billion for the period from 1963 to 1977.
6. It should be noted that other issues besides Ethiopia divided the two governments; for instance, they clashed over the use of Berbera, the creation of an "Arab lake" in the Red Sea, the role of Islam and the lack of political structures in Somalia (see Patman, 1989, pp. 185–90, 211–12).
7. Communication between the US and the Somali governments was fraught with misunderstandings. One especially obscure link was Siad Barré's longtime US physician, Dr. Kevin Cahill. He came to Mogadishu in mid-June telling Barré, supposedly on good authority, that the US was not averse to Somali control over the Ogaden. His claim that this view was relayed by Matthew Nimitz, a high-level administration official, was later officially denied (see Ayoob, 1980b, p. 155; Porter, 1984, p. 208).
8. The vicissitudes of US statements reflected internal policy divisions. "Globalists" such as Zbigniew Brzezinski wanted to grab the chance to weaken the Soviet geostrategic position, while State Department "regionalists" under Cyrus Vance counseled against an alignment with the rogue Somali government. In the end, the US delivered no weapons prior to the war, but the Somali side anticipated US support in a crisis situation with the Soviet Union. It was claimed that "it is highly probable that the ambivalence of US policy immediately prior to the Ogaden war has influenced the Somali decision to go to war" (Napper, 1983, p. 245).
9. The Ethiopian air force had air superiority almost throughout the war. This was of limited relevance for the early Ethiopian war effort, though, because only a few aircraft could actually fly sorties and because an essential element of Ethiopian air defense, the Karamara radar station above the Gara-Marda Pass, was lost early in the war.
10. The total number of Cubans involved in the operation is generally given as eleven-to-twelve thousand (*Österreichische Militärische Zeitschrift,* vol. 16, no. 3, 1978, 241); Porter, 1984, p. 183, gives fifteen thousand, and Brzezinski, 1983, p. 184, ten-to-eleven thousand.
11. After unsuccessful direct attacks, the offensive forces moved about seventy ASU-57 air-transportable light tanks, transport vehicles, and light artillery with heavy helicopters over the mountain ridge to the

rear of the defenders on March 4 and 5. In addition, the Fifth and Sixth divisions moved around the flanks. Paratroopers were dropped behind the Somali lines.
12. Matthies, 1987, 255. The Somali government disputed this UN High Commission on Refugees (UNHCR) figure and claimed about one-million refugees.
13. In February 1978 Somalia first admitted that its regular forces had intervened in the Ogaden.
14. Compare *Africa Research Bulletin,* vol. 15, February 1–28, 1978, p. 4741, with Ottaway, 1982, p. 118.
15. Brzezinski, 1983, p. 181, reports that in mid-January President Sadat offered to send Egyptian troops to Somalia. "We agreed to that initiative . . . but Sadat did not follow through."
16. National Security adviser Brzezinski proposed to station a carrier group in the Red Sea, possibly supported by a similar French show of force. Secretaries Harold Brown (Defense) and Vance strongly disagreed (Brzezinski, 1983, p. 182–83).

Chapter 12: The Tanzania-Uganda War, 1978–79

1. Estimates of the number of victims run between 250,000 and 300,000 (see Mudoola, 1988; Rupesinghe, 1989).
2. The major incident was an attack by about one-thousand troops loyal to former Ugandan President Milton Obote on September 17, 1972. The operational plan, which was remarkably similar to the eventual 1979 invasion, faltered because of a lack of heavy weapons, ammunition, and logistics, as well as a miscalculation about the willingness of the local population to support the intruders (see *Africa Contemporary Record,* 1972, pp. B246–49, B275–78; Avirgan and Honey, 1982, pp. 34–36).
3. Former CIA officials reportedly claimed that the Amin coup was planned by British intelligence in cooperation with the Israeli Mossad (Avirgan and Honey, 1982, p. 10).
4. Flight personnel on this plane were US-recruited. When the US Securities and Exchange Commission later brought foreign payoff charges against Page, the company that had handled the transaction, the CIA testified that the disclosure might "reveal security secrets." It is assumed that during these flights, intelligence on Libyan military operations was gathered (see Avirgan and Honey, 1982, p. 18).
5. After the fall of Kampala, it was found that a number of companies, including British and American firms, had sent dual-purpose goods, such as communication equipment, for which no export licenses were needed. Other companies transported goods illegally. The State

Research Centre, where thousands had been tortured, continued to do business with US and British firms until the end of 1978 (see Smith, 1980, p. 176).
6. The Chinese, who also supplied significant economic aid, judged Tanzania to be a showcase for their preferred type of economic development and political nonalignment. Good relations with Tanzania also allowed Beijing to gain influence with a number of Southern African liberation movements.
7. It was not until late March 1979 that a political conference of the Ugandan exile forces was organized in Moshi, Tanzania, with the aim of forming a government.
8. Early in the campaign, Tanzanian antiaircraft fire had downed a number of Tanzanian MiGs, mistaking them for Ugandan aircraft.
9. In addition, at least one ship loaded with weapons worth about $10 million, including ten T-55 tanks, was sent from Libya to the Kenyan harbor of Mombasa in early March 1979. But the Kenyans refused to let the ship unload when it docked between April 4 and 18, so the weapons never reached Uganda. After an odyssey along the East African coast, the ship finally docked in Durban, South Africa, on April 25. There, the weapons were unloaded and bought by the South African government from the shipping company. They were probably later sent on to Angolan rebel UNITA forces (see Oakes, 1985, pp. 4–11).
10. Both were concerned about Amin's internal violence and external adventurism. Arab leaders were upset that Amin had not invested much of the money given to him, and the Soviets did not want to alienate frontline African states, such as Mozambique and Angola, that favored Tanzania.
11. Reports about the Kenyan policies are contradictory. Officially, the Kenyan government maintained that as a signatory of the Convention of Landlocked Countries it could not stop deliveries to Uganda. On the other hand, there are several examples of Kenyan blockage of military goods on their way to Uganda, including trucks from Spain and weapons from Libya (see *Africa Research Bulletin,* vol. 16, April 1–30, 1979, pp. 5220–21).

Chapter 13: Recent Trends, Analysis, and Projection

1. In the 1973 war, supplies to Israel as the initially defending state, though delayed, ultimately enhanced its capacity to fight back, although there is controversy over how crucial these supplies were. Confronted with the prospects of negative long-term arms-supply patterns, though, Israeli leaders, wanting to deliver a decisive blow,

settled finally for a breakthrough in direct negotiations. The subsequent disengagement talks also benefitted Egypt considerably by moving the Israelis some distance away from the Suez Canal and established the pattern of "land for peace" exchanges.

2. Nonetheless, the Chinese Foreign Ministry maintained that since it had supported UN Security Council Resolution 660, sales of arms to Iraq would be stopped (see *Defence,* October, 1990, p. 615).

3. Long-range South African artillery ammunition was shipped via Jordan; it had been designed by a Dr. Bull, who also had designed the Iraqi "supergun." Indeed, the South African connection was ironic in view of that country's reputed military connections with Israel (see the *Independent,* January 28, 1991, p. 4).

4. In all, the West German government received more than 150 British and American allegations concerning embargo violations. After initial screening, the German authorities decided to open criminal proceedings in sixteen cases (see Deutscher Bundestag, May 8, 1991).

5. While behind the scenes diplomacy was attempted, public statements by the parties defined their respective bargaining positions. On December 24, Saddam Hussein announced that Israel would be the first Iraqi target if war broke out. The statement came during the weeks of preparation in the US Congress for debate on the use of force against Baghdad, and might have been intended to generate doubts about a US military attack. Israel, however, pledged not to attack Iraq without consulting Washington. After a heated debate, Congress voted to authorize the use of force on January 12. The days between the Congressional vote and the US deadline for compliance saw frantic diplomatic efforts to avert war. On January 12, UN Secretary General Perez de Cuellar visited Baghdad with "no specific proposals" beyond the wish for a peaceful settlement (*Keesings Contemporary Archives*, vol. 37, January 1991, p. 37935). Specific proposals were brought by many of the other high-level delegations attempting mediation, including Nicaragua, Zambia, Yemen, Japan, Libya, Yugoslavia (on behalf of the nonaligned movement), Syria, Jordan, and Saudi Arabia.

6. Many of Iraq's seven-hundred planes survived the war in British designed fortified underground hangars or in the north of the country; about one hundred were moved to Iran (*Facts on File*, vol. 51, January 24, 1991, p. 42). Iraq's few offensives are easily counted: three F-1 Mirages, believed to have been armed with Exocets, tried to attack allied vessels in the Gulf on January 24, but were intercepted by a Saudi F-15; two battalion-sized armored columns invaded Saudi Arabia but were soon repulsed; and in his most spectacular but militarily insignificant exploit, Saddam Hussein made good on his prior pledge and promptly launched seven Scuds towards Tel Aviv

within hours of the allied attack, raising political headaches for Washington concerning possible Israeli retaliation and splits in the coalition amidst mass Arab uprisings. Allied commanders remained puzzled as to why Iraq's Exocet-armed Mirages were not deployed against ships in the Gulf.
7. This was controversial in light of Bonn's arms export restraints regarding areas of tension. Tel Aviv for some time had complained about the flow of US arms to Saudi Arabia, and was able to make good political use of allied concerns about keeping the coalition together.
8. The guerrillas were photographed in new uniforms and with modern weapons (*Economist*, July 13, 1991, p, 35).
9. In June, Soviet officials offered India their latest V/STOL fighter, the YAK-141 "Freestyle" (see *Jane's Defence Weekly,* June 29, 1991, p. 1164).
10. Of course, the 1982 Falklands-Malvinas example showed that domestic political problems can sometimes make parties more likely to seek foreign adventures. Ms. Bhutto, for example, would have been under considerable pressure to stand firm on the issue of Kashmir, and perhaps to extend additional support to the dissidents.
11. The Hungarian firearms manufacturer FEG was threatened by bankruptcy in late 1991 when the Hungarian government enforced stringent export restrictions following discovery that a large quantity of Kalishnikov-type rifles had been sold to Croatia (*Jane's Defence Weekly*, November 30, 1991, p. 1073).
12. Another complication is the question of whether the attacking force is completely and effectively under centralized or civilian control. Throughout the Yugoslav war, the question of whether the JNA was acting on its own or under federal or Serbian authority has been debated, and the role of ethnic militia in various republics has at times reminded many of the anarchic violence of Lebanon. Of course, if Serbia had wanted to enforce discipline on Serbian militias, it conceivably could have done so, but sanctions against Serbia (or Croatia in relation to Croat militia) could at the same time weaken its ability to enforce such discipline.

Bibliography

Newspapers, Periodicals, Chronologies, and Radio Broadcasts

Africa Contemporary Record.
Africa Research Bulletin.
Africa South of the Sahara.
All India Radio.
Arab Observer.
Asia-Pacific Defence Reporter.
Arab World.
Asian Recorder.
Aviation Week and Space Technology.
Christian Science Monitor.
Congressional Record.
Defence.
Defense and Armament International.
Defense and Foreign Affairs.
Defense Electronics.
Defense News.
Der Spiegel.
Detroit News.
Economist.
Facts on File.
Far Eastern Economic Review.
Foreign Broadcast Information Service.
Frankfurter Rundschau.
Independent.
International Defense Review.
International Herald Tribune.
Jane's Defence Weekly.
Jerusalem Post.
Keesings Contemporary Archives.
London Times.
Los Angeles Times.
Middle East Economic Digest.

Middle East Journal.
Milavnews.
New African.
New York Times.
Newsweek.
Österreichische Militärische Zeitschrift.
Washington Post.
Wehrtechnik.
World Weapon Review.

Books and Articles

Abdulghani, J. M. 1984. *Iraq and Iran: The Years of Crisis.* Baltimore: Johns Hopkins University Press.
Abolfathi, Farid. 1979. "Defense Expenditures in the Persian Gulf: Internal, Interstate, and International Factors in the Iraqi-Iranian Arms Race, 1950 to 1969." In W. Ladd Hollist, ed. *Exploring Competitive Arms Processes.* New York and Basel: Marcel Dekker.
Adams, James. 1990. *Trading in Death.* London: Hutchinson.
Adelman, Kenneth L. 1980. "Facts and Fantasies." *Comparative Strategy.* Vol. 2, no. 1, pp. 97–108.
Agyeman-Duah, Baffour. 1986. "The U.S. and Ethiopia: The Politics of Military Assistance." *Armed Forces and Society.* Vol. 12, no. 2, pp. 287–307.
Aker, Frank. 1985. *The Arab-Israeli War.* Hamden, Conn: Archon Books.
Albrecht, Ulrich and Birgit Sommer. 1974. *Waffen für die Dritte Welt?* Reinbek: Rowohlt.
Alford, Jonathan. 1984. "Conventional Conflicts in a Nuclear Age: Falkland Islands, the Limited Use of Limited Power." *Jerusalem Journal of International Relations.* Vol. 7, no. 1/2, pp. 79–91.
Al-Khalil, Samir. 1989. *The Republic of Fear: The Politics of Modern Iran.* Berkeley: University of California Press.
Alnasrawi, Abbas. 1986. "Economic Consequences of the Iraq-Iran War." *Third World Quarterly.* Vol. 8, no. 3, pp. 869–95.
Amin, S. H. 1984. *Political and Strategic Issues in the Persian-Arabian Gulf.* Glasgow: Royston Limited.
Anderson, Thomas P. 1981. *The War of the Dispossessed: Honduras and El Salvador, 1969.* Lincoln: University of Nebraska Press.
Anthony, Ian. 1990. "The International Arms Trade." *Disarmament.* Vol. 13, no. 2, pp. 231–55.
———, ed. 1991. *Arms Export Regulations.* London: Oxford University Press.
———, ed. 1992. *The Arms Trade and Medium Powers.* Brighton: Harvester Wheatsheaf.

Anthony, Ian, Paul Claesson, Elisabeth Sköons, and Siemon T. Wezeman. 1993. "Arms Production and Arms Trade." *SIPRI Yearbook 1993: World Armaments and Disarmament.* Oxford: Oxford University Press, ch. 10.

Arbeitsgruppe Rüstung und Unterentwicklung. 1980. Data in the Socio-Military Field, Report Prepared for the United Nations Study on Disarmament and Development. Hamburg: University of Hamburg.

Archer, George D., and Paulos Milkias. 1979. "The Second Scramble for Africa." *Horn of Africa.* Vol. 2, no. 3. pp. 55–66.

Armstrong, Robert, and Janet Shenk. 1982. *El Salvador: The Face of Revolution.* Boston: Southend.

Assidon, Elsa. 1978. *Sahara Occidental. Un Enjeu pour le Nord-Ouest Africain.* Paris: Francois Maspero.

Avery, William P., and Louis A. Picad. 1980. "Pull Factors in the Transfer of Conventional Armaments to Africa." *Journal of Political and Military Sociology.* Vol. 8(Spring), pp. 55–70.

Avirgan, Tony, and Martha Honey. 1982. *War in Uganda.* Westport, Conn.: Lawrence Hill.

Axelgard, Fredrick W. 1988. *A New Iraq? The Gulf War and Implications for U.S. Policy.* Washington, D.C.: The Center for Strategic and International Studies.

Ayoob, Mohammed. 1978. *The Horn of Africa: Regional Conflict and Super Power Involvement.* Canberra: Strategic and Defence Studies Centre, The Australian National University.

———, ed. 1980a. *Conflict and Intervention in the Third World.* London: Croom Helm.

———. 1980b. "The Horn of Africa," in Ayoob, 1980a, pp. 136–70.

Ayoob, Mohammed, and K. Subrahmanyam. 1972. *The Liberation War.* New Delhi: S. Chand.

Azid, Ali. 1987. "USA-Iran Arms Deal: The Israeli Connection." *Middle East.* Vol. 13 (January), pp. 46–52.

Bailey, Martin. 1975. "Tanzania and China." *African Affairs.* Vol. 74, no. 294, pp. 34–50.

Bailey, Sidney. 1982. *How Wars End: The UN and the Termination of Armed Conflict, 1946–64.* Vol. 1. Oxford: Clarendon Press.

———. 1990. *Four Arab-Israeli Wars and the Peace Process.* Basingstoke, Eng.: Macmillan.

Barbier, Maurice. 1982. *Le Conflit du Sahara Occidental.* Paris: l'Harmattan.

Bar-Siman-Tov, Yaacov. 1987. *Israel, the Superpowers, and the War in the Middle East.* New York: Praeger.

Baugh, William H., and Michael J. Squires. 1983a. "Arms Transfers and the Onset of War, Part I: Scalogram Analysis of Transfer Patterns." *International Interactions.* Vol. 10, no. 1, pp. 39–63.

———. 1983b. "Arms Transfers and the Onset of War, Part II: Wars in the Third World States, 1950–1965." *International Interactions.* Vol. 10, no. 2, pp. 129–41.

Bavly, Dan, and Eliahu Salpeter. 1984. *Fire in Beirut: Israel's War in Lebanon with the PLO*. Briarcliff Manor, N.Y.: Stein and Day.
Beer, Francis A. 1981. *Peace Against War*. San Francisco: Freeman.
Beer, Francis, and Thomas Mayer, 1986. "Why Wars End: Some Hypotheses." *Review of International Studies*. Vol. 12, no. 2, pp. 95–106.
Beit-Hallahmi, Benjamin. 1987. *The Israeli Connection*. New York: Pantheon Books.
Bender, Gerald J., James S. Coleman, and Richard L. Sklar, eds. 1985. *African Crisis Areas and U.S. Foreign Policy*. Berkeley: University of California Press.
Bennett, Alexander J. 1985. "Arms Transfers as an Instrument of Soviet Policy in the Middle East." *Middle East Journal*. Vol. 39 (Autumn), pp. 745–74.
Benoit, Jean, and Catherine Gollian. 1986. "L'interminable Guerre du Sahara Occidental." *Les Temps Modernes*. No. 478, pp. 66–78.
Bertram, Christoph, ed. 1982. *Third World Conflict and International Security*. London: Macmillan.
Bhargava, G. S. 1972. *Their Finest Hour: Saga of India's December Victory*. Delhi: Vikas.
Bidwell, Shelford, ed. 1979. *Brassey's Artillery of the World*. New York: Bonanza Books.
Bienen, Henry. 1980. "Perspectives on Soviet Intervention in Africa." *Political Science Quarterly*. Vol. 95 (Spring), pp. 29–42.
Biger, Gideon. 1989. "The Shatt-Al-Arab River Boundary: A Note." *Middle Eastern Studies*. Vol. 25 (April), p. 250.
Birth of a Nation: The Story of How East Pakistan Turned into Bangladesh. 1971. Calcutta: Bangladesh Mukti Sangram Sahayak Samity.
Blackman, Raymond V. B., ed. 1972. *Jane's Fighting Ships*. London: Haymarket.
Blake, Bernard, ed. 1988. *Jane's Weapon Systems*. London: Jane's.
Bloomfield, Lincoln P., and Amelia Leiss. 1969. *Controlling Small Wars*. New York: Knopf.
Bock, Walter De, and Jean-Charles Deniau. 1988. *Des Armes Pour L'Iran: L'Irangate Européen*. Paris: Gallimard.
Bontems, Claude. 1984. *La Guerre du Sahara Occidental*. Paris: Presses Universitaires Françaises.
Bowles, Chester. 1969. *A View From New Delhi: Selected Speeches and Writings*. New Haven: Yale University Press.
———. 1971. *Promises to Keep: My Years in Public Life, 1941–1969*. New York: Harper and Row.
Brecher, Michael, Jonathan Wilkenfield, and Sheila Moser. 1988a. *Crisis in the Twentieth Century. Volume 1: Handbook of International Crises*. Oxford: Pergamon Press.

———. 1988b. *Crisis in the Twentieth Century. Volume 2: Handbook of Foreign Policy Crises.* Oxford: Pergamon Press
———. 1989. *Crisis in the Twentieth Century. Volume 3: Crises, Conflicts and Instability.* Oxford: Pergamon Press.
Brecher, Michael, and Patrick James. 1988. "Patterns of Crisis Management." *Journal of Conflict Resolution.* Vol. 32 (September), pp. 426–56.
Brines, Russell. 1968. *The Indo-Pakistani Conflict.* London: Pall Mall.
Brogan, Patrick, and Albert Zarca. 1983. *Deadly Business: Sam Cummings, Interarms, and the Arms Trade.* New York: Norton.
Brown, W. Norman. 1972. *The United States and India, Pakistan, Bangladesh.* Cambridge, Mass.: Harvard University Press.
Bruce, James. 1986. "Crucial Phase Beginning in Gulf War." *Jane's Defence Weekly.* September.
Brzezinski, Zbigniew. 1983. *Power and Principle.* London: Weidenfeld and Nicolson.
Brzoska, Michael. 1982. "Arms Transfer Data Sources." *Journal of Conflict Resolution.* Vol. 26, no. 1, March, pp. 77–108.
Brzoska, Michael. 1984. "Ein Geschenk fur die Rustungsindustrie: Waffenlieferungen an Irak und Iran." *Der Überblick.* Vol. 20 (June), pp. 63–65.
———. 1987. "Profiteering on the Iraq-Iran War." *Bulletin of the Atomic Scientists.* Vol. 43 (June), pp. 42–46.
———. 1991. "Ild pa Olien: 1980s Vabenoverforsler till Irak." *Vandkusten (Copenhagen).* No. 5 (January), pp. 197–210.
Brzoska, Michael, and Thomas Ohlson, eds. 1986. *Arms Production in the Third World.* London: Taylor and Francis.
———. 1987. *Arms Transfers to the Third World 1971–85.* London: Oxford University Press.
Bueno de Mesquita, Bruce. 1981. *The War Trap.* New Haven, Conn.: Yale University Press.
Bulloch, John, and Harvey Morris. 1988. *The Gulf War.* London: Methuen.
Burden, Rodney A., ed. 1986. *Falklands: The Air War.* London: Arms and Armour Press.
Burke, S. M. 1973. *Pakistan's Foreign Policy: An Historical Analysis.* Oxford: Oxford University Press.
Burt, Richard. 1977. "Development in Arms Transfers: Implications for Supplier Control and Recipient Autonomy." *Rand Paper P-5991.* Santa Monica, Calif.: Rand Corporation.
Butterworth, Robert Lyle, with Margaret E. Scranton. 1976. *Managing Interstate Conflict, 1945–74: Data with Synopses.* Pittsburgh: University Center for International Studies, University of Pittsburgh.
CARDRI. 1989. *Saddam's Iraq: Revolution or Reaction?* London: Zed Books Ltd.
Carrington, Lord Peter. 1978. *Reflections on Things Past.* London: Collins.

Carus, Seth, W. 1991. "Ballistic Missiles in Modern Conflict." *The Washington Papers.* No. 146. Washington, D.C.: Praeger for the Center for Strategic and International Studies.
Cassen, Robert, ed. 1985. *Soviet Interests in the Third World.* London: SAGE Publications.
Catrina, Christian. 1988. *Arms Transfers and Dependence.* New York: Taylor and Francis/UNIDIR.
Chaigneau, Pascal. 1986. "Les Transfers d'Armements en Afrique Australe." *Etudes Polémologiques.* No. 40, pp. 75–89.
Chaudhri, M. A. 1966. "Pakistan's Relations with the Soviet Union." *Asian Survey.* Vol. 6, September, pp. 492–500.
Chatterjee, Sisar. 1972. *Bangladesh: The Birth of a Nation.* Calcutta: The Book Exchange.
Choudhary, Sukhbir. 1972. *Indo-Pak War and Big Powers.* New Delhi: Trimurti Publications.
Choudhury, G. W. 1975. *India, Pakistan, Bangladesh and the Major Powers: Politics of a Divided Subcontinent.* New York: Free Press.
Chowdhury, Subrath. 1972. *Genesis of Bangladesh.* Bombay & New York: Asia Publishing House.
Chubin, Shahram. 1982. *Security in the Persian Gulf 4: The Role of Outside Powers.* London: International Institute for Strategic Studies.
———. 1983a. "La France et le Golfe: Opportunisme ou Continuite?" *Politique Etrangére.* Vol. 48, no. 4, pp. 879–87.
———. 1983b. "The Soviet Union and Iran." *Foreign Affairs.* Vol. 61 (Spring), pp. 921–49.
———. 1985. "Israel and the Iran-Iraq War." *International Defense Review.* Vol. 18, No. 3.
———. 1986. "Reflections on the Gulf War." *Survival.* Vol. 28 (July-August), pp. 306–21.
———. 1987a. "Hedging in the Gulf: Soviets Arm Both Sides." *International Defense Review.* Vol. 20, no. 6, pp. 731–35.
———. 1987b. "Les Conduite des Operations Militaires dans le Conflit Iran-Iraq." *Politique Etrangere.* Vol. 52, no. 2, pp. 303–16.
———. 1989. "The Last Phase of the Iran-Iraq War: From Stalemate to Ceasefire." *Third World Quarterly.* Vol. 11, no. 2, pp. 1–14.
Chubin, Shahram, and Charles Tripp. 1988. *Iran and Iraq at War.* Boulder, Colo.: Westview.
Cimbala, Stephen J., and Sidney R. Waldman, eds. 1991. *Controlling and Ending Conflict. Issues Before and After the Cold War* (Contributions in Military Studies, Number 119). New York: Greenwood Press.
Clapham, Christopher. 1981. "The Soviet Experience in the Horn of Africa." In Feuchtwanger and Nailor, 1981, pp. 202–23.
Claude, Inis L. 1985. "UN Efforts at a Settlement." In Coll and Arend, 1985, pp. 118–31.

Clausen, Ursel. 1975. "Der Konflikt um die Spanische Sahara." *Orient*. Vol. 16, no. 4, pp. 21–38.
Clément, Jean-François. 1985. "Le Conflit du Saharien." Paris: Institut Francais de Polémologie et Centre Droit et Defense, Université de Paris V. Colloque Transferts d'armements et conflits locaux. 21–22 Mars.
———. 1986. "Le Conflit du Sahara Occidental." *Etudes Polémologiques*. No. 40, pp. 91–142.
Coll, Albert R., and Anthony C. Arend, eds. 1985. *The Falklands War: Lessons for Strategy, Diplomacy and International Law*. Boston: Allen & Unwin.
Colombo, Jorge Luis. 1984. "`Super Etendard' Naval Aircraft Operations During the Malvinas War." *Naval War College Review* Vol. 37, no. 3, pp. 12–22.
Cordesman, Anthony. 1987a. *The Arab-Israeli Military Balance and the Art of Operations: An Anthology of Military Lessons and Trends and Implications for Future Conflicts*. Washington, D.C.: American Enterprise Institute.
———. 1987b. *The Iran-Iraq War and Western Security, 1984-87*. London: Jane's Publishing Company.
———. 1987c. "Arms to Iran: The Impact of US and Other Arms Sales on the Iran-Iraq War." *American-Arab Affairs*. Vol. 20 (Spring), pp. 13–29.
Cordesman, Anthony H., and Abraham R. Wagner. 1990a. *The Lessons of Modern War, Volume II: The Iran-Iraq War*. Boulder, Colo., and San Francisco: Westview.
———. 1990b. *The Lessons of Modern War, Volume III: The Afghan and Falklands Conflicts*. Boulder, Colo.: Westview.
Costa Mendez, Nicanor. 1985. "El Papel de los EEUU an la Fase Inicial del Conflict del Atlantico Sur." *Revista Argentina de Estudios Estrategicos*. No. 6 (October–December).
Cottam, Richard. 1988. *Iran and the United States: A Cold War Case Study*. Pittsburgh: University of Pittsburgh Press.
Coulson, Andrew. 1982. *Tanzania: A Political Economy*. Oxford: Clarendon Press.
Dacoudi, M. S., and M. S. Dajani. 1983. "Sanctions: The Falkland Episode." *World Today*. Vol. 39, no. 4, pp. 150–60.
Damis, John. 1982. "The Role of Third Parties in the Western Sahara Conflict." *Maghreb Review*. Vol. 7, no. 1–2, pp. 1–15.
———. 1983a. *Conflict in Northwest Africa: The Western Sahara Dispute*. Stanford, Calif: Hoover International Press.
———. 1983b. "The Western Sahara Conflict." *Middle East Journal*. Vol 37, No. 2, pp. 169–79.
Dartford, Mark, ed. 1985. *Falklands Armoury*. Poole, Eng.: Blandford Press.

Davis, H. David, ed. 1962. *The Economic Development of Uganda.* Baltimore: Johns Hopkins University Press.
Davis, Thomas M. 1987. *40 Km. Into Lebanon.* Washington, D.C.: National Defense University Press.
Dawisha, Karen. 1981. "Sowjetische Entscheidungsfindung im Nahen Osten: Der Oktoberkrieg 1973 und der Krieg zwischen Irak und Iran 1980." *Beiträge fur Konfliktforschung.* Vol. 11, no. 3, pp. 33–55.
Day, Alan J., ed. 1982. *Border and Territorial Disputes.* Detroit: Gale Research.
De Lillo, Don. 1988. *Libra.* New York: Viking Penguin.
Deutscher Bundestag, 1991. "Unterrichtung durch die Bundesregierung, Bericht der Bundesregierung über legale und illegale Waffenexporte in den Irak und die Aufrüstung des Irak durch Firmen der Bundesrepublik Deutschland." *Drucksache,* 12/407. May 8.
Diehl, Paul. 1985. "Arms Races to War." *Sociological Quarterly, pp.* 331–49.
Dietl, Wilhelm. 1986. *Waffen fur die Welt. Die Milliardengeschäfte der Rüstungsindustrie.* München: Droemer Knauer.
Dillon, Mick. 1988. *The Falklands: Politics and War.* London: Macmillan.
Dodd, Norman. 1982. "Einige Lehren aus dem Falklandkrieg." *Europäische Wehrkunde.* Vol. 31, no. 9, pp. 392–97.
Donaldson, R. H., ed. 1981. *The Soviet Union and the Third World: Successes and Failures.* Boulder, Colo.: Westview.
Dougherty, James E. 1980. "The Polisario Insurgency: War and Minuet in North-West Africa." *Conflict.* Vol. 2, no. 2, pp. 93–120.
Dunkerly, James. 1985. *The Long War: Dictatorship and Revolution in El Salvador.* London: Verso.
Dunn, Keith A. 1981. "Constraints on the USSR in Southwest Asia: A Military Analysis." *Orbis.* Vol. 25, no. 3, pp. 607–29.
Dupuy, T. N., and Wendell Blanchard. 1972. *Almanac of World Military Power,* 2nd ed. New York: R. R. Bowker Co.
Dupuy, Trevor, and Paul Martell. 1986. *Flawed Victory: The 1982 War in Lebanon.* McLean, Va: Hero Books.
Durham, William H. 1979. *Scarcity and Survival in Central America: Ecological Origins of the Soccer War.* Stanford: Stanford University Press.
Edwards, Geoffrey. 1984. "Europe and the Falkland Islands Crisis, 1982." *Journal of Common Market Studies.* Vol. 22, no. 4, pp. 295–313.
El Azhary, M. S. 1984. *The Iran-Iraq War.* New York: St. Martins Press.
El Badri, Hassan, El Magdoub Taha, El Din Zohdy, and Mohammed Din. 1977. *The Ramadan War, 1973.* Boulder, Colo.: Westview.
Ethell, Jeffrey, and Alfred Price. 1983. *Air War: South Atlantic.* London: Sidgewick & Jackson.

Evron, Yair. 1973. *The Middle East: Nations, Superpowers, and Wars.* New York: Praeger.
Falcoff, Marc. 1990. *A Tale of Two Policies: US Relations with the Argentine Junta.* Philadelphia: University of Pennsylvania Press.
Farhang, Mansour. 1985. "The Iran-Iraq War: The Feud, the Tragedy, the Spoils." *World Policy Journal.* Vol. 3 (Fall), pp. 659–80.
Fei, Edward T. 1979. "Understanding Arms Transfers and Military Expenditures: Data Problems." In Neuman and Harkavy, pp. 37–46.
Feldman, David Lewis. 1985. "The United States Role in the Malvinas Crisis, 1982: Misguidance and Misperception in Argentina's Decision to go to War." *Journal of Interamerican Studies and World Affairs.* Vol. 27, no. 2, pp. 1–24.
Feldman, Herbert. 1972. *From Crisis to Crisis: Pakistan—1962-69.* London: Oxford University Press.
Feuchtwanger, E. J., and Peter Nailor, eds. 1981. *The Soviet Union and the Third World.* New York: St. Martin's Press.
Flitner, Michael. 1987. "Krieg als Geschaft: Waffenexporte in Iran und Irak." In Anja Malanowski, ed., *Bis die Gottlosen vernichtet sind.* Reinbek: Rowohlt, pp. 56–68.
Foreign Affairs Chronology, 1978-1989. 1990. New York: Foreign Affairs.
Freedman, Lawrence. 1983. "Bridgehead Revisited: The Literature of the Falklands." *International Affairs.* Vol. 59 (March), pp. 445–52.
———. 1988. *Britain and the Falklands War.* London: Basil Blackwell.
Freedman, Lawrence, and Virginia Gamba-Stonehouse. 1990. *Signals of War.* London and Boston: Faber and Faber.
Fricker, John. 1983. "The Falklands: Air Claims and Losses Analysed." *Air International.* Vol. 24, no. 5, pp. 244–59.
Friedman, Norman. 1983. "The Falklands War: Lessons Learned and Mislearned." *Orbis.* Vol. 26, no. 4, pp. 907–40.
Fukuyama, Frances. 1980. "The Soviet Union and Iraq since 1968." *RAND N-1524-AF.* Santa Monica, Calif.: RAND.
Fuller, Graham E. 1989. "War and Revolution in Iran." *Current History.* Vol. 88 (February), pp. 81–100.
Gabriel, Richard A. 1984. *Operation Peace for Galilee: The Israeli-PLO War in Lebanon.* New York: Hill and Wang.
Galaydh, Ali Khalif. 1988. *International Negotiation: Soviet-Somali Relations and the Ogaden War, 1978-9.* Case 113. Pittsburgh: Pew Program in Case Training and Writing in International Affairs.
Gamba, Virginia. 1987. *The Falkland/Malvinas War: A Model for North-South Crisis Prevention.* Boston: Allen & Unwin.
Ganguly, S. 1986. *Origins of War in South Asia: Indo-Pakistani Conflicts Since 1947.* Boulder, Colo.: Westview.
George, Alexander, ed. 1983. *Managing U.S.-Soviet Rivalry: Problems of Crisis Prevention.* Boulder, Colo.: Westview Press Special Studies in International Relations.

———. 1986. "U.S.-Soviet Global Rivalry: Norms of Competition." *Journal of Peace Research.* Vol. 23 (September), pp. 247–62.
———. 1993. *Bridging the Gap: Theory and Practice in Foreign Policy.* Washington, D.C.: United States Institute of Peace.
George, Alexander L., Alexander Dallin, and Philip J. Farley, eds. 1988. *U.S.-Soviet Security Cooperation: Achievements, Failures, Lessons.* New York: Oxford University Press.
George, Alexander L., and Richard Smoke. 1974. *Deterrence in American Foreign Policy: Theory and Practice.* New York: Columbia University Press.
Gill, R. Bates. 1991. "Fire of the Dragon: Arms, Influence and Chinese Security Policy." *PSIS Occasional Papers No. 1, 1991.* Geneva: Programme for Strategic and International Security Studies.
Goldblat, Jozef, and Victor Millan. 1983a. *The Falklands/Malvinas Conflict: A Spur to Arms Build-ups.* Stockholm: Stockholm International Peace Research Institute.
———. 1983b. "The Falklands/Malvinas Conflict: A Spur to Arms Build-ups." *SIPRI Yearbook 1983.* London: Taylor & Francis, pp. 467–515.
Goodman, Allan E., and Sandra Clement Bogart. 1992. *Making Peace. The United States and Conflict Resolution.* Boulder, Colo.: Westview.
Grimmett, Richard F. 1989. "Trends in Conventional Arms Transfers to the Third World by Major Suppliers, 1981–1988." Washington, D.C.: Congressional Research Service, August.
Gupta, Hari Ram. 1967. *Indian-Pakistan War 1965.* 2 vols. Delhi: Hariyana Prakashan.
———. 1969. *The Kutch Affair.* Delhi: W. C. Kapur.
Habib, Philip. 1985. Personal interview with the author. St. Louis, Mo.
Haffa, Annegret I. 1987. *Beagle-Konflikt und Falkland/Malwinen-Krieg: Zur Aussenpolitik der argentinischen Militärregierung 1976 bis 1983.* München: Weltforum Verlag.
Haig, Alexander. 1984. *Caveat.* London: Weidenfeld & Nicolson.
Halliday, Fred. 1985. "East-West Conflict and the Horn of Africa." *Vierteljahresberichte der Friedrich-Ebert-Stiftung,* No. 100, pp. 199–206.
———. 1988. "Iran-Iraq: The Uncertainties of Peace." *World Today.* Vol. 44 (October), pp. 165–66.
Halliday, Fred, and M. Molyneux. 1981. *The Ethiopian Revolution.* London: New Left Review.
Handel, Michael. 1978. "The Study of War Termination." *Journal of Strategic Studies.* Vol. 1, no. 1, pp. 51–75.
Harkavy, Robert. 1975. *The Arms Trade and International Systems.* Cambridge, Mass.: Ballinger.
———. 1979. "The New Geopolitics: Arms Transfers and the Major Powers' Competition for Overseas Bases." In Neuman and Harkavy, 1979, pp. 131–51.

———. 1985. "Arms Resupply During Conflict: A Framework for Analysis." *Jerusalem Journal of International Relations.* Vol. 7, no. 3, pp. 5–41.

———. 1989. "Arms Resupply During Conflict: A Framework for Analysis." In C. Schmidt, ed., *The Economics of Military Expenditures.* London: Macmillan, pp. 239–79.

Harkavy, Robert E., and Stephanie G. Neuman, eds. 1985. *The Lessons of Recent Wars in the Third World: Approaches and Case Studies. Volume 1.* Lexington, Mass.: D. C. Heath.

Harshe, Rajen. 1980. "Political Implications of French Military Interventions in Africa: Three Case Studies." *IDSA Journal.* Vol. 12, no. 3, pp. 270–85.

Hartung, William. 1987. "Nations Vie for Arms Market." *Bulletin of the Atomic Scientists.* Vol. 43 (December), pp. 27–35.

Hastings, Max, and Simon Jenkins. 1983. *The Battle for the Falklands.* London: Michael Joseph.

Heller, Mark, ed., 1986. *The Middle East Military Balance 1985.* Jerusalem: Jerusalem Post Press.

Henderson, Sir Nicholas. 1983. "America and the Falklands." *Economist.* Vol. 289 (November 12), pp. 31–38.

Henze, Paul B. 1983. "Arming the Horn 1960–80." *International Security Studies Working Paper 43.* Washington, D.C.: Woodrow Wilson Center for Scholars.

———. 1984. "Arming the Horn 1960–80: Military Expenditures, Arms Imports and Military Aid." *Proceedings of the Seventh International Association of Ethiopian Studies,* East Lansing, Mich., pp. 637–56.

———. 1985. *Rebels and Separatists in Ethiopia: Regional Resistance to a Marxist Regime.* Santa Monica, Calif.: Rand Corporation Paper Series.

———. 1991. *The Horn of Africa: From War to Peace.* London: Macmillan.

Hersh, Seymour M. 1991. "U.S. Cleared Iran Arms Sales." *International Herald Tribune,* December 9, p. 1.

Herzog, Chaim. 1982. *The Arab-Israeli Wars: War and Peace in the Middle East.* New York: Random House.

Hiro, Dilip. 1988. *The Longest War.* London: Grafton Books.

Hodges, Tony. 1980. "U.S. Arms and the Desert War." *Africa Report.* Vol. 25 (May–June), pp. 42–49.

———. 1983. *Western Sahara: The Roots of a Desert War.* Westport, Conn.: Lawrence Hill.

———. 1985. "At Odds with Self-Determinism: The United States and Western Sahara." In Bender, Coleman, and Sklar, 1985, pp. 260–76.

Hooglund, Eric. 1989. "The Islamic Republic at War and Peace." *Middle East Report.* Vol. 17 (January–February), pp. 5–12.

Hosmer, Stephen T., and Thomas W. Wolfe. 1983. *Soviet Policy and Practice Toward Third World Conflicts.* Lexington, Mass: Lexington Books.

Howarth, H. M. F. 1983. "Die Auswirkungen des Irakisch-Iranischen Kriegs auf den Militärbedarf in den Golfstaaten." *Internationale Wehrrevue*. Vol. 16, no. 10, pp. 1405–9.

Howe, Geoffrey. 1985. *House of Commons Official Report, Written Answers*. London: Hansard, vol. 84, no. 172. October 29.

Hubel, Helmut. 1988. "Nordafrika in der sowjetischen Auâenpolitik." In H. Hubel, ed., *Nordafrika in der Internationalen Politik*. München: Oldenbourg, pp. 202–19.

Huertas, Salvador Maf, and Jesus Romero Briasco. 1987. *Argentine Air Force in the Falklands Conflict*. London: Arms and Armour Press.

Hughes, Denis. 1982. "Israeli Air Force in Close-up." *Jane's Defence Review*. Vol. 3, no. 4, pp. 413–14.

Hunt, Ben W. 1990. "Port Access and [Soviet] Arms Sales: The Unspoken Quid Pro Quo." *Journal of Conflict Resolution*. Vol. 34 (June), pp. 335–65.

Huth, Paul. 1988. *Extended Deterrence and the Prevention of War*. New Haven, Conn.: Yale University Press.

Huth, Paul, and Bruce Russett. 1984. "What Makes Deterrence Work? Cases from 1900 to 1980." *World Politics*. Vol. 36, no. 4, pp. 496–526.

———. 1988. "Deterrence Failure and Crisis Escalation to War." *International Studies Quarterly*. Vol. 32 (March), pp. 29–45.

Huyser, Robert E. 1986. *Mission to Teheran*. New York: Harper & Row.

International Institute for Strategic Studies (IISS). Annually. *The Military Balance*. London: IISS.

———. Annually. *Strategic Survey*. London: IISS.

Jackson, Robert. 1975. *South Asian Crisis: India, Pakistan, and Bangladesh*. New York: Praeger.

Jacob, Abel. 1971. "Israel's Military Aid to Africa, 1960–66." *Journal of Modern African Studies*. Vol. 9, no. 2, pp. 165–87.

Jasani, Bhupendra. 1983. "The Military Use of Outer Space." *SIPRI Yearbook 1983*. London: Taylor & Francis, pp. 427–56.

Johansen, Robert, and Michael Renner. 1985. "Limiting Conflict in the Gulf." *Third World Quarterly*. Vol. 7, no. 4, pp. 803–38.

Jouve, Edmond. 1985. "France and Crisis Areas in Africa." In Bender, Coleman, and Sklar, 1985. pp. 297–320.

Kahn, M. Asghan. 1979. *The First Round, Indo-Pakistani War, 1965*. Sahibabad Dist., Ghaziabad, Pakistan: Vikas.

Kamil, Leo. 1987. *Fueling the Fire: US Policy and the Western Sahara Conflict*. Trensbury, N.Y.: Red Sea Press.

Kaplan, Stephen S. 1981. *Diplomacy of Power: Soviet Armed Forces as a Political Instrument*. Washington: Brookings Institution.

Karsh, Efraim. 1982. "Military Lessons of the Iran-Iraq War." *Orbis*. Vol. 33, no. 2, pp. 209–23.

———. 1987. "The Iran-Iraq War: The Military Implications." *Adelphi Paper 220*. London: IISS.

———. 1988. "Military Power and Foreign Policy Goals: The Iran-Iraq War Revisited." *International Affairs.* Vol. 64 (Winter), pp. 83–95.
———. ed. 1989. *The Iran-Iraq War.* London: Macmillan.
Katz, James E., ed. 1984. *Arms Production in Developing Countries.* Lexington, Mass.: Lexington Books.
Kaufman, Chaim. 1988. *U.S. Mediation in the Falklands/Malvinas Crisis: Shuttle Diplomacy in the 1980s.* Pittsburgh, Pa.: Pew Program in International Case Studies Teaching and Writing.
Kaul, B. M. 1971. *Confrontation with Pakistan.* New York: Barnes and Noble.
Keegan, John, ed. 1983. *World Armies.* 2nd Ed. Detroit: Gale Research.
Kemp, Geoffrey. 1990a. "Regional Security, Arms Control, and the End of the Cold War." *Washington Quarterly.* Vol. 13 (Autumn), pp. 33–51.
———. 1990b. *Remarks at Conference on Conflict Resolution in the Post–Cold War Third World.* U.S. Institute of Peace, Washington, D.C.
Kemp, L. 1988. "The International Arms Industry: A Final Casualty of the Gulf War." *Jane's Defence Weekly,* July 30, pp. 164–65.
Kerr, Malcolm. 1971. *The Arab Cold War: Gamal 'Abd al-Nasir and his Rivals, 1958–1970.* 3rd ed. London: Oxford University Press for the Royal Institute for International Affairs.
Khadduri, Majid. 1988. *The Gulf War: The Origins and Implications of the Iraq-Iran Conflict.* New York: Oxford University Press.
Khan, Fazal Muqeem. 1973. *Pakistan's Crisis in Leadership.* Islamabad: National Book Foundation.
Kidron, Michael, and Dan Smith. 1983. *The War Atlas: Armed Conflict— Armed Peace.* New York: Simon and Schuster.
King, Ralph. 1987. "The Iran-Iraq War: Political Implications." *Adelphi Paper 221.* London: International Institute for Strategic Studies.
Kinney, Douglas. 1989. *National Interest/National Honour: The Diplomacy of the Falkland Crisis.* New York: Praeger.
Kissinger, Henry. 1979. *The White House Years.* London: Weidenfeld and Nicolson.
———. 1987. *Years of Upheaval.* London: Weidenfeld and Nicolson.
Klare, Michael T. 1984. *American Arms Supermarket.* Austin, Tex.: University of Texas Press.
———. 1986. "The State of the Trade: Global Arms Transfer Patterns in the 1980s." *Journal of International Affairs.* Vol. 40 (Summer), 1986, p. 1–21.
———. 1987. "The Arms Trade: Changing Patterns in the 1980s." *Third World Quarterly.* Vol. 9, no. 4, pp. 1257–81.
Kliemann, Aaron. 1985. *Israel's Global Reach: Arms Sales as Diplomacy.* Washington, D.C.: Pergamon-Brassey's.
Klinghofer, Arthur Jay, with Judith Apter. 1985. *Israel and the Soviet Union: Alienation or Reconciliation?* Boulder, Colo.: Westview.

Kolodziej, Edward A. 1979. "Measuring French Arms Transfers: A Problem of Sources and Some Sources of Problems with ACDA Data." *Journal of Conflict Resolution.* Vol. 23 (June), pp. 195–227.
———. 1989. *The Making and Marketing of Arms.* Princeton: Princeton University Press.
Kolodziej, Edward, and Roger Kanet, eds. 1991. *The Cold War as Cooperation: Superpower Cooperation in Regional Conflict Management.* Basingstoke, Eng: Macmillan.
Koppe, Holger, and Egmont R. Koch. 1990. *Bomben-Geschafte: Tödliche Waffen für die Dritte Welt.* München: Knesebeck Schuler.
Kramer, Mark. 1987. "Soviet Arms Transfers to the Third World." *Problems of Communism.* Vol. 36, no. 5 (September–October), pp. 52–68.
Krause, Joachim. 1985. *Sowjetische Militärhilfepolitik gegenüber Entwicklungslandern.* Baden-Baden: Nomos Verlag.
Krause, Keith. 1987. "Arms Transfers, Conflict Management and the Arab-Israeli Conflict." In David Dewitt and Gabriel Ben-Dor, eds., *Conflict Management in the Middle East.* Lexington, Mass: Lexington Books.
———. 1990. "Constructing Regional Security Regimes and the Control of Arms Transfers." *International Journal.* Vol. 11 (Spring), pp. 386–423.
———. 1991. "Military Statecraft: Power and Influence in Soviet and American Arms Transfer Relationships." *International Studies Quarterly.* Vol. 35, no. 2, pp. 313–16.
———. 1992a. *Arms and the State: Patterns of Military Production and Trade.* Cambridge, Eng.: Cambridge University Press.
———. 1992b. "Transferts d'Armement et Gestion des Conflits: le Cas de la Guerre Iran-Irak." *Cultures et Conflits.* No. 4 (Hiver), 91–92, pp. 13–40.
La Feber, Walter. 1984. *Inevitable Revolutions: The United States in Central America.* Expanded ed. New York: Norton.
Laitin, David O. 1979. "The War in the Ogaden: Implications for Siyaad's Role in Somali History." *Journal of Modern African Studies.* Vol. 17, no. 1, pp. 95–115.
Langley, Lester D. 1985. *Central America: The Real Stakes.* New York: Crown.
Lapper, Richard, and James Painter. 1985. *Honduras: State for Sale.* London: Latin America Bureau.
Laqueur, Walter. 1968. *The Road to Jerusalem: The Origins of the Arab-Israeli Conflict, 1967.* New York: Macmillan.
———. 1974. *Confrontation: The Middle East and World Politics.* New York: Quadrangle.
Laurance, Edward J. 1992. *The International Arms Trade.* Lexington, Mass.: Lexington Books.
Laurance, Edward J., and Ronald G. Sherwin. 1978. "Understanding Arms Transfers through Data Analysis." In Uri Raanan, Robert T. Pfaltzgraff,

Jr., and Geoffrey Kemp, eds. *Arms Transfers to the Third World: The Military Buildup in Less Industrial Countries.* Boulder, Colo.: Westview, pp. 87–106.

Lawless, Richard, and Leila Monahan, eds. 1988. *War and Refugees: The Western Sahara Conflict.* London: Pinter.

LeBorgne, Claude. 1983. "Le conflit du Sahara occidental." *Defense Nationale,* Vol. 39 (Mai), pp. 111–31.

Lebow, Richard Ned. 1981. *Between Peace and War.* Baltimore: Johns Hopkins University Press.

Lebow, Richard Ned, and Janice Gross Stein. 1990. "When Does Deterrence Succeed and How Do We Know?" *Occasional Papers No. 8.* Ottawa: Canadian Institute for International Peace and Security.

Lefebvre, Jeffrey A. 1981. "American Foreign Policy and the Horn of Africa: A Cold War Reaction?" *Northeast African Studies.* Vol. 3, no. 1, pp. 31–42.

———. 1987. "Donor Dependency and American Arms Transfers to the Horn of Africa: The F-5 Legacy." *Journal of Modern African Studies.* Vol. 25, no. 3, pp. 465–88.

Legum, Colin. 1981. "Angola and the Horn of Africa." In Stephen S. Kaplan, *Diplomacy of Power: Soviet Armed Forces as a Political Instrument.* Washington, D.C.: Brookings, pp. 570–642.

Legum, Colin, and Bill Lee. 1979. *The Horn of Africa in Continuing Crisis.* New York: Africana.

Lewis, John W., Hua Di, and Xue Litai. 1991. "Beijing's Defense Establishment: Solving the Arms-Export Enigma." *International Security.* Vol. 15 (Spring), pp. 87–109.

Lewis, William H. 1985a. "War in the Western Sahara." In Harkavy and Neuman, 1985, pp. 117–38.

———. 1985b. "Ethiopia-Somalia (1977–1978)." In Harkavy and Neuman, 1985, pp. 99–117.

Leyendecker, Hans, and Richard Rickelmann. 1990. *Exporteure des Todes.* Göttingen: Steidl.

Licklider, Roy. 1991. "How Civil Wars End. Preliminary Results from a Comparative Project." In Cimbala and Waldman, 1991, pp. 219–38

Lifschultz, Lawrence, Rabia Ali, and Steven Galster. 1991. *Bordering on Treason? The Trial and Conviction of Arif Durrani.* East Haven, Conn.: The Pamphleteer's Press.

Linde, Gerd. 1972. *Bangladesh: Indien und die Grossmächte im Pakistanischen Konflikt.* Stuttgart: W. Kohlhammer.

Litwak, Robert. 1984. *Detente and the Nixon Doctrine: American Foreign Policy and the Pursuit of Stability, 1969–76.* Cambridge, Eng.: Cambridge University Press.

Luard, Evan. 1988. *Conflict and Peace in the Modern International System.* 2nd ed. London: Macmillan.

Luckham, Robin, and D. Bekele. 1984a. "Foreign Powers and Militarism in the Horn of Africa, Part I." *Review of African Political Economy*, No. 30, pp. 8–20.

———. 1984b. "Foreign Powers and Militarism in the Horn of Africa, Part II." *Review of African Political Economy*, No. 31, pp. 7–28.

McGowan, Pat, and Charles W. Kegley, Jr., eds. 1980. *Threats, Weapons, and Foreign Policy.* Vol. 5. Beverly Hills: Sage Publications.

McNaugher, Thomas L. 1984. "Arms and Allies on the Arabian Peninsula." *Orbis.* Vol. 28 (Fall), pp. 486–526.

———. 1985. *Arms and Oil: U.S. Military Security Policy Toward the Persian Gulf.* Washington, D.C.: Brookings Institution.

———. 1990. "Ballistic Missiles and Chemical Weapons: The Legacy of the Iran-Iraq War." *International Security.* Vol. 15 (Fall), pp. 5–34.

McWilliams, James P. 1990. *Armscor: South Africa's Arms Merchant.* London: Brassey's.

Makin, Guillermo. 1983. "Argentine Approaches to the Falklands/Malvinas: Was the Resort to Violence Foreseeable?" *International Affairs.* Vol. 59, no. 3, pp. 391–403.

Mankekar, D. R. 1966. *Twenty-Two Fateful Days: Pakistan Cut to Size.* Bombay: Manaktalas.

Marquina, Antonio. 1988. "Libya, the Maghreb and Mediterranean Security." *Adelphi Paper 231.* London: International Institute for Strategic Studies.

Martz, Mary J. R. 1978. *The Central American Soccer War: Historical Patterns and Internal Dynamics of OAS Settlement Procedures.* Columbus: Ohio State University Press.

Matthies, Volker. 1976a. "Somalia—Ein sowjetischer 'Satellitenstaat' im Horn von Afrika?" *Verfassung und Recht in Übersee.* Vol. 9, no. 4, pp. 437–56.

———. 1976b. *Das 'Horn von Afrika' in den internationalen Beziehungen Internationale Aspekte eines Regionalkonfliktes.* München: Weltforum Verlag.

———. 1977. *Der Grenzkonflikt Somalias mit Ethiopien und Kenya.* Hamburg: Weltforum.

———. 1987. "Der Ogadenkrieg zwischen Somalia und Äthiopien von 1977/78." *Afrika-Spectrum.* Vol. 22, no. 3, pp. 237–53.

———. 1990. "Krieg am Horn von Afrika: Historische Aspekte von Gesellschaft, Rüstung und Verheerung." *Afrika-Spectrum.* Vol. 25, no. 1, pp. 5–33.

Maull, Hans W., and Otto Pick. 1989. *The Gulf War.* London: Pinter.

Medalia, Jonathan. 1986. "Arms Transfers to Iran Since 1979: Reports from the Media." *Report No. 86-187 F.* Washington, D.C.: Congressional Research Service.

Mets, David R. 1986. *Land Based Air Power in Third World Crises.* Maxwell Air Force Base, Ala.: Air University Press.

Miall, Hugh. 1990. "Peaceful Settlement of Post-1945 Conflicts: A Contemporary Study." Paper for the U.S. Institute of Peace Colloquium on Conflict Resolution in the Post Cold War Third World, Washington, August.

Middlebrook, Martin. 1985. *Operation Corporate: The Story of the Falklands War 1982*. London: Viking.

———. 1989. *The Fight for the 'Malvinas': The Argentine Forces in the Falkland War.* London: Viking.

Millan, Victor. 1986. "Argentina: Schemes for Glory." In Brzoska and Ohlson, 1985, pp. 35–54.

Moeini, Nasser. 1981. "The Iranian Position." *The Iran-Iraq War: Issues of Conflict and Prospects for Settlement.* Princeton, N.J.: Princeton University Press.

Moneta, Carlos. 1984. "The Malvinas Conflict: Some Elements for an Analysis of the Argentine Military Regime's Decision-Making Process 1976–82." *Millenium.* Vol. 13, no. 3, pp. 311–24.

Monroe, Elizabeth, and A. H. Farrar-Hockley. 1974. "The Arab-Israeli War, October 1973: Background and Events." *Adelphi Paper 111.* London: International Institute for Strategic Studies.

Montgomery, Tommie Sue. 1982. *Revolution in El Salvador: Origins and Evolution.* Boulder, Colo.: Westview.

Moore, John, ed. 1983. *Jane's Fighting Ships 1982/1983.* London: Jane's.

Moran, Theodore H. 1978. "Iranian Defense Expenditures and the Social Crisis." *International Security.* Vol. 3 (Winter), pp. 178–92.

Morgan, Patrick M. 1977. *Deterrence: A Conceptual Analysis.* Beverly Hills, Calif.: Sage.

———. 1983. *Deterrence: A Conceptual Analysis.* 2nd ed. Beverly Hills, Calif.: Sage.

Moro, Ruben Oscar. 1989. *The History of the South Atlantic Conflict: The War for the Malvinas.* New York: Praeger.

Morris, James A. 1984. *Honduras: Caudillo Politics and Military Rulers.* Boulder, Colo.: Westview.

Most, Benjamin, and Randolph M. Sieverson. 1987. "Substituting Arms and Alliance 1879–1914: An Exploration in Comparative Foreign Policy." In C. F. Hermann, C. W. Kegley, and J. N. Rosenau, eds. *New Directions in the Study of Foreign Policy.* Winchester, Mass.: Allen & Unwin, pp. 131–51.

Mottale, Morris Mehrdad. 1986. *The Arms Buildup in the Persian Gulf.* Lanham, Md.: University Press of America.

Moynihan, Patrick. 1979. *A Dangerous Place.* London: Secker & Warburg.

Mudoola, Dan. 1988. "Political Transitions Since Idi Amin: A Study in Political Pathology." In Holger Bernt Hansen and Michael Twaddle, eds. *Uganda Now.* Athens: Ohio University Press, pp. 280–98.

Mulira, James. 1981. "Soviet Bloc: Trade, Economic, Technical and Military Involvement in Independent Africa: A Case Study of Uganda." *Genéve-Afrique.* Vol. 19, no. 1, pp. 39–79.

Murguizur, Juan. 1983. "Der Konflikt im Südatlantik aus argentinischer Sicht." *Internationale Wehrrevue.* Vol. 16, no. 2, pp. 135–40.

Myroie, Laurie. 1989. "Iraq's Changing Role in the Persian Gulf." *Current History.* Vol. 88 (February), pp. 89–99.

Nachmias, Nitza. 1988. *Transfer of Arms, Leverage, and Peace in the Middle East.* Contributions in Military Studies, No. 83. New York: Greenwood Press.

Napper, Larry C. 1983. "The Ogaden War: Some Implications for Crisis Prevention." In George, 1983, pp. 155–86.

Navias, Martin. 1990. "Missile Proliferation in the Third World." *Adelphi Paper 252.* London: Brassey's.

Nelson, H. D., ed. 1982. *Somalia: A Country Study.* Washington, D.C.: American University Press.

Nelson, H. D., and I. Kaplan, eds. 1981. *Ethiopia: A Country Study.* Washington, D.C.: American University Press.

Neuman, Stephanie G. 1978. "Security, Military Expenditures and Socioeconomic Development." *Orbis.* Vol. 22 (Fall), pp. 569–94.

———, ed. 1984a. *Defense Planning in Less-Industrialized States.* Lexington, Mass.: Lexington Books.

———. 1984b. "International Stratification and Third World Military Industries." *International Organization.* Vol. 38 (Winter), pp. 167–97.

———. 1986a. "Military Assistance in Recent Wars: The Dominance of the Superpowers." *The Washington Papers No. 122.* Washington, D.C.: Praeger Publishers for Center for Strategic and International Studies.

———. 1986b. "The Arms Trade in Recent Wars." *Journal of International Affairs.* Vol. 40 (Spring), pp. 77–99.

———. 1987a. "Third World Military Industries: Capabilities and Constraints in Recent Wars." In Harkavy and Neuman, 1987, pp. 157–98.

———. 1987b. "The Role of Military Assistance in Recent Wars." In Harkavy and Neuman, 1987, pp. 115–56.

———. 1988. "Arms, Aid and the Superpowers." *Foreign Affairs.* Vol. 66 (Summer), pp. 1044–66.

———. 1990. Remarks at panel on arms sales. International Studies Association, Washington, D.C.

Neuman, Stephanie G., and Robert E. Harkavy, eds. 1979. *Arms Transfers in the Modern World.* New York: Praeger.

———. 1987. *The Lessons of Recent Wars in the Third World, Volume II.* Lexington, Mass.: Lexington Books.

Nielsson, Gunnar P. 1988. *Mediation Under Crisis Management Condition: The United Nations Secretary General and the Falkland/Malvinas*

Crisis. Pittsburgh: Pew Program in Case Teaching and Writing in International Affairs, Case #127.

N'Yongo, Peter Anyang'. 1989. "Crisis and Conflict in the Horn of Africa." *Genéve-Afrique.* Vol. 22, no. 2, pp. 59–70.

Oakes, John. 1985. "The Durban Arms Link." *Seatrade.* Vol. 15 (March), pp. 4–11.

O'Ballance, Edgar. 1987. *The Gulf War.* London: Brassey's.

Ohlson, Thomas, ed. 1988. *Arms Transfer Limitations and Third World Security.* London: Oxford University Press.

Okoth, P. Godfrey. 1984. "The O.A.U. and the Uganda-Tanzania War." Paper presented at the Twenty-Seventh Annual Meeting of the African Studies Association, Los Angeles, Calif., October 25–28, 1984.

Olson, William J. 1984. "The Iraq-Iran War and the Future of the Persian Gulf." *Military Review.* Vol. 64, no. 2, pp. 17–29.

———, ed. 1987. *U.S. Strategic Interests in the Gulf Region.* Boulder, Colo.: Westview.

Osmanczyk, Edmund Jan. 1985. *Encyclopedia of the UN and International Agreements.* Philadelphia: Taylor and Francis.

Østerud, Øyving. 1989. "War Termination in the Western Sahara." *Bulletin of Peace Proposals.* Vol. 20 (September), pp. 309–17.

Ottaway, Marina. 1982. *Soviet and American Influence in the Horn of Africa.* New York: Praeger.

Ovendale, Ritchie. 1984. *The Origins of the Arab-Israeli Wars.* London: Longman.

Palit, D. K. 1972. *The Lightening Campaign: The Indo-Pakistani War, 1971.* New Delhi: Thomson.

Parson, Sir Anthony. 1983. "The Falkland Crisis in the United Nations, 31 March–14 June, 1982." *International Affairs.* Vol. 59 (Spring), pp. 169–78.

Patman, Robert G. 1989. *The Soviet Union in the Horn of Africa.* Cambridge: Cambridge University Press.

Payne, Robert. 1973. *Massacre.* New York: Macmillan.

Payton, Gary D. 1979a. "Soviet Military Presence Abroad: The Lessons of Somalia." *Military Review.* Vol. 59, no. 1, pp. 67–77.

———. 1979b. "The Soviet Ethiopia Liaison: Airlift and Beyond." *Air University Review.* Vol. 31 (Nov.–Dec.), pp. 66–73.

Pearson, Frederic S. 1979. "Netherlands Foreign Policy and the 1973–74 Oil Embargo: The Effect of Transnationalism." In Forest L. Grieves, ed. *Transnationalism in World Politics and Business.* New York: Pergamon, pp. 114–38.

Pearson, Frederic S., and Edward Kolodziej. 1989. "The Political Economy of Making and Marketing Arms: A Test for the Systemic Imperatives of Order and Welfare." *Occasional Paper 8904.* St. Louis: Center for International Studies, University of Missouri—St. Louis, April.

Pearson, Frederic S., Robert A. Baumann, and Gordon N. Bardos. 1989. "Arms Transfers: Effects on African Interstate Wars and Interventions." *Conflict Quarterly*. Vol. 9, no. 1, pp. 36–62.

Petterson, Donald K. 1985. "Somalia and the United States, 1977–1983." In Bender, Coleman and, Sklar, pp. 194–204.

Pierre, Andrew. 1982. *The Global Politics of Arms Sales*. Princeton, N.J.: Princeton University Press.

Porter, Bruce D. 1984. *The USSR in Third World Conflicts: Soviet Arms and Diplomacy in Local Wars, 1945–80*. London: Cambridge University Press.

Pretty, R. T., and D. H. R. Archer, eds. 1971. *Jane's Weapon Systems 1969–1970*. London: Haymarket.

Price, David Lynn. 1979. "The Western Sahara." *The Washington Papers*. Vol. VII. Beverly Hills, Calif.: SAGE.

Quandt, William. 1978. "Influence through Arms Supply: The U.S. Experience in the Middle East." In Uri Ra'anan, Robert Pfaltzgraff, Jr., and Geoffrey Kemp, eds. *Arms Transfers to the Third World: The Military Buildup in Less Industrial Countries*. Boulder, Colo.: Westview, pp. 121–30.

Ra'anan, Uri. 1978. "Soviet Arms Transfers and the Problem of Political Leverage." In Ra'anan, Robert Pfaltzgraff, and Geoffrey Kemp, eds. *Arms Transfers to the Third World: The Military Buildup in Less Industrial Countries*. Boulder, Colo.: Westview, pp. 131–58.

Ramazami, R. K. 1989. "Iran's Foreign Policy: Contending Orientations." *Middle East Journal*. (Spring), pp. 202–17.

Randle, Robert F. 1973. *The Origins of Peace*. New York: The Free Press.

Razi, Hossein. 1988. "An Alternative Paradigm to State Rationality in Foreign Policy: The Iran-Iraq War." *Western Political Quarterly*. Vol. 41 (December), pp. 688–717.

Reese, Cynthia M. 1987. *U.S.-Soviet Competition for Influence in the Horn of Africa*. Ann Arbor, Mich.: University Microfilms International.

Reiser, Stewart. 1989. *The Israeli Arms Industry*. New York and London: Holmes & Meier.

Remnek, Richard B. 1981. "Soviet Policy in the Horn of Africa: The Decision to Intervene." In Donaldson, 1981, pp. 125–49.

Roberts, C. A. 1983. "Soviet Arms Transfer Policy and the Decision to Upgrade Syrian Air Defenses". *Survival*. Vol. 35 (July/August).

Roeder, Philip G. 1985. "The Ties That Bind: Aid, Trade, and Political Compliance in Soviet-Third World Relations." *International Studies Quarterly*. Vol. 29 (June), pp. 196–216.

Rose, Gregory F. 1989. "Fools Rush In: American Policy and the Iraq-Iran War, 1980–88." In M. E. Ahrari, ed. *The Gulf and International Security*. London: Macmillan, pp. 89–100.

Rose, H. M. 1987. "Toward an Ending of the Falkland Islands War, June 1982." *Conflict*. Vol. 7, no. 1, pp. 1–13.

Rosen, Steven J. 1980. "On Weaning Iraq Away from Moscow." *Rand Paper P-6484.* Santa Monica, Calif.: Rand Corporation.

Rosenberg, Mark B., and Philip L. Shepherd. 1986, eds. *Honduras Confronts its Future: Contending Perspectives on Critical Issues.* Boulder, Colo.: Lynn Rienner.

Rosh, Robert. 1990. "Third World Arms Production." *Journal of Conflict Resolution.* Vol. 34 (March), pp. 57–73.

Ross, Dennis. 1984. "Soviet Views Towards the Gulf War." *Orbis.* Vol. 28 (Fall), pp. 437–47.

Roth, Jürgen. 1986. *Die illegalen deutschen Waffengeschäfte.* Frankfurt: Eichborn.

Ruf, Werner. 1988. "The Great Powers." In Lawless and Moynihan, 1988, pp. 65–97.

———. 1992. "Der Krieg in der West-Sahara." In J. Siegelberg, ed. *Die Kriege 1985–90.* Münster: Lit Verlag.

Ruhe, William J. 1984. "Submarine Lessons." In Watson and Dunn, 1984, p. 7–12.

Rupesinghe, Kumar, ed. 1989. *Conflict Resolution in Uganda.* Athens: Ohio University Press.

Safran, Nadav. 1969. *From War to War: The Arab-Israeli Confrontation, 1948–67.* New York: Pegasus.

Saivetz, Carol R. 1989a. *The Soviet Union and the Gulf in the 1980s.* Boulder, Colo.: Westview.

———. 1989b. *The Soviet Union in the Third World.* Boulder, Colo.: Westview.

Sanders, Ralph. 1990. *Arms Industries: New Suppliers and Regional Security.* Washington, D.C.: National Defense University.

Sarfo, Kwasi. 1987. "US Policy on African Conflicts." *Africa and the World.* Vol. 1, no. 1, pp. 21–29.

Schahgaldian, Nikola B. 1987. "The Iranian Military under the Islamic Republic." *Rand Report R-3473-USDP.* Santa Monica, Calif.: Rand Corporation.

Scheina, Robert L. 1983. "The Malvinas Campaign." *United States Naval Institute Proceedings.* Vol. 109 (May), pp. 98–111.

———. 1984. "Where Were Those Argentine Subs?" *United States Naval Institute Proceedings.* Vol. 110 (March).

Schilhan, Hans-Werner. 1983. "Rüstungsindustrie in islamischen Ländern." *Österreichische Militarische Zeitschrift.* Vol 21, No. 1, pp. 41–48.

Schmid, Alex P. 1985. *Soviet Military Interventions Since 1945.* New Brunswick, N.J.: Transaction Books.

Schmidt, Steffen W. 1983. *El Salvador: America's Next Vietnam?* Salisbury, N.C.: Documentary Publications.

Schrodt, Philip A. 1983. "Arms Transfers and International Behaviour in the Arabian Red Sea Area." *International Interactions.* Vol. 10, no. 1, pp. 5–37.

Schultz, Ann Tibbitts. 1989. *Buying Security.* Boulder, Colo.: Westview.
Seddon, David. 1987. "Morocco and the Western Sahara." *Review of African Political Economy.* Vol. 456, no. 38, pp. 24–47.
———. 1988. "Morocco at War." In Lawless and Monahan, 1988, pp. 98–136.
Segal, David. 1988. "The Iraq-Iran War: A Military Analysis." *Foreign Affairs.* Vol. 67 (Summer), pp. 946–63.
Sethi, Surinder Singh. 1972. *Decisive War.* New Delhi: Sagon Publications.
Sherwin, Ronald G. 1983. "Controlling Instability and Conflict Through Arms Transfers: Testing a Policy Assumption." *International Interaction.* Vol. 10, no. 1, pp. 65–99.
Sichor, Yitzhak. 1988. "Unfolded Arms: Beijing's Recent Military Sales Offensive." *Pacific Review.* Vol. 1, no. 3.
Sick, Gary. 1985. *All Fall Down: America's Tragic Encounter with Iran.* New York: Random House.
———. 1987. "Iran's Quest for Superpower Status." *Foreign Affairs.* Vol. 65 (Spring), pp. 697–715.
———. 1989. "Trial by Error: Reflections on the Iran-Iraq War." *Middle East Journal.* Vol. 43 (Spring), pp. 230–45.
———. 1990. "Slouching Toward Settlement: The Internationalization of the Iran-Iraq War, 1987–88." In Nikki R. Keddie and Mark Gasiorowski, eds., *Neither East Nor West: Iran, The Soviet Union, and the United States.* New Haven, Conn.: Yale University Press, pp. 219–46.
Siddiq, Sallik. 1979. *Witness to Surrender.* Delhi: Oxford University Press.
Siddiqui, Kalim. 1972. *Conflict, Crisis, and War in Pakistan.* New York: Praeger.
Sigler, John H. 1986. "The Iraq-Iran Conflict: The Tragedy of Limited Conventional War." *International Journal.* Vol. 41 (Spring), pp. 424–56.
Singer, J. David. 1990a. "Peace in the Global System: Displacement, Interregnum, or Transformation?" In Charles W. Kegley, ed., *The Long Postwar Peace.* New York: Harper Collins, ch. 3.
———. 1990b. Quoted in *Detroit News,* Dec. 17, p. 3E.
Singh, B. 1982. 1965. *War and the Role of Tanks.* Patiala, Punjab, India: B. C. Publishers.
———. 1983. *Indo-Pak: Conflicts Over Kashmir.* Patiala, Punjab, India: B. C. Publishers.
Singh, Jagdev. 1988. *Dismemberment of Pakistan: 1971 Indo-Pak War.* New Delhi: Lancer International.
Singh, K. R. 1988. "The Sand Wall is Crumbling." *Strategic Analysis.* Vol. 12 (August), pp. 479–95.
SIPRI (Stockholm International Peace Research Institute). Annual, 1969– . *SIPRI Yearbook: World Armaments and Disarmament.* London: Oxford University Press.

SIPRI, 1971. *The Arms Trade with the Third World.* Stockholm: Almquist & Wicksell.
SIPRI. *Fact Sheet 1988.* "Iran-Iraq War 1980-1988: Military Costs and Arms Trade." Stockholm: Stockholm International Peace Research Institute, August 8.
SIPRI. *Fact Sheet 1990.* "Military Expenditure and Iraqi Arms Imports." Stockholm: Stockholm International Peace Research Institute.
Sisson, Richard, and Leo E. Rose. 1990. *War and Secession: Pakistan, India and the Creation of Bangladesh.* Berkeley, Calif.: University of California Press.
Sivard, Ruth Leger. 1987–88. *World Military and Social Expenditures.* 12th ed. Washington, D.C.: World Priorities.
Slaughter, Ronald. 1983. "The Politics and Nature of the Conventional Arms Transfer Process During a Military Engagement: The Falklands/Malvinas Case." *Arms Control.* Vol. 4, no. 1, pp. 16–30.
Smith, George I. 1980. *Ghosts of Kampala.* London: Weidenfeld and Nicolson.
Solarz, Stephen. 1980. "Arms for Morocco?" *Foreign Affairs.* Vol. 58 (Winter), pp. 278–99.
Sorley, Lewis. 1983. *Arms Transfers Under Nixon: A Policy Analysis.* Lexington: University Press of Kentucky.
Staudenmaier, William O. 1985. "Iran-Iraq (1980–)." In Harkavy and Neuman, 1985, pp. 211–38.
———. 1987. "Conflict Termination in the Third World: Theory and Practice." In Harkavy and Neuman, 1987, pp. 227–40.
Stein, Janice G. 1975. "War Termination and Conflict Reduction or, How Wars Should End." *Jerusalem Journal of International Relations.* Vol. 1, no. 1, pp. 1–28.
———. 1980. "Proxy Wars—How Superpowers End Them: the Diplomacy of War Termination in the Middle East". *International Journal.* Vol. 35, pp. 478–519.
Tahir-Kheli, Sharin, and Shaheen Ayubi, eds. 1983. *The Iraq-Iran War: New Weapons, Old Conflicts.* New York: Praeger.
Taylor, John W. R., ed. 1970. *Jane's All the World's Aircraft 1968–1969.* London: Jane's Yearbooks, Sampson Low, Marston and Co.
———. 1978. *Jane's All the World's Aircraft 1976–1977.* London: Jane's Yearbooks, Sampson Low, Marston and Co.
Tessler, Mark. 1988. "Moroccan-Israeli Relations and the Reasons for Moroccan Receptivity to Contact with Israel." *Jerusalem Journal of International Relations.* Vol. 10, no. 2, pp. 76–108.
Thayer, George. 1969. *The War Business: The International Trade in Armaments.* London: Weidenfeld and Nicolson.
Tilford, Earl H., Jr. 1984. "Air Power Lessons." In Watson and Dunn, 1984, pp. 37–50.

Timmerman, Kenneth R. 1988. *Öl ins Feuer: Internationale Waffengeschäfte im Golfkrieg.* Zurich: Oreill Füsli.
———. 1991. *The Death Lobby: How the West Armed Iraq.* Boston: Houghton Mifflin.
Tower, John. 1987. *Report of the President's Special Review Board.* Washington, D.C.: Government Printing Office.
Treverton, Gregory F., and Don Lippincott. 1988. *Falklands/Malvinas.* Case #406. Pittsburgh: Pew Program in International Case Study Teaching and Writing.
Treverton, Gregory F., and Stephen Flanagan. 1988. *Falklands/Malvinas.* Case #406A&B. Pittsburgh: Pew Program in International Case Study Teaching and Writing.
Uban, Sujan Sin. 1985. *Phantoms of Chittagong: The "Fifth Army" in Bangladesh.* New Delhi: Allied Publishers.
United Kingdom. 1982. Secretary of State for Defence. *The Falkland Campaign: The Lessons. Report Presented to Parliament. Cmnd 8758.* London: Her Majesty's Stationery Office.
———. 1983. *Report of a Committee of Privy Councellors, Chairman: Lord Franks. Falkland Islands Review. Cmnd. 8787.* London: Her Majesty's Stationery Office.
United Nations Year Book. 1969. New York: UN.
United States Arms Control and Disarmament Agency (ACDA). 1988. "High Costs of the Persian Gulf War." Washington, D.C.: Government Printing Office, pp. 21–24.
———. Annual, 1972– . *World Military Expenditures and Arms Transfers.* Washington, D.C.: Government Printing Office.
United States Congress. 1975. House Committee on Foreign Affairs, Subcommittee on International Political and Military Affairs, 94th Congress, 1st Session. "U.S. Policy and Request for Sale of Arms to Ethiopia." Hearing March 5, 1975. Washington, D.C.: Government Printing Office.
———. 1977a. House Committee on International Relations, Subcommittee on International Organizations and Africa, 95th Congress, 1st Session. "The Question of Self-determination in Western Sahara." Hearings October 12, 1977. Washington, D.C.: Government Printing Office.
———. 1977b. House Committee on International Relations, 95th Congress, 1st Session. "United States Arms Policies in the Persian Gulf and Red Sea Areas: Past, Present and Future." Hearings December 1977. Washington, D.C.: Government Printing Office.
———. 1978. House Committee on International Relations, 95th Congress, 2nd Session. "War in the Horn of Africa: A Report by Rep. Bonker and Tsongas." Hearings February 3, 1978. Washington, D.C.: Government Printing Office.

———. 1979. House Committee on Foreign Affairs, Subcommittee on International Organizations and Africa, 96th Congress, 1st Session. "U.S. Policy and the Conflict in the Western Sahara." Hearings July 23 and 24, 1979. Washington, D.C.: Government Printing Office.

———. 1980. House Committee on Foreign Affairs, Subcommittee on International Security and Scientific Affairs, 96th Congress, 2nd Session. "Proposed Arms Sale to Morocco." Hearings January 24 and 29, 1980. Washington, D.C.: Government Printing Office.

———. 1981a. House Committee on Foreign Affairs, Subcommittee on International Security and Scientific Affairs, 97th Congress, 1st Session. "Arms Sales in North Africa and the Conflict in the Western Sahara: An Assessment of U.S. Policy." Hearing March 25, 1981. Washington, D.C.: Government Printing Office.

———. 1981b. Subcommittee on Human Rights and International Organizations and on Inter-American Affairs, 97th Congress, 1st Session. "Review of U.S. Policy on Military Assistance to Argentina." Hearing April 1, 1981. Washington, D.C.: Government Printing Office.

———. 1983. House Subcommittee on International Organizations and Africa, 98th Congress, 1st Session. "Review of U.S. Policy toward the Conflict in the Western Sahara." Hearing March 15, 1983. Washington, D.C.: Government Printing Office.

———. 1984. Senate Committee on Foreign Relations. 98th Congress, 2nd Session. *War in the Gulf: A Staff Report.* Washington, D.C.: Government Printing Office.

———. 1987a. House Committee on Foreign Affairs. 100th Congress, 1st Session. "Overview of the Situation in the Persian Gulf." Hearings May 27, June 14. Washington, D.C.: Government Printing Office.

———. 1987b. House Committee on Armed Services. 100th Congress. 1st Session. "U.S. Military Forces to Protect `Reflagged' Kuwaiti Oil Tankers." Hearings June 5, 11, and 16, 1987. Washington, D.C.: Government Printing Office.

———. 1987c. Senate Committee on Foreign Relations. 100th Congress, 1st Session. "War in the Persian Gulf: The U.S. Takes Sides: A Staff Report." Washington, D.C.: Government Printing Office.

United States Department of Defense. 1986. *Soviet Military Power.* 5th ed. Washington: Government Publishing Office.

United States Government Accounting Office. 1979. "Financial and Legal Implications of Iran's Cancellation of Arms Purchase Agreements." FGMSD-79-47, July 25. Washington, D.C.: Government Accounting Office.

Urquhart, Brian. 1988. "The UN and the Iran-Iraq War." In *SIPRI Yearbook 1988,* pp. 507–19.

———. 1989. "Conflict Resolution in 1988: The Role of the United Nations." In *SIPRI Yearbook 1989,* pp. 445–60.

Vance, Cyrus. 1983. *Hard Choices.* New York: Simon and Schuster.
Wallace, Michael. 1982. "Armaments and Escalation: Two Competing Hypotheses." *International Studies Quarterly.* Vol. 26, no. 1, pp. 37–51.
Walters, Vernon. 1978. *Silent Missions.* New York: Doubleday.
Watson, Bruce W., and Peter M. Dunn, eds. 1984. *Military Lessons of the Falkland Islands War: Views from the United States.* Boulder, Colo: Westview.
Watson, Paul. 1986. "Arms and Aggression in the Horn of Africa." *Journal of International Affairs.* Vol. 40 (Summer), pp. 150–70.
Wayman, Frank W., Jr., J. David Singer, and Gary Goertz. 1987. "Capability Allocation and Conflict Avoidance Among Major Powers 1816–1976: A Research Note." Unpublished paper. Ann Arbor: University of Michigan.
Weede, Erich. 1985. "Some (Western) Dilemmas in Managing Extended Deterrence." *Journal of Peace Research.* Vol. 22, no. 3, pp. 223–38.
———. 1988. "Deterrence by Mutual Assured Destruction or Strategic Defense?" *International Interactions.* Vol. 14, no. 4, pp. 283–97.
Wellmann, Arend, ed. 1988. *Irak-Iran: Internationale Dimensionen eines regionalen Konfliktes.* Berlin: ASTA der Freien Universitat Berlin, Das Arabische Buch.
Westander, Henrik. 1988. *Bofors Svindlande Affärer.* Stockholm: Ordfront.
Wheelock, Thomas. 1978. "Arms for Israel: The Limits of Leverage." *International Security.* Vol. 3 (Fall), pp. 123–37.
Whetten, Lawrence L. 1974. *The Canal War: Four Power Conflict in the Middle East.* Cambridge, Mass.: MIT Press.
Wilber, Richard Morgan. 1990. "The Iran-Iraq War: An Analysis of the Cease-Fire." *Fletcher Forum of World Affairs.* Vol. 14, no. 1, pp. 111–26.
Wilcox, Wayne. 1973. *The Emergence of Bangladesh: Problems and Opportunities for a Redefined American Policy in South Asia.* Washington, D.C.: American Enterprise Institute.
Williams, Rushbrook L. F. 1972. *The East Pakistan Tragedy.* New York: Drake.
Wöhlcke, Manfred. 1986. *Brasilien als Produzent und Exporteur von Rüstungsgütern.* Baden-Baden: Nomos.
Wolf Jr., Charles. 1990. "The Third World in U.S.-Soviet Competition: From Playing Field to Player." *Rand Paper P-7625.* Santa Monica, Calif.: Rand Corporation.
Wood, Derek, and Mark Hewish. 1982. "Der Falklandkonflikt." *Internationale Wehrrevue.* Vol. 15, nos. 8, 9, and 10, pp. 977–1343.
World Bank (I.B.R.D.). *Annual Reports.* Washington, D.C.
Wright, Claudia. 1983a. "Neutral or Neutralized? Iraq, Iran and the Superpowers." In Tahir-Kheli and Ayubi, 1983, pp. 172–94.
———. 1983b. "Journey to Marrakesh: U.S.-Moroccan Security Relations." *International Security.* Vol. 7 (Spring), pp. 163–79.

Yaniv, Avner. 1987. *Dilemmas of Security: Politics, Strategy, and the Israeli Experience in Lebanon.* New York: Oxford University Press.
Zabih, Sepehr. 1988. *The Iranian Military in Revolution and War.* London: Routledge.
Zartman, I. William. 1977. "Les Transferts d'armements en Afrique." *Etudes internationales.* Vol. 8, no. 3, pp. 478–86.
———. 1989. *Ripe for Resolution: Conflict and Intervention in Africa.* 2nd ed. New York: Oxford University Press.
———. 1991. "Superpower Cooperation in North Africa and the Horn." In Kolodziej and Kanet, 1991, pp. 147–70.
Ziegler, David. 1987. *War, Peace, and International Politics.* 4th ed. Boston: Little, Brown.
Ziring, Lawrence. 1984. *The Middle East Political Dictionary.* Santa Barbara, Calif.: ABC-Clio.

Index

Aaron, David, 195
Abdessalam, Ali, 211
Adrisi, Mustafa, 204
Air warfare, 91–92; in 1965 South Asian war, 33–34; in 1971 South Asian war, 55–56; in 1969 Central American war, 66; in 1982 South Atlantic war, 79–81; in 1973 Middle Eastern war, 100–101; in 1982 Lebanon war, 119; in Iraq-Iran war, 140–41; in Western Sahara war, 164; in 1991 Iraq war, 225–26
Algeria: involvement in Middle East 1982, 124; involvement in Western Sahara, 161–64, 168–71, 173–74, 176–79; support of Tanzania, 210
Algiers Accord, 134
Alliances, 54–55, 57, 84–85; reassessment in war, 5; as consideration in arms transfer decision-making, 12; NATO, 36, 73, 77, 84–85; SEATO, 39; Soviet friendship treaties, 47, 124, 139, 151, 186,192, 197; CENTO, 55; intra-alliance war, 73; strategic cooperation, 118
Amin, Idi, 199–211
Anaya, Isaac, 72
Angola: civil war 178, 202
Arab League, 112, 126, 128, 153, 187, 202
Argentina: decision making in South Atlantic War, 71–72, 76, 87–88; domestic arms industry, 73–74
Armor warfare: in 1965 South Asian war, 32–33; in 1973 Middle Eastern war, 100–102; in 1982 Lebanon war, 120–121; in Iraq-Iran war, 140–42, 152; in Western Sahara war, 165–66; in Ogaden war, 189–90; in Tanzania-Uganda war, 205–207
Arms production: in the Third World, 2; role of India's domestic industry, 26, 38, 45; role of Argentina's domestic industry, 74. *See also* Egypt; El Salvador; Iran; Iraq; Pakistan; Yugoslavia
Arms races: as field of research, 4–5; cases, 30, 69–70, 134–35
Arms transfers: control, 1, 239–40, 158–59; pre-World War I, 2; affecting the relationship between armaments and warfare, 5–12, 59, 88, 90–91, 129–30, 214–21; in conflict management, 7, 15–16, 240; importance of timing, 17–18; data sources, 18–22, 239–40; specialist publications, 19
Ascension Island, 78
al-Assad, Hafiz, 121, 124, 130
Australia: arms sales to India, 27; to Israel, 114; to Pakistan, 229
Austria: arms sales to Argentina, 76, 83; to Iran, 147, Iraq 150, to Morocco, 167; to ex-Yugoslavia, 233

Awami League, 44–49, 56
Aziz, Tariq, 148

Balance of forces: in deterrence, 3–4, 15–16; changes through arms transfers, 6–7, 9; affecting wars, 11, 13–16; in 1965 South Asian war, 26–30; in 1971 South Asian war, 50–55; in 1969 Central American war, 63–64, 69–70; in 1982 South Atlantic war, 75–77, 81–82; in 1973 Middle East war, 95–99; in 1982 Lebanon war, 113–19; in Iraq-Iran war, 134–40, 146–48; in Western Sahara war, 163–67; in Ogaden war, 182–88; in Tanzania-Uganda war, 200–206; in 1991 Iraq war, 223–27; in Kashmir Crisis-1991, 227–29
Bangladesh: war of independence, 12, 43–55
Bani-Sadr, Abdolhassan, 135, 140–41
Barré, Siad, 186, 188, 192, 195–97, 275
Base rights, 1, 13, 119, 162, 170, 182, 186
Begin, Menachim, 122–24, 127
Belaunde Terry, 86
Belgium: arms sales to India, 27; to Pakistan 49, 53; to Argentina, 75; change in export law, 159
Benjedid, Chadli, 173
Bhutto, Benazir, 231, 279n10
Bhutto, Zulfiqar Ali, 44, 58–59
Black market, 83, 135, 145, 148, 152–53, 193, 202–203, 212, 239
Bosnia-Herzegovina: involvement in 1991 ex-Yugoslavia war, 237–38
Boumedienne, Houari, 107, 161
Brazil: arms sales to Argentina, 75; support request from United Kingdom, 84; arms sales to Iraq, 146–47, 223; to Iran 150
Brezhnev, Leonid, 47, 149, 153
Brines, Russell, 26–27, 42
Brzezinski, Zbigniew, 169, 180, 194, 275n8
Bulgaria: arms sales to Iraq, 149
Bush, George, 227, 239

Canada: arms sales to India, 27–28, 52; to Argentina, 83; to Iraq, 147; to Morocco, 163; to Tanzania, 210
Canary Islands, 172
Carter, Jimmy, 168–70, 185, 187, 194
Castro, Fidel, 191–92
Castro, Raul, 195
Central American Common Market, 61
Central American Defense Council, 63
Chemical Weapons, 142–43, 148, 154, 157
Cheney, Dick, 224
Cheysson, Claude, 126
Chile: support request from United Kingdom, 84; arms supplies to Iraq, 150
China: war with Vietnam, 11–12; arms supplies, 13–14; relations to India and Pakistan prior to 1965 war, 26–30; arms supplies to Pakistan, 27, 29, 35–36, 40–41, 48–50, 52–53, 59, 228; diplomacy in 1971 South Asian war, 31–39, 40–41; diplomacy in 1971 South Asian war, 43–44, 46, 48, 57–59; arms sales to Iraq and Iran, 144–54, 224, 278n2; diplomacy in Iraq-Iran war, 153; arms sales to Tanzania, 204–205, 210; diplomacy in Tanzania-Uganda war, 210

Christopher, Warren, 169
Chou En-lai, 39
CIA reports, 57, 129, 273n4
Clark, Dick, 168
Clausewitz, 141
Conference on Security and Cooperation in Europe (CSCE), 236
Croatia: war in 191, 232–37
Cuba, 62; advisors and troops in Ogaden war, 180, 189–90, 194, 275n10
Czechoslovakia: arms supplies, 8, 13; to India, 52; to Syria, 97, 115–16; to Iraq, 136, 146–49

Denmark: arms sales to Iraq, 146; to Morocco, 167
Dependency: on arms deliveries, 35, 51, 55, 66, 70, 86, 87, 93, 107–11, 132, 163, 176–79, 214; diversification of arms supplies, 35–37, 41, 44, 66–68, 82–86, 139, 148, 156–57, 171–72, 185, 209, 217; reverse leverage, 49, 102–103, 129, 177, 195
Dergue, 180
Deterrence: as field of research, 3–4; during conflicts, 4, 6, 13–16; in 1971 South Asian war, 47–48, 55; in 1973 Middle East war, 98; in 1982 Lebanon conflict, 128; in Western Sahara conflict, 168; in 1991 Kashmir conflict, 238–39
Diplomacy: substituted by arms transfers, 7; of arms acquisition, 8; to end wars, 10, 15–16, 217–18, 239–40; as variable cluster, 23–24. *See also* China; France; Soviet Union; United Kingdom; United States
Dobrynin, Anatoli, 195
Dual use equipment, 83, 148, 153

East Timor, 222
Economic assistance: suspension of, 46, 58, 124; offered to hold Yugoslavia together, 236–37, 239–40
Ecuador: arms sales to Argentina, 83
Egypt: war of 1956, 8; 1973 Middle East war, 90–111; domestic arms production, 93, 272n2; support of Iraq, 146–47, 149; support of Morocco, 167, 172
El Salvador: decision making on 1967 war, 65–70; domestic arms production, 65
Embargo: effects of arms embargoes on warfare, 6–7, 15–16, 87–89, 216–18, 221; changes in effectiveness over time, 16; on arms transfers in 1965 South Asian war, 25, 31–42; before and during 1971 South Asian war, 48–50; in 1969 Central American war, 66–67; economic sanctions, 68, 107, 126, 200–201, 208, 210–21, 236–37; during 1982 South Atlantic war, 82–86; in connection with 1967 Middle East War, 91; on arms transfers during 1982 Lebanon war, 123–26, 129; during Iraq-Iran war, 135, 151, 153, 154–56; during Western Sahara war, 169, 171; against Uganda, 199–200; against Iraq, 224; concerning ex-Yugoslavia, 239–40
Ethiopia: war with Somalia, 12, 180–98; arms transfers to Iran, 147; support of Tranzania, 210
European Community: role in South Atlantic war, 82–83; involvement in 1991 Yugoslav war, 236–37

as-Faisal, Saud, 188
France: relationship to US, 11, 177;

arms sales to India, 27–28, 51–53; to Pakistan, 49, 53–54, 74–75; to Argentina, 82; arms transfer restraint, 91, 107, 171; arms sales to Iraq and Iran, 135–36, 146–47, 149–51, 156; diplomacy in Iraq-Iran war, 157–58; arms sales to Morocco, 163, 165–68,183; diplomacy in Western Sahara war, 168, 171–72; arms sales to Iraq, 223

Galbraith, John Kenneth, 30
Galtieri, Leopoldo, 72, 268n7, 269n8, 270n12
Gandhi, Indira, 47, 51, 55, 266n1
Gandhi, Rajiv, 231
Garba, Joseph N., 191
Gemayel, Beshir, 113, 128
George, Alexander, 7, 22
Germany: arms transfer restraint, 2; arms sales to Pakistan, 27, 29, 49, 53; to El Salvador, 64, 66; to Argentina, 74–77, 82; to Iran, 136, 139; arms sales from East Germany, 146, 150, 152, 264n5; arms sales to Iraq, 146–47, 150–51, 225–26, 278n4; lack of control of arms transfers, 148; arms sales to Morocco, 166, 172; to Ethiopia, 183, 185; East German advisors, 187; meeting on Horn of Africa, 193; arms sales to Israel, 227, 279n7; to ex-Yugoslavia, 232–33;
Gonzáles, Felipe, 172
Gorbachev, Mikhail, 149, 159
Great Britian. *See* United Kingdom
Green March, 160–61
Grey markets, 135, 145, 152, 212
Grimmett, Richard, 21
Guerrilla warfare: in 1965 South Asian war 32, 35, 38; in 1971 South Asian war, 43–46, 48; in Ogaden war, 188–90; in Tanzania-Uganda war, 199, 204–205; in Kashmir 1991, 227

Habib, Philip, 113, 125, 127, 130
Haig, Alexander, 84–86, 118, 123, 125, 170, 268n7, 269n8, 270n12
Haile Selassie, 180–81
Harkavy, Robert, 7–15
Hassan II, King of Morocco, 160, 164, 168–70, 176–77
Heikal, Mohammed, 102
Hernandez, Sanchez, 70
Hodges, Tony, 177
Honduras: war with El Salvador, 61–70
Hoopes, Townsend, 41
Hungary: arms sales to Iraq, 146; to ex-Yugoslavia, 279n11
Hussein, Saddam, 1–3, 7, 73, 134–35, 139, 141, 155, 224, 278n5, 279n6

India: 1965 war with Pakistan, 25–42; arms produced domestically, 26, 28, 38, 44–45, 51–54; 1962 war with China, 29–30; 1971 war with Pakistan, 44–60; conflict over Kashmir 1991, 227–32
Indonesia: arms sales to India, 28; support of Pakistan, 34–36
Intelligence data: from Space intelligence, 105; USA-Israel sharing, 118–19, 129
International Court of Justice: on Western Sahara, 160–61, 168
International Monetary Fund: pressuring to reduce military budgets, 228–29
Iran: 1980–88 war against Iraq, 1, 6, 11–12, 134–59;relations with Iraq in the 1970s, 7; support of Pakistan, 34–36, 40, 53; involvement in Lebanon war, 120;

Iran (*continued*)
  domestic arms production, 137–38, 152; support of Morocco, 172; arms sales to Ethiopia, 183, 185; assistance to Somalia, 193
Iraq: invasion of Kuwait, 1–3, 222–27; war with Iran, 1, 6, 11–12, 134–48; relations with Iran, 7; involvement in 1973 Middle East war, 100, 102; domestic arms production, 150, 223
Israel: war involvement, 8, 12; arms sales to India, 51; 1967 war as example in Central America, 65; arms sales to Argentina, 75, 83, 268n5; domestic arms production, 93–94, 118; arms sales to Iran, 135, 148, 272–73n4; to Morocco, 166; to Ethiopia, 185, 195; advisors, 195, 201; arms sales to Uganda, 201; Entebbe raid, 203; non-involvement in Kuwait war, 226; US relations, 119
Italy: arms transfer restraint, 2, 159; arms sales to Pakistan, 49; to India, 52; to Argentina, 75, 83; to Iraq, 136, 146–47; to Iran, 147; to Morocco, 163, 166, 172

Japan: arms sales to India, 27; embargo against Argentina, 83
Jordan: arms sales to Pakistan, 53; potential US proxy, 57; expulsion of PLO, 92; involvement in 1973 war, 102; arms acquisitions, 119; arms sales to Iraq, 146–47, 150; to Morocco, 165–72

Kenya: stopping Ugandan supplies, 210, 277n11
Khalid, King of Saudi Arabia, 122
Khameini, Ali, 155

Khan, Ayub, 36–37, 39
Khan, Yahya, 44–46, 48, 51, 58
Kirkpatrick, Jeane, 84, 270n10, 270n12
Kissinger, Henry, 43, 46, 49, 51, 55, 58–59, 100, 102, 104–105, 266n2, 267n8
Kosygin, Aleksei, 105
Koutakhov, P. S., 48
Krause, Keith, 12; 107–108
Kuwait: invasion and liberation, 1–3, 222–27; involvement in 1973 war, 101–102; arms transfers to Iraq, 146

Lebanon: arms sales to ex-Yugoslavia, 233
Libya: arms supplies to Pakistan, 57–58; to Argentina, 83; involvement in 1973 war, 102; arms supplies to Syria, 115–16; to Iran, 147–49, 151; to Uganda, 201–203, 210, 277n9; involvement in Western Sahara war, 161–65, 173–74, 177; involvement in Tanzania-Uganda war, 200, 203, 208–209
Lopez Arellano, Oswaldo, 70

Machel, Samora, 210
Mao Tse-tung, 44, 186
Mauritania: involvement in Western Sahara, 161, 164–65
Mediation: by international organizations, 68–70, 86, 153, 174–75, 191–93, 210–11; by governments, 84–86, 112–13, 210–11, 278n5
Meir, Golda, 102
Mengistu Haile Mariam, 185
Mercenaries, 203
Methodology: range of issues studied, 2, 9; in the study of deterrence, 3–4; in the study of

arms races, 4–5; concurrent chronologies, 9, 24; research hypotheses, 9, 13–16; use of newspapers, 20; of pricing arms transfers, 21; focussed case-study approach, 22–23; selection of variables, 23

Military intervention of foreign troops: relations to arms transfers, 9–10, 218, 264n1; threat of Chinese intervention in 1965 South Asian war, 37–38; Indian intervention in 1971 Bangladesh war, 45–48; US intervention in 1971 Bangladesh war, 57; threat of Soviet intervention in 1973 Middle East war, 91–92; Israeli intervention in 1982 Lebanon war, 117–21; French intervention in Western Sahara, 164–65; Cuban intervention in Ogaden, 189–90; discussion of US intervention in Ogaden, 195; principle of non-intervention, 199; Libyan intervention in Tanzania-Uganda war, 200, 218–19

Missiles: air-to-air, 80; anti-ship, 80–81, 142, 144; ground-to-ground, 100, 114–15, 142, 144, 152

Mitterand, François, 171, 225, 239

Moose, Richard, 192

Morocco: war with Polisario, 12, 160–79; involvement in 1973 Middle East war, 101–102

Mohammad Reza Pahlevi, Shah of Iran, 137, 139–40, 188

Mozambique: support of Tanzania, 210

Mujibur Rahman, Sheikh, 44–45, 56, 266n1

Nachmias, Nitza, 119

Nasser, Gamal Abdel, 130

Naval warfare: in 1971 South Asian war, 56; in 1982 South Atlantic war, 79–81; in 1973 Middle East war, 104; in Iraq-Iran war, 144

Negotiations: affected by arms transfers, 9–14, 217; timing in conflict, 16, 220–21. *See also* Mediation

Netherlands: arms sales to Pakistan, 29; to Argentina, 75; to Iran 147–48

Neuman, Stephanie G., 6–12

Neutrality: Law of, 2; as motive for arms suppliers, 5

Nixon, Richard M., 43, 51, 55, 106, 137

Nonalignment, 470

North Korea: arms sales to Pakistan, 51; to Iran, 143, 147–48, 151–52

Nuclear Weapons: in 1982 South Atlantic war, 82; in 1991 Kashmir conflict, 228–31; in 1973 Middle East war, 271n3

Numeiry, Gafar, 211

Nyerere, Julius, 203, 206–207, 209–11

Obote, Milton, 200, 210

Ogaden, 194

Operation Desert Storm, 225

Operation Peace for Galilee, 121–22

Operation Staunch, 135, 152–53

Oreja, Marcelino, 172

Organization of African Unity (OAU), 162, 191, 200, 202, 206, 208, 210; peacemaking attempts, 174–75, 191, 193, 210

Organization of American States, 66–70, 84

Organization of Arab Petroleum Exporting Countries (OAPEC), 107

Pakistan: 1965 war with India, 25–42; dependence on arms from US, 35; 1971 Bangladesh war, 43–60; domestic arms production, 54; conflict over Kashmir 1991, 227–32
Palestine Liberation Organization (PLO), 92; involvement in 1973 war, 101; in Lebanon, 112–13, 116–17, 120–33; mediation effort in Iraq-Iran War, 153
Palme, Olof, 153
Peacekeeping forces: in Lebanon, 120, 123, 126; in Iraq and Iran, 156; in ex-Yugoslavia, 237
Perez de Cuellar, Javier, 85–86, 155, 175, 278n5
Peru: arms sales to Argentina, 75, 83; mediation effort, 86
Petrov, V. I., 190
Phalange, 112–13, 129
Podgorny, Nikolai, 191
Poland: arms sales to India, 52; to Iraq, 146–47, 149
Polisario: war with Morocco, 12, 160–79, 220
Proxy arms sales, 8, 49, 57, 158

al-Qaddafi, Muammar, 192, 203, 208

Rafsanjani, Hashemi, 151
Rann of Kutch fighting, 25, 30–31, 39, 40
Ratanov, Anatoly, 185
Reagan, Ronald, 84, 122–24, 125–27, 129, 131, 170, 269n8
Realism: as basis for research hypotheses, 9
Recipients of arms, 6–16; diversification of suppliers, 7, 13–16; calculations about supply restrictions, 13–16. *See also* individual countries
Refugees, 43, 61–62, 70
Regional order: in the Middle East, 2, 118; challenges to, 2; Soviet proposed South Asian security system, 47; Soviet attempts in the Horn of Africa, 191. *See also* Alliances
Revolutionary Guards, 140
Richardson, Lewis F., 4
Roberto, Holden, 202
Rockefeller, Nelson, 67
Romania: arms sales to Pakistan, 51; to Iraq, 146, 149; to Morocco, 172
Russia: arms trade data, 19

as-Sadat, Anwar, 92–94, 105, 271n3
Satellite information, 84, 230
Saudi Arabia: as potential US proxy, 57; involvement in 1973 war, 102; involvement in 1982 Lebanon war, 113, 124, 128; financial assistance to Syria, 119; involvement in Iraq-Iran war, 135, 147; financial assistance to Morocco, 170–72; involvement in Ogaden war, 188, 193; armaments before 1990 Kuwait invasion, 223
Saunders, Harold, 169–70
Schwartzkopf, Norman, 226
Serbia: war in 1991, 236–41
Sharon, Ariel, 113, 118, 129, 133
Shultz, George, 126
Singapore: arms sales to Croatia, 233–34; lack of control, 264n1
Singer, J. David, 3–4
Singh, V. P., 230
Slovenia: war in 1991, 233–38
Solarz, Stephen, 170
Somalia: war with Ethiopia, 12, 180–98
South Africa: arms sales to Argentina, 83, 268n6; to Iraq, 147,

150, 224–25, 278n3; to Morocco, 166–67, 172; to ex-Yugoslavia, 233
South Atlantic War: effects in Middle East, 125
South Korea: arms sales to Iran, 148; to Morocco, 172; lack of control, 264n1
South Yemen, 186, 194
Soviet Union: deliveries to Egypt in 1955, 8; behavior during cold war, 10–11; influence over other arms suppliers, 11–12; presence in Vietnam, 12; arms trade data, 18; arms transfers and policy toward India and Pakistan, 27, 35, 41, 48–50, 53–54; diplomacy in 1965 South Asian war, 31–41, 43–44; diplomacy in 1971 South Asian war, 46–47, 54, 57–60; arms offers to Argentina, 84; arms transfers and policy toward Middle East, 91–94, 96–98, 101–108, 115–16, 123, 127; diplomacy in 1973 Middle East war, 91–92, 105–108; diplomacy in 1982 Lebanon war, 119, 122–25, 128–29; arms transfers and policy toward Iraq and Iran, 136–37, 139, 146–49, 151; diplomacy in Iraq-Iran war, 154–59; arms transfers to Algeria and Morocco, 162–64; arms transfers and policy toward Ethiopia and Somalia, 182–95; arms transfers and policy toward Uganda and Tanzania, 199–205, 208–10; diplomacy in Second Gulf war, 225–26; diplomacy in 1991 Kashmir conflict, 230; arms transfers to Yugoslavia, 234; military personnel in 1973 Middle East war, 271n2
Spain: arms embargo toward Argentina, 83; arms supplies to Iraq, 146–47, 150; role in West Sahara conflict, 161–62, 168, 171–72; arms transfers and policy toward Morocco, 166–67, 172
Sri Lanka, 222
Stockholm International Peace Research Institute (SIPRI), 20–21
Sudan, 222; involvement in 1973 war, 101; arms sales to Iraq, 136
Superpowers: differences in arms transfer patterns, 10; changes in arms supplies during conflict, 10; cooperation, 11, 34, 41, 60–61, 105–106, 158–59, 195; conflict, 103–104, 118, 195, 271n3; reversal of alliance, 181
Suppliers of arms: motives, 1, 5–6, 13–14; change of motives during war, 11; testing equipment in war, 31, 110. See also individual countries
Sweden: supply of military technology to Iran, 139, 144, 152, 157, 273n6; change in arms transfer law, 160
Switzerland: arms transfer restraint, 2; arms sales to India, 51–52; to Argentina, 75; to Iraq, 136, 146–47; 273n7; to Iran, 147; to Uganda, 201
Syria: support of Iran, 148; arms supplies to Iran, 147, 151 also

Tafari-Banti, 180
Taiwan: arms sales to Morocco, 172
Thatcher, Margaret, 270n11
Thayer, George, 27, 30
Third-party arms sales, 77, 149–50, 172, 174, 233
Trade statistics, 18–19
Training, 64, 113, 170, 189, 202

Tudeh Party, 149
Tudjman, Franjo, 234
Tunisia: involvement in 1973 war, 102
Turkey: arms sales to Pakistan, 34–36, 40; allowing Soviet overflights, 103, 125

Uganda National Liberation Army (UNLA), 206–209
United Kingdom: relationship to US, 11; arms transfers and policy, toward India and Pakistan, 26–29, 51–52; diplomacy in South Asian wars, 35, 37,58; 1982 South Atlantic war, 71–89; arms transfers to Argentina, 75–76; arms embargo toward Middle East 1973, 108; arms embargo toward Israel 1982, 126; arms sales to Iran, 137, 147–48; to Iraq, 146; arms sales and policy toward Uganda, 200; economic boycott of Uganda, 200–201, 210; arms sales to Tanzania, 205
United Nations: role in 1965 South Asian war, 31–32, 34–39; role in 1971 South Asian war, 47, 54, 58–60; mediation effort in 1969 Central American war, 69; role in 1982 South Atlantic war, 86–87; references to UN in 1973 Middle East war, 106; efforts to stop 1982 Lebanon invasion, 122–23, 126–27; efforts to end Iraq-Iran war, 153–56; efforts to influence Western Sahara war, 160, 168, 174–75; proposals for mediation of Ogaden war, 193, 195; forum for measures against Iraq, 224–29; involvement in Yugoslav crisis, 236–37; arms trade register, 240
United States: Nixon Doctrine, 5, 7, 137, 264n1; behavior during cold war, 10–11; arms trade data, 18, 20–21; diplomacy in 1965 South Asian war, 25–42; arms transfers and policy toward Pakistan and India, 26–30, 41–42, 48–50, 53–54; diplomacy in 1971 South Asian war, 47–48, 54–55, 57–60; arms transfers and policy toward El Salvador and Honduras, 63–64, 68–70; arms transfers and policy toward Argentina, 75–76, 83; arms transfers and policy toward United Kingdom, 78, 82, 84, 87–89; mediation effort in 1982 South Atlantic war, 84–86; arms transfers and policy toward Israel, 95–96, 100, 114–15, 117, 127; diplomacy in 1973 Middle East war, 100, 104–107; suggestion of arms deliveries to Egypt, 107; diplomacy in 1982 Lebanon war, 112–13, 123–30; Rapid Deployment Force, 119, 170; legal arms export restrictions, 125, 185; arms transfers and policy towards Iran, 135–38, 148, 152, 159–60, 272n4; arms transfers and policy toward Iraq, 151, 223; diplomacy during Iraq-Iran war, 153–56; arms transfers and policy toward Morocco, 165–67; diplomacy during Western Sahara war, 168–70; arms transfers and policy toward Ethiopia and Somalia, 181–85, 191–96; arms transfers to Uganda, 201; arms transfers to Tanzania, 205; arms sales to Saudi Arabia, 224; diplomacy in Second Gulf war, 224–25; diplomacy during 1991 Kashmir conflict, 229–30; arms sales to ex-Yugoslavia, 233

United States Arms Control and Disarmament Agency (ACDA), 20–21
United States Congress, 49, 125–26, 129, 132, 169; Congressional Research Service (CRS), 20–21

Vance, Cyrus, 172, 195, 275n8
Venezuela: arms sales to Honduras, 66; to Argentina, 75, 83
Vergetius, 3–4
Victims: of 1969 Central American war, 67; of 1982 Lebanon war, 122; of Ogaden war, 190–91; of Tanzania-Uganda war, 209; of 1965 South Asian war, 275n3; of 1971 South Asian war, 267n9; of 1973 Middle East war, 271n2
Vietnam: relations with Soviet Union, 12; possible arms sales to Iran, 273n5

Walters, Vernon, 170, 269n10
War of Attrition, 91
Wars: costs, 1, 145, 178, 209, 273n5; level of violence, 14, 214–16; World War I, 3, 140–41, 143–44; dangers of preparation, 4; effect of arms transfers on decision making, 4, 8–9, 30, 214–16; importance of length, 8, 10–11, 90–91, 219–21; Suez Crisis of 1956, 85. *See also* individual countries
Weinberger, Caspar, 84, 118, 269n8
Wright, Quincy, 4

Young, Andrew, 170
Yugoslavia: arms sales to India, 28; granting overflight right to Soviet Union, 103; arms sales to Iraq, 146; to Iran, 152; to Ethiopia, 183; to Uganda, 202; war in 1991, 232–39; domestic arms industry, 234

Zablocki, Clement, 170
Zaire: Shaba crisis, 12, 178, 274n5
Zewde, Gebre-Selassi, 185
Zimbabwe, 204